Upheaval in Charleston

UPHEAVAL

in Charleston

EARTHQUAKE
AND MURDER
ON THE EVE OF
JIM CROW

Susan Millar Williams
Stephen G. Hoffius

The University of Georgia Press

Athens

Publication of this work was made possible, in part, by a generous gift from the University of Georgia Press Friends Fund.

Published by the University of Georgia Press
Athens, Georgia 30602
www.ugapress.org
© 2011 by Susan Millar Williams and Stephen G. Hoffius

Designed by April Leidig-Higgins
Set in Arno by Copperline Book Services, Inc.
Printed and bound by Thomson-Shore

The paper in this book meets the guidelines for permanence and durability of the Committee on Production Guidelines for Book Longevity of the Council on Library Resources.

Printed in the United States of America

15   14   13   12   11   C   5   4   3   2   1

Library of Congress Cataloging-in-Publication Data
Williams, Susan Millar.
   Upheaval in Charleston : earthquake and murder on the eve of Jim Crow / Susan Millar Williams and Stephen G. Hoffius.
   p. cm.
Includes bibliographical references and index.
ISBN-13: 978-0-8203-3715-9 (hardcover : alk. paper)
ISBN-10: 0-8203-3715-3 (hardcover : alk. paper)
   1. Charleston (S.C.) — History — 19th century.   2. Charleston Earthquake, S.C., 1886 — Social aspects.   3. Charleston (S.C.) — Race relations — History — 19th century.   4. Charleston (S.C.) — Social conditions — 19th century.   5. African Americans — Segregation — South Carolina — Charleston — History — 19th century.   6. Dawson, Francis Warrington, 1840–1889.   7. Murder — South Carolina — Charleston.   I. Hoffius, Stephen G.   II. Title.
F279.C457W55   2011
975.7'915041 — dc22   2010045462

Contents

Preface

LIVING WITH DISASTER

Susan Millar Williams

CHARLESTON HAS ALWAYS stood on shaky ground. Vulnerable to the fury of nature and the brutality of man, the old port city has served as the stage for the major acts of the great American drama. It landed more enslaved Africans than any city in the original thirteen colonies, reaped a vast fortune from their labor, surrendered to the British during the Revolution, led the charge for secession, and fired the first shots of the Civil War. When that war was lost, the city was occupied by federal troops and bound by U.S. laws that turned the state's racial hierarchy on its head.

By the early 1880s catastrophe had become a way of life. Wars, hurricanes, fires, floods, epidemics, and riots had come and gone. Most black Charlestonians had endured the galling yoke of slavery, as had their parents and their parents' parents. Most white men over the age of forty had fought and bled in the Civil War. The city was burdened with more than its share of widows and orphans. The citizens of Charleston, white and black, thought of themselves as survivors.

On August 31, 1886, the city was struck by a new and unforeseen calamity: the most powerful earthquake ever recorded on the east coast of North America. Buildings collapsed, dams broke, railroad tracks buckled and derailed trains. Fissures split the ground and water spouted two stories high. Miraculously, fewer than one hundred people died, though many more were injured.

The terror of the experience stayed with people all their lives.

I FIRST STARTED thinking about the earthquake in 1988, when one of my students at the College of Charleston wrote a research paper about it. She simply intended to find out what had happened — what fell down, who was injured, how people coped. Instead, she uncovered conflicts that surprised us both. Why were whites so angry when black people prayed and held religious services in the public encampments? Why would a white Episcopal minister threaten to beat a black woman with his walking stick if she didn't stop singing hymns? Why were the police called to halt a children's baseball game? These were intriguing questions, but they seemed extremely remote from my life.

A year later, on September 21, 1989, Hurricane Hugo flattened parts of my little town, McClellanville, thirty miles north of Charleston, and left the rest looking like a French battleground after World War I. My house weathered the winds and the twelve-foot storm surge; the homes of many of my friends did not. Life as we had known it was swept away.

I still catch myself referring to something that happened "during the storm" when what I really mean is five months, or ten months, or even eighteen months later. Only on the nightly news does disaster pass quickly. And when I recall the long trudge back to normality, the memories that haunt me are not the images that show up on television every year on September 21 — shrimp boats in the streets, a house that floated fifty yards from its foundation — or the ones in our family album — umbrellas poking through holes in the roof, my baby daughter climbing a mountain of donated sweet potatoes, dead fish on the front steps. Instead I remember feeling flayed alive, and knowing that everybody else must feel that way too. It was as if the storm had stripped away every shred of the emotional padding that, in normal times, allows people to ignore pain, smile politely, and go about their daily routines. There was a sense that help would never come, that we were doomed to spend the rest of our lives foraging in the wilderness.

Help did come, of course. Lots of help. Huge trucks rolled into town carrying water, ice, donated socks, diapers, mattresses, generators, even sofas. Volunteers and National Guardsmen wielded chainsaws and power washers.

But almost before the first bag of ice had melted, suspicion and greed set in. The storm hit in the middle of a prolonged fight over whether to establish a new public school in the heart of the village. Many whites supported the local private school, established to resist integration, and they loudly opposed the idea. Blacks and whites who favored public education saw the struggle as a crusade for equal rights. And far from laying aside their differences after the storm, these factions quarreled more bitterly than ever.

Perhaps it is a natural human impulse to want to help the people most like oneself — after all, the basic motive behind relief efforts is the knowledge that something like this *could* happen to you. Yet I was shocked when white people in vans tried to press diapers and baby clothes on me and visibly recoiled when I suggested they take their donations to Lincoln High School, where harder-hit black residents could get them.

I sometimes found myself thinking about the earthquake and wishing I knew more. But I was working on a biography of the novelist Julia Peterkin, who revolutionized American fiction in the 1920s by writing seriously about the lives of black farming people. As I labored to pin down the source of her subversive genius, the struggles Peterkin dramatized were playing out all around me. Blacks and whites inhabited the same expanse of earth but lived in different worlds. The trauma of the disaster itself was magnified by the experience of subsisting in a blasted landscape, looking, day after day, at splintered trees and mangled houses. Two decades after the storm, these images still appear in my dreams.

When the Peterkin book was finally finished, I did some research on the earthquake. I wanted to know more about how black people reacted, but all of the letters and diaries I found had been written by whites. I decided to try my hand at fiction and make up characters to fill in the blanks. But as I found out more, my friend Steve Hoffius, a skilled historian and the author of a highly acclaimed novel for young adults, convinced me that at least in this case, truth was more interesting than fiction. Steve had just finished a novel about three young girls living in the aftermath of the hurricane, and the same questions that troubled me fascinated him. Why did city authorities set up a comprehensive system to provide food and shelter, only to dismantle it less than three weeks later? And why did the city council try to discourage further donations when people still needed help? Before long we were collaborating on a nonfiction book about the earthquake.

With Hugo we had seen firsthand the havoc nature can unleash. Yet the earthquake, by all accounts, was far more surreal. What was it like to see the ground under your feet writhing, spouting, and lurching? Was it really true that the earth trembled for thousands of miles around? Could we verify bizarre reports that boggled the imagination? One by one, we checked out the stories. Most of the strangest proved to be true.

EVERY TIME A new disaster hit the news, Steve and I watched as governments tripped over each other trying to provide relief. People were fed and sheltered. Houses, schools, and businesses were rebuilt. While many questioned whether various agencies were responding in the correct way, no one debated, as they had in 1886, whether state and national governments should come to the rescue. In that sense, public attitudes have changed dramatically. But in another, more primal, sense, the trajectory of human emotions has stayed remarkably constant. After the Indonesian tsunami, after Hurricane Katrina, and even after the attacks of September 11, 2001, conflicts that had simmered before the cataclysm came back in more virulent forms, just as they had after the Charleston earthquake. The initial surge of harmony gave way to resentment, paranoia, and spite.

FOR YEARS Steve and I hunched over microfilm readers and blurry photocopies of century-old newspapers, trying to understand the dynamics of the city that was shattered by the earthquake. The details were endlessly absorbing, artifacts of a forgotten time that came to life in the pages of the *Charleston News and Courier*.

The editor of that paper, Francis Warrington Dawson, was the hero of the earthquake. He led the relief effort, rebuilt morale, and controlled much of what the rest of the world heard about the crisis. Standing amid the rubble of his newspaper office, Dawson predicted that Charleston would build a new city on the ruins of the old. The calamity, he declared, would bring people closer together. But as New Orleans reminded the world after Hurricane Katrina, natural disasters do not erase old conflicts. They reveal dirty secrets.

Born and raised in England, Dawson had a broader vision than almost anyone else in Charleston. He consulted with presidents and recognized the need to industrialize when most southerners only wanted to force more cotton from their fields. Brilliant, well traveled, and arrogant, he never doubted his own judgment or hesitated to tell the people of his adopted state what they should do.

Twenty years before, he had come to the South at its most perilous moment, drawn to what he perceived as the nobility and romance of the Confederacy's ideals. He stayed on through military defeat, occupation, economic disaster, and the bloody revival of the first state government to secede from the Union. He acquired an American accent and admission to Charleston's most exclusive clubs and societies. Scars on his arms, legs, and chest bore witness to Dawson's loyalty: this man had put his life on the line, not only in the Civil War but in the wave of violence that swept the state ten years later.

Yet he would always remain an outsider in one crucial respect: he would never share white South Carolina's conviction that racial inequality was a higher law.

Dawson was horrified by the intransigence of native-born white southerners, who would stop at nothing — including mass murder — to resurrect white supremacy. His was often a lone voice, pushing and prodding the postwar South to rejoin the nation. But Dawson's South was not a place where differences were easily resolved. Slavery had been dead for less than a generation in 1886, and emancipation had transformed millions of dollars worth of human chattel into citizens who demanded wages, land, education, and votes. For either race to make gains, the other race had to suffer losses. Naive as he was about his countrymen's ingrained caste system, Dawson was sure that if the economy boomed, there would be enough for everybody. Blacks and whites would rise together, buoyed by the tide of prosperity.

Frank Dawson spent the years between the war and the earthquake transforming himself into the "Czar of South Carolina" — no small feat for anyone, much less a transplanted foreigner, a Catholic in a Protestant land, a man who condemned violence in a culture where bloodshed was equated with honor.[1] But like Booker T. Washington, who was also feeling his uneasy way through the minefields of racial uplift, Frank Dawson had learned over the years that to keep white southerners on his side, he had to speak their language. His voice, to our twenty-first-century ears, seems less than heroic, echoing the paternalistic — and sometimes racist — sentiments of his audience. But by the standards of his time and place he was extremely progressive, courting the North, supporting blacks who challenged segregation, and branding white nationalists as butchers and barbarians. He dreamed of a time when the South would heal and prosper, no longer haunted by the ghosts of war and slavery. The aftermath of the earthquake put an end to those fantasies.

THE "GREAT SHOCK" of 1886 has been eclipsed in memory by the earthquake and fire that devastated San Francisco twenty years later. But as a turning point in U.S. history, Charleston's seismic disaster was far more significant, exposing a country torn between the fading ideals of racial justice and the lure of white reunion. The earthquake shook Charleston exactly midway between 1876, when white "Redeemers" snuffed out Reconstruction, and 1896, when the U.S. Supreme Court legalized segregation in *Plessy v. Ferguson*. But in 1886 no one was sure what path the country would follow. African Americans were still pushing for an expansion of their rights. Labor organizations were recruiting blacks as well as whites, women as well as men. As historian C. Vann Woodward wrote in his classic study, *The Strange Career of Jim Crow*, it "was a time of experiment, testing and uncertainty — quite different from the time of repression and rigid uniformity that was to come toward the end of the century."[2]

The city where the Civil War began had been far slower to segregate the races than other parts of the South. Blacks and whites lived side by side even in the wealthiest neighborhoods. But the enormous relief effort after the quake outraged many whites, who felt that blacks were being given too much help. The destruction created a windfall for the black craftsmen who dominated the city's construction trades, allowing them to command higher wages and better working conditions. This, too, infuriated those who were used to making the rules. Dawson was caught in the middle, pushing for more relief even as he railed against those who, in his view, were trying to exploit the crisis for personal gain.

Less than three years after the earthquake, Frank Dawson was murdered, an act that silenced his moderate voice and left South Carolina in the grip of virulent white supremacists. The trial of his killer made headlines across the nation, triggering a campaign to prevent blacks from serving as jurors. Soon South Carolina passed a new constitution that legalized segregation and disfranchised black voters. And rather than building a new city on the ruins of the old, Charleston constructed a fresh set of walls to separate the races.

Upheaval in Charleston is the story of one man and one city confronting the awesome destructive power unleashed by a sudden geologic upheaval. But it is also the story of a crucial turning point in our country's tragic history, when the nation began rushing headlong toward segregation and Jim Crow.

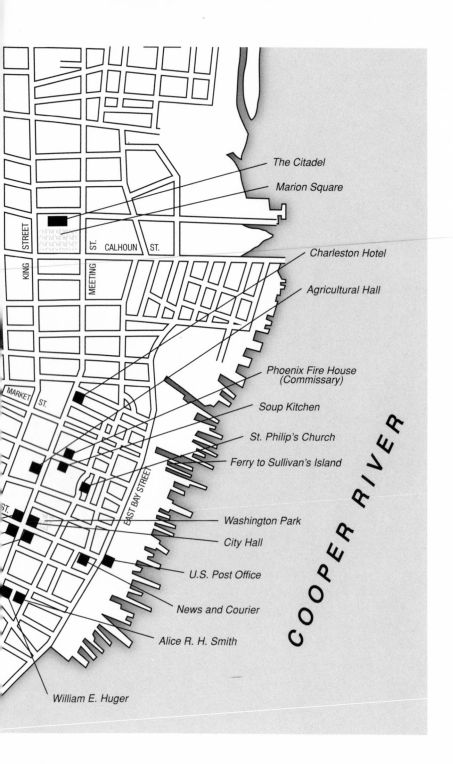

The Citadel

Marion Square

Charleston Hotel

Agricultural Hall

Phoenix Fire House
(Commissary)

Soup Kitchen

St. Philip's Church

Ferry to Sullivan's Island

Washington Park

City Hall

U.S. Post Office

News and Courier

Alice R. H. Smith

William E. Huger

KING STREET

MEETING ST.

CALHOUN ST.

MARKET ST.

EAST BAY STREET

COOPER RIVER

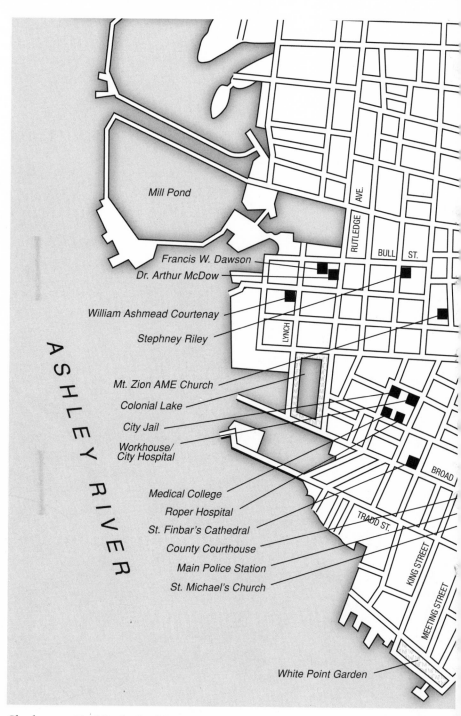

Mill Pond

RUTLEDGE AVE.

BULL ST.

Francis W. Dawson

Dr. Arthur McDow

William Ashmead Courtenay

Stephney Riley

LYNCH

A S H L E Y

Mt. Zion AME Church

Colonial Lake

City Jail

Workhouse/
City Hospital

R I V E R

Medical College

Roper Hospital

St. Finbar's Cathedral

County Courthouse

Main Police Station

St. Michael's Church

BROAD

TRADD ST.

KING STREET

MEETING STREET

White Point Garden

Charleston, 1886. Map by Paul Rossmann.

Upheaval in Charleston

Chapter One

THE GREAT SHOCK

O N THE EVENING of Tuesday, August 31, 1886, shock waves swept across North America at 7,200 miles an hour, accelerating when they reached rigid rock and lagging in softer sand and clay soils. They surged through pastures and pavements, factories and farms, through the mountains and valleys of Appalachia and the flats of Chesapeake Bay. They pulsed through tall buildings and one-room shacks, sent worshippers scrambling through church windows, stampeded audiences in opera houses, and broke up lodge initiations. They ruffled the leaves of cornstalks and cotton plants, set tomatoes and melons trembling, and shook green apples from the trees.[1]

In Yellowstone National Park a huge geyser that had been dormant for the past four years began to spout, while in the Caribbean a strange light flashed across the Cuban sky, frightening sleeping families from their beds. The captain of a schooner off the coast of Maine saw a "black wall" rising, a mighty wave that tore off his ship's sails, snapped the mast, and lifted the vessel to a fantastic height before it came to rest in a mountain of foam. Flames shot from caverns in the mountains of North Carolina, leaving a cloud of smoke that smelled like burning coal.[2]

On the third floor of a brick house in Washington, D.C., William John McGee jerked awake. His holstered knife and pistol swung on the bedpost. McGee, an employee of the U.S. Geological Survey, knew at once that he was feeling an earthquake, and he was thrilled. His grandfather had lived in Missouri during the New Madrid upheavals in 1811–12, and the old man's tales of fissures and waterspouts inspired the boy to study geology. McGee leaped out of bed. Using his watch and a tumbler of water, he improvised a crude instrument to measure the time and duration of two separate shocks.[3]

In a nearby drugstore, McGee's boss, John Wesley Powell, watched beakers and bottles dance along the shelves. He too pulled out his watch and carefully noted the time: 9:53 p.m. Powell expected the motion to cease quickly. Instead, the glassware continued to rattle as if it were possessed. Powell had lived in earthquake country, on the West Coast and in South America, but this shock was the most intense he had ever experienced.[4]

At the Virginia state penitentiary in Richmond, eight hundred prisoners hammered on their cell doors and screamed to be let out. Guards rang bells to summon the militia. Word spread that one of the walls had fallen and convicts were escaping. Ten thousand armed men converged on the prison, ready to stop an uprising.[5]

In Terre Haute, Indiana, a man was thrown out of the balcony at a minstrel show but saved himself by clinging to a rail. A large hotel in Louisville, Kentucky, rocked "like an egg in the surf." Two men playing pool in New Haven, Connecticut, watched the billiard balls creep across the felt as if prodded by an invisible cue. Two women in Savannah, Georgia, jumped out of second-story windows, one of them holding a baby.[6]

In southeastern South Carolina, at a small settlement known as Ten Mile Hill, a commuter train jumped the tracks and hurtled down an embankment. Passengers bounced off their seats like kernels of corn in a popper. Beside the tracks, cracks split the earth.[7]

Not far away, near the tiny hamlet of Woodstock, another train flew into the air. Newspapers, cigars, and spectacles took wing; pocket change skittered down the aisles. The engineer mashed the brakes, but the train kept going. Lights strobed outside the windows — warning flares. The engine screeched to a stop on the brink of a gully.[8]

IN ATLANTA a policeman out on night patrol felt as if he were riding a giant turtle. High above him, in the six-story building that housed the *Atlanta Constitution*, the floor began to vibrate. The engineer shut down the generator, plunging the building into darkness. Henry Grady, the newspaper's managing editor, was sitting in a pedestal rocker at his home on Peachtree Street when the chandeliers began to swing. The house rattled and shook. Grady jumped up and ran outside, pushing his wife and two children ahead of him. A chimney thundered through the roof next door.[9]

Grady dashed to the newspaper office. Terrified people thronged the streets. By the time he got there, the lights were blazing and telegrams were streaming in from all over the country. The *Constitution*'s correspondent in Columbia, South Carolina, had been thrown into a brick drain, dislocating his shoulder.[10] People talking on the telephone in Chicago had been suddenly cut off. Newspaper reporters at the *Detroit Free Press*, running from their offices, had leaped from rooftop to rooftop.

Reporters rushed in with odd bits of news about incidents on Atlanta's streets. A building had collapsed, cans had tumbled from grocery store shelves, slates had fallen off roofs, and fire bells had rung. It would take all night to write the stories and set them in type, and by then even more startling accounts would have arrived.

High above the streets of Atlanta, looking out over the lights of the city toward the comforting bulk of Stone Mountain, Grady shuffled his stack of telegrams and stared at a map. The wires reported strong tremors from Florida to Maine and as far west as Chicago. In South Carolina, where there had been several accounts of small earthquakes in the past few days, a bridge near Charleston "was shaken from its foundations," yet no word had been received from the city's leading newspaper, the *News and Courier*. It was not like Frank Dawson and his men to fall down on the job.

Something, Grady realized, must be terribly wrong in Charleston.

Chapter Two

SEEDS OF DESTRUCTION

T WO HOURS EARLIER on that Tuesday evening, Grady's friend and rival Frank Dawson was sitting in his Broad Street newspaper office in Charleston sifting through a stack of stories. Over the weekend, a series of mild earth tremors had rocked the city and the nearby town of Summerville. Superstitious people were saying that the end of the world was near. Thunder and lightning had split the sky. Stars were falling, the sky had turned to blood, and the earth had trembled. When two more comets and a cyclone arrived, the prophecies of Revelation would be fulfilled. The righteous would be swept off to heaven, while the wicked would plunge into hell. Some who believed Judgment Day was approaching had stopped reporting to work.[1]

Charleston was no stranger to earthquakes. At least twenty-five tremors, mostly "dish rattlers" or "baby earthquakes," had shaken the city since its founding, the first in February 1698. When the New Madrid earthquakes — named for a town destroyed by one of the quakes — jolted the Mississippi River out of its bed in the winter of 1811–12, a comet hovered in the sky over Charleston. Over the course of three months, a series of seven shocks stopped clocks, rang the bells of St. Philip's Church, and broke the glass in picture frames. Convinced that the quakes were a rebuke from God, the city declared a day of prayer, fasting, and "humiliation." In the summer of 1869, a quake uprooted trees at a military encampment near the city, throwing soldiers off their feet and opening a "huge chasm" that spewed dark liquid. But in the two centuries since records had been kept, no quake had ever been strong enough to cause serious damage.[2]

Frank Dawson left the office a little early that night because he had already prepared the annual economic report that would fill most of the next day's paper. The numbers were disheartening: Charleston's gross trade had fallen off by almost a million dollars in the last year. The all-important cotton and rice crops had been damaged by spring floods. The upstate had "wrested away" a significant chunk of Charleston's trade, largely because its railroads transported cargo that had once traveled by water. Yet, according to Dawson, there was "no good reason to be dissatisfied with the business of Charleston" in this time of "depression of trade and industry throughout the United States, and indeed, throughout the civilized world." Dawson tried to emphasize the positive. Cotton and rice prices were off, but not as much as had been expected. Manufacturing was down some, but the city was "holding its own." His report predicted a time when Charleston would move ahead "not with a halting or hesitating step, but by leaps and bounds."[3]

In the moments before disaster struck, the city seemed strangely becalmed. The sun sank in a blood-red blaze, veiled with black clouds. The air hung heavy, dead still. Breathing was a burden and walking a trial in the soggy heat. The upper classes suffered most, the women trussed up in whalebone stays and layers of heavy linen while the men were firmly encased in vests and coats, starched shirts, and leather boots. The poor wore lightweight clothing and often went barefoot. In the winter, their condition was pitiable. In summer, they were the lucky ones, free from the sweaty encumbrances of convention.

Dawson strolled to the corner of Meeting and Broad streets and perched on the base of one of the pillars of St. Michael's Church, founded when England still ruled and the city was known as Charles Towne.[4] He glanced down the street toward his own church, St. Finbar's Catholic Cathedral. Joining either of the elite Episcopal churches, St. Michael's or St. Philip's, would have been a wise move for a man who hoped to rise to the top in this class-conscious Protestant city. Yet Dawson was Catholic to the bone: brother to a priest, a member of the vestry, knighted by the pope for his opposition to dueling.

Across the street was the Guard House, its portico supported by six huge columns extending over the sidewalk. City Hall was on the right, the county courthouse, once the colony's capitol, on the left. When a streetcar arrived, Dawson boarded it and rattled north along Meeting Street.

Dawson was far more interested in the city's potential than in its glorious past. The crude line of telegraph poles that marched up Meeting Street did not mar the view for him. They were a sign that Charleston at last was getting in step with the world.

At the corner of Rutledge and Bull streets, Dawson leaped off the

streetcar and strode toward his home at 25 (now 99) Bull Street. A vigorous, athletic man who worked out with dumbbells and Indian clubs, he had
spent many hours sailing in the harbor. Ordinarily his wife Sarah would be
waiting to share a cold supper and a chat, but she was traveling in Europe
with their two children, Ethel and Warrington. Sarah's sister Miriam and
her fifteen-year-old daughter Lucile had been living with the Dawsons off
and on since Miriam left her alcoholic husband four years before, but this
week Frank had arranged for them to stay in a beach house on nearby Sullivan's Island. The cook, a high-strung German immigrant who had married
and buried a husband in the last month, had retired for the evening to her
quarters behind the main house.[5]

Frank Dawson was a self-made man in more ways than one. He was born
in London to a moneyed Catholic family and christened Austin John Reeks.
As he was about to enter college, his father's investments had forced him
to declare bankruptcy. An aunt, Mrs. William Dawson, offered to pay the
boy's tuition, but before she could follow through she suffered a stroke and
died. The young Reeks did not let these misfortunes stop him, but instead
turned to singing and writing plays, one of which appeared on the London
stage.[6]

He turned twenty in May 1861, soon after the South Carolina militia fired
on federal troops at Fort Sumter, shots that would go down in history as the
start of the American Civil War. Poring over newspaper accounts of the early
battles, he compared southern secession to the stands of other oppressed
people through history, like the English barons in 1215 whose demands led
to the adoption of the Magna Carta. The "American war," he later wrote,
was "most delightfully romantic."[7] At a family dinner that fall, young Reeks
announced that he wanted to join the rebel army and the freedom fighters'
quest for liberty. His father tried to talk him out of it — if the boy were captured and hanged, he said, he would disgrace the family name. Austin John
shot back that if he were captured, he would hang under a name of his own.
From then on he called himself Francis Warrington Dawson. "Dawson" he
took from his kind-hearted aunt, and "Francis" from St. Francis of Assisi.
"Warrington" was an embellishment of the family name Warren.

Searching for a route to the southern states, he discovered a Confederate
steamship, the *Nashville*, lying in the port of Southampton. Dawson convinced the captain to take him on. Four months later, after the ship passed
through the federal blockade and reached Morehead City, North Carolina,

he resolved to join the army, where he thought he might see more action than in the navy. One of his comrades later claimed that Dawson jumped off his own ship and swam through a barrage of gunfire to join a company that was about to engage the enemy.[8] He fought in the bloody battles of Second Manassas and Gettysburg, was wounded three times and taken prisoner twice. When the war ended he owned nothing but a penknife and a five-dollar bill. But he was smart, energetic, and alert to opportunity. He tried several jobs before he found work as an editor and reporter for the *Richmond Daily Examiner*. A year later he acquired a half interest in one of Charleston's two important newspapers; he and his partner soon bought the other. By 1886 the Charleston *News and Courier* boasted "the largest circulation in the cotton states."[9]

Frank Dawson stayed on in the battered South and became a U.S. citizen for the same reason that earlier generations of immigrants had come to America: it promised an opportunity to rise above the rigid limits of Old World caste systems. "Here I have a high position and a high reputation," he wrote his mother in 1866. "In England I should be less than nobody."[10] He would always be known as "Captain Dawson" out of respect for his Confederate service. He married a genteel young Charlestonian named Virginia Fourgeaud, who died of consumption just seventeen months later. There were no children, but the connection with Virginia's family made him less of an outsider.

A few weeks after his wife's death he met Sarah Morgan, the older sister of one of his wartime chums. The sixth child in a family of seven children, Sarah was a tiny, fragile-looking woman with large violet eyes — smart, opinionated, and feisty. A fall from a carriage when she was young had twisted her spine, so pain was her constant companion. At thirty-one she was over the hill by nineteenth-century standards. Men had been proposing to Sarah for more than a decade, but she had turned them all down.

Dawson was smitten. Still officially in mourning, he wrote Sarah love letters on stationery bordered in black. She protested that a Catholic man was an unsuitable prospect for a good Episcopal girl, but Frank did not give up. He invited her to write for his newspaper, supplied her with subjects, and polished and published her essays, many of which set forth her notions about men and women. "Man is unquestionably a tyrant, but woman was made for him. Consequently reasonable submission is a duty," she declared in "Young Couples."[11]

Frank was anything but a tyrant while he was courting Sarah. He took over the care of her twelve-year-old nephew, shopped for fabric when she needed clothes, and sent her mother brandy — for medicinal purposes, of course. After a year of this treatment, Sarah finally gave in, and the two were married in 1874. She bore him three children and buried one of them, a six-month-old baby named Philip, who died of heat stroke during one of Charleston's sweltering summers.

Dawson always came to the rescue when Sarah's family got in trouble, a situation that was not uncommon. Not only had he taken in Miriam and Lucile and paid the debts of Sarah's older brother Philip, but he had just spent over a year calling in favors for her brother Jimmy, a charming but irresponsible man who had helped Frank out of trouble countless times. In mid-August 1886 Jimmy Morgan had been named consul-general to Australia, a post he owed solely to Dawson's political connections and relentless string pulling. President Grover Cleveland himself made the appointment, in spite of Jimmy's Confederate service, a reward to Dawson for delivering thousands of votes in the 1884 election.[12]

Grover Cleveland was not the only political figure who owed Frank Dawson favors. In his twenty years in Charleston, Frank had turned himself into a kingmaker, though he never ran for political office himself. He was as relentless about politics as he had been in courting Sarah. As the national committeeman for the Democratic Party, he eagerly did his party's bidding. Was money needed for a campaign? He raised it. Were party officials concerned about getting out the vote? He made sure the polls were full. He had allies in every ward of the city and far beyond the borders of South Carolina.

The *News and Courier* was his base, the foundation of his power. If, to make his point, he needed to slant the news, he did not hesitate. A small gathering could be described as a numberless throng. A lackluster speech might be reported as having provoked thunderous applause. Awkward events could be ignored. Dawson was determined to rejuvenate the city of Charleston, and to raise himself in the process.

EVERY EVENING about nine o'clock, the work of putting out the *News and Courier* moved from the editorial offices facing Broad Street to the new brick building out back. There the curved, freshly set type beds, or "turtles," were hoisted into place on the steam-powered press, which could print, cut, fold, and count twelve thousand newspapers an hour.

On August 31, 1886, the boxes of type were brand new, never touched by ink. Dawson had saved the pristine characters to set his economic report.[13] The press throbbed, the lights blazed; the smells of ink and newsprint and hot metal poured out the open doors and windows into Elliott Street, where some of the poorest residents of Charleston inhabited a warren of run-down tenements.

In his office upstairs, reporter Carlyle McKinley bent over a stack of papers. As long as Dawson was in the building, the air seemed to vibrate with nervous tension. His head wreathed in cigar smoke, the editor ranted, cursed, fumed, scolded, and ordered people around. No one ever moved fast enough to suit him. When he left for home, calm settled over the staff.[14] McKinley picked up a pencil and started marking copy.

A FEW BLOCKS AWAY from Dawson's office, in a big Georgian house on Church Street, ten-year-old Alice Ravenel Huger Smith rolled her mother's wheeled chair in from the piazza. Alice wriggled into her cool cotton night-gown, happy to be free of the heavy dress and petticoats she wore during the day.[15]

Alice's grandmother popped her head in the door. A fan attached to a long ribbon peeked from the folds of her heavy black skirt. "I am *always* glad when August is over," Eliza Smith declared, snapping her fan. "All the *worst* things in my life come to me in August." Young Alice had heard this lament many times. The Yankees started to shell Charleston in August 1863. A week later, Eliza's son died on his twelfth birthday. In August of the following year, another son died from wounds suffered at the battle of Cold Harbor, where eight thousand soldiers were killed in a single hour. And just last summer, on August 25, 1885, Alice and her family had huddled in a hallway as a hurricane pounded the city.[16]

August is the height of storm season in Charleston. Gales, tempests, cyclones, hurricanes — the awesome, destructive energy systems that originate as tropical waves — spin their way across the summer Atlantic, gathering force until they either veer north across open water or slam into land. "June, too soon," goes an old rhyme; "July, stand by; August, come it must."[17]

In August 1886 much of the previous year's storm damage had not yet been repaired. The top of the steeple at Citadel Square Baptist Church still lay smashed in the churchyard. Parishioners at the French Huguenot Church had just printed a pamphlet asking for contributions to fix their building. On the morning of August 31, a small crowd had watched as a gilded cypress ball was replaced atop St. Michael's steeple, complete with weathervane and lightning rod. The ball had crashed down at the height of the 1885 storm, denting the pavement. Along the Battery, the seawall at the tip of the peninsula where guns were once mounted, railings and flagstone walkways had been washed out by the storm surge. They had just been reset. Ten thousand cartloads of tree limbs had been collected by city crews, and the refuse had been recycled as fill for low-lying roadways and lots.[18]

When the long, narrow peninsula was first settled by the British in the late seventeenth century it was mostly marsh, crisscrossed by countless small creeks. King and Meeting streets were laid out along a spine of slightly higher ground. For two hundred years residents dumped garbage and discarded ballast from ships, construction debris, and soil in the lowest areas, trying to raise the city a few precious inches higher above sea level. By 1886 Charleston sat atop a more-or-less solid spit of land, with mill ponds on the banks of the Ashley River to the west and wharves forming a serrated edge along the Cooper River on the east. There were still pockets of marshland, especially along the Ashley, but more than a sixth of the city stood on former wetlands. The eradication of these interior swamps was a feat of primitive engineering, accomplished with shovels and sweat. An 1883 map indicates this "made ground" with a symbol that looks like a child's drawing of waves.[19]

Both the City Market building and the Charleston Hotel straddled one former creek. Two hospitals, the Medical College of the State of South Carolina, and the city jail sat at the edge of another. So did hundreds of dwellings and stores, including the home of Francis Dawson. No one gave much thought to this long-buried topography. The city flooded whenever rainfall coincided with high tide. People waded through streets turned to rivers until the water flowed along its old courses and found its way to the sea. Children paddled in flooded intersections. No one imagined that these long-vanquished streams would ever cause trouble. Yet deep in the sand beneath the city, the seeds of destruction had been sown.

IN THE late afternoon of August 31, 1886, in a house built on one of the filled-in lots, Charlotte Hayden sank into a chair with the sense of a job well done. She and her daughter had worked for days, cleaning out closets, hemming sheets, scrubbing, dusting, and polishing. The house was ready for their new boarders, due on the next steamer from New York. Like many of the formerly well-to-do families, the Haydens had learned to make ends meet by renting out rooms. They lived beside "the Pond," a reservoir carved from the mud flats along the Ashley River just north of Broad Street. Officially christened Colonial Lake, it had only recently been landscaped as a "pleasure-ground."[20]

Open spaces were scarce in most parts of the city. A typical block was filled with narrow houses, their sides almost touching, though often a small private garden was tucked somewhere toward the rear. Larger lots were crowded with outbuildings — kitchens, stables, carriage houses, servants' quarters, and sheds — some of which had, in the lean years after the war, been converted to rental property. The Haydens leased a cottage behind their main house to a family of seven expatriate Cubans.

Mrs. Hayden's husband had not yet returned from his insurance office on Broad Street, and their son, a student at the medical college down the street, was due home at any minute. Like Frank Dawson, most men worked late into the evening, after breaking for a long dinner and a nap in the middle of the hot afternoon. Savannah, a hundred miles south, was about to abolish this quaint custom in order to bring the city into line with the ways of the bustling world.[21] Charleston clung to its traditions, though men like Dawson were nudging it toward a reluctant modernity.

Charleston in 1886 boasted streetcars, a paid fire department, electric fire alarms, a gas works, an electric lighting plant, and running water, though still no sewage system. Many relied on cisterns for water, or on public artesian wells. A few families and businesses — the Dawsons and the *News and Courier* among them — had telephones, but the service was so rudimentary and rare that most people sent letters to communicate with friends across town. Cows and chickens in tiny pens were a common sight even in fashionable parts of the city, while horses and mules were stabled in the rear of the finer houses. One little girl often brought her pet lamb to graze on the lawn of the old federal courthouse just south of Broad Street.[22]

WELL-TO-DO WHITE Charlestonians were set in their ways, and most recoiled at the idea of spending money on public projects, especially those aimed at bettering the lot of the poor. But in 1879 the city had elected a mayor who believed in civic improvement. William Ashmead Courtenay insisted that the city replace its old plank roads with cobblestones or block, brick the sidewalks, and install curbs. His most recent crusade was a campaign to upgrade the City Hospital, located in a structure built as the city's Workhouse, a dungeon where slaves were punished. The building was a dank and airless old hulk with no place to isolate those suffering from fevers and communicable diseases. The city council had balked at funding improvements, but Courtenay insisted that the city needed a decent charity hospital.[23]

Mayor Courtenay was not in Charleston on the night of August 31. He was on a ship heading home across the Atlantic. Seven years of running the city had taken a heavy toll on his health. The summer before, his son Campbell had been expelled from the Citadel, the Military College of South Carolina, a situation that was all the more hurtful since Courtenay had been a major force in persuading the federal government to allow its reopening after occupying troops were sent home. Courtenay asked the board of visitors to reinstate Campbell, who had accumulated 202 demerits for "neglect of study." The board refused. An anonymous letter in the *News and Courier* charged that Courtenay had joined forces with Ben Tillman, the rough Upcountry populist who declared the military college nothing but a "Dude Factory" that should be converted into a girls' school.[24]

Three times Mayor Courtenay had considered resigning, only to be persuaded that city government would collapse without him. In August 1885 he was about to make his move — and then the cyclone hit. In December, when the crisis was over, he submitted his resignation, but the city council begged him to stay. In January he agreed to a compromise: the city would grant him a three-month leave of absence, appoint an acting mayor to serve in his place, and try to make do until he got back on his feet. He had left as soon as possible for England and the continent, where, above all, he visited rare-book dealers.[25]

Books were Courtenay's first love. He collected rarities, cherished examples of fine printing, and haunted the aisles of the Charleston Library Society. Before the Civil War, he had worked for ten years in a successful Broad Street bookshop run by his older brother. Then he took a job selling ads for the *Charleston Mercury*, the South's "leading secessionist organ." Right after the war, when the railroads were out of service and the bookstore was closed, he went into business hauling cotton in wagons.[26]

In addition to his duties as mayor of Charleston, Courtenay managed a shipping company. Business was booming when he left home, but since he'd been away his accountant had sent some alarming news to him in Europe. The slump Dawson had tried to gloss over in his annual report was hitting the cargo business hard. Exports and imports had fallen off, and vessels were leaving the wharves half full. Courtenay needed to get home to take charge of his affairs.

At a little after nine on the evening of August 31, 1886, Courtenay's accountant J. A. Riols was drafting another letter in the shipping office on East Bay Street. He had done exactly what his boss had ordered: called in all possible accounts due, including an advance on Courtenay's mayoral salary for September, and used the money to stave off creditors. But it was not enough. Since his last letter, he reported, "the bottom seems to have dropped out of every thing."[27]

To Courtenay, Dawson, and their fellow businessmen, this was a familiar refrain. Once the hub of the richest colony in British North America, Charleston clung to a glorious vision in which it was still a major port, a powerhouse of business and finance, and a bastion of high culture. In truth, its glory days were long past, and the economy had been faltering since before the Civil War. Whenever things seemed to be picking up, another disaster struck.

Charleston was a city of heroic architecture, proudly embellished with Greek and Roman columns. But a gash cut from river to river through residential and business neighborhoods where the great fire of 1861 had swept through the heart of the city. The vine-shrouded shell of Circular Congregational Church, once the largest domed building in North America, loomed over Meeting Street. The hollow gothic arches and spires of St. Finbar's Cathedral towered over bustling crowds at the corner of Broad and Friend streets. Neither had been repaired since the fire swept the city.

Ashmead Courtenay knew these ruins like he knew his books. He had been home on leave from the Confederate army when the fire broke out. Before the smoke cleared he had inspected almost 540 acres, noting every building that had burned, along with its owner, its occupants, and the extent of the damage.[28]

Four more years of war, including eighteen months of heavy bombardment, had left other scars. By September 1865, according to one visitor, Charleston was a city "of desolation, of vacant houses, of widowed women, of rotting wharves, of deserted warehouses, of weed-wild gardens, of miles of grass-grown streets, of acres of pitiful and grass-grown barrenness."[29] Some of the destruction had been repaired by 1886, but a great deal had not. Out in the harbor, pounded to pieces, lay the remains of Fort Sumter. Upriver, the ruins of Magnolia and Middleton Place plantations bore witness to the torches of General Sherman's raiders, who had spared the city proper but destroyed structures to the south, west, and north.

About three-fifths of Charleston's people were white on the eve of the Civil War. By 1886, the balance was reversed: three-fifths were black.[30] Whites felt dangerously outnumbered and viewed the growing ranks of black residents as a drain on the city's resources. Blacks felt cheated and betrayed. For a few years after the Civil War, when the federal government controlled South Carolina institutions, they had tasted equal opportunity and access to law and government. During Reconstruction, black men filled the South Carolina House and Senate and the Charleston City Council, took seats on city and state commissions, wore the uniforms of the police and fire departments, and attended the South Carolina College and Law School. Then in 1876 white men banded together, determined to push blacks back into submission and regain total control. Most of the opportunities of Reconstruction were long gone by 1886, but they were not forgotten.

While the nation prepared to dedicate the Statue of Liberty as a tribute to freedom and equality, Charleston stonemasons were laying the granite base for a massive shrine to white supremacy. In Marion Square, the old Citadel parade ground newly landscaped as a public park, a thirty-three-foot tall pedestal was being built to hold a statue of John C. Calhoun, South Carolina's fire-eating statesman who never wavered in his conviction that slavery was "a positive good."[31] When the Calhoun Monument was completed, Calhoun's image would face south, at the boundary between the august business and residential areas downtown and the city's hardscrabble upper wards, inhabited mostly by blacks and working-class whites. It was a stern if wordless warning that the values of the slaveholding South were alive and well.

ON THE EVENING of August 31, a sunburned young Englishman named Robert Alexander strolled up Meeting Street. He worked as a chemist for Kiawah Phosphates, one of the many fertilizer companies on the Ashley River. The phosphate works were hellish places, stinking of sulfur. The smell clung to everything: clothes, skin, and hair. Dredges sucked mud from the river bottoms and men used picks and shovels to strip-mine deposits on the banks. "Every foot of ground is turned up," wrote an appalled observer in 1883, "and a field that has just been mined, with the trees uprooted, resembles more than anything the track of a tornado."[32]

Phosphate mining had raped the land, but it lined the pockets of a new generation of Charleston businessmen. Robert Alexander drew a hefty salary, and he had just bought himself an extravagant present: a small steam-driven yacht. Today he had taken his new boat out for the first time, and he was bursting to tell about it.

Alexander strode up the front walk to the home of William Elliot Huger, Alice Ravenel Huger Smith's first cousin once removed, who was acting mayor of the city until Ashmead Courtenay returned from Europe. Huger wasn't home yet, so Alexander sat down at the dining-room table to talk with the houseguests, a professor from Tulane University and his wife. Alexander was still fizzing with excitement. There had been no wind on the harbor, so the sailboats were all becalmed. But his little steam yacht had chuffed merrily along, borne on the wings of a modern engine. Alexander snatched up a piece of paper to illustrate how it worked.

ACROSS THE HARBOR, at a beach house on Sullivan's Island, Frank Dawson's sister-in-law Miriam DuPré sat on a darkening porch, talking to a guest. Her daughter Lucile was in the hallway playing cards with a crowd of young people. From the open windows came giggles and the slap of cards. Miriam had sat through supper without eating, unsettled by the sunset. Walking toward the end of the island, she had seen the steeples of the distant city silhouetted against a red cloud. The ball of the sun sank while the sliver of a new moon rose. A dying earth, she whispered to her companion, might wrap herself in just such gorgeous robes. The man shrugged her off.[33]

Miriam had always been theatrical. As a young woman she had been prone to impulsive acts like betting her hand in marriage as the prize in a card game.[34] It was a trait that worried her sister Sarah, who had to rescue her from scrapes. Now Miriam was forty-six, divorced, and still an incorrigible flirt.

AT 9:51 P.M., people across the city of Charleston heard a strange noise. On Sullivan's Island Miriam DuPré imagined railroad cars booming down a hollow track. Frank Dawson, in his empty house on Bull Street, thought it must be a streetcar grumbling up nearby Rutledge Avenue. Sitting at his desk in the *News and Courier* office on Broad Street, Carlyle McKinley pictured a large iron safe trundling across the floor.[35]

Everywhere people paused, trying to understand what they were hearing. One man thought the sound resembled the thunder of balls in a ten-pin alley. Another envisioned a hogshead rolling through a warehouse. Railroad magnate George Walton Williams believed he heard an approaching train. Cotton factor Edward Wells compared it to the "horrid singing . . . of machinery in operation." A visitor from Richmond was reminded of the roar of a waterfall. A ship's captain believed that a squall was churning into a tornado.[36]

The roar grew louder, gathered force, began to rattle the buildings. It seemed to rise from everywhere at once, an "infernal drum-beat."[37]

And then all hell broke loose.

Chapter Three

"THE EARTHQUAKE IS UPON US!"

C RYSTAL DROPS from a chandelier exploded on the floor around Frank Dawson. His desk and writing table bumped across the bedroom. Cracks ripped through the plaster ceiling. Windows shattered. Pictures and mirrors leaped from the walls, scattering broken glass. Outside, someone shouted, "God save us!" Water from the rooftop cistern poured down the hall wallpaper and cascaded over the stairs. Dawson picked up the telephone to call his office. The line was dead. Then the shaking began again, and the screaming outside grew louder. He stepped carefully through the torrent on the stairs. In the entranceway statues sprawled, wrenched from their pedestals.[1]

He stepped out the front door to survey the damage and fell six feet, landing hard on a pile of jagged marble. The front porch had collapsed. Blood dripped from his knee. Dawson staggered to his feet, considered trying to climb back inside, then turned and limped toward his newspaper office, thirteen blocks away.

Half-clothed people jostled and milled around him. The sidewalks and streets were strewn with debris. Strands of telegraph wire clutched at his ankles. Gritty dust hung in the air. A red glow filled the sky. The explosions, the ruins, the screams, the blood: this was disaster on a grand scale, worse, Dawson thought, than the war. He was glad that Sarah and the children were not home.

A FEW BLOCKS from Dawson's home, an old seaman stared into the shadows of Vanderhorst Street. His wife had already gone to bed, just beyond the open door of their second-floor piazza. Without warning, a corner of their house leaped into the air. The captain staggered and shouted, "Stay in bed!" Cups and glasses skidded off the night table. Books flew off the shelves.

The structure began to rise and fall "like a flat boat in a chop sea." Earth waves rolled toward him like "ground swells in deep water." The buildings across the street flashed with light as a gas street lamp swayed. A sulfurous stench filled the air while a thin vapor hovered near the ground. A deafening barrage of explosions reminded the former soldier of artillery fire. His war wounds began to throb as though he had brushed a live wire.

His ship, the *Caroline*, was docked near the West Point Rice Mill. Standing on the pitching deck, the old man's son watched the huge brick building collapse. The crash was swallowed up in a thundering tumult as shock waves swept across the city.

Mayor Courtenay's accountant dropped his pen and dashed out to East Bay Street, leaving his letter about debts unfinished. George Walton Williams, the richest man in town, tried to climb out of bed but was "tossed from side to side like a foot-ball." The curator of the Charleston Museum watched a pitcher full of water sail across his room. A physician was thrown across Tradd Street by earth waves two feet high.[2]

Chickens screamed, cows lowed, cats cried, dogs howled. Church bells and doorbells clanged. Granite covers flew from well shafts, propelled by geysers of water and mud. The newly repaired bridge over the Ashley River slid off its foundations, snapping the telegraph cable slung under its belly.[3]

Yards and streets flooded with bubbling water. Small springs that smelled like gunpowder trickled through the old Washington Race Course. On lower King Street a waterspout dumped six inches of sand across a patch as big as a baseball diamond. Water and gas mains ruptured, flooding the streets and extinguishing lights. Heavy marble funeral urns vaulted from their pedestals and rammed into the ground. In the cemetery at Circular Congregational Church, a stream of water and sand vomited from a grave.

At Disher's Farm, just north of the city, a field erupted with hundreds of cones that spilled liquid like tiny volcanoes. In the village of Cainhoy, just up the east branch of the Cooper River from Charleston, the earth split apart, leaving a gap twenty-five feet wide. Blisters appeared on the beach at Sullivan's Island, oozing fresh water. At the village of Adams Run, west of the city, geysers twenty feet high turned the streets into rivers, and near Ravenel, the ground broke open in a gash two and a half miles long. A man trying to reach his screaming grandchildren was cut off by a jet of water. The earth caved in under a stable, swallowing a horse and shooting water high into the air. Thousands of clocks and watches stopped. Thirty miles southwest of Charleston on Edisto Island, a four-year-old boy ran to the door just in time to see the ground going "twisty, twisty." His parents shouted "Merceeee! Judgemennnnnnnt!"[4]

Before he threw down his pen and fled, one compulsive Charleston diarist took time to scrawl, "Great God the earthquake is upon us!"[5]

INSIDE THE STORES in Charleston's northern wards, kerosene lamps pitched to the floor and exploded. Windows blazed with fire. Fabrics and ready-made clothing burst into flame. Men rushed inside and grabbed sheets of burning cloth. People sleeping in second-floor bedrooms were cut off by walls of flame. Mothers and fathers dashed into burning buildings and emerged carrying their children "wrapped in a circle of fire." A cry arose: "Get to the Green!" A river of humanity poured down King Street toward Marion Square, a ten-acre park that was also called Citadel Green. A five-year-old girl was trampled.[6]

"It's the night of Sodom and Gomorrah!" shouted a black man. "Pray, my white people. Why don't you pray?" An old black woman seized passersby and ordered, "Praise the Redeemer!" A few whites drifted near and bowed their heads.

"Look for the rock of Horeb to split!" exclaimed another black man, recalling how Moses brought water to the people fleeing slavery. There was rapture in his words, a sense of liberation. In ordinary times, no sane black man or woman would have said such things within earshot of whites. But these were not ordinary times. "The city of St. Michael is down to the ground!" bellowed an old man in triumph.[7]

Last year's hurricane now seemed a mere foretaste of what an angry God could do. In less than a minute and a half, shock waves ripped away the city's classical facade. Grand pillared porticoes and columned porches tumbled to earth as if some supernatural force had decided to strip the city of its pretensions. The sudden impact was so extreme that Charlestonians instinctively turned to the Old Testament to describe its enormity. The new owner of an afternoon newspaper immediately thought of the book of Revelation, confirming that this was "the grand wind-up." Even those few who knew something about geology were seized by "helplessness and hopelessness and horror beyond expression."[8]

The vertical thrust of the primary waves made buildings spring from their foundations. Oscillating secondary waves tore them joint from joint.[9]

Brick houses, safe havens against storm and fire, fared worse than the humblest frame dwellings. The mortar that held the bricks together was ground to dust that hung suspended in the night air.

Nothing was as it had been five minutes before, and nothing would ever be quite the same again. Shattered were the walls that separated rich from poor, white from black, neighbor from neighbor. Gone was the extreme physical modesty of genteel nineteenth-century city life. Men and women ran through the streets naked or half-dressed in nightclothes and underclothing, their bare feet slashed by broken glass and jagged shards of brick. The rules that governed everyday behavior were suspended, exhilarating the powerless and terrifying the powerful. The very foundation of the earth had turned treacherous, and man's dominion over nature was challenged. In the words of one awed resident, the only steady objects now were the stars, "shining peacefully in a cloudless sky."[10]

THE *NEWS AND COURIER* office shivered, though no more at first than it normally did when a streetcar passed along Broad Street. Pencils skittered across desks. The window sashes and gas fixtures rattled. Reporter Carlyle McKinley, absorbed in his work, did not even look up. Then the floors heaved and the walls swayed as if the building were being struck by an "angry hand." Enormous blocks of stone crashed down outside the windows.

In the new printing plant out back, heavy equipment bumped across the floor. Pieces of lead type flew through the air like knife-edged hail. The staff took off, any way they could. One of the typesetters jumped from a third-floor window. He hit the ground and rolled hard, injuring his head and shoulder. Three of his colleagues burst out the door and were pelted by chunks of brick. The jarring stopped, and McKinley thought the worst must be over.

Then it began again.

McKinley raced for the stairs with a crowd of other men, though he expected to die whether or not he made it out the door. And then the roar died away. Silence fell, the earth lay still, the men sagged with relief. McKinley sucked air into his lungs. The dust nearly choked him.

A chorus of human misery rose over the city. A man carried a limp woman in his arms, whispering in her ear.

Light flared in a second-story window. "Fire!" someone cried. In the glare of the flames McKinley glimpsed a man's bloody legs. He moved nearer to look at the face. It was a bookstore clerk who lived in a third-floor apartment. A typesetter asked the clerk whether he jumped or fell. He said he didn't know.[11]

Abruptly the noise started up again. This time it seemed to come from all directions at once, even underground. To McKinley, it sounded like "a wild beast swiftly approaching its prey." The crowd shrank together as the throbbing swelled and rolled.

McKinley thought about his wife and children on the other side of the Cooper River, but he assumed the steam ferry *Sappho* would not be running and gave up hope of reaching them. Uncertain of what else to do, he started walking north toward his rented rooms on Coming Street. As always, he was armed with a notebook and pencil.

Meanwhile, Dawson saw water spewing from a broken main as he approached the *News and Courier* building on Broad Street. The pools covered his shoe tops. He climbed over piles of marble that blocked the door and called to his staff. His voice echoed in the empty halls.

ROBERT ALEXANDER, the young British chemist who worked for Kiawah Phosphates, dropped the diagram of his yacht and sprinted for the door. Just as he crossed the threshold, part of the stone parapet broke loose and fell on the young man, crushing his skull. Behind him, the professor's wife groped for the iron stair rail, but it came loose in her hands. Her husband tried to wrestle the heavy stone off Robert Alexander's body. Under the rubble lay a plaque that had been embedded in the steps to commemorate the moment in 1783 when Acting Mayor William Huger's great-great-grandfather had been struck by a piece of stone that broke loose from the roof. Huger had lived to tell the tale. Alexander was dead.[12]

A block north on Meeting Street, the roof of the old federal courthouse collapsed, shattering the janitor's leg. The stone portico of the Main Police Station fell on two women who were taking an evening stroll. One man ran out of a bar and was crushed by a block of sandstone. Another was buried under a wall at his home in Cow Alley. A German cabinetmaker was crushed by falling bricks as he headed home for supper, a loaf of bread still tucked under his arm.

A chimney collapsed through the roof of a house on Rutledge Avenue. Thirteen-year-old Keitt Walker pulled a pillow over his face and rolled to the floor, calling for his younger brother. The boys' mother was out of town, but their grandmother ran outside for help. Five men charged into the house and tugged at the beams. Soon the floor began to buck, and the would-be rescuers turned and ran. The old woman hurried after them and begged them to try again. The men reluctantly followed her inside, and this time they were able to lift the boy out of the wreckage. A black man picked him up and carried him to White Point Garden near the Battery, away from other structures.[13]

JAMES ROBSON WAS waiting at the depot with two of his sons for his wife's train to arrive from Columbia. All of a sudden the platform shuddered, the lights blinked out, and carriage horses bolted. People screamed and dropped to their knees. A crowd pushed and shoved toward the exits, trampling a nine-year-old girl. Robson thought a runaway train must have rammed the station.[14]

"Earthquake!" someone cried. The crowd milled and waited for news. Strangers arrived with bizarre reports: the Northeastern Railroad Station had split in half. The Unitarian Church had caved in. The front wall of the Meeting Street School had fallen off.

The stationmaster announced that the telegraph wires were dead. The train probably wouldn't arrive anytime soon. The Robson men headed home.

Driving down Coming Street, they could see that something was wrong. Neighbors crowded their yard, hacking at a pile of rubble lying in the garden. One of Robson's daughters ran out to meet her father and brothers, her dress in tatters, tears on her cheeks. She and her sister and brother had been sitting on the second-story piazza when it started to shear off. They tried to jump over the railings, but the falling structure carried them down. She found a way to crawl out, but the other two were trapped.

James Robson sprinted toward the pile, his heart in his mouth. The crowd parted to let him through. He could hear both of his children's voices. Robson reached into a gap and touched a cold hand. From beneath the wreckage Robson's son Ainsley whispered that his head hurt but he did not fear death.

Robson moved out of the way to let the men try to lift the wreckage with a makeshift lever. A beam slipped free and his daughter crawled out. Then Ainsley was lifted clear, his body hanging limp. Robson laid an ear on his son's chest to listen for a heartbeat. There was none.

ALICE SMITH stood on the landing, watching her family stamp out flames from an overturned kerosene lamp. Her uncle shouted, "Steady, now, steady." Alice thought he sounded like a man trying to calm a herd of frightened horses. Her grandmother rushed by with an armload of blankets. "*Prompt obedience!*" she snapped.[15]

Alice's mother cried to her husband, "Huger! Suppose there is a tidal wave?"

"Then, my dear," he calmly replied, "we shall all be drowned." He hurried them out of the house and into the garden. A chimney crashed through the piazza roof as Smith led his children away from the tall brick house.

All of a sudden, the air turned cold. The cool came as a relief after the stifling heat of the day, but even Alice knew that such a chill was freakish on an August night. The men went inside for quilts and mattresses. Her father set off to check on a relative who lived several blocks away. Glancing down an alley, he saw two naked women. "Go home and put on some clothes!" he snapped.

"I ain' got no house, I ain' got no clothes! I'se gwine to Jesus jes' as I is!" one woman chanted in a nasal voice, as if she were singing a Psalm.

ON SULLIVAN'S ISLAND, Miriam and Lucile DuPré leaped to their feet when the beach house began to rock. Mother and daughter crossed the sand dunes, then ran back into the house twice to retrieve their possessions. Across the harbor Miriam could see the city, blazing orange as if illuminated by a sunset. But the sun, she knew, was long gone. Then there was a flare, another, and another. "He will come to us," she whispered to Lucile, speaking of her brother-in-law Frank Dawson.[16]

Miriam decided that she and Lucile should walk down the beach to the home of Dawson's friends, Charles and Mollie Glidden. Two young boys carrying a lantern were pressed into service as their escorts. A crowd had gathered on the wooden sidewalk that ran by a grocery and saloon. One woman muttered prayers, another nursed a sprained ankle. Girls in party dresses arrived to tell how the quake broke up a "hop" at the Moultrie Hotel. Someone spotted a point of light far out on the water, a tiny spark that bobbed larger and larger until they could make out the *Sappho*. A cheer went up as the side-wheel steamer chugged up to the pier.

The captain brought chilling news: Charleston destroyed, flames spreading, hundreds dead and injured. The newspaper office had collapsed. Miriam turned away. Mollie Glidden scribbled a note to Frank: "All safe and sound, though somewhat shaken. . . . We are all heroes, except those who are heroines. We shall spend the night on Keenan's piazza, because it is low down — that is near to *terra* — I had almost said *terra firma*, but I refrain." She handed it to two young fishermen who were about to set off across the harbor in a rowboat.

A CROWD SWEPT Carlyle McKinley down Broad Street toward Washington Park. He passed a stencil factory with its front wall gone. At the Confederate Home, built to provide for the widows and orphans of southern soldiers, the roof perched at an odd angle. Terrified people jammed the park, screaming and shouting prayers, trampling the flowerbeds. McKinley skirted the crowd. He pulled the notebook and pencil from his pocket and began taking notes as he walked north.

On Meeting Street, the massive portico of Hibernian Hall had hurtled to the ground. Only the jagged stumps of columns remained. The curved staircases of the Fireproof Building across the street, where county offices were housed, were reduced to heaps of rubble. McKinley could see flames along King Street, but people were so intent on listening for tremors that they acted oblivious to the fire.

A few doors south of Market Street, women screamed from an upstairs window that the staircase was blocked with debris. Some men below called, "Jump!" The women hesitated. At last the bravest climbed out and hung from the window ledge by her fingertips. Her feet dangled high above the street, tiny clappers in the bell of her skirt. Then she dropped, petticoats fluttering, into the waiting arms of the men below. Her friends followed, one by one, until all eight were safe.

At the corner of Meeting and Market streets, the Steitz building looked like an enormous dollhouse, all three floors laid open to the public view. One room was lighted. McKinley watched as a woman inside the yellow square removed the mosquito netting over her bed and folded it neatly. She turned down the bedside lamp and walked slowly, calmly from the room.

ALTHOUGH THE CITY fire alarms were knocked out, the impact of the quake rang the emergency gong at every firehouse in the city. The state-of-the-art system was set so that a single peal would trip a lever and release a team of horses at the station nearest the fire, ready to haul the heavy engines. This feature was supposed to speed response, but now all the frightened horses took off at a gallop, leaving the fire engines behind.[17]

People mobbed the fire stations, screaming directions. Some of the trucks were trapped in their bays by fallen debris. Firemen shouldered aside rubble to drag out the engines, and, taking the place of the runaway horses, pulled the heavy carriages themselves.

Smoke billowed over the city. Firemen dragged hoses to hydrants and screwed them onto spigots, only to find that the pipes had broken. Precious time was wasted before two engineers could improvise a solution and the firemen's hoses drenched the burning buildings.[18]

Flames leaped from a dozen houses on King Street across from Marion Square. Behind them stood a massive gasoline tank, a bomb waiting for a spark. A block farther south was the Orphan House, where two hundred sleepy children huddled in the courtyard. Fire vaulted from rack to rack in Mintz's clothing store, where the family lived above their shop. The owner, his parents, his wife, and their two small children fought their way through the inferno. In the space of a few minutes, everything they owned was destroyed. Down the block, a dentist's office, four apartments, and a fruit stand burned to the ground.

The fire chief ordered his men to open the tidal drains and pump salt water out of these natural reservoirs. He commandeered passing black men to chop wood for the voracious steam engines. Alderman Francis Rodgers, who had organized the city's first public fire department five years before, took charge of one of the pumps. Nine buildings along upper King Street were gutted, but the firemen managed to prevent the flames from reaching the gas tank and the Orphan House.

A smaller fire near the College of Charleston burned for an hour before the engines arrived. In the meantime, residents soaked their roofs with buckets of water passed hand to hand. Two houses were destroyed. Another fire incinerated two houses at the northeastern edge of the city, nearly burning itself out before word reached the fire department.

Engine No. 2 headed south of Broad to a corner where two schoolteachers watched helplessly as the flames spread from their small wooden home to buildings on both sides. One fireman sank to the ground, paralyzed by a stroke.

The biggest fire began after one o'clock in the morning, while the fire department was concentrating its efforts in the northern part of the city. It engulfed a dozen buildings on lower King Street, just north of Broad. The blaze started when a kerosene lamp shattered in a room on the second floor of a wooden tenement. Flames spread quickly to the windows, floors, and beams of the adjacent brick buildings. A fireman emerged from a burning doorway carrying a six-year-old girl. Her mother and two sisters were rescued moments later. A woman tied her baby in a feather mattress and tossed the bundle from a second-story window. A passerby reached up to catch it and the baby landed unharmed.

Flames jumped across the street to a bakery, devouring every building on the east side of the street until they reached the Quaker cemetery and the open lots next door. Since the great fire of 1861, which destroyed the Friends' Meeting House and everything around it, this area had stood empty. Now, the open space checked the march of a new conflagration.

HUNDREDS OF PEOPLE converged on the Cooper River waterfront, where the passenger steamer *Delaware* lay at Union Wharf. Men, women, and children, hysterical with fear, scaled the sides of the ship. Some hurled themselves into lifeboats and rowed out into the harbor. Sixteen ships lay in port, hailing from Norway, Russia, Italy, Spain, Austria, and Germany. Many of the sailors did not speak English. Most had been using their time off to tap the city's liquor supply. They surged out of the bars near the docks and milled around the dark streets, disoriented and dazed.[19]

"Come, boys, this won't do," a voice rang out. "We've got to do something here!" The sailors fell into line. Their self-appointed leader organized them into companies and sent them out in all directions — up and down East Bay Street, along Market and Broad streets. Huge warehouses along the waterfront had collapsed, and the narrow streets leading to the wharves had become "avenues of ruins." Sailors pulled victims from broken buildings and helped people salvage their possessions. From on board the ships, they retrieved spare sails to set up temporary shelters, carrying the injured to the Mariner's Church at the corner of North Market and East Bay streets and laying them on the pews.

PRISONERS IN THE city jail on Magazine Street shook the bars and screamed. Cracks split the thick brick walls. The foundation sank so that an octagonal cellblock leaned like the Tower of Pisa. The head jailer drew his pistol and fired into the air. Inmates dashed themselves against the bars, begging for release. The jailer relented, opened the cells, and herded all sixty-four prisoners into the exercise yard. One woman, a convicted murderer, broke away to scale the high brick wall. Forty-two other prisoners followed, leaving twenty-one in the yard.[20]

Within the same square of streets as the jail were most of the city's hospitals, now all heavily damaged. Down the block, the portico of the medical college collapsed. A tower imploded at Roper Hospital, bringing down part of the front wall and blocking the main entrance. Two passersby were killed. Students groped their way to a side door and began to evacuate patients, discovering two men lifeless in their beds, covered with debris. An eighteen-year-old nurse was also dead, crushed in the act of helping someone else crawl to safety. At City Hospital, where the poorest patients were treated, the walls had crumbled and heavy buttresses lay shattered on the ground. Bodies sprawled on doors and shutters torn from wrecked buildings for use as stretchers.[21]

Dr. Thomas B. McDow roamed the streets looking for people who needed help. When a woman was pulled unconscious from under a pile of rubble at a saloon, McDow was called to treat her. The battered victim was beyond help, and there was little the doctor could do but sign her death certificate. Within a few years McDow would become infamous, his name eternally linked with that of Frank Dawson. But on this night he was still unknown, just a doctor doing his job.[22]

Charlestonians went out of their way to avoid the city-supported hospitals. In spite of Mayor Courtenay's efforts, they were dark, smelly, hopeless places where beggars went to die. A man injured just across the street from City Hospital crawled five blocks to Washington Square looking for a physician. There, stretchers clustered near the gates. One woman who was visiting from Savannah gave birth to a son in the park, and her husband promptly named him Charleston.[23]

From a makeshift pulpit two black men called the people to repent. Their voices rang out over the park. God was punishing Charleston for its sins! The end of the world was near! "Amen!" cried a crowd of worshippers, many weeping in terror. "Do, my master Jesus, have mercy!"

The park was small, the clamor inescapable. Genteel old women who seldom left their houses stood elbow to elbow with rowdy tenement dwellers. To the whites huddled nervously on blankets and quilts, the preacher's point was clear: white people had better beware. God was angry *at them*.

Six indignant white men ordered the preachers to quiet down. The black throng jeered. A policeman on duty in the park refused to intervene, so the whites went off in search of the police chief, complaining that the demonstrations were "boisterous and maddening." Their wives and children were terrified. No one could sleep. The chief sent two more officers to confront the noisemakers. This time they obeyed.

Back at the *News and Courier* office, Frank Dawson shouted orders. One by one his reporters showed up. Most of the typesetters were still missing; of the pressmen, only the foreman and one other man remained on duty.[24]

Carlyle McKinley knew how to set type — he had started his newspaper career working as a compositor. He grabbed a composing stick and glanced at his notes. On page one he cleared enough space to squeeze in two inches of copy, announcing that an earthquake had struck and voicing the wistful sentiment that always follows disaster: "Perhaps our misfortune will bring our people nearer and closer together." Otherwise he left the first seven pages intact, so that the city's annual economic report remained the lead story. The headline now seemed bitterly ironic: "Charleston's Firm Stand in 1885–86."

McKinley tore up the eighth page and inserted a new headline: "A Terrible Earthquake. The Whole City Injured. The Most Disastrous Event In The City's History." His fellow reporters crowded near, ready to call out bulletins. "We cannot pretend to give more than a rough sketch of the consequences of the disaster," Frank Dawson dictated. "It must be scrappy, and, in a sense, less or more than the truth." Determined to control public opinion, he added, "The loss is not as great as it seems to be."

WITH THE TELEGRAPH and phone lines down, the newspaper staff could only report what each of them had seen. Dawson told his story first, describing the streets as he stumbled through them to the office. His reporters related what had happened to important buildings, as far as they could determine the damage in the dark and the dust: "The Main Station was crushed in, as if some mighty weight had fallen upon it. The City Hall, St. Michael's, and the Courthouse show no evidence yet of the shocks." Carlyle McKinley captured with lyric melancholy one of the most powerful and disorienting emotions sweeping through the devastated city — a sense that the catastrophe, though unforeseen, was inevitable. "The wild tremors of the earth which startled the people of Charleston early Friday morning were but the precursors of the more terrible visitation which fell upon the city last night." Dawson printed Mollie Glidden's note from Sullivan's Island as she wrote it.

Under the heading "The Very Latest," Dawson and his men squeezed in a report that the train from Columbia — Anna Robson's train — had not been heard from, and that "all efforts to secure connection by telegraph with any point outside of the city [had] proved futile." The last inch of space was occupied by a note, no doubt dictated by Dawson: "All our arrangements have been disturbed by the terrible calamity last night, and it is with the utmost difficulty that the paper is published at all.... The confusion and trouble — far beyond anything ever before experienced in Charleston — will account for all deficiencies."

BY 3:30 ON THE morning of Wednesday, September 1, the paper was ready to go to press. Carlyle McKinley found an old blanket and headed for Washington Park, hoping to grab some sleep. The preachers had quieted, but the crowd was still restless and loud. McKinley found a clear spot and lay down on the grass.

Dawson ordered the night editor to meet his sister-in-law at the dock with a copy of the paper. Then he headed home and fell into bed.

At White Point Garden a black man held a flask to Keitt Walker's lips, feeding the boy sips of whiskey. Two blocks north, on Meeting Street, the Tulane professor and his wife stared down at Robert Alexander's battered body. Outside City Hospital a nurse drew a sheet over the six-year-old girl who had been pulled from the burning building. Over the roof of the Main Police Station, a patrolman thought he saw a glowing cross. He laid his hand on his heart and exclaimed, "Ah, that is what saved us!"[25]

In Washington Park, two women lifted the corner of a blanket to gawk at a body. The corpse stirred and lifted its arm. The women gasped and shrank away. Carlyle McKinley turned over and pulled the covers back over his head.

One of the Robson boys returned to the Line Street depot to ask about his mother's train. The stationmaster told him that two of his men were about to set off by rail toward Summerville, some sixteen miles northwest of Charleston. There was no telling what they would find, but he was welcome to ride along. Robson boarded the engine with a heavy heart. He needed to find his mother and tell her that her oldest child was dead.[26]

Chapter Four

A WORLD TURNED UPSIDE DOWN

S THE SUMMER SUN rose over Charleston Harbor on Wednesday, September 1, people streamed out of the parks, heading home to see what was left. Few had slept, except in snatches. They had endured a long night, with four hard shocks before midnight and others at two and four in the morning.[1] Houses slumped on their foundations. Gutted buildings smoldered. Mills and warehouses sprawled along the wharves like broken toys. A white dust shrouded everything — streets, ruins, grass, and people. In some places the ground was covered with wet sand.

Atop the Orphan House, the huge wooden figure of Charity tilted as though preparing to dive off the dome. A large brick building behind the post office had caved in, and the walls of the post office itself were cracked and visibly leaning. The portico had pulled away from St. Michael's Church, and large cracks ran up the wall that faced Broad Street. St. Philip's steeple had shed part of its brick casing. The old federal courthouse behind the Guard House had lost its upper story. William Bird's oil and paint store on East Bay was an avalanche of broken lumber and torn canvas awnings.

The hands of the clock on St. Michael's steeple were frozen at 9:54. No chimes to mark the quarter hours broke the silence. The stillness seemed, as Frank Dawson would later write, "a sign of the shadow of death." Most pendulum clocks facing north or south had stopped; those facing east or west had speeded up. Watches had gone haywire because the jewels used to reduce friction on the gears had either broken or popped out of their housings. Nothing but the blazing sun marked the passage of time.[2] The damage seemed random and often counter to the laws of physics. A glass shade had tumbled from a lamp but landed intact. The ceiling of a drugstore had collapsed onto a showcase without shattering the glass. Some objects seemed to have floated up instead of falling down. Had gravity somehow lost its force during the shock?[3]

AT ROPER HOSPITAL, attendants carried the patients into the frame out-buildings — kitchens, washhouses, and morgues. Some lay in the open air on top of newly built coffins. Injured people poured in from other parts of the city. Feet, legs, and arms were so crushed that often the only treatment was amputation. Knees and ankles had been dislocated, skulls were frac-tured, arms and legs broken. Practically everyone had cuts, bruises, and lacerations. The death toll stood at twenty-seven that morning, and no one knew what might emerge from under the piles of rubble.[4]

For the lucky, bad news was minor — furniture overturned, plaster fallen, chimneys on the ground. Silver had tarnished overnight, and white paint had turned black. Charlotte Hayden, who had worked so hard the day before cleaning, returned home and opened the front door to see daylight pouring into the parlor through a crack in the wall. A heavy wardrobe stood on end, and a fracture ran through the marble mantel. The wallpaper hung in shreds as if clawed by a giant talon. One of a pair of china vases perched in its usual spot. The other lay in pieces.[5]

Alice Smith awakened outdoors and saw a gap in the brick wall that sepa-rated her house from the First Baptist Church cemetery next door. She and her brothers and sisters were hustled into the pantry, where the cook handed them cups of hot coffee laced with milk and sugar. Alice had never before been allowed to drink coffee; she thought there must be some mistake, but she gulped down the delicious drink and kept very quiet. Men hauled jugs of water into the yard, even though the house had taps that brought water inside. It was just a precaution, someone told Alice, in case the city water system was contaminated.[6]

FOR A COUPLE of hours after sunrise, it was possible for most people to believe that the worst must be over. At a bakery on King Street, six em-ployees cleared their workspace and started making dough. Carts of freshly baked bread went out as usual, the drivers picking their way around the piles of rubble. William Bird inspected the ruins of his paint store, located a relatively undamaged building, and negotiated a lease.[7]

Many returned to their battered homes and took comfort in small things — coffee, breakfast, clean clothes, a visit to the privy. A ninety-two-year-old man slipped away from his family and entered his house, though one whole side had collapsed. He took a bath, dressed in fresh clothes, and emerged to find his children plotting to send him to safety. The old man declared in no uncertain terms that he found the earthquake very exciting and "meant to stay and see it through."[8]

And then, at 8:25, the treetops began to thrash and sway though the air was dead calm. Waves moved along the ground in "slow and quivering" swells. Bricks and shingles pelted down. Everybody who had gone inside raced back to the street.[9]

The city seemed to hold its breath, tense and hyperalert. People complained of nausea and headaches. Ladies swallowed sedatives: morphine, laudanum, red lavender, valerian, and alcohol-based patent medicines. Men joined them or fled to the bars, which were open for business. A young man named Ned Cantwell smoked dozens of cigars he had stuffed in his pockets at the height of the shaking. "The fragrant weed," Cantwell wrote his cousin, "is such a comfort in troublous times." Few people thought of going to work.[10]

Edward Wells, Alice Smith's uncle, walked down to the Battery and squinted at the sea, anxiously trying to figure out if the land he stood on had risen or sunk during the night. Wells imagined that the sun greeted him with a "sickly smile."[11]

ON SULLIVAN'S ISLAND, Dawson's sister-in-law Miriam DuPré and her daughter Lucile, Mollie and Charles Glidden, and the seven Glidden children boarded the *Sappho*. They rode across Charleston Harbor toward the shattered city. Waiting for them at the dock was a young man carrying a copy of the *News and Courier* and a scrawled note from Frank Dawson. Miriam sagged with relief. Her hero had not been killed — he had even managed to publish a paper. Frank had not come to rescue them, as she had promised Lucile, but they would soon join him at home.[12]

The two families crossed East Bay Street and struggled west along Market. Buildings were laid open like stage sets, exposing tumbled furniture. Cornices dangled over the streets. Telegraph poles leaned at crazy angles, trailing wires. The DuPrés and the Gliddens ducked inside the long market sheds, breathing the pungent essence of yesterday's fresh produce. For three blocks they tramped along, until Miriam noticed that Lucile seemed to be stumbling. Frantic with worry, she hovered over her daughter. Lucile brushed her off.

But when they emerged on Meeting Street, Lucile staggered over to the steps of Market Hall and collapsed. The Glidden children gaped at Lucile while their father rushed off for a carriage. Finally they all sat down on the steep stairs, watching dazed people struggle over heaps of debris. All at once a policeman appeared and shouted at them. They must move away from the building, he insisted. The heavy portico above their heads was about to fall.

Miriam pulled Lucile to her feet and draped her daughter's arm over her shoulder. Mollie Glidden took the other side and, half-carrying Lucile, they headed north toward the Charleston Hotel, where taxi drivers normally waited to pick up fares. Today there were no cabs, no streetcars — only people trudging through wreckage, as far as the eye could see.

At last a carriage appeared, driven by Charles Glidden. Lucile was boosted in and the others crowded around her, three adults and eight children in a vehicle designed for four. They made slow headway.

When they finally arrived at Dawson's gate, Miriam stared. Vines trailed over a heap of brick and stone where the front staircase had stood. The grass was white with dust. Miriam elbowed her way out of the carriage, leaving Lucile behind. Oblivious to propriety, she dashed around the house, up the back stairs, through the hallways, and into Frank's bedroom. There he lay, fast asleep, in a bed covered with broken plaster.

Frank sat up, scoffed at her fears, and insisted on coming down at once to greet the Gliddens. They were about to move to Florida and had just sold their town house, so he invited the whole family to stay with him until the danger was over. Miriam bustled out back to see about breakfast. She found Emma, the German cook, moaning and crying in the kitchen house. Miriam calmed her enough to produce some food, but it was clear that Emma was still a nervous wreck.

Frank bolted some ham and eggs and headed back to the office. Paperboys hawked the *News and Courier* wherever there was a crowd, and his reporters were already on the streets, filling in the details of an increasingly surreal picture. Buildings that had seemed untouched the night before, including City Hall and the courthouse, now appeared ruined. St. Michael's newly repaired steeple listed. St. Philip's looked like a "total wreck." The steeple at the Unitarian Church had fallen through the roof, pulling down the ribbed ceiling that had been its most beautiful feature.[13]

TELEGRAPH REPAIRMEN worked their way down the wires, searching for breaks. The Western Union office was mobbed with people, and employees took down their messages, promising to send them out as soon as the lines were repaired. Two of the operators, Charles Rittenhouse and a colleague named Scott, scooped up these slips of paper along with dispatches from the newspapers. Their plan was to leave the earthquake zone and find a working terminal. At the railroad station Rittenhouse saw an engine puffing steam. He ran into the office and asked to catch a ride to wherever the train was going. Permission was granted. The engine crept out of town, moving at a snail's pace, but after about four miles it halted. The engineer explained that the rails had spread, and he and the fireman jumped out to straighten them by hand. Their slow journey resumed. Finally the locomotive stopped before a wide crevasse where the tracks had twisted. Seeing that repairs would take a long time, Rittenhouse and Scott continued on foot.[14]

They walked about ten miles along the tracks, arriving in Summerville hot, hungry, and thirsty but still clutching the precious sheaf of messages. They found telegraph instruments inside the railroad station, but the whole place was deserted. Rittenhouse sat down and searched for a live wire. Scott took off to "skirmish" for something to eat. He wandered into a deserted grocery and helped himself to crackers and cheese.

Meanwhile, Rittenhouse managed to make contact with Washington, D.C. Operators all along the line broke in to ask for news of the city. "Now, boys," Rittenhouse tapped, puffed up with his new renown. "Listen and you will hear the news." He started to "rattle off" messages, eating cheese and crackers with his left hand and working the key with his right. Finally the rest of the world got word of Charleston's plight.

At Asheville, North Carolina, the news came in pieces. First a wire arrived from the South Carolina state capital, Columbia: "We are all safe, but poor Charleston." Rev. A. Toomer Porter, an Episcopal minister who ran a private academy in Charleston, heard this news from friends. Like many well-to-do Charlestonians, he was vacationing in the cool mountains, though his mother, aunt, and niece were all at home in Charleston. Porter hurried down to the telegraph office in Asheville and waited nervously for more information. Around eleven that night, half a sentence came through. There was a break, and another fragment, then another. Finally the operator told Porter that Charleston had been destroyed.[15]

In Flat Rock, not far from Asheville, rumors flew: only fifty houses were still standing in Charleston. The land for twenty miles around the city was a "quagmire" that would never again support a railroad.[16]

From Summerville, Rittenhouse and Scott took turns sending messages over the single wire. They worked frantically until midnight, when they reached the bottom of the pile. Then they curled up on the floor and slept like the dead.

AT THE *News and Courier* office, stories piled up on Frank Dawson's desk that Wednesday morning. Still flushed with last night's triumph — who else would have even tried to put out a paper in the middle of an earthquake, much less succeeded? — he shouted orders and made plans to print extra editions. Thousands were clamoring for a fuller account of the disaster. But then things started to go wrong. The foreman of the pressroom was there, and compositors were expected to start setting type around ten that morning. But the hour came and went, and no compositors appeared. A few sent word that they were busy with their families. Others simply failed to show up. Dawson was exasperated. He tracked down one of the men who refused to report for work. The composing room was too dangerous, the man explained. He would not set foot inside until it had been inspected.[17]

Just two years before, in a front-page article, the *News and Courier* had proudly announced that the walls of its new pressroom were "so thick and solid that nothing less than an earthquake could harm them."[18] Now that an earthquake had arrived, Dawson continued to insist that his building was safe.

A tremor shook the damaged walls at one that afternoon. Still no typesetters appeared. Dawson exploded. The compositors were cowards, a disgrace to the profession. Yet they had him over a barrel. If he fired them, where would he find replacements? And the last thing Dawson wanted was to butt heads with the typesetters' union, a powerful and well-organized group that could bring a newspaper to its knees. Typesetters had walked out at Henry Grady's *Constitution* four years before, and the dispute had dragged on until arbitrators were brought in. Dawson was stymied. The *News and Courier* would not be issued on September 2.[19]

Aftershocks usually follow strong earthquakes. Though generally less destructive than the main shock, they are not harmless — they can shake loose parts of damaged buildings and cause structural damage. In most cases, the tremors, caused by readjustments along a fault as it settles into a new position, gradually decrease, their magnitude diminishing. Yet there are exceptions to this rule, and the first big shock is not always the strongest. As many older Charlestonians would have remembered, the first New Madrid earthquake, which occurred along the Mississippi River near present-day Memphis in December 1811, was followed by two more massive shocks in January and February, both stronger and more destructive than the first.[20]

Those who read newspapers and history books feared that the 1886 earthquake would trigger a "tidal wave," what we now call a seismic sea wave or a tsunami. On the heels of the great Lisbon earthquake of 1755, an enormous wave drowned thirty thousand people. In 1883, the eruption of the Krakatoa volcano in the Dutch East Indies (today Indonesia) had triggered an even larger surge. Charleston is nearly surrounded by water, a low tongue of sandy ground only a few feet above sea level. It was easy to envision a giant wave engulfing the peninsula.[21]

The earthquake triggered many strange afflictions, even in cities far from the epicenter. According to the *Savannah Morning News*, at least a dozen people went insane and had to be sent to lunatic asylums, including "the wives and daughters of prominent citizens." A drugstore clerk started walking on Tuesday night and didn't stop until he reached a town fifty miles away, where he sent a postcard to his parents saying he could not return. A woman in Winston, North Carolina, lost the ability to speak. A fourteen-year-old girl who lived in Smoaks Crossroads, South Carolina, was taken to the South Carolina Lunatic Asylum in Columbia when she started raving after the earthquake and exhibited "a strong homicidal tendency."[22]

In Augusta, there were multiple reports of earthquake-induced insanity. The city collector wandered the streets, talking "in a wild way" about terrible warnings sent by God. The daughter of a factory worker cried for help as she jerked in response to imaginary aftershocks. A family of three tied themselves together and jumped into Horse Creek. All drowned. A shoe salesman, "prostrated" by the quake, sat down on the floor of his room and blew his brains out with a pistol. Another man heard about this suicide and told his wife that he, too, was going to "end his anguish by death." He locked himself in a room, made a noose, and strung himself up. But his wife called the police, and they burst in and pulled him down in time to save him. At least four women were said to have been "frightened to death."[23]

Sometimes the shocks seemed to heal people. Reports spread that fifteen-year-old Minnie Martus of Savannah, who had been mute since she suffered a bout of meningitis three years before, abruptly started talking. In Columbia, there were reports that the shocks had cured "many chronic cases of partial paralysis, spinal weakness, &c."[24]

Animals were affected, too. Thousands of earthworms crawled out of the ground in one Savannah yard. So many piled up that the owner removed them with a shovel, only to find more accumulating as soon as he was done. Countless fireflies congregated in a swamp close to Kingstree. Roosting birds tumbled from the trees on Pawley's Island. Seamen who were out in the harbor during the quake swore that "numbers of fish jumped out of the water, apparently frightened to death." In Charleston, armies of rats and roaches were observed evacuating damaged houses.[25]

ALMOST NO ONE tried to begin making repairs. Paths were cleared through the rubble, but otherwise little move was made toward cleaning up the mess. Those whose houses were fit to inhabit took in crowds of refugees. Attorney and state senator Augustine Smythe invited his neighbors, the burned-out schoolteachers, to sleep in his spare room. Smythe's cook and her whole family moved into the entryway, and another servant's family set up camp in his study. A playhouse in the back yard sheltered more of his employees. At his wife's insistence, Smythe roamed the streets looking for their butler and a woman who sewed for them.[26]

But undamaged houses were few and far between, and by early afternoon shelters had mushroomed in every open space. Night air was thought to cause disease, especially malaria and the dreaded yellow fever. An epidemic could kill hundreds or even thousands, and to sleep outdoors was to gamble with death. Yet for most people it was more frightening to stay inside a damaged house while the aftershocks continued. At least one family built a large fire "to purify and dry the air," which at least would have driven away the mosquitoes.[27]

In the Dawsons' yard, children sprawled everywhere, playing or napping. Nearly everybody was nauseated, and most had diarrhea. Dawson's sister-in-law found a bottle of valerian, a sedative, and passed it around. She and Mollie Glidden coaxed Emma the cook to lie down between them. At last Emma drifted off and everything quieted. Then another tremor hit and she leaped up in tears. Charles Glidden and his son Philip headed to the harbor to retrieve a sail from their yacht, which they draped over an arrangement of poles as a tent.[28]

The cook pulled herself together to prepare a meal — ham, coffee, bread, and milk. Dawson and his guests sat down in the dining room and tried to pretend they were having a normal supper. Then they heard a rumble and the walls began to shake. They all ran outside, leaving the food on the table.

The Cuban physician whose family rented space from the Haydens used his position as a government employee to procure a large hospital tent. When it was set up on the banks of Colonial Lake, the Haydens brought out chairs and mattresses and invited the neighbors in. A woman with a newborn baby was put to bed on a sofa. As dusk began to fall, twenty-seven people, including the infant, huddled under the canvas.[29]

Alice Smith's father rigged a shed with old tin and a strip of carpet. The servants carried mattresses from the house and lined them up underneath. Alice crawled inside and lay down, gazing at the rug above her head. The floor she had walked across last night was now her ceiling.[30]

At last darkness shrouded the ruins. Candles, lanterns, and flickering campfires cast eerie shadows over the trampled ground. In the parks and the vacant lots, blacks and whites bedded down side by side. It was a strange new world, unlike anything the old city had ever known.

Chapter Five

THE EARTHQUAKE HUNTERS

AT THE *CONSTITUTION* offices in downtown Atlanta, the lobby was so crowded around the bulletin board by eight on the morning after the earthquake that employees had to squeeze in and out of the building. Around ten, a telegram arrived and the newspaper posted a notice: Charleston had been hit by an "awful catastrophe." Unconfirmed reports said that the city had been engulfed and ocean waves were breaking over the historic steeples. The only landmark still visible was the top of the Custom House on East Bay Street. At least sixteen hundred people had died.[1]

Henry Grady's heart beat faster. This was the story of a lifetime, and he yearned to go to Charleston to cover it himself. Grady took his request to the editor-in-chief, Evan P. Howell, expecting him to object. Managing editors were supposed to stay in the office, not go out in search of news. But Grady had made his reputation by covering breaking stories, and he was part owner of the newspaper. Howell surprised him by saying that he wanted to go, too. Soon it was settled — Grady and Howell would travel to Charleston and meet the *Constitution*'s Columbia correspondent, who was already on his way.

Around eleven that morning, someone in the newspaper lobby shouted that Southern Telegraph had received a wire about Charleston. Hundreds of people ran down the street and mobbed the telegraph office. "A terrible earthquake last night at 9:50 p.m. destroyed the principal business portion of the city," read the telegram. "Hundreds are rendered homeless. Men are frantic and women are beseeching mercy from the Almighty and the children are in tears. The Union station house, the City Hall, the Hibernian Hall and many other well known public buildings including the never-dying St. Michael's Church, all irreparably damaged. Many people are terribly if not fatally injured. Broad Street presents a spectacle of the utmost horror. Even women armed with hatchets fought valiantly to rescue the imprisoned unfortunates."

Western Union, Southern's rival, soon made contact with Charleston, too, thanks to the efforts of Charles Rittenhouse, and part of the Atlanta crowd moved down the street to the Western Union office. Reports continued to come in, hair-raising, preposterous-sounding tales of twisted train tracks, gaping fissures, and spouts of boiling water. The bulletin board was moved outside, and whenever new details arrived, a man was sent to post them. At two, newsboys appeared with an extra edition of the *Constitution*, and the papers "sold as fast as a dozen men could count them out." "Charleston Shocked! Over Sixty Lives Lost In The Earthquake! The Streets Filled With Ruins And The Dead!" Printing after printing sold out, and when the press was finally shut down for the day, people still clamored for additional copies. More than five thousand papers sold in less than half an hour, a record. The paper promised to print another edition as soon as more news came in.[2]

Grady and Howell boarded a train for Charleston in high spirits. Atlanta's damage was minor, and at first the stories they gathered were comical. At Crawfordville, an old man got on holding a lantern and a "stout stick." He was, wrote the amused Grady, "evidently patrolling the town and looking up the earthquake, pretty much as a town marshal looks up a burglar, assuredly bound to collar it when found." The old man searched under the seats, Grady wrote, "as if he thought we had the earthquake concealed somewhere in the car."[3]

"It's . . . still in the neighborhood," he said, "for I've heer'd it twice and felt it three times this very night." Then he took his "bludgeon" and departed, lantern glimmering in the darkness.

Grady knew that his readers wanted drama, so he also played up the danger of his mission. "Since Don Quixote charged the windmill, I doubt if ghastlier work has been done than the advance I now begin against an earthquake," his first dispatch began. "It was 'kiss and go' with Atlanta and her 'quake — a tremor, a sigh and an *au revoir*. But the earthquakes still linger in the lowlands, and I go to seek them there."

Grady described his journey in the melodramatic prose of dime novels. "The empty cars admonish me," he wrote, "that when the earth's crust is smoking, one should not leave Atlanta, buttressed as she is on her everlasting hills. . . . I feel that I have left the gates of granite land, and am henceforth liable to be smote down, swallowed up or spit out at any moment."

The train pulled into Augusta, Georgia, near the South Carolina border and about 120 miles from Charleston, "in the cool gray of the morning" on

September 2. Beds had been set up under the trees, and people were cooking breakfast over open fires. Babies slumbered outdoors on improvised cots. Two hundred people were camped in a graveyard. Grady saw wagons parked in the middle of the streets, filled with sleeping people. Even the whorehouses were deserted, and the occupants stood in the streets "praying for mercy and forgiveness."

"The earthquake hunters," as Grady called his group, soon discovered that getting closer to Charleston would be a considerable challenge. The tracks beyond Augusta were damaged. No trains could get through. Grady waved rolls of bills and offered to charter an engine. The railroad officials turned him down, claiming that the tracks from Yemassee, South Carolina, to Charleston had been deformed by volcanic eruptions. Grady asked about driving to the coastal town of Beaufort, South Carolina, and hiring a tugboat there to take him the remaining seventy miles. He was told that no tugs would put out to sea "while the earthquakes are around."

Finally, Grady sent a wire to John H. Averill, master of transportation on the South Carolina Railway. Averill replied that if Grady and his colleagues could get to the mill town of Langley, fifteen miles northeast of Augusta, he would have an engine try to take them the rest of the way to Charleston. Grady hired a wagon pulled by "four handsome grays," and he and Howell set off with the editor of the *Augusta Chronicle*.

The destruction at Langley was awesome. Cracks and fissures ran through a huge dam that had once confined a mill pond. The forest looked as if a tornado had ripped through, and the rushing water had washed out more than a thousand feet of railroad track, plowed down the forest, and swallowed a train, drowning two of the crew. Five miles away at Horse Creek, another train pulling stock cars had plunged into forty feet of water. One crewman had been killed there and four horses had drowned. Yet Grady was surprised to note that there were no signs of a volcanic eruption. "It was simply as if some tremendous power had torn the earth apart, cutting the tracks clean and definite."

Everywhere Grady looked he saw fear and despair. People ran through the woods, screaming. At every turn he heard tales of men and women driven insane by the quake. Yet there was also a tendency to make do, to make the best of things. Grady saw several men fishing, and the scent of frying fish seasoned with vinegar hung in the air.

He spied a small boat on the opposite side of the mill pond and paid a local man to strip and swim for it, then row them all across the water to the promised locomotive. The engineer warned them that they would be traveling at their own risk. Then the train pulled out toward Charleston, chugging backward up the track.

Each time the engine stopped, people swarmed the train, begging for news. Charlestonians crowded in, trying to get home. Passengers clung to the wood tender and the cowcatcher. At Branchville, an important junction where the two sets of tracks came together, the depot was crowded with refugees who had trudged along the tracks from Summerville. Some begged for scraps of food.

The train steamed slowly on, approaching the town of Jedburg as darkness fell. Hundreds of people stood on the platform. In other villages crowds had run up to meet the incoming train. Here the terrified group ignored its arrival. "The women were crying. The children's features were tense with fear. Some had fainted," Grady noted. People finally approached the train, tears streaming down their cheeks, and begged to be let on. When the engine pulled away without them, the "wails of the children" followed Grady down the track.

In Summerville, the streets were empty. The ground was pocked with craters "vomiting sand and water." They passed a family of fifteen camped near a collapsed house. "Beds, tables, books, and work" were spread under a tree. As they inched their way toward Charleston, gangs labored in front of the train, straightening the tracks. Sometimes the train hardly moved. One man told Grady he had spent all day cutting out pieces of twisted rail; that morning a jet of water had erupted between him and his fellow workers. Someone handed Grady a cup of water dipped from a fissure. He took a mouthful and swished it around. It tasted of sulfur and iron.

Campfires flickered in the woods along the tracks, and most of the houses were dark. Grady was reminded of the Civil War, though he had been too young to fight. Suddenly the train began to lurch, and a telegraph lineman sitting on the tender was thrown to the ground. The engine stopped. Someone came aboard and announced that they had just experienced an earthquake shock, and that another tremor thirty minutes before had shot a stream of water fifteen feet in the air. The train started again and crept down the straightened rails, rising, sinking, and swaying. An odor like rotten eggs hung in the night air.

Rolling into Charleston that Thursday night, the train passed a long line of railroad cars stopped on a side track. At the Line Street station, Grady hired a carriage, and the men made their slow way into the city. It was long after dark, yet the streets were filled with people carrying babies and bed-clothes. A policeman halted their cab. "That street is full of beds and peo-ple," he said. "You can't go down it."

At eleven Henry Grady drew up in front of Frank Dawson's house. The gate was shut and locked, so Grady, who had been traveling for about twenty-four hours, pulled a knob that rang a bell. Miriam and the children were asleep, but Dawson was still up, talking to the Gliddens. He had finally made time that day to compose a letter to Sarah. "I am perfectly well and about as serene as usual," he insisted. But the crisis was taking its toll. Daw-son was tense and apprehensive, uncertain whether the city could bounce back as it had so many times before.[4]

Henry Grady shook Dawson's hand and started asking questions. Sleep-deprived and caught off guard, Dawson admitted that his city was trauma-tized. It was possible that people might move away in the wake of the disas-ter. Yet the city was ready for business, he hastened to add, and he was sure that people would recover and "turn their faces toward the future."

At midnight Grady moved on to interview Acting Mayor Huger, who was still up and attending to his official duties. The body of Robert Alexan-der had been taken away, though the rubble that killed him still lay by the door. Grady asked if a relief committee had been formed, and Huger said there was no need. "What about crime?" Grady asked. Huger said that order had prevailed and no arrests had been necessary.

At two in the morning on Friday, September 3, Grady leaned on the counter at the telegraph office in Charleston, posting his report. The city was "worn and weary," he wrote, in better shape than Summerville, but in ruins nevertheless.

Later that morning, he was out and about as soon as people began to stir. His basic assessment did not change: "Charleston is laid down in dust." People were just beginning to clear paths through the streets, and small groups of men searched the ruins for bodies and survivors. The official death toll was thirty-three, with at least one hundred injured.

Grady's story was wired to papers all over the nation, and it was pub-lished under his byline although very few reporters at the time were ac-knowledged by name. Often Grady's account ran side by side with the sto-ries sent in by Dawson's reporters, many of whom were stringers for big-city papers. Carlyle McKinley's earthquake story had beaten Grady's by a whole day, yet Grady's over-the-top descriptions were the ones that grabbed the public's attention. The city, he declared, "is one vast holocaust, a mighty charnel house. . . . Corpse after corpse has been exhumed from the debris, and yet the dreary work is not near finished. . . . How many of these dead bodies will be taken out no one can answer. Grim surprises have attended the work of recovering the victims' remains. In one building, where it was thought that a single person had perished, three mangled corpses were laid bare. Most of the bodies are frightfully disfigured. Many of them have not yet been identified. Some of them never will be. In the ruins of some of the buildings which were burned have been found human bones and skulls and half roasted bodies."

As both Grady and Dawson knew, bad news is good news for journalists. In one day in late August 1886, before Charleston's own spectacular disaster came to dominate the news, the *News and Courier* reported a double drowning, a bridge collapse, a fire that killed a mother and two children, a man gored by a steer, an explosion at a factory, and the murder of a black youth who was suspected of chopping a white woman to death with a hoe — all on the front page. So the news of a U.S. earthquake drew reporters by the dozens. By Sunday, representatives from the *New York Times, Star, Sun,* and *World,* the *Boston Globe,* the *Baltimore Sun,* the United Press, and the Associated Press had arrived in Charleston. They had to wait in line to telegraph their stories.[5]

Other newspapers ran sensational tales that rivaled Grady's for melodrama. The *Savannah Morning News* promised accounts of hair-raising peril:

A Yawning Inferno
Charleston On The Crust Of a Crater
Huge Bottomless Pits
Lava And Water Hurled High in the Air
Nature's Hideous Jaws
Great Seams in the Earth Opening and Shutting[6]

The *New York Herald* depicted Charleston as "paralyzed" by the shock. Many bodies lay unburied, it said, especially those of poor blacks. Workmen were demanding "outrageous" sums to repair damaged houses. Proprietors, instead of reopening their stores, "wandered up and down the streets all day looking at the scenes of desolation and destruction." The black population was out of control, and the police were "utterly incapable." Instead of going after criminals, they spent their time warning people away from dangerous buildings. Mounted officers were patrolling the streets, but so were gangs of burglars, who showed "alarming boldness." "Millions of dollars in the shape of help have been offered," the paper scolded, "and as yet no means have been provided for . . . distribution."[7]

"Charleston's Citizens Demoralized," the *Herald* reported, using a word that had specific connotations in the late nineteenth century. Applied to the upper classes, "demoralized" meant depressed, dispirited, sad with good reason. Applied to the poor, especially blacks, it meant lazy, weak-willed, insane with fright, unwilling to work, and waiting for a handout. The *Herald* jeered that Charleston's problem was mostly fear.

Terror might threaten to paralyze the city, but some Charlestonians could still joke about their condition. McElree's Jewelry Palace offered to repair clocks "demoralized" by the quake, as well as "magnetized watches" and other timepieces "suffering from any other complaint caused by the late 'Shock.'" Another jeweler invented a useful new adjective when he offered to pay special attention to "earthquaked" watches and clocks.[8]

THE AGGRESSIVE, circulation-hungry *New York World* printed Henry Grady's earthquake story hot off the wires on its front page. Joseph Pulitzer, the publisher, called in his favorite illustrator, Walt McDougall, and told him to get to Charleston. McDougall, who was twenty-six but looked younger, had already made a name for himself as a political cartoonist — his biting caricatures of Republican presidential candidate James G. Blaine had helped turn the tide for Grover Cleveland in 1884. But McDougall also functioned as a kind of human camera, illustrating news stories. His pictures were crude, dashed off in a few minutes, but they had the power to bring events to life and sell thousands of papers.[9]

Pulitzer asked McDougall before he left to look at photographs and make quick sketches of the standard Charleston attractions — King Street, the Battery, City Hall, the Custom House, and St. Michael's. Then he put the artist on a train to Charleston, accompanied by a telegraph operator named Fisher. It was a difficult journey. The two men rode the last twenty miles on horseback, arriving around ten in the evening on September 3, the day after Grady's arrival. Mr. Fisher went off to find a working wire, while Walt

McDougall stowed his bags in a third-floor room at the Charleston Hotel. He called for a carriage and sat down to rest in the crowded lobby. As soon as he had settled into his seat, the hotel began to shudder. A clerk leaped over the counter. A bellboy carrying a pitcher of ice flew down the stairs and sprinted away. The men sitting in rocking chairs dashed outdoors. When the earth settled, everyone drifted back in, pale and shaking. One man turned to McDougall and inquired, "When does the next train leave?"

The city had been silent when McDougall arrived; now people were milling everywhere. Even the rumble of a passing carriage brought campers running out of their tents, convinced that another shock was on its way.

McDougall joined a group of reporters who were trying to make up their minds whether to sleep in the hotel or camp in one of the parks. A few decided to stay outside. The rest got into McDougall's carriage and rode back to the hotel, where they drank themselves "into a spirit of calm" and went upstairs to bed. McDougall, at least, slept well, having been awake for almost forty-five hours.

The next morning he went out to sketch, followed by crowds of spectators. McDougall tried his best to record dialect, an attempt at verisimilitude that sometimes made his stories from Charleston sound racist. "Put me in dare, boss!" he claimed the people cried. Whenever a little head popped up, an adult voice shouted, "Go way from dah, you chile, de gentium cawn't see frough you." Sometimes adults tried to sneak into the picture and were taunted by the crowd. "See dat ar black wench sticking her head outen dat ar winder," one woman sneered. "She tinks she's gwine in dis yere picture!"

Then another shock rolled through, and the crowd began to pray. "Laud! Hold up dese yere houses in de palms of yer hands," McDougall heard a woman cry. Finally someone raised a song, and they all joined in. McDougall kept on drawing.

"Say, boss, how long dis yere gwine to last?" an old man inquired. "Does yer tink de ground gwine to open and swaller de chillen of Israel?"

The illustrator said he thought that the ground felt pretty stable. "Well, if dat's so," an old woman shot back, "I'd like to know what's de meaning ob all dese little 'breviations dat we'se a-gittin?"

McDougall found a barbershop and went in for a shave. The barber's hands were trembling. "S'cuse me, boss," he apologized. "I'se jist frighted to deff. De'se yere shocks is breakin' me all up. I'se gitten so as I can't do nuffin' at all." McDougall assured him that the danger was over. The barber shook his head and said that a man could never tell when he was about to be yanked into everlasting fire.

WALT MCDOUGALL'S earthquake drawings still have the freshness of immediate observation — they provide the kind of informal snapshot that nineteenth-century cameras were incapable of taking. McDougall sketched a family looking for a place to sleep, lugging blankets and pots. He drew someone lying in a hospital bed, covered in fallen boards and plaster. And his pen was better than a lens at depicting the scale of the disaster. "Camp in the Old Cathedral Ground" shows a cluster of tiny tents in the towering shadow of the ruins.

McDougall soon took the train back the way Grady had come, ostensibly to look at fissures. As it turned out, however, the people interested him more. Disembarking at Ten Mile Hill, a settlement northwest of the city where geysers and craters were abundant, he met a man who claimed the shocks were "the Evil One" and tried to shoot them with his gun.

Then he encountered a group beating the ground with sticks. "What kind of a religion is this?" he asked. An old man replied, "Honey, don't you say nuffin agin dat beatin' on de groun' wid sticks; ef we hadn't a-beaten on de groun' wid dem sticks we all bin swallered up long ago." Another man observed that the earthquakes had never struck in "de ole times," and said he thought that "pokin' in de groun' for phosphate an drillin' dem 'tesian wells way in de bowells ob de yarth is what's adoin' it."

An Irishman, shoveling dirt into a crater that had engulfed a peach tree, said he had agreed to fill the hole in exchange for a dollar. "Begob, sir," the man exclaimed, "I'm thinkin' I've bit off more than I kin chew! Shure I've put three wagon-load of mud in the hole, and it's as big as iver it was."

A crowd gathered to watch him work. "Why do you waste your time?" asked a woman who was smoking a pipe. "Let the dead bury the dead. The Lord made that hole: let him fill it."

At a hotel in Summerville, McDougall ordered corn on the cob. He was presented with a worm-eaten ear that was "almost bald." When he complained, the waiter clasped his hands. "Lord, sah, you'se mo' peticular dan mos' folks dese times. Dis de bes' we kin do, and de Laud have mercy on our souls. It's 'nuff to wait on de table, when we ought to be in de meetin' prayin', sah, widout bein' 'bused fo' bringin' dat kine ob' coun." McDougall dashed off a quick sketch of the wretched cob.

Walt McDougall had a number of close calls. On his last day in Charleston, he sat down on a camp stool at the corner of Meeting and Hasell streets to sketch the ruins of Mrs. Benjamin Lazarus's house. The usual crowd of spectators pushed close to watch. Without warning, a brick wall crashed down behind him. McDougall got up and walked away, carrying his sketch box and stool. The crowd was sure he had been crushed and rushed into the pile of ruins to search for his body. That night he checked in at the telegraph office, only to discover that his colleague Fisher had sent out a mournful telegram announcing his death. McDougall wired New York just in time to prevent the *World* from printing his obituary.[10]

THE SAME TRAINS that brought the reporters also carried another group of earthquake hunters. The U.S. government had recently appointed Professor J. C. Mendenhall, William John McGee, Clarence E. Dutton, and three other distinguished scientists to a new Earthquake Commission. Before the Charleston earthquake, the commission had very little seismic work to do. Now they hastily prepared a questionnaire to be distributed throughout the country. The head of the U.S. Geological Survey (USGS), John Wesley Powell, dispatched Mendenhall and McGee to Charleston, along with a photographer named C. C. Jones.[11]

Mendenhall was a professor of electrical science with the U.S. Signal Corps. He had become interested in earthquakes while teaching in Japan and had set up several stations to collect data on seismic phenomena. Forty-five years old, bald, and bespectacled, Mendenhall was strong willed and contentious, always sure that his was the right way. Before leaving on his mission, he told the press that the Charleston shock had been felt over a wider area than any earthquake on record. Using a world globe ten inches in diameter, he demonstrated that the area shaken by most earthquakes, even severe ones, could be covered by the end of his little finger. The Charleston quake had agitated half the North American continent — a truly astonishing sweep.[12]

McGee, who was twelve years younger than Mendenhall, had worked for the USGS since 1883, compiling a detailed study of the geology of the southeastern coastal plain. To the despair of proofreaders everywhere, McGee was an impatient man who insisted that his initials be printed without the conventional periods — W J McGee. He liked fine clothes and was always well dressed, even when working in the field.[13]

The thirty-year-old Jones was from Maryland. Though more experienced at making prints and slides of maps than at photography in the field, he had just accompanied McGee on a tour of the Chesapeake Bay area, where they recorded evidence of geological stratification.[14]

McGee strode out into the wreckage almost as soon as he arrived in Charleston on Friday, September 3, carrying a small notebook. Within an hour, he had reached several conclusions. Walls facing east had sustained the greatest injury. Walls and ornaments facing north were most likely to have been thrown outward. Chimneys seemed to have fallen either north or south. Everywhere McGee went he scribbled notes and drew diagrams. He concentrated first on places where water had burst through the ground. On Savage Street, near the Ashley River, jets of water had dislodged clumps of sod. A yard on Queen Street had been submerged in more than a foot of water.[15]

The next day, Saturday, he set out to look for the center of the disturbance. As his train pulled out for Summerville, McGee noticed that buildings made of wood seemed to be undamaged. Even their brick chimneys were intact. Then, as the train moved into open country, he began to see fissures and craters along the tracks and in the fields. The number of craters increased as they neared Ten Mile Hill, then decreased beyond. McGee observed many fissures between the towns of Woodstock and Ladson, northwest of Charleston along the South Carolina Railway line. He saw none at the black settlement of Lincolnville, farther out, though many houses and chimneys there had been badly damaged. As the train rolled into Summerville around five in the afternoon, McGee spotted hundreds of fissures. Large fields were covered by films of yellow or blue sand and crossed by "long lines of little hillocks." McGee noted these phenomena with scientific detachment — unlike the excitable Edward Wells, who visited the same territory a few days later and noted with wonder that anyone who had been in the right spot on the night of the quake might have witnessed "a fountain with more numerous jets than the celebrated Basin of Neptune at Versailles."[16]

Summerville was a mess. About three-fourths of the chimneys were damaged, and McGee could see that most had been crushed instead of thrown to the side. Even the frame houses had been knocked askew. Every half hour or so, tremors rocked the ground. Someone offered McGee a tent, but he scoffed at the idea of sleeping outside. Instead, he calmly lay down on the first floor of a wooden house. In the middle of the night the earth roared. The building strained, the floor "sprung and twisted," and the furniture shifted and rocked. McGee was thrown up and down so fast that it seemed as if his bed were beating him. A slender glass vial danced over the surface of his dressing case. McGee stayed calm enough to notice that his head was being pushed to the west and his feet to the east. At last the nightmarish growl died away, and McGee could hear dogs barking, chickens cackling, ducks quacking, horses neighing, and people "screaming, shouting, praying." Several times during the night, the earth shuddered again. Each time, humans and animals raised an "indescribable wail."

The next day was Sunday. As McGee went about his work, dazed by lack of sleep, he was often startled by detonations. Sometimes the earth also moved, and sometimes it didn't. Horses and dogs stared at the ground for no apparent reason. That night McGee returned to Charleston, desperate for a good night's rest. The city was quieter than Summerville, but not by much. He was relaxing at a house on Meeting Street when "a pretty severe quake" rocked the city.

McGee and Mendenhall, presumably accompanied by Jones, took the train up to Ten Mile Hill. McGee noted that a two-acre sweet potato field was blanketed with sand a foot deep. It was clear from marks on the fences and plants that water must have covered the ground to a depth of eighteen inches.

McGee was guided by the work of Robert Mallet, an Irish engineer who some three decades before had used dynamite and gunpowder to measure how fast elastic waves could travel through surface rocks. Mallet was famous for suggesting that objects moved by a quake — such as displaced tombstones and overturned columns — could be used to deduce the direction of earth waves and how fast they were moving. He had also proved that earthquake waves travel at different speeds through different types of soil.[17]

Following Mallet's lead, McGee paid special attention to the way heavy monuments had been twisted and thrown in graveyards and stone-carving shops. At Viett's marble yard on Broad Street, an obelisk had been pitched against an iron fence, landing so that McGee was convinced that the earth waves had traveled from north to south. A column made of Tennessee marble had lifted off its base and spun around, suggesting a "rotary motion." One of a pair of granite globes atop the gateposts at George Walton Williams's mansion had "rocked," leaving behind a telltale chip on its support.[18]

The *News and Courier* quickly adopted McGee's obsession with twisted tombstones, reporting every example that could be discovered. "The single most significant fact which I garnered [in Charleston]," the irreverent Walt McDougall would later joke, "was that every single-shafted monument in the graveyard was speared into the ground for a foot or two by the sudden jerk of the earth." But most people put tremendous faith in what Professor McGee had to say, and Frank Dawson published an article on his activities almost every day he was in the area. McGee delivered his conclusions quickly, and with an air of comforting certainty. "It is simply a seaward slip," he announced as soon as he rolled into town. The Atlantic Coastal Plain was inching toward the sea.[19]

McGee demonstrated with a slice of bread he had cut almost in half. He held the bread at an angle and attempted to slide the two halves across each other. "If I had cut it clear through there would have been no resistance except the friction," he explained. "But as it is joined together at the end there is additional resistance." He asked his listeners to imagine fifty saucers strung like beads on a single elastic string. If you pulled the train of saucers along a surface, he said, they would move along in jerks. The coastal plain worked like this — each part operated independently.

The visiting members of the Earthquake Commission hoped to calm the fears of local residents who expected further shocks. But the experts did not agree as to what had caused the earthquake. In fact, Professor Mendenhall "hoot[ed]" at McGee's seaward-slip theory.[20] The interior of the earth was hot, he said, and the cooling crust contracted from time to time, causing "adjustments." Mendenhall's report, published in the *Monthly Weather Review of the Signal Service* for August, located the epicenter in the neighborhood of Summerville. Mendenhall described the sandblows and craters, noting that there was no evidence that the ejected water had been hot, much less "boiling." He pointed out that structures built on "made ground," or fill, had suffered severe damage, and that brick structures had fared worse than those made of wood. He refrained from making larger judgments until all the evidence was in.

None of the original earthquake hunters stayed more than a week. Professor Mendenhall left on September 7. And despite the fact that William McGee saw in the quake "the most interesting problem that has been presented to th[is] generation of scientists," he returned to Washington on September 8. Before leaving, he wrote a letter to Frank Dawson reiterating that there was no reason to fear future shocks. There was "not the slightest

danger of tidal waves, volcanic eruptions, or other catastrophic disturbances." McGee expressed his heartfelt sympathy for Charleston and claimed
— falsely, as his field notes reveal — that he himself had slept on the third
story of a brick house every night since his arrival.[21]

Most journalists left the city by Monday night, less than a week after the
first shock. Walt McDougall departed for New York after five days. Henry
Grady, the first to arrive, claimed he had slept two nights on the grass; in
fact, he spent only one. Grady returned to Atlanta boasting that he had
"sought the earthquake and found its tracks, . . . heard its roar, felt its sigh,
smelt its breath, drunk its sweat, [and] examined its handwriting."[22]

Of all the scientists and reporters who had sought the earthquake, only
Henry Grady would be catapulted to fame on the strength of his observations. It was Grady who brought the horror of the disaster into America's
drawing rooms. "The city is a wreck," he scrawled as his train sped back
toward Atlanta. "A complete, pitiful, hopeless wreck. Its people are wrecked
as hopelessly as its houses. . . . When Sherman put the torch to Atlanta and
Columbia he did not inflict on both cities one-tenth the damage that has
been done to Charleston."[23]

Chapter Six

AFTERSHOCKS

JUST TWO DAYS after the quake, frantic people jammed the sidewalks outside the Charleston telegraph companies, begging to send messages. Western Union brought in extra operators from Washington and Savannah. The local office owned only one horse and buggy, so the manager scrambled to rent other vehicles in order to deliver incoming messages. None could be found. Forty additional men were hired and sent out on foot, but it was almost impossible to find recipients amid the wreckage. Soon the company gave up attempting deliveries.[1]

At least forty thousand people were "tenting" in Charleston by September 3. A new city had sprung up on top of the old grid, complete with a new system of addresses. Encampments bloomed on every scrap of open ground, and every camp, no matter how small, soon acquired a name. Robb's Lot on King Street, cleared by the fire of 1861, became home to three hundred people, all black. Nearby, at the corner of King and Queen, a group of two hundred blacks bunked in an old cellar in what came to be known as Queens Camp. A hundred fifty whites took over the Artesian Park on the corner of Wentworth and Meeting streets, sleeping in buses, ice wagons, and carts with the wheels tied to prevent them from "lurching." In the northwest part of the city, Rev. A. Toomer Porter, who had returned from the North Carolina mountains, opened his academy to house six hundred.[2]

Sails were commandeered to serve as temporary shelter, and soon there was more billowing canvas on land than in the harbor. A mainsail dubbed the Doran Tent sheltered three hundred. A grape arbor was transformed into a "pavilion" for a hundred when the occupants gathered dozens of awnings and sewed them together for a roof. Captain Thomas Young provided a hundred refugees with a floor as well as a roof — he had a wooden platform built and covered it with a huge piece of canvas. The steamship *Delaware* took in a hundred and fifty. Bennett's Rice Mill was rechristened Bennett's Hotel. The grounds of St. Finbar's Cathedral, left in ruins by the great fire of 1861, became Camp Duffy in honor of the rector who allowed more than five hundred people to set up housekeeping there despite earlier fears that the wreckage would collapse.[3]

Marion Square was a warren of shelters made of sheets, blankets, carpets, clothing, and empty barrels. About a thousand people slept there every night. Washington Park held six hundred campers lying shoulder to shoulder. White Point Garden, at the Battery, was home to six hundred more, mostly the white gentry and their black servants. Tent cities also appeared in the upper wards at Hampstead Mall, Wragg Square, Gadsden Green, and the farms above Sheppard Street. One camp was turned into a laundry by black washerwomen, who brought their tubs and set up shop. Linguard Street, near the Market, was soon crisscrossed with rope lines hung with drying clothes. Fortunately, it had not rained since before the quake, so the grass in the parks was as "dry as a carpet."[4]

In some places blacks and whites continued to camp side by side, notably at Marion Square and Camp Duffy. But whites soon began moving out of areas where they felt outnumbered. Washington Park, next door to City Hall, was the open area closest to home for many of the city's oldest and most distinguished white families. They had fled there the night of the quake, left to check on their property, and, terrified by aftershocks, returned to discover that almost every inch of ground had been staked out into "claims" by blacks from the notorious slums lining Princess and Elliott streets. Sticks had been driven into the ground and draped with sheets, matting, carpets, rags, and salvaged tin. One shanty was made of panels from the News and Courier's delivery wagon, which had been smashed the night of the earthquake by a falling cornice. In the not-so-distant past, blacks had been forbidden even to cross Washington Park. Now they refused to give way to whites.[5]

On Thursday afternoon the tension in Washington Park came to a head. A crowd of black boys and girls started playing baseball, racing through the campsites, jostling people as they ran. Men and women who were already anxious grew increasingly testy. Acting Mayor Huger happened to be walking through the park on the way to his office. A group of white men waylaid him and insisted that he confront the romping children. Huger called in the police and the game was shut down. However, the few remaining white campers soon retreated to the more peaceful cathedral grounds.[6]

FEAR OF WHAT might come next kept the city on edge. "Everybody was looking for the earthquake all the time," Henry Grady observed. "A sudden footfall would startle a crowd. The sharp ring of a telephone would make men jump. The quick roll of the burglar alarm would empty half of the desks in the telegraph office. The drop of a piece of plastering in a hotel would bring the few guests running down stairs."[7]

One man observed that his fellow citizens went about their business "with minds racked and stretched to an intensity that no one can even imagine who has not passed through this ordeal"; he claimed that each tremor caused a "sickening terror" to wash over them.[8]

And as if another earthquake wasn't frightening enough, people expected a volcano to erupt at any minute. "Volcanic outbursts" were reported all around Charleston, on James Island and Sullivan's Island, in Mt. Pleasant and Summerville. "Volcanoes Belching Mud!" screamed headlines in the *New York Herald*. "Yawning Chasms and Fissures Breathing Forth Sulphurous Fumes!" A volcanic fissure near Summerville was said to be "vomiting heated bluish mud . . . to a height of twenty feet." Lava was rushing down in "boiling torrents."[9]

The "volcanoes" were really phenomena that scientists now call sandblows or liquefaction features. The water table in coastal South Carolina lies close to the surface, and when saturated ground is severely shaken, the soil is destabilized. Pressure forces water upward, carrying particles of sand. Sandblows are generally harmless, unless a very large waterspout erupts directly under a person or animal. Because the waterspouts bubbled and appeared to boil, many people believed they were hot, like thermal springs. In fact, they were generally the same temperature as well water. An old man from Remley's Point near Mt. Pleasant offered firsthand proof—when a waterspout upended a kennel, it "did not scald the dog." The fissures and chasms were caused by lateral spread, another form of liquefaction.[10]

Professors McGee and Mendenhall insisted that these frightening phenomena had nothing to do with volcanic action, yet volcano mania spread across the country. The *New York World* reported that a volcano was erupting on a farm near Mooney, Indiana. The earth was torn up for yards around, and a cloud of smoke and dust rose sixty feet in the air. When a soft, ashy powder fell near Wilmington, North Carolina, citizens jumped to the conclusion that it was dust from "the volcanic manifestation near Charleston."

In the Pondtown District of Georgia, a one-room log cabin began to shake so hard that the clock on the mantel stopped and cups turned over; the locals feared that a "volcanic terror" was about to spring from underground. When a huge plume of smoke appeared near Tybee Island, Georgia, the *Savannah Morning News* suggested that it was "of volcanic origin." The next day, incoming ships' pilots observed marsh grass burning on the south end of the island.[11]

One night not long after the quake, Alice Smith's uncle Edward Wells heard a deafening roar. His nerves frayed by the constant talk of volcanoes, he was sure that he must be hearing an eruption. Wells cursed and threw down his cigar. His first impulse was to gather his family — his wife, a newborn baby, two little girls, and their nurses — and put them all aboard a rowboat he had tied up at a nearby wharf. Then he decided he should take time to find out the location of the vent and move everyone away from the flow of boiling lava. He was plotting his route when he discovered that the sound had come from a ship in the harbor releasing steam.[12]

On Friday the tide ran unusually high in Charleston, reviving fears that the area would be inundated by the ocean. A number of people staying on Sullivan's Island hastily evacuated. Some moved into the city. Others, taking no chances, headed further inland. "It is very well in the day, but when night comes it is simply awful," wrote a Charleston woman to a friend in Flat Rock, North Carolina. "Some people say the worst is yet to come, also that we are to slide off into the sea — but I suppose we won't know it."[13]

THE HOSPITALS were inspected and declared unsafe, but Dr. Arthur B. Rose, chairman of the Agricultural Society of South Carolina, came to the rescue. The society owned a large hall on Meeting Street, where, in happier times, flower shows were held. Rose gave permission to convert the hall, which appeared to be structurally sound, to hospital wards. Just after noon on Wednesday, a caravan of wagons holding 165 patients began rolling three blocks east toward the Agricultural Hall, which was partitioned with cloth to make separate compartments for white and black patients. There were no privies and no running water, yet Dawson's *News and Courier* marveled that the makeshift hospital was "a model of neatness."[14]

Impatient with the city council's lack of initiative, the Charleston Cotton and Merchants exchanges sent a telegram to President Grover Cleveland, asking the federal government for a loan. "A city has been wrecked and its people are without means to rebuild it," they wrote. "The situation is grave and without precedent in this country, and the remedy can be only in equally grave measures."[15]

Congress could and sometimes did appropriate large sums for disaster relief, as it had to aid recovery from the great Chicago fire of 1871, yellow fever epidemics in Memphis and Shreveport, floods on the Mississippi and Missouri rivers, storms in Texas and Mississippi, and a locust plague in the Southwest. Charleston officials hoped that their representatives would introduce a bill providing funds, but the politicians showed little interest. The president was on vacation, fishing and deer hunting in Saranac, New York. He listened "with astonishment and sincere regret" while accounts of the "ruin and suffering in Charleston" were read to him. Yet he behaved as if the calamity had nothing to do with him or any part of the federal government and sent no response at all to the stricken city. The *Savannah Morning News* found it hard to believe that President Cleveland would not at least send "a message, a proclamation, an offer of Federal aid — even the supplying of tents" to show that he was "impressed with the gravity of the calamity." But, as the paper sarcastically noted, the only evidence U.S. citizens had that Cleveland even existed was a running total of "the size and weight of the pickerel and trout [he] caught . . . and the bites and nibbles he missed."[16]

Cleveland did not believe in spending money on public assistance. And unless authorized by the president, the Departments of the Army and Navy could not send tents or other equipment. Many state constitutions, including South Carolina's, prohibited the use of state property for such "private purposes" as relief, and most state officials, no matter how sympathetic they might have felt toward Charleston, were reluctant to challenge the law. Only a few had the courage to act on their convictions. The governor of New Jersey immediately dispatched to Dawson a load of canvas shelters owned by the state militia. "Take the tents," he wrote. "We will amend the constitution later." The governor of Ohio followed his lead, shipping 166 tents belonging to the state National Guard.[17]

Dawson was dismayed by Cleveland's rebuff, but he had other connections to pursue. His wife's sister Lavinia was married to Gen. Richard Coulter Drum, adjutant general of the army. Dawson telegraphed General Drum, who went straight to the president and asked for permission to send whatever Charleston needed. Cleveland relented. He dispatched a telegram to the secretary of war asking him to do everything in his power to aid the relief effort. Soon a hundred large hospital tents were on the way.[18]

Many people were skeptical of the dire reports from the scene of the disaster. General Drum asked one of his officers to visit Charleston as soon as possible to provide an unbiased account of the damage. The word came back that, if anything, conditions were worse than had been reported. Money and condolences poured in, many of them addressed to Frank Dawson, the best-known public figure in the city. Queen Victoria sent a cable to President Cleveland. "I desire to express my profound Sympathy with the sufferers by the late Earthquake, & await with anxiety fuller intelligence, which I hope may show the affects to have been less disastrous than reported," she wrote, signing herself "Victoria Rex." Charleston was abuzz, as if the city were still a British colony — its suffering had been acknowledged by the queen of England! A facsimile of the text, forwarded to Charleston, would soon become a holy relic, trotted out on every occasion and reproduced as the frontispiece to the official account of the earthquake in the 1886 *City of Charleston Yearbook*. President Cleveland acknowledged the queen's gesture with a terse cable: her concern was "warmly appreciated."[19]

In Charleston, the acting mayor was slow to organize a response, so Dawson stepped forward to offer his leadership. He urged the city council to help the homeless and hungry. There was only one thing to guard against, he announced: giving aid to the able-bodied. "We want no loafers, no drones," he declared. "There is work for all who are . . . willing to work."[20]

The question of whether to provide relief was not new in Charleston. The year before, after the hurricane, the city council had refused to accept outside assistance even though half the houses in the city were damaged and only four people held insurance that covered storm damage. Nonetheless, suffering did not seem to increase. The City Almshouse, which routinely cared for the poor, reported that fewer people had applied for rations after the storm than before. At least two inmates, a tinner and a carpenter, had found work and left the institution. But the earthquake was clearly different — a bigger, nastier calamity in every possible way.[21]

The city of Charleston, like most nineteenth-century cities, maintained a fund for emergency financial aid. After the earthquake, a lucky few with connections were immediately given small sums to tide them over. However, it was widely believed that women of good breeding would rather starve than ask for charity. Alderman J. Adger Smyth lost no time in petitioning the city council to provide for the Misses Gibbes who had lost their house in a fire. His brother Augustine Smythe, who had added a final "e" to his surname to keep people from mispronouncing it "Smith," procured money from a private source for his burned-out neighbors "so that their names will not go before a public Committee." "There's a great deal of quiet distribution going on," Smythe wrote his wife, "besides the public money which will be distributed later."[22]

For the first few days after the quake, city officials were too stunned by their own losses to act in the public interest. It was Friday, September 3, more than sixty hours after the disaster, before Acting Mayor William Huger convened a special meeting of the city council, and then the first item on his agenda was not relief but the legalities of repair and rebuilding. An ordinance required the city to condemn and remove any damaged building that posed a threat to public safety. Thousands of structures, public and private, now fell into that category. Huger asked the council that a committee be appointed to carry out this task, which was guaranteed to enrage property owners already reeling from the quake. The aldermen balked, and in the end agreed only that they would all undertake to report any unsafe buildings.[23]

Alderman Edward Sweegan proposed that the city ask the state legislature to rescind a law prohibiting the erection of wooden buildings in downtown Charleston. The law had been intended to minimize damage from fires and hurricanes. Now, in the face of a new enemy, it was clear that masonry cracked and crumbled when shaken, while wood was able to bend. The council members debated which kind of disaster they should prepare for next.

Charleston had been one of the first U.S. urban areas to adopt a building code. After a devastating fire in 1838, the city passed a law requiring all new structures to be made of brick. Areas where the poor concentrated were exempt, as long as the buildings stood at a safe distance from more valuable property. The penalty for noncompliance was steep: the owner could be fined between $300 and $1,000, almost as much as it cost to build a house, and every workman employed on the project could be charged $5.00 a day, more than twice what most skilled laborers were making for a day's work. Now it seemed that the old law had led the city astray, and the aldermen quickly voted to ask the legislature to change it.[24]

Finally, almost as an afterthought at the Friday council meeting, Alderman Smyth moved that the city "gratefully accept the aid" offered by outside sources. Alderman Sweegan seconded the motion, and it was duly passed. Everyone agreed that this disaster called for drastic measures. But accepting donations meant that the city would have to devise a system of distribution that would not offend the northern philanthropists who might contribute. While Reconstruction was long past and there was little official interest in enforcing civil rights for blacks in the South, there were still plenty of people who blamed Charleston for starting the Civil War and who assumed that city leaders would not deal honestly with its black population.

The very word *relief* was tainted for white Charlestonians. Shortly after the first shots of the Civil War were fired at Fort Sumter, a Free Market was set up to provide relief for the families of servicemen. There was soon a separate fund for "fire sufferers," those who lost their homes in the conflagration of 1861. Then, in late 1862, Union ships blockaded the harbor. Food prices went through the roof. The city council named a subsistence committee, which sold goods at cost. Those who could not pay were given food at no charge. After the war, the federal government established the Bureau of Refugees, Freedmen, and Abandoned Lands, an agency designed to help former slaves make the transition to freedom. The bureau provided rations for blacks, which whites resented bitterly. Free food, they felt, removed the only incentive that could induce former slaves to work. So the city mounted an even bigger relief effort to keep its white citizens fed. The work was organized by wards, with a committee for each district. Wagons delivered supplies to the elderly and infirm.[25]

In the eyes of most middle- and upper-class Charleston whites, a return to large-scale public assistance would bring back the bad old days of Reconstruction. And yet in the present crisis, with thousands hungry and homeless while donations poured in, the city had no choice. At the Friday meeting, Huger announced the appointment of a three-man relief committee, to include the acting mayor, the chairman of the ways and means committee (Francis Rodgers), and a citizen to be named later. The next day, he changed his mind about the number and composition of the relief committee. Now it was made up of chair Col. Joseph A. Yates, treasurer Frank Dawson, William B. Guerard (a civil engineer and surveyor), and Thomas A. Huguenin (the city superintendent of streets). A subcommittee on shelter was set up to determine how to allocate the tents that would soon arrive. Most of the men on the relief committees were Confederate veterans. All of them were white.[26]

After the council meeting adjourned on September 3, Dawson and the other men emerged from City Hall to find a huge crowd waiting for word about relief. Speeches seemed in order, and they conferred among themselves about what to say. Without warning, the gable end of the county courthouse crashed to the ground. The crowd gasped and backed away from the new heap of rubble. No one had been hurt, but only because no one happened to be standing in the wrong spot.

Dawson was torn. This was news, and the collapse could be used to argue for speedier government action. But reporting it might alarm workers, halt progress, and drive away business. Danger still lurked around every corner, and the seat of local government was literally falling apart. In the end, Dawson acted in his unofficial role as protector of the city rather than his official position as newspaper editor. He killed the story. Yet the crumbling of the courthouse was reported in the *New York World*, the *Savannah Morning News*, and other out-of-state papers. Only to Sarah would Dawson admit the truth: the calamity, he wrote, was "far worse than the News and Courier has told. . . . I had rather go through the Confederate War again than through that Earthquake."[27]

Dawson turned much of his boundless energy to directing the recovery. Nobody really knew what to do or how to do it, but the editor, unlike so many others, was not frozen with uncertainty. Charleston city government was obsessed with prudent budgets and meticulous paperwork. Above all, the members of the city council were loath to set up a slapdash system that might spin out of their control. Dawson shared their basic philosophy, but he realized that, like it or not, this situation demanded quick action on a large scale. With Mayor Courtenay away, he was willing to plunge in and work out the details later. Swept along by his encouragement, the other men on the committees got down to business.

The first priority was shelter. People were still living in the streets, with nothing but "stones for their pillows and no roof but the firmament," as a reporter for the *Philadelphia Inquirer* put it. Dawson himself pointed out in the pages of the *News and Courier* that the number of habitable rooms in Charleston had "been diminished enormously by the earthquake." Women and children would have nowhere to live unless the city came to their aid. And many of those who owned homes would not be able to repair them without assistance. No one was likely to die of the cold, at least not yet. Charleston's daytime temperatures tend to hover in the eighties during

September, and heavy frosts rarely occur until late November. Yet people had begun to die of what the doctors called "exposure." It was still the peak of hurricane season, and violent storms were likely to come in the next few months. People crammed together in unsanitary conditions would be more vulnerable to cholera, typhoid fever, and, worst of all, yellow fever.[28]

The first tents were sent to the orphanages, the City Almshouse, and St. Francis Xavier Infirmary. The others were set up in the city parks. The committee estimated that at least five hundred more tents were needed, since only about one-tenth of the homeless had been provided for. Letters began arriving at City Hall from families who hoped to get their names on the tent list. Some demanded that portable shelters be assigned only to families, so that, as the News and Courier explained, the "disorderly element of the colored people might be kept out and the respectable white and colored families who are homeless be made as comfortable as possible."[29]

Despite a nationwide call for tents, it was clear that canvas alone could not solve the problem. On Monday morning, September 6, the shelter subcommittee began erecting rows of "sheds" on Marion Square. These wooden structures resembled stables and were intended to house fifteen hundred blacks. An identical set, intended for whites, was planned for the west side of the park, and others would be erected at Colonial Lake and Hampstead Mall, ensuring that every quadrant of the city had its share of shelters. Each structure would contain twenty-five "apartments," and the committee estimated that every room could hold about twenty people. The authorities assumed it was necessary to keep the races apart.[30]

Food was the next item on the agenda. Dr. Rose, the man who had already solved the problem of where to locate a temporary hospital, was well suited for chairing the subsistence subcommittee. Trained as a physician, he had spent the last few years helping Mayor Courtenay establish one of his pet projects, the William Enston Home, an attractive and humane residence for elderly citizens. The son of a plantation owner, Rose had gone into the phosphate business after the war and now owned one of the larger mining companies. All the other members of the committee were wholesale grocers. There was a certain logic in this — these men were experienced at ordering food in bulk — but it was a bit like putting the fox in charge of the henhouse, since the grocers would obviously be in a position to profit from donated funds.[31]

Acting on Rose's advice, the relief committee voted to set up a commissary and employ clerks to staff it. Dr. Rose knew that before his subcommittee could buy or hand out food, they needed a large, intact building to use as a warehouse and distribution center. His first choice was the Citadel, conveniently located on Marion Square, the site of the largest encampment and midway between the upper and lower wards. The committee sent a telegram to Governor John C. Sheppard asking for permission to use the state-supported school. As with the pleas to President Cleveland, there was no reply.[32]

Rose turned then to his second choice. The old Phoenix Engine House on Cumberland Street, a former volunteer fire station, now vacant, was near Washington Park, the second-largest encampment. Permission to use the firehouse as a commissary was easily obtained. Two passageways were built to channel lines of applicants into and out of the building. Ten men were hired to measure and package groceries, and several "ladies" were recruited to hand them out. Across the street, on a vacant lot, a soup kitchen was established by building a large shed and hauling in wood cookstoves. The subcommittee bought huge iron kettles, knives, and ladles, and hired cooks and servers. No food was actually distributed yet, but things were starting to look up.[33]

Dawson urged people to calm down and go back to work. The danger was over, and the best thing for everyone would be to ignore the aftershocks, clean up, and get the city running again as soon as possible. McGee and Mendenhall backed him up, but not everyone believed the scientists. Roaming the city before he left for New York, artist Walt McDougall discovered a group of frightened Irish immigrants sitting in chairs and rockers under the glow of a street lamp, "as if they were in a parlor." Hats and bonnets firmly in place, cradling children on their laps, they said they were waiting for the tidal wave. Two men perched on telegraph poles were gazing at the sea, acting as lookouts.[34]

ON THE GROUNDS of his academy in the northern part of the city, Rev. A. Toomer Porter lay down to sleep on the floor of a small wooden house, nursing a sore foot. He had not slept in three nights. His elderly mother lay on a pallet nearby. Porter could hear a constant "whirling" sound, and every so often there was a shock, as if the ground had been struck by a "tremendous sledge hammer." Outside the walls, a group of black people shouted to the Almighty to save their souls, a sound that might have thrilled the white minister in normal times. Now he "could not stand" it. He stalked out to confront "the ringleader," an old gray-haired man. The gates of hell were open, the man proclaimed, and everyone was going to go down into those burning jaws.[35]

Porter put his hand on the man's head. "My friend," he said, "look at me; you know who I am; and that I am a preacher, too. I believe in prayer, but you can't fool the Lord. . . . He knows it is fright, not conversion, that is bringing out all this excitement. . . . The most religious thing you can do now is to keep quiet and go to sleep and let everybody else do the same. Just over that wall is a lady not two weeks out of the lunatic asylum, and you have nearly made her wild again."

Porter assumed the man would know that he served as minister to an elite black church, St. Mark's Episcopal, made up mostly of well-educated descendents of free people of color. He was well known in Charleston among both blacks and whites, and, of course, they were standing on the very grounds of Porter Academy, which he had founded. But these people seemed indifferent to his status.

An old woman lashed out at him: "Just like you buckra. Here we is all going down to hell, and you won't let us even say a prayer." The exhausted Porter boiled over. He raised his cane as if to beat her. "Look here," he shouted. "I never struck a woman, but if you do not hush up, this instant, I will wear this out on you." The woman backed off, but the crowd broke into song. And not just any song, but "Oh, pretty yaller gal, can't you come out to-night," a bawdy number about interracial sex. Porter gave up.

TOWNS AND CITIES all over the region offered to take in refugees. Florence, with a total population of only three thousand, offered accommodations for up to five hundred people. Little Barnwell sent word that it could take two or three hundred. A. W. Rhodes of Hephzibah, Georgia, near Augusta, telegraphed Dawson: "I tender you or anyone you may send free of rent for the volcanic occasion a house of three rooms in our village." Even the impudent Ben Tillman, leader of the burgeoning Farmer's Movement, got into the act from the upstate town of Edgefield. "My house is small," he wrote Dawson, "but I will share it with any family you may send me. . . . A visit to the country will do more to reknit shattered nerves than anything I know. . . . I do not write this to get my name in the paper, for I do not want it put there."[36]

As Dawson well knew, Tillman *did* want his name in the paper. He always wanted his name in the paper, and Dawson regularly obliged. A one-eyed plantation owner and the younger brother of U.S. Congressman George Tillman, he had first caught Dawson's attention when he demanded that the state establish an agricultural college to train South Carolina farmers. Dawson was amused by Tillman's earthiness and impressed by his mono-maniacal drive. They made strange bedfellows, to be sure — Dawson came across as snooty and patrician, while Tillman posed as a salty, down-home populist — but Dawson had a long history of taking up with unlikely allies, and both men were far more complex than they seemed. Dawson and Tillman had met secretly three months before the earthquake to discuss the agricultural movement. Dawson agreed to support the agricultural college if Tillman would drop his attacks on the Citadel, which he said should be converted to a girls school. Word got out, however, and Tillman began to fear that he would lose followers if people knew about his alliance with Dawson. "We must *never never never* meet again," Tillman wrote Dawson on August 24, a week before the quake. "I think it will be advisable for you once & a while to give me or the 'movement' a punch just to keep [people] from thinking I am running your paper. . . . Of course I will understand your motive and regard them as 'love licks.'"[37]

Ben Tillman had a thick skin and would do almost anything to get his message out. On August 28 he had mailed Dawson a long letter about fertilizer analysis for publication in the *News and Courier*. Two weeks later, in the middle of one of the worst natural disasters in U.S. history, he sent a testy note asking why his missive had not appeared. "Of course the Earthquake shook you up . . . [but] this is important," he persisted. Tillman hoped Dawson would find the letter among the thousands that had poured in and print it in a conspicuous place, along with his call for a farmer's convention. Only in a hasty postscript did he remember to add a brief note of sympathy: "I watch the clouds & pray that it may not rain in your devoted city yet awhile." Dawson located the letter and published it at once.[38]

Officials would later estimate that more than two thousand people evacuated Charleston in the first week after the quake. About two thousand more delayed returning from their summer homes in the mountains. But some people did not want to leave. Persuaded that she must take her children out of the city, one woman reluctantly departed on Friday. "It was a terrible blow to me," she later wrote. "I did not want to go at all. If Charleston was to be destroyed I wished to be destroyed at the same time."[39]

AROUND ELEVEN o'clock on Friday night, September 3, not long after his panic over the imaginary volcano, Edward Wells sat on his piazza about a block from Charleston Harbor, petting his pointer, Luck. All at once the dog pulled away and retreated to the corner of the room. Wells heard a roar in the distance, followed by a "zip" that reminded him of an electric shock. Doorbells began to chime, one after another, moving up Water Street. At last his own bell rang. "It seemed the Devil himself were striding bodily through the Town," he later wrote, "pulling the doorbells of the poor shattered dwellings and laughing in derision to find the wretched owners 'not at home.' "[40]

The ringing was triggered by the strongest shock since the night of the earthquake. All over the city "cries of thousands of wailing voices united in one vast chorus expressive only of the utmost human misery." One reporter was reminded of the stories told by shipwreck survivors. The sounds gradually died away, he wrote, "as though voice after voice were being silenced as life after life were quenched beneath the tossing waves."[41]

In the composing room of the *News and Courier*, the windows rattled and the cracked walls shook. Typesetters raced outside, and when the shock died down, they refused to go back in. They were not about to risk death in order to put out a newspaper.[42]

When the shock hit, Frank Dawson was sitting in his backyard, chatting with Miriam and the Gliddens. He leaped to his feet and ran for the office. When he got there, the compositors were gone. Many stories had already been set, but the columns were still incomplete and none had been mounted on the cylinders that fit into the press. He hit the streets and found two out-of-town printers who were willing to set the remaining columns. Pressmen, paper carriers, mail clerks, and reporters were drafted to help mount them on the press. Somehow they managed to produce a paper that looked almost normal. But as readers would discover the next morning, many of the stories had been reprinted from the previous day's edition.

Dawson's small stock of patience was exhausted. "The custom to set type in the teeth of an earthquake seems to be above the ability of the average Charleston compositor," he raged in an editorial. Eventually he called it a night and went home to bed.[43]

But the excitement at the newspaper office was far from over. Around 2:30 a.m. on Saturday, the night crew heard a sound like hail beating down. They ran outside to investigate. In a vacant lot behind the building they found a scattering of small stones. Someone reached down to pick one up and discovered that it was hot.

The graveyard shift went home and the day workers arrived. Most of the compositors showed up that day, but they refused to work in the damaged pressroom. Dawson was still furious, but he had begun to realize that he would have to bend a little if he wanted to continue publishing a newspaper.

Around 7:30 that morning, more pebbles hit the roof. A few even bounced through the open windows into the pressroom. These stones, too, were warm. The employees raced outside, but they could not find a source. By this time, some people were convinced that a volcano was forming under their feet. How else could these showers of hot stone be explained? Few would admit to feeling fear, but tensions ran high.

Early that afternoon, more hot stones pattered down into the alley. A couple again bounced into an open window. The stones were small, smooth, worn, and polished, ranging "from the size of a grape to that of an egg." Most of them appeared to be flint, and the largest one looked suspiciously like a Native American ax head.

Dawson did not print the story in the Sunday paper, but a short, dry report was wired to the Associated Press, and a reporter for the *New York Herald* repeated rumors that the falling pebbles must have come from a volcano. McGee and Mendenhall were brought in to examine the evidence. There was no volcano, they said. The incident was a prank. But no one confessed, and the story soon made its way around the world. Newspapers in London and Paris reported that a volcano was erupting in Charleston.[44]

Forty-nine years later, one of Dawson's employees, Robert Richardson, the print-shop foreman who had been so faithful on August 31, and who would name a son after Frank, disclosed that a typesetter named Walter Daggett had indeed played a practical joke. Daggett apparently heated someone's rock collection in the stereotyping oven, then threw handfuls of the hot pebbles out of the windows of the main building. Richardson claimed that Daggett was trying to scare refugees camping in the streets. But the timing suggests that he was really trying to get back at Frank Dawson, who had insisted that the typesetters work in a dangerous building and then insulted them in print.[45]

However they did it, the typesetters got Dawson's attention. He arranged that day to move the typesetting equipment out of the damaged annex to a wooden building a half mile away, around the corner from the charred remains of the large King Street fire. Carts and barrows filled with type and cases rolled down Broad Street, and by late evening a new composing room had been set up. Many stories had to be delayed until the next day, and again the paper was less than complete. Still bitter, Dawson wrote Sarah that his staff could be divided into "quakers" and "nonquakers." But he breathed a sigh of relief that the typesetters had agreed to return to work. The compositors' rebellion was a foretaste of many conflicts to come. Skilled workmen had seized the moment to demand better treatment.[46]

CAUGHT UP IN THE pressures of work and running the relief effort, Frank Dawson was oblivious to the drama unfolding in his own backyard between his sister-in-law Miriam DuPré and the Gliddens, who had made the trek from Sullivan's Island together. One of the large government tents sent by his brother-in-law had been set up as a private bedroom for Miriam DuPré, Lucile DuPré, and Mollie Glidden. Each of the ladies had her own sofa. They ate breakfast and dinner in the main Dawson house but had their evening meal in the kitchen building. A ramp of rough planks was built over the fallen porch so they could get in the front door, but they preferred to use the back entrance.[47]

The giddy, improvident Glidden family had begun to grate on Miriam's nerves. Each one demanded breakfast at a different time, she complained in a letter to her sister Sarah, still in Europe with the Dawson children. "They take life so easy that I saw at a glance it would be impossible to make them understand that . . . an earthquake every three hours would render it inconvenient to have a regular hot breakfast from 8 a.m. to 11, dinner and desserts at 4 p.m., and a well set supper table of cold meats and hot coffee between 10 p.m. and 12 with no servant to prepare it." Mollie's cook and maid came to the Dawsons' every day, but they left before dark.[48]

Miriam was a wreck. She drove Frank to work each morning, leaving Lucile at home. Each time she left the house, she worried that her daughter might be "buried under the ruins" before she could make it back. When she was home, she worried that Frank's office would collapse and kill him. When their horse, Brownie, stepped on a nail, Miriam tried to treat the wound herself. Brownie developed an infection and they had to hire another horse to pull the carriage.[49]

Every morning Charles and Mollie Glidden declared that that night they were going to sleep in the house. Their mattresses were carried in — and then they changed their minds. Miriam reminded them that Emma, the cook, was sick and that William, the other servant, did all that one man could do. "*Everybody* is frazzled," Charles retorted. "I am, Mollie is, so are you. . . . Mollie and I *almost* quarrel!" Their son Philip put on a stoic mask, but Miriam noticed that after each shock he "would shake with nervousness." Lucile, a music student, remarked that the worst part was that she could never tell whether the shake she felt was an "overture or a finale." They all slept in their clothes and boots, ready to make a run for it. When rain fell, Miriam moved to a sofa in the back parlor and Frank slept on the carpet in the front parlor.[50]

People were nervous about crime, too. When he wasn't worrying about volcanic eruptions or imagining the devil ringing doorbells, Edward Wells fretted about what might happen "when the disorderly classes recovered a little from fright and realized how easy it would be" to rob the deserted houses. A well-read and well-traveled man, he recalled bloodcurdling accounts of the "robberies and violence" that had swept Lisbon in 1755 long after the earthquake had ceased and the flood receded.[51]

Though Dawson never admitted it in print, others were quick to observe that the city's ninety policemen were unprepared for this kind of emergency. Sam Stoney, a Charleston resident who ran several nearby plantations, complained to his mother that the police were "badly demoralized" and "all fools." Homes and businesses were broken open, ripe for looting. One man claimed that gambling houses, barrooms, and whorehouses had sprung up all over the city. More than forty prisoners had escaped the night of the quake, and several more had been released for lack of a place to keep them. The police warned that there were many "experienced thieves" among the escapees. At first the prisoners who had not run off slept in the yard of the jail, where two policemen were put on duty to guard the crack in the wall. But other arrangements would have to be made. On Saturday evening, the twelve remaining prisoners were marched up to the Citadel, where they were confined in the watch room. That night, a shock rocked the building, and the inmates were evacuated to Marion Square. Two more escaped.[52]

In fact there was some looting in Charleston, but far less than people feared. A few seconds after the first shock, a man sneaked into an abandoned store and stole some money; he was, as the *News and Courier* observed, "a daring and enterprising thief." Between the first and second shocks, a bar on King Street was robbed of $160. Someone broke into an undertaker's parlor and stole a child's coffin. Eight boys entered a damaged shop and made off with some fishing lines, pens, pencils, and inkstands. A man was caught removing lead from the shattered windows of the Unitarian church. Ten black women were arrested for taking bedding and clothing from un- occupied houses. All, according to the police, were habitual criminals. The stolen goods were soon discovered at a campsite on Marion Square, and the police were ordered to search "all the colored encampments." Several hundred arrests could be expected, the News and Courier predicted, though those numbers never appeared in the newspaper's crime reports.[53]

On the other hand, a few people were apparently scared straight. Ed- ward Wells reported that one man who had been losing chickens before the earthquake found all his missing fowl returned to their yard on the morning after, along with the sack in which the thief had brought them back.[54]

Thomas A. Huguenin, who served as a deputy state constable in addition to superintendent of streets, took matters into his own hands and called out two rifle companies, the Hussars and the Light Dragoons. (He later wrote the governor asking for authority to do so.) Soon white men, many of them Confederate veterans, mounted their horses and rode patrols through the streets of the city. One of them wrote that his first night out, September 7, everything was as "still as death . . . the only sound to be heard being the crackling of the ruined brick houses, or the dull thud of a brick loosened from its place and falling on the floor of some deserted house." Sam Stoney, who rode with the Dragoons, claimed, "Everyone tells us that the clatter of our horsehoofs over the pavements night after night has been a great com- fort to them, and they feel that life and property is safer." By "everyone," Stoney of course meant white citizens.[55]

Whether from fear of crime, aftershocks, tidal waves, or volcanoes, or simply because life in the camps was harsh, refugees continued to pack out- going trains. Whites rode comfortably in passenger cars while blacks were crammed into boxcars like livestock. When one train pulled into Columbia on Saturday night, it was, according to Narciso Gonzales, Dawson's Colum- bia correspondent, "the saddest sight seen here since the burning of Co- lumbia" in 1865.[56]

The Columbia Board of Trade appointed a committee to meet the trains. White women and children were taken to dormitories at local colleges. If men were with the group, they were escorted to hotels or private homes. Black refugees "quickly disappeared," presumably into the homes of "those of their own race," though the paper never investigated this point. Many people refused to leave the rail cars until early the next morning, when the police chief sent patrolmen to remove them in a horse-drawn omnibus. Even a hundred miles from Charleston, they were afraid to spend the night inside buildings.[57]

Yet as the refugees were rolling out of town, tourists were rolling in. An "earthquake excursion" was announced on September 5, a fast train from Savannah and two slower trains of ten coaches each. The next day, another thousand visitors came. Less than a week after the quake, the streets were crowded with people who had come to gawk at the ruins. The tourists wanted souvenirs, including samples of "earthquake sand" that had erupted from the craterlets. A man who lived at Ten Mile Hill, near one of the largest fissures, found five different colors of clay thrown up on his property. He dug a quantity of each kind and arranged the colors in glass bottles to sell as earthquake "mementos." Youngsters were soon employed to collect the extruded soil and pour it into containers for the tourists.[58]

ON SATURDAY, September 4, four days after the quake and before the tourists flooded in, Governor Sheppard arrived to inspect the damage. Acting Mayor Huger drove him around the city. On September 3, the governor had written Frank Dawson for advice, and Dawson told him that the city needed money for relief and repairs. Governor Sheppard issued a proclamation "advising and earnestly requesting all the people of this State to contribute as promptly and as generously as their means will permit" to the relief fund. He himself sent a check for fifty dollars. However, the state government itself appropriated no funds.[59]

On the day after Henry Grady returned to the "firm granite backbone" of Atlanta, he prepared another long account of what he had seen in Charleston and took the opportunity to boast again that Atlanta was much safer than Charleston. Grady felt "oppressed with the sense of having told inadequately" what he had seen. "No American city," he wrote, had ever "been in such straights [sic]." Then he went on to blame Charleston for creating much of its own misery. "The last citadel of the old regime" had failed to adapt itself to conditions after the war. The people, he said, were excessively proud. They "preferred martyrdom to huckstering," and had let the modern world pass them by. "Impoverished to a pitiful degree, with no appetite for the new methods of business, they held their splendid homes and proudly kept their counsel there.... The shock of the earthquake has thrown them out, as birds are shaken from a falling ruin."[60]

The next day, Grady repeated his charge in even blunter terms: "There is a class of people for whom we are extremely sorry," he wrote. "It is those who were once very rich, who have been reduced since the war, who now live in houses that they are unable to keep up; this calamity falls very heavy on them. But it would have been better for these people to have given up those houses years ago, and sold them when they could, and have put the money in other business."[61]

Grady's report convinced some people that the city was getting along just fine. Worse still, he boasted that the *Constitution* had given its subscribers "a fuller account of the Charleston earthquake than was printed in the Charleston papers." Frank Dawson would never forgive him.[62]

Chapter Seven

AN ANGRY GOD

O N SUNDAY MORNING, September 5, Frank Dawson knelt with hundreds of other Catholics beneath the ruins of St. Finbar's Cathedral, surrounded by fallen stones and sagging tents. Smoke from dozens of campfires mingled with the smell of incense and unwashed bodies. The bishop of Charleston, speaking under a hastily erected shed, told his flock that God had sent the earthquake to punish the city for its arrogance. "We have been too vain," he thundered, "too fond of the world, and the things of the world, and God has made the earth to roll under our feet like the waves of the sea. . . . How foolish is it for us to spend our labor and energy to build for this world when at any moment the earth might open and we be engulfed."[1]

Dawson must have cringed on hearing those words. He had been trying all week to rally Charleston to rise from the rubble and begin the long task of rebuilding, and the bishop's message could obstruct the city's recovery. Educated, well-to-do whites might scoff publicly at black superstitions, yet in private they were often prey to dark forebodings. "It seems as if the powers of heaven and earth are combined against [Charleston]," planter T. P. Stoney wrote his mother, "and it will choke almost anyone's belief and faith to compare its visitations of evil with any other ever brought down in this world." Epidemics, wars, fires, and hurricanes Charlestonians understood — but why an earthquake?[2]

At Bethel Methodist Church, the minister announced that God was angry at the way his children had acted: "Ice cream gardens, music and dancing are the popular amusements for the Sabbath afternoons in Charleston." Excursionists often sailed around the harbor on Sundays in "gay and frivolous" abandon.[3]

Walt McDougall asked a white woman camping at the Battery if she really believed God would pass over sinful Chicago and chastise Charleston.

"Yes," she said. "I was very worldly. I loved fine dresses and dancing and good living, and this is my punishment."[4]

This idea had its roots deep in the Puritan tradition. In 1727 an earthquake terrified much of New England. The young Jonathan Edwards, who would go on to write the most famous sermon in American history, "Sinners in the Hands of an Angry God," told his parishioners in Northampton, Massachusetts, that while earthquakes might have natural causes, they were also signs of God's displeasure.[5]

The Great Awakening, a revival of religious fervor that swept across the American colonies from 1730 to 1780, was spurred by Puritan ministers attempting to bring people back to God. Scientific discoveries were beginning to demystify the universe, and a host of inventions promised to put man in control of his fate. Faith in science had a tendency to undermine belief in God, but theologians like Edwards struggled to reconcile the two systems of thought.[6]

When in 1755 New England was hit by another earthquake, "a violent, prodigious shock" felt from Halifax, Nova Scotia, to the West Indies, ministers preached sermons and published pamphlets titled *Earthquakes the Works of God, and Tokens of His Just Displeasure* and *Earthquakes a Token of the Righteous Anger of God.*[7]

"What ailed the earth, that it shook in such a dreadful Manner?" asked a minister named Thomas Prentice. "Why it was because the Lord was angry," he answered. "It was under the heavy Burden of our sins that the Earth groaned, and shook and trembled, in so amazing a Manner."[8]

On both sides of the Atlantic Ocean, 1755 was an earthquake year. The great Lisbon earthquake, which spawned a fire and three surges that swept over the banks of the Tagus River into Europe's fourth-largest city, had occurred just seventeen days before the shock that rattled New England.

The same questions that worried Puritan New England polarized Europe. Protestants claimed the destruction meant that God was angry with Catholic Lisbon, a center of the bloody Inquisition and a hotbed of superstition and idolatry. Enlightenment philosophers argued that there were rational scientific reasons to explain the earthquake, reasons that had nothing to do with God or with sin. Voltaire satirized the debate in his novel *Candide*, published in 1759. The hero, having been taught that God is good and that this is the best of all possible worlds, arrives in Lisbon Harbor just in time to watch a friend drown. His tutor assures him that the wave was sent by a benevolent God especially to chasten the sinful. "If this is the best of all possible worlds," cries Candide, "what must the others be like?"[9]

The Portuguese government outlawed sermons suggesting that the earthquake might be a punishment for Lisbon's sins. The call for repentance, it feared, might lead people to stop working at a time when the city needed every hand to clean up and rebuild. Charleston would not take such drastic measures, but its official attitude, as expressed by Dawson, was remarkably similar.

In order to defuse the threat of religious mania, Lisbon officials offered scientific-sounding explanations that the public could understand. Probably it was no coincidence that eighteenth-century theories of earth science often seemed to describe hell. Vast caverns of molten lava and sulfurous gas were thought to lie beneath the surface of the globe, producing earthquakes and volcanoes when the crust settled and cracked.

In 1727, a few weeks after the first New England quake, Rev. Josiah Smith preached a sermon in the village of Cainhoy, just upriver from Charleston. "The God who shook New England," he said, "can, with equal ease, make Carolina tremble. . . . We know not what vast Subterraneous Caverns We stand over and what store of *nitrous Sulphurious Particles* are lodged below us. . . . We are, perhaps, *greater* Sinners than [the people of New England], though justice has smote them and spared us. . . . It may be, God reserves for us far *severer* Rebukes of Providence."[10]

The pulpits of Charleston rang again with talk of wickedness and punishment 159 years later, in the wake of what Smith would surely have interpreted as a fulfillment of his prophecy. At St. Philip's Church, Episcopal bishop William B. Howe recalled Charleston's many calamities — the war, the fire, the hurricane, the earthquake — but insisted that these scourges were not the fault of their victims. "We must look beyond the ruins of Charleston, which are being shaken day after day, to the Kingdom of God which cannot be shaken," he said. The battered old city would rise from her ruins if everyone did his duty. At a combined meeting of several white churches, the ministers talked about hope, love, and faith. An open-air service at the Battery dwelt on the fragility of human life and God's readiness to pardon all who asked.[11]

By far the most popular message was delivered by Rev. Robert Wilson of St. Luke's Lutheran Church, who drew on what the *News and Courier* called his "special study of the geological formations underlying Charleston . . .

concerning which he has written papers in the *Popular Science Monthly* and in *Lippincott's Magazine*." Wilson assured his listeners that it might be ten thousand years before another big shock hit Charleston. "There will be no more earthquake!" he thundered. Dawson must have smiled when he heard about this sermon. Most reassuring of all, Wilson declared in no uncertain terms that "the man who calls this a 'visitation of God's wrath for sin' is a fanatic who ought to be silenced." Wilson's scientific approach soothed the frayed nerves of the middle and upper classes. People begged him to repeat his message over and over to reassure them of their own innocence. He was urged to go to Summerville and deliver the sermon amid the ruins there. Other white ministers adopted his reasoning and made it their own.[12]

Most blacks were not calmed by such claims. A great many of them felt that slavery and oppression were the sins responsible for the upheaval, and the earthquake was just a foretaste of the destruction still to come. Newspapers across the nation reported that during the earthquake, an unnamed black woman thought to be dead had sat up in her coffin somewhere in Liberty County, Georgia, and announced that the world would end on September 29. From then on, she would always be referred to as the "Liberty County prophetess." Black street preachers held forth on the prophecies in Revelation that foretell Judgment Day. Soon an angel would send a star to earth, they shouted, opening the bottomless pit of hell and sending plagues of stinging locusts to torture the unredeemed. God would release the four horsemen of the Apocalypse, a stronger earthquake would roll across the land, and the faithful would be called to heaven. The Lord's temple would be opened, revealing the Ark of the Covenant. Then the earth would quake again. Finally, in the largest shock of all, "such as had never been since men were on the earth," islands and mountains would be swept away, and huge hailstones would drop from heaven. The world would be destroyed.

The sounds of blacks preaching and singing could be extremely disconcerting to whites. Deprived of other ways to communicate freely, black men and women had long used worship services as a way to register protest. Before the war, whites had felt free to flog slaves who disturbed their rest with loud demonstrations. Now, as the voices of freedmen and their descendents rang out across the city in 1886, whites looked for ways to silence them.[13]

Off-duty police were installed in a tent near the edge of Washington Park, and by Friday night the preaching there was quieter, or perhaps it just seemed so since whites by then had moved out. Many of the exhorters migrated uptown, to the much larger mixed encampment at Marion Square. There, in the eerie glow of tents lit by kerosene lamps, no less than a dozen camp meetings were organized, each occupying its own section of the park. In a large tent near the center of the square, an old black woman raised the hymn, "Oh Raslin Jacob, let me go." The crowd swayed and clapped. One man dropped to the ground, and a group of women crowded in to grasp his hands. He cried for mercy and then "swooned away." Six young boys fell down, grinding their faces in the grass. "Lord look on last Tuesday night," shouted a preacher. "Some is alive and some is dead and gone. Oh, my handsome God, dear sir, look down on us. We know what the little finger of the Lord can do. Sometimes the world can kick up in thunder, but do take care of our brothers. Ain't the black lamb and the white lion done lie down together in peace?" The crowd began to sing. "Fight the battle, fight the battle," the speaker continued. "Fight it out girl, fight it out boy. Oh, yes, ma'am, the time is come. Wake up! Wake up! The last chance is come to save old Charleston."[14]

Before the earthquake, the preacher said, he hadn't expected to see Jesus. But now, "Look at these in the valley. Didn't you hear Gabriel's horn blow? Oh, Gabriel, turn that horn to the land of Egypt on the miserable sinners and not on we!" For whites who couldn't escape such speeches day in and day out, it didn't take too much imagination to suspect that the "miserable sinners" in question might not be Egyptian.

And the sinning against blacks had not ended with the abolition of slavery. A black woman told a roving reporter that she had been expecting an earthquake "ever since the McKnight murder."[15] Dawson ran her remark in the *News and Courier* without comment, and certainly his fellow Charlestonians needed no explanation. Only a year before the quake, two murders had exposed the city as a place where officials talked about equal justice but failed to practice it.

On the night of July 7, 1885, a young black woman named Matilda McKnight ducked into a grocery store on the northern outskirts of Charleston. McKnight told the white storekeeper that she was bone weary. She had buried her grandmother that afternoon, and while the funeral was going on, her aunt had dropped dead. The storekeeper ordered his helper, a one-armed black man named Abram Gathers, to carry McKnight's groceries to her house down the street.[16]

But Gathers claimed Matilda McKnight was not at home when he showed up a short while later. Her body was discovered the next morning a few hundred yards from the boardinghouse she owned, her corpse so brutally battered that the eyeballs had popped out of their sockets. The police were stumped — they had no suspect and there was no apparent motive. Matilda McKnight was widely respected as hard working and honest, a churchgoing woman and a loyal wife. She was married to a man well known in the city because he had once owned a newspaper. When the *Palmetto Press* folded, Joe McKnight had moved north to work on the railroad. Mrs. McKnight stayed behind to run their boardinghouse.

The murder of Matilda McKnight took place at the northern edge of the city, far removed from the antebellum homes and churches of downtown Charleston, on a dirt road that skirted strawberry, bean, and potato fields owned by a man named Silas Daly, an adventurer who had been born in Kentucky, sold sewing machines in Cuba, and raised coffee in Jamaica. McKnight sometimes worked for Daly, sorting and packing produce, and it was Daly who discovered her body and called the police.

McKnight and Daly were hardly prominent, and their neighborhood was so remote that most people from downtown thought of them as country folk. One of the attorneys described the scene of the crime as a rural village, "Snapbeanboro," and much was made of the fact that Daly walked the streets without a coat and hat, flouting convention in a way that pegged him as less than a gentleman. Yet the case had an immediate impact on every layer of society.

Sweating in the muggy heat of a Charleston summer day, hundreds of black men and women laid down their tools and showed up for the inquest at the Fireproof Building. "Old washerwomen left their wash-tubs, cooks deserted their kitchens and house servants abandoned their places," the *News and Courier* reported. "Draymen and hackmen stopped their vehicles as they passed by, and lingered for hours around the building."[17]

Suspicion pointed to Gathers, the deliveryman. Investigators questioned several people known to have quarreled with McKnight. For two weeks the inquest continued as more suspects were detained, but they were all released for lack of evidence. Finally the coroner's jury concluded only that Matilda McKnight had been killed by "some person or persons unknown."

Black Charlestonians assumed that white officials would simply drop the case. In the first decade after the Civil War, federal troops occupied the city to enforce Reconstruction laws that granted blacks rights they had never had before, including equal protection. Then whites had launched a ruthless quest to regain power, a terrorist campaign they glorified with the name "Redemption." In most ways, their strategy succeeded, though laws that gave blacks the right to vote and serve on juries remained on the books. The city's response to the McKnight murder would test whether those laws still had teeth.

In the early days of the investigation, officials said that whoever had murdered Matilda McKnight must be brought to justice. The city council offered a large reward for information leading to the arrest of the murderer. The governor of South Carolina matched it. Appeals went out in the black churches, and Dawson urged Charlestonians of both races to contribute more. Murderers, he said, must be called to account, whether they were white or black, sober or drunk, of good families or not. "It is absolutely essential to the peace of society and the security of human life that the murderers of Mrs. McKnight be punished to the full extremity of the law," he declared.[18]

The city hired a private detective from the renowned Pinkerton Agency in Philadelphia, a stout mustached man who posed as an itinerant farmhand in order to get McKnight's neighbors to talk. A month after the murder, Abram Gathers was cleared and four new suspects were taken into custody: Silas Daly and three of his black employees.

Because the coroner's jury had been dismissed, a judge had to decide whether to hold a trial. More testimony was collected, during which Daly's lawyer hammered away at the "Pinkerton man," trying to establish that he was a Yankee profiteer bent on framing an innocent man. Yet all the evidence the detective had collected pointed straight to Silas Daly, who seemed increasingly mysterious as new information about him was revealed. Daly was listed in the city directory as "colored" though his friends regarded him as white. He was sixty-two years old, blind in one eye, and nearly deaf. He claimed to suffer from debilitating back pain, though he took a walk every day "on account of the sickness in his head." His cook testified that the day after the murder, he tried to keep her from coming into his kitchen, which she saw had been freshly mopped. Witnesses testified that he had offered to give McKnight a second house if she would have sex with him. There were many other suspicious circumstances, and the "Pinkerton man" concluded that Matilda McKnight had been murdered when she resisted a sexual assault. Nevertheless, the judge ruled that there was not enough evidence to charge Daly. The investigation ended.

Black people were incensed, "too mad to talk." The verdict confirmed what they had known all along—a white man would never be held accountable for assaulting a black woman. All the witnesses against Daly were black, and one white spectator brazenly declared, "No white man shall be convicted in this county on nigger testimony."[19]

To the dismay of most whites in town, Dawson sided with the black citizens. In his newspaper he announced that the inquest provided "abundant reason" to try Daly for murder. The public fury grew.[20]

The next Sunday, the white minister of a black church preached a fiery sermon about the failure to indict Daly. "What do you think would have been the result if Mrs. McKnight had been a white woman and her slayer a black man?" asked Rev. W. H. Lawrence. He recalled watching the sheriff of a nearby rural county place a noose around a black man's neck with an air of such profound indifference that "all that was wanted was a lively air upon the piano to accompany the dying sinner to eternity."[21]

Lawrence characterized Charleston's city fathers as falling into two camps: one group was "Liberal," the other inclined to "cry down the negro as a beast." Frank Dawson, Mayor Ashmead Courtenay, and the rest of the men who had hired the outside investigator had "linked themselves" with "the thinking and representative colored men of this city," while the other side had said to blacks, "Here you are and no farther shall you go." Lawrence advised his parishioners to trust Dawson and his allies and to run from their enemies. A reporter from the News and Courier was sitting in the audience, taking down the minister's words, and the next day they appeared in print.

Dawson was in a quandary, knowing such praise was guaranteed to raise the hackles of his white subscribers. He tried to distract them by insisting that the city government was united in its attitude toward racial justice. He even claimed that there was no place in the United States where the rights of blacks were better protected.[22]

Dawson's editorial appeared on August 28, 1885, the very day the hurricane swept in to rip the city apart. Tin and slate, boards and branches whirled through the air. An iron steamship tore free from its moorings and flew up the Ashley River, taking out a drawbridge. Wharves, warehouses, and piers collapsed. The steeple of Citadel Square Baptist Church crashed to the ground. At the southern tip of the Charleston peninsula, the ocean swallowed White Point Garden, where the white aristocracy liked to promenade. A large bathhouse at the foot of King Street vanished into the sea. The storm was a "carnival of havoc," wrote Carlyle McKinley. "Wreck was piled on wreck, ruin heaped on ruin." Few buildings escaped injury, and twenty-one people died. The storm inflicted far more damage on the rich than on the poor, and it was said that those who protected Silas Daly suffered the most.[23]

And then, in the fall, just as the McKnight murder was fading from the headlines, another brutal killing alarmed the city. This time, both the victim and the assailant were prominent men.

Stephney Riley, a former slave, had made a small fortune after the Civil War operating a fashionable livery stable and bucking the usual racially divided politics. During Reconstruction in the South, the Republican Party, the party of Lincoln, was made up overwhelmingly of blacks; the Democrats were white. Yet nearly all of Riley's clients were white, and he had adopted their Democratic politics. He was viewed by most of his race as a man who had turned his back on the party of freedom. Riley lived in a substantial house just two blocks from the Dawsons, with stables adjoining.[24]

On the night of October 1, 1885, Dr. Amos Bellinger stopped by Dawson's house to look in on Sarah, who suffered from chronic pain. Frank trusted Dr. Bellinger absolutely and believed that only his friend's care was keeping his wife alive. Even while Sarah and the children were in Europe, Frank consulted Bellinger about their health problems and passed on his advice by letter. As Dr. Bellinger made his way home he saw Stephney Riley out on the street, whipping a balky horse. Bellinger cursed Riley and ordered him to stop. Riley told Bellinger to mind his own business. "I am no God damned servant of yours, to be ordered by you," Riley said. "I am my own boss."

The next morning, witnesses noticed Dr. Bellinger hovering near Riley's home. When Riley emerged from his house, Bellinger shouted that he was a "damned nigger son of a bitch." The two argued. Bellinger grabbed hold of Riley and drew his pistol. "Doctor, what you want to shoot me for?" Riley asked. "I've done nothing to you."

Bellinger pulled the trigger three times. The black man slumped against his legs. Bellinger drew back and let him fall, then gave him a kick. He fired a shot into one side of Riley's head, then calmly shifted position to pump another into the other side. Dr. Bellinger retrieved his hat, wiped the revolver on the tail of his coat, and walked off down Bull Street.

At the police station, Bellinger confessed but claimed self-defense. He was locked up in the very jail where he served as the official physician.

Stephney Riley's body was carried into his carriage house and an autopsy was performed by Dr. George Kinloch, assisted by his brother Dr. Robert A. Kinloch and a third physician, Thomas B. McDow. News of the murder spread from street to street. A throng of black men and women gathered around the dead man's house, tearing boards off the fence so they could peer into the yard. "Kill for kill, dat's what we want," shouted one of the women.

City authorities prepared for the worst. Black Charlestonians were as livid as they had been after the McKnight murder.

Frank Dawson found himself in a difficult position. White Democrats had spent the last twenty years protecting Riley from attack by members of his own race. If there was a single black man in the city whose white killer might be declared guilty by a white court system, it was Stephney Riley. But Dr. Bellinger was a close friend, and he was also the family doctor. Caught between his principles and loyalty to a pal, Dawson deplored the killing but accepted Bellinger's explanation that he had acted in self-defense. "There will be a rigid investigation," he wrote, but he was confident that the coroner's inquest would exonerate Bellinger. And despite eyewitness reports that attested to Bellinger's harsh language, Dawson stoutly declared that there was "absolutely no question of race concerned in this affair."[25]

Riley's body lay for three days in a magnificent "refrigerated coffin," ingeniously constructed with double walls to hold crushed ice. Hundreds of black people filed by to gaze at his face. They might not have liked or trusted Riley when he was alive, but in death he was one of their own.

Bellinger was charged with murder. A week before his trial was to begin, a group of black ministers, including Rev. William Henry Harrison Heard, called a mass meeting to discuss not just the Riley killing but the condition of the colored race. "The strong tyrannize over the weak," they observed. "The whole machinery of the courts is in the hands of white men." Blacks were always in danger of being dragged from their homes, beaten, or even killed. If a man as prominent as Stephney Riley could be shot down in cold blood, what safety could an average man expect?[26]

Bellinger claimed that Riley had pulled a knife on him. There were many witnesses to the killing — people who had been washing Riley's carriages, selling vegetables door to door, tending their nearby shops, or just looking out their windows when the commotion started. Only one of them, a white man, said he saw Riley attack Bellinger with a knife. The others, all of whom were black, said there was no knife. One witness reported that on the morning of the murder, Riley had angrily remarked that in the years before emancipation Dr. Bellinger had whipped his slaves and rubbed salt in their wounds.

Bellinger's lawyer insisted that his client had been understandably enraged when Riley called him a bastard. No man, he said, white or black, could stand by and hear his mother's good name dragged through the mud. In fact, Bellinger had exercised "remarkable forbearance" by waiting until the next day to kill Riley. The defense lawyer claimed that all the black witnesses were untrustworthy, while the white ones, including Bellinger himself, were incapable of lying. The lawyer for the other side, who was supposed to be making the case against Bellinger, politely suggested that there probably was no knife, but otherwise he agreed with his opponent that Dr. Bellinger was an upstanding citizen.

At the end of the three-day trial, the eleven white jurors voted for acquittal. The lone black juror held out for a charge of manslaughter. The judge declared a mistrial and released Bellinger on bail.

Black ministers protested the ruling, and outrage spread through the streets. Only come Judgment Day, declared Heard from the pulpit of Mt. Zion African Methodist Episcopal (AME) Church, would true justice be served.[27]

In an editorial published the next day, Frank Dawson contradicted everything he had written about the McKnight killing. He noted that Dr. Bellinger had fought for the Confederacy and that the doctor and his family had always been honorable people. Here was someone who "would not tread on a worm." It was inconceivable that a man whose life was devoted to healing could have "wantonly [shot], again and again, a dead or dying man, who had power no longer to injure him."[28]

Seven months later, at Amos Bellinger's second trial, an all-white jury was seated. This time, the jury deliberated for less than an hour before returning a verdict of not guilty.[29] Even the pretense of equal justice had been abandoned.

In September 1886, Silas Daly and Amos Bellinger walked the streets as free men, but their city had been laid low by a pair of natural disasters. Small wonder that many blacks saw both the storm and the earthquake as God's punishment for sin.

REV. WILLIAM HENRY HEARD did not join the chorus of black voices blaming whites for the earthquake. Like Frank Dawson, Heard was more concerned about hunger and homelessness. And he knew whom to blame for those conditions. Just before the quake, Heard had published an angry article in the pages of the *New York Freeman*, a black newspaper that was distributed across the nation. Fifteen hundred farm workers and their families were starving on plantations along the Santee River, just forty miles northeast of Charleston, Heard wrote. The planters who employed them claimed there was no way to provide them with rations, since for several years in a row the rice crop had been killed by flooding. Gardens and livestock had died, too, and the farm hands were so desperate for food that they were foraging for rotten fish in the mud along the river. "What kind of Nation is this," Heard asked, that "allows hundreds to starve and to be murdered and does not raise its little finger?" The victims "are colored," he answered, so the nation and the state were willing to let them suffer.[30]

Born into slavery, sold twice before he was ten, Heard remembered the promises and disappointments of Reconstruction. A slim man who sported a stylish goatee, he radiated a determination born of lifelong struggle. After gaining his freedom in 1865, Heard had paid a white man to teach him to read and had attended South Carolina College on a scholarship. But when whites took back power in 1876, they purged black students from the university and Heard was "turned out." He worked on the railroads and ran for office before being called to preach at Mt. Zion AME Church in Charleston.[31]

Religion had been a covert form of resistance for slaves, whose songs and prayers often expressed anger under the cloak of metaphor. After the Civil War, churches were the center of African American life, and black ministers served as political leaders as well as spiritual guides. Whites might form their opinions about the world from newspapers, magazines, books, and politicians, but a black minister was often the sole source of guidance for his parishioners.

Just after the earthquake, Heard received many letters from donors who wanted to send money directly to black Charlestonians, and he began contacting his fellow black pastors to decide how to proceed. Among them were George C. Rowe of Plymouth Congregational Church and John Dart of Morris Brown Baptist. Heard also consulted two prominent black Republicans, Samuel W. McKinlay, a former postal carrier, and Dr. William Demosthenes Crum. Together they were ready and willing to challenge the white city leaders who were directing the relief effort — including Dawson.

Heard and Rowe were newcomers to the city. Heard had lived in Charleston for less than two years, and Rowe had been called to Plymouth Church from Hampton, Virginia, just six months before. Both men were known and respected outside the provincial world of Charleston — Heard wrote a regular column for the *New York Freeman* and Rowe contributed to the *Missionary*, the weekly journal of the American Missionary Association. Dart had grown up in Charleston but had spent time working in Rhode Island and Georgia. McKinlay's family was well known among Charleston's mixed-race elite.[32]

Crum was the son of a white father and a free black mother. He had grown up on his father's Orangeburg plantation, sixty miles northwest of Charleston, where forty-three slaves raised cotton. The family lost everything in the war. Like Heard, Crum attended the state university during the brief window in the 1870s when it was open to black men. His four older brothers pooled their money and sent him north to medical school. There he married Ellen Craft, a light-skinned, well-educated woman who had grown up in England. Mrs. Crum was the daughter of William and Ellen Craft, fugitive slaves who fled to England and wrote an acclaimed book about their escape, *Running a Thousand Miles for Freedom*.[33]

Crum, Heard, Rowe, Dart, and McKinlay were all well-educated, eloquent men who had learned from experience how far to trust whites. Convinced that the relief committee would pay insufficient attention to the needs of black victims, they decided to call a public meeting at Heard's church. Exalted leaders in the small worlds of their own churches and social groups, they were poised to step out onto a much larger stage.

Chapter Eight

LABOR DAY

REV. WILLIAM HEARD and his colleagues were not alone in mistrusting Charleston's official relief committee. On September 5 the city received a petition from the local chapters of the Knights of Labor (KOL), a national organization of working men and women that included artisans of all kinds, including carpenters and joiners, window glassworkers, telegraphers, cigar makers, machinists, and blacksmiths. The petition was signed by nine labor leaders, who asked that the committee turn over a portion of the relief fund for them to distribute. They would appoint three Knights from each ward to search out those "who are in distress and worthy of help and assistance."[1]

Founded by nine Philadelphia tailors in 1869, the KOL was more a fraternal organization than a traditional trade union. Led by Grand Master Workman Terence V. Powderly, a charismatic former machinist, the organization officially discouraged strikes, yet in the years preceding 1886 it had been associated with several high-profile work stoppages, some of which had won stunning concessions from national corporations. Unlike almost any other group in 1880s America, the KOL actively recruited blacks and whites, men and women. In cities across the country, they fought for an eight-hour day, child-labor laws, and equal pay for black and female workers. In 1886 these ideas were considered radical if not downright seditious, a sure way to ruin business and bankrupt employers.[2]

The KOL was the largest labor organization in America. Nationwide, it claimed 750,000 members, and Charleston supported four local assemblies, with almost 4,000 members. A joint meeting of the Charleston assemblies in mid-August, just before the earthquake, had attracted nearly a thousand participants, about half of whom were black. And the larger and stronger the KOL grew, the more business leaders feared and hated it.[3]

Until just three weeks before, the Knights had kept a low profile in Charleston, meeting in secret and refusing to talk to Dawson's reporters about their business. Now, five days after the earthquake, their leaders called for a mass meeting of working men to set a new scale of wages for all tradespeople and laborers. The letter closed with a threat: either the city agreed to these conditions or the work of restoration would grind to a halt. If they were compensated fairly, the men promised to "work with all their honest might" to "blot out every sign of this mighty visitation."[4]

The relief committee was astounded at the audacity of the letter. After what was surely a heated discussion, they drafted a polite reply saying they would welcome the Knights' assistance in identifying those who needed aid, but they could not give money to any organization for redistribution. (They would soon contradict themselves by giving banker Morris Israel $1,000 to be used "for the relief of needy Hebrew sufferers.")[5]

The civility of the committee's letter was just a facade. As the group stepped onto Broad Street from the News and Courier office, one of the members was overheard saying that "any man who signed that paper ought to be hung to a lamp-post." The Knights took this remark as a declaration of war.[6]

On Monday, a small notice appeared in the News and Courier: "A mass meeting of the mechanics and day laborers of the city of Charleston, under the auspices of the Knights of Labor, will be held to-night at 8 o'clock . . . for the purpose of establishment of a specific rate of wages for mechanics and day laborers in restoring our beloved city to its former beauty and grandeur."[7]

Monday, September 6, happened to be Labor Day, a holiday so recently created — or, perhaps, so controversial — that the News and Courier did not even mention it. The first Labor Day parade had taken place in New York City just four years earlier, but by 1886 KOL members in many cities simply assumed that Labor Day was a holiday and took off work the first Monday in September. While the Knights in Charleston were holding their mass meeting to set wages, fifteen thousand people were parading through the streets of Baltimore. In Buffalo two thousand marched, in Albany five thousand. Boston turned out fifteen thousand and put on a "monster picnic." In Chicago, thirty thousand walked or rode trucks and wagons. The largest Labor Day celebration of 1886 took place in New York City, where some thirty-four thousand marchers were accompanied by brass bands and drum corps. This procession included representatives of every possible trade, from the Amalgamated Society of Fresco Painters and the United Umbrella and Walking Stick Dressers to bricklayers and carpenters. Waving blue silk banners were 130 typesetters employed by the *New York World*. The workers marched alongside extravagant floats shaped like steamships, sailing ships, lions, horses, and horseshoes.[8]

There was no such celebration in Charleston. South Carolina, in fact, was the only southern state where the Knights of Labor had failed to establish a strong foothold. Yet through an act of God — or was it nature? — the laborers of Charleston, skilled and unskilled, were suddenly in a position to demand higher wages and better working conditions. A space was cleared among the tents in Marion Square and two wooden dry-goods boxes were pushed together to make a speaker's stand. Three lanterns flickered at its foot. Master Workman W. P. Russell, state organizer for the Knights of Labor, read the letter to the relief committee and the committee's reply. Then he told his listeners that a member of the committee had proposed lynching the signers. The crowd jeered and booed. Finally, he turned to the main order of business, an increase of fifty cents a day for most workers. First-class bricklayers, at the top of the heap, would now command $3.50 instead of $3.00 a day. Laborers, at the bottom, would make from $1.50 to $2.00 instead of $1.00. The scale was quickly approved. Frank Dawson declared the increase "moderate," at least in comparison to the $6.00 a day many workmen had recently been demanding. The Charleston laborers did not seem as belligerent as many had feared.[9]

The year 1886 was turbulent nationally for organized labor, the height of what historians call "the Great Upheaval," an explosion of working-class solidarity and resistance to exploitation. Factories, mines, and mills across the nation were hit by protests associated with the KOL. Successful strikes against the railroads, especially against magnate Jay Gould, had given the Knights an almost mythic reputation as a "giant killer."

Blacks and whites, men and women, natives and immigrants, skilled and unskilled — hundreds of thousands of laborers believed that the Knights of Labor could change the world and bring them justice. In Charleston, blacks who were members of the KOL had just asked for a black organizer to help them fight local prejudice. Six months before, the KOL had mounted a strike at the National Cotton Compress Company in Richmond, Virginia, because it paid its black employees less than whites for doing the same work. The strike failed to accomplish its goal — the company simply replaced the strikers with more black workers, whom they continued to pay at lower rates — but the Knights' challenge to racial discrimination sent a powerful message. A few weeks later, Richmond was in the throes of another strike, as those in the construction trades successfully held out for higher wages.[10]

In early May, a work stoppage in support of an eight-hour day at the McCormick Harvester plant in Chicago had turned into an anarchist demonstration on Haymarket Square. When police attempted to disperse the crowd, a homemade bomb exploded, killing eleven people and injuring more than a hundred. Police arrested dozens of suspected socialists and radicals. The trial had been front-page news everywhere, including in the *News and Courier*, for most of the summer of 1886, stirring up fears that foreign agitators might organize disgruntled workers to commit acts of terrorism.[11]

But for Charlestonians, the strike that hit closest to home had been unfolding since early July in the textile mills around Augusta, Georgia. It was led by a Charleston native, J. Simmons Meynardie, a Baptist minister and master workman of the Augusta local. Employees at a mill on Horse Creek had demanded a raise, which the owners had refused. On August 11 management shut down all the mills in the Augusta area and attempted to starve out the strikers by pressuring local grocers to refuse them credit. Dawson branded the demand for higher wages "utterly unreasonable and unjustifiable." Master Workman W. P. Russell pointed out in a letter to the editor that skilled adult mill workers in Augusta were making only eighty-one cents a day, while children were paid the "miserable pittance" of ten cents a day. Was it "unreasonable," he asked, for the strikers to request a few cents more? If they got what they were asking for, a child worker would make only a penny more each week. Whether their demands were reasonable or not, the strikers were evicted from company housing and replaced with nonunion labor.[12]

Then came the earthquake. The textile plants were badly damaged when the dam broke on the Langley mill pond. "The mill wheel stands still as death," Meynardie wrote Dawson in a letter to the editor. The striking mill workers and their families were going hungry.[13]

Meanwhile, back in Charleston, laborers were poised to take advantage of the desperate need for workers. Regardless of the official scale, carpenters and bricklayers asked for and got up to ten dollars a day. Even unskilled laborers could now command five dollars a day, more than double the usual rate. Early on the morning of Wednesday, September 8, banners appeared in Marion Square: "Mass Meeting of Working Men, 2 p.m." But storm clouds moved in around noon, and rain poured down on the makeshift shelters. Tents collapsed, the flat roofs of the new wooden sheds leaked, and everything inside was soaked. An hour later, the storm passed. One of Dawson's reporters watched as a hundred black men crowded around a white house-painter who said that as soon as Mayor Courtenay returned "everything would be attended to." He was voicing a sentiment the reporter approved, one that seemed likely to lead to cooperative workers and quick repairs. The crowd nodded but did not disperse. A black man, an "old politician" named Butler Spears, climbed onto the stand. Whites could not be trusted, he shouted, launching into what one of Dawson's reporters described as a "harangue" intended to "divide the races."[14]

The reporter asked the men around him why they were not working, since there were plenty of jobs. They replied that even though wages had gone up, they still weren't high enough. Twenty-five men had just walked off a job because the pay was too low. Another black bystander mounted the stand. "You are all damned fools to be talking to that man!" he cried, pointing to Dawson's reporter. "He is no friend of yours. Stand up for your rights!" A policeman pushed through the crowd and dragged the protestor away. As soon as he was gone, several other black men hastened to repudiate his remarks. They said they were willing to "bear their sufferings and await the relief which must come in time." The News and Courier claimed that the outspoken critic was a convict who had served time in the penitentiary for burglary and larceny. "It is just such characters as he," wrote Dawson, "who are trying to arouse race prejudice in Charleston, and it is that class of men who should be shunned alike by white and colored."

A sharp critique of the relief committee was published in the Charleston Dispatch, a small weekly newspaper. The man who made the lamp-post comment was identified as Gen. Thomas A. Huguenin, who had earlier called out the militia forces, sending Confederate veterans on horseback throughout the city. He claimed that he was misquoted; he had not said that the Knights of Labor should be lynched but that "any man or set of men who at this time of dire calamity would combine together to oppress their suffering fellow-citizens" should be punished. And, he said, he still felt that way. To profit from the earthquake in any way was to commit treason.[15]

WILLIAM HENRY HEARD's coalition of Colored Clergy, as he called them, also met on Labor Day, again at Mt. Zion AME Church. A committee of seventeen black men was officially appointed, including Heard, Dart, Rowe, McKinlay, and Crum. The men drafted an appeal for disaster relief "in this trying hour." They submitted the document to the *News and Courier*, and Dawson printed it the next day. Yet Heard and his colleagues also sent their letter to newspapers and churches in other parts of the country.[16]

Dawson branded this "an ill-advised attempt to divide the contributions of the American people." The *Cleveland Gazette*, a black newspaper, urged its readers to send funds directly to the black ministers, since "the large amount of funds and clothing being sent daily to Charleston by the *whites* will reach the *suffering whites*, and unless we take hold at once and assist our own suffering they will continue to be in dire need." At least two groups in New York contacted Acting Mayor Huger asking for the name and address of "a leading colored citizen or pastor to whom we can send money or clothing." Huger referred them not to Heard but to William Ingliss Jr., a black man who ran the barber shop at the Charleston Hotel. Ingliss, predictably enough, said he would direct all funds to the mayor.[17]

Having worked so hard to feed the hungry and shelter the homeless, Dawson was livid that anyone would question the fairness of the system he had helped create. In an editorial titled "No Sectional Line, No Color Line," he insisted that aid was being distributed with no "distinction of class or color." The relief committee had provided more shelter for blacks than for whites, he claimed, and in some respects it was better shelter.[18]

The editorial infuriated Heard and his colleagues, who pointed out in a new proclamation that they and other prominent black men had been "entirely ignored" by Mayor Huger's relief committee. No one had asked them for information or approached them in any way. There were many needy blacks, they said, who would rather do without than "submit to impertinent questioning," and "a committee of their own race would open the way for relief without humiliation."[19]

Dawson was correct that more blacks than whites were served by the committee. After all, blacks made up the majority of the population and had fewer resources, while thousands of whites hadn't yet returned from their summer vacations or had fled the city in the first days after the quake. But most of the largest and strongest tents had been allocated to whites, along with sixty-seven wooden shelters. Only twenty-six of these wooden sheds had been designated for blacks. There were no government tents or frame structures in all-black Washington Park, though just down the street at White Point Garden, where most of the campers were well-to-do whites, the relief committee had provided thirteen sturdy hospital tents equipped with wooden floors, and ditches had been dug around the bases to carry away rainwater.[20]

Still, Dawson insisted, "we are all in the same boat." The Colored Clergy, like the Knights of Labor, were welcome to make recommendations that the relief committee might or might not follow. He published the Colored Clergy's appeal in the *News and Courier*, but he suggested that they could help most by screening out people who were able to work. The separate appeal, he warned, might "cause uncharitable people to think that the colored people, who are in distress, had been neglected or otherwise ignored." That, of course, was exactly the point. "The newspapers of this and other cities may picture as they please, but the people are demoralized and the earthquake will set us back at least ten years," Heard declared in the *New York Freeman*. And as Heard and Master Workman Russell well knew, not one black man or labor leader sat on any of the committees established to coordinate the relief. Most committee members, in fact, were Confederate veterans. The same group that had defended slavery at gunpoint was still in charge.[21]

Dawson continued to insist that there was enough paid work for every able-bodied man and boy. Anyone not busily occupied must be "too lazy to work." Many hands were needed to pick up fallen bricks, clean off the old mortar, and stack them in neat piles so they could be relaid. But even for wages well above the usual rate, there were few takers. Working in the ruins was dangerous, and many laborers were injured. Two men tearing down a two-story brick building were nearly killed when the walls caved in, burying them in the wreckage. Five more were thrown to the ground when a scaffold collapsed. Aftershocks came almost every day, dislodging more bricks and stones.[22]

The *News and Courier* vilified workers who demanded "earthquake prices." When a black man named Henry Lesesne was accused of raising his haulage rates and shortening his wagon to cheat people who needed to move their possessions into safer quarters, the paper called his actions "The Quintessence of Meanness" and went on to remark, "It takes an earthquake to bring out the full character of the Charleston coon." The man showed up at the newspaper office and demanded a retraction, protesting that he had not raised his prices and that he had sawed off part of the wagon only because it had splintered in the quake. Dawson published a correction, but he did not apologize for the racial slur.[23]

Dawson's increasingly harsh tone no doubt was caused in part by stress. He himself was working overtime: running his newspaper, bossing the relief committee, and keeping peace inside his own crowded household. He had been too busy even to exercise and had given up his usual routines — sailing, boxing, working out with weights.[24] Almost single-handedly, he was attempting to prod his fellow citizens to buck up and rebuild their city. A military man who was used to running his business without interference, he felt that his efforts were being attacked by the very people they were meant to help. He was stretched to the limit and ready to explode.

But Dawson was also responding to lessons he had learned ten years earlier, during one of the most dramatic years in the history of the country, 1876. Though that date no longer resonates with nonhistorians, white southerners in 1886 thought of it as one of the major watersheds of history. They spoke of *1876* the way others would later think of December 7, 1941, or of September 11, 2001. To them, everything was different after 1876, and the sight of black laborers joining together in 1886 brought back memories of the violent clashes that had shaken the South during that turbulent year. To understand the rifts that divided Charleston after the earthquake of 1886, and to understand Frank Dawson, it is essential to know what had happened in South Carolina just ten years before.

BETWEEN 1866 AND 1876, blacks still played major roles in the governments of the southern states. With pride they voted and held office. They could walk any street, ride any streetcar. Schools offered them opportunities for the future.

South Carolina was occupied by federal troops whose mission was to enforce the new laws that gave blacks their citizenship. The state government was overwhelmingly Republican, made up of mostly blacks and a few whites, natives and newcomers, some idealistic, some hoping to enrich themselves in the new order of things. The vast majority of the Democratic Party were whites who had been born in the state, who had suffered wartime defeat, and who now saw some of their former slaves, most of whom had little education, holding positions that they thought weren't deserved. They spoke with dismay of living "under the bootheel" of black rule in "the Prostrate State."

In 1874, a truly corrupt Republican governor, Franklin J. Moses, who stole and swindled his way through the state treasury, had been replaced by a new kind of southern Republican, Daniel Chamberlain. A man much like

Dawson, Chamberlain was a nonnative, polished, temperate, and reasonable. Raised in Massachusetts and educated at Yale, he had spent the last
two years of his governorship attempting to purge the state's Republican
Party of greed and corruption.[25]

Dawson felt that the best thing for the state was to make sure Chamberlain would be reelected in 1876. This required refusing to nominate a
Democratic candidate for governor, crossing party, color, and class lines,
and cooperating with open-minded Republicans to elect candidates both
parties could stomach. It made perfect sense to Dawson, and he used his
newspaper that July, while the nation was celebrating its centennial, to present eighteen reasons to vote for Daniel Chamberlain, with lengthy disquisi-
tions on each. He had faith in the power of the press, especially the power
of his own press, and he believed that South Carolinians would follow what
he saw as a rational plan for restoring good government. He was wrong.[26]

The summer of '76 taught Dawson a hard lesson: South Carolina, his
adopted state, was anything but a rational place. As Dawson's biographer,
E. Culpepper Clark, observes, Dawson and Chamberlain had put themselves in untenable positions by behaving like "moderate men" in a "revolu-
tionary society." A few years earlier, Dawson might have been able to persuade his readers to compromise and cooperate. But now all eyes were on
Mississippi, where a bloody campaign of fraud and terror had suppressed
the black vote so completely that white Democrats swept the elections of
1875. Congress was halfheartedly investigating the matter, but it was rap-
idly becoming clear that the federal government did not have the will to
intervene. The people in the southern states — former slaves and masters
— would have to resolve their grievances themselves.[27]

To many whites, the most infuriating feature of Republican rule was that
the federal government had organized armed militias made up of black men.
In retaliation, whites formed their own "rifle clubs," groups that pretended
to be social fraternities while their members rode around the countryside
terrorizing blacks. Many of the nightriders wore red flannel shirts as a kind
of paramilitary uniform, as frightening as the white robes of the Ku Klux
Klan. They called themselves Redshirts.[28]

South Carolina blacks did not back down as whites mustered forces to
take away their newly granted rights. In May 1876 farm laborers in the rice
fields along the Combahee River, some fifty miles south of Charleston, near
Beaufort, went on strike. In a move that shocked their white employers,

these black workers demanded higher wages and cash payments instead of checks that could only be used in the plantation store. Otherwise, they would refuse to cultivate and harvest the crop.[29]

By the end of August, the rice was cut and stacked in the fields. Unless the hands agreed to bring it in, the crop would rot. Beaufort County officials called out a white rifle club to end the standoff, but the strikers fought back. Congressman Robert Smalls, a former slave who had first made his mark by stealing a Confederate gunship and giving it to the Union forces, convinced the landowners to compromise and persuaded the rioters to disperse. It seemed the trouble was over.

But then, just a few days later, the laborers went on strike again, beating and whipping other workers who refused to join them. Again Robert Smalls intervened, telling the strikers that they had a perfect right to organize and demand higher wages, but others had a right to work for less if they chose.

His words fell on deaf ears, and by early September 1876 the strikes had spread to other rice rivers in the Lowcountry. Planters begged federal troops to keep the peace, a measure of their desperation, since the soldiers were part of an occupying army whose purpose was to protect the rights of freed slaves. A prominent black man announced that if even one striker lost his life, "not a white man would be left" in the region. In the end, the strikers got their raise, and no one was killed.[30]

In the rest of South Carolina, however, a bloodbath was beginning. On the Fourth of July 1876, the nation's one-hundredth birthday, two white men forced a black militia company to move off a road near the mostly black settlement of Hamburg, in Ben Tillman's home district of Edgefield. Most scholars of the period now agree that the white men hoped to start a fight that would give them an excuse for bloodshed. They got their wish.[31]

Four days after the initial showdown, a white rifle club rode into Hamburg. The men in the militia took refuge in a building near the river. Shots were exchanged. When a white man was killed, his buddies hauled in a cannon and began to bombard the building. The black men sneaked out the back way and tried to make their escape.

If the incident had ended there, it probably would have made only local headlines. Instead, the Hamburg riot would become a potent symbol for both North and South. The whites chased down and captured some of the blacks, who surrendered and gave up their guns. Five of the prisoners were then taken aside, one by one, and shot to death while they begged for mercy.

Dawson was outraged. His first headline on the event called it "The Hamburg Slaughter." A day later he branded it "butchery" and condemned the killings as "barbarous in the extreme." He said he knew no words strong enough to express his horror at the crime. Dozens of white men were arrested and charged with murder. Hamburg shared the headlines with Gen. George Armstrong Custer's ignominious defeat at Little Bighorn, whipping up southern white fears that people of color were on the attack everywhere. But Dawson knew that the North would be outraged by the massacre. And it was. A Thomas Nast cartoon published in *Harper's Weekly* shows outraged Justice standing in front of copies of the Declaration of Independence, the Constitution, and a handbill that reads "Negroes Shot in Cold Blood at Hamburg, S.C." Justice points angrily to her scales, where a heap of six black bodies on one side far outweighs the single white body on the other.[32]

Carlyle McKinley, who was then the *News and Courier*'s Columbia correspondent, was sent to investigate the incident. He turned up even more sickening details: the mob had cut out one man's tongue and put it in his hand. Another of the injured black victims lay helpless as a white man shredded his flesh with a hatchet and offered two black children who were watching a handful of this "sausage meat."[33]

Many other whites in the state were also outraged, not at the massacre but at Dawson for condemning it. Martin Witherspoon Gary, one of the most virulent of the white supremacists, challenged him to a duel. The editor of a rival newspaper, Col. Robert Barnwell Rhett Jr., branded Dawson as an "ingrate, liar, and coward," and he, too, challenged Dawson to fight.[34]

Three years before, Dawson had denounced dueling as barbaric, illegal, and against the doctrine of the Roman Catholic Church. This was, in some ways, self-serving, since, as one historian points out, Dawson's newspaper coverage made so many men angry that he "would have had a duel on his hands every week" if he had once agreed to exchange shots. As a young man, Dawson had fought one duel in Tennessee and served as a second many times while he lived in Virginia. After he met Sarah, who had lost one of her brothers in a duel, he had come to detest the practice and frequently criticized it. But this attitude set him apart from "real" white South Carolina men and marked him as a foreigner no matter how many battles he had fought on behalf of the Confederacy.[35]

Dawson's cool response to Colonel Rhett would become a Charleston legend. At a little before noon on August 11, 1876, Rhett came out of his office and strolled up Broad Street. Dawson, accompanied by Sarah's brother Jimmy Morgan, emerged from his own office a few blocks away and sauntered toward Rhett on the opposite side of the street. Spectators hung from every door and window, hoping for a fight. Rhett was honor bound not to shoot first, since according to the *code duello* the man who hurled the first insult must allow the man he had insulted a chance to shoot at him. Dawson refused to fight. The two men passed each other in silence. The next day they repeated the performance, and again nothing happened. After that, the incident was considered closed.

Dawson escaped with his life, but he paid a heavy price for denouncing white atrocities. Businesses pulled their ads from the *News and Courier* and readers canceled their subscriptions. In the end, he ate crow. When the whites who were on trial in Hamburg said that the black men had lied, he did not challenge them.

Even while white supremacists were threatening to shoot him and trying to bankrupt his paper, Dawson had been busy figuring out which counties would go Republican in the November 1876 elections based on whether they had black majorities. He concluded that his party was bound to lose big if it refused to compromise with Daniel Chamberlain and the Republicans. What he failed to understand was that white Carolinians, who were almost all Democrats, were in no mood to "fuse" with the enemy and would not hesitate to break the law in order to win the election.

The Democratic Party convention was held on August 16 in Columbia. Until that first day of the convention, Dawson was sure that most delegates agreed with him and would abstain from nominating a candidate for governor, leaving the field open for Chamberlain. But his party voted overwhelmingly to ignore his advice and nominated Wade Hampton, a former Confederate cavalry general. The Democrats were determined not to compromise but instead to ram through a "straight-out" ticket that would sweep all Republicans out of office. Then there would be no more black militias parading on the public roads, raising fears that they would attack whites. Elect a Republican governor? Never![36]

Dawson was shocked, but he quickly abandoned Daniel Chamberlain and backed Wade Hampton for governor, praising him with the same fervor he had earlier used to support his opponent.[37]

Up to that point Dawson had not fully grasped the fury pent up inside people who felt that the emancipation of slaves had perverted the laws of nature. Now he saw that he was fundamentally different from the white men and women of his adopted state. Though he had come from England to fight for the Confederacy, and though he had married a southern woman as unreconstructed as any, he did not really think and feel like a native South Carolinian.

Events moved so quickly that bloody summer and fall that there was little time to contemplate right and wrong and even less time to figure out what to say or do next. On the evening of September 6, 1876, a group of white men set out to escort two black men home from a Democratic political rally in Charleston. One of the black Democrats was Stephney Riley, the owner of a livery stable whose death would later bring the city to the brink of another race riot. The group was jumped near the Citadel Green by a gang of black men. Someone fired a gun, and everyone started shooting. One of Dawson's reporters watched in terror as black men stripped a white man, knocked him down, and beat him up. Then the mob turned on the reporter and hit him with a chunk of brick launched by slingshot. Twenty men armed with clubs shouted death threats.[38]

Other white men were assaulted that night and "beaten almost to a jelly." One, a young bookbinder, died the next day. Dawson himself was attacked, though he escaped injury. The Upper Guard House near the Citadel was filled with bleeding men. Rioters smashed plate-glass windows, looted stores, and ripped out fences, shouting words few white Charlestonians would ever forget: "Kill them! Kill them all! This town is ours!"[39]

About two weeks later, near Ellenton in Aiken County, a white rifle club roamed the countryside for a week, killing seventeen black men. Among them was a Republican state senator, who was snatched from his wife's side and executed in full view of passengers on a train as he knelt in prayer. The mob emptied his pockets and even stole his wedding ring.[40]

And the bloodshed continued. One of the Democrats' favorite tactics was to ask Republicans to make their rallies bipartisan, then take them over. On October 16 Republicans and Democrats gathered in Cainhoy, a tiny settlement on the Wando River, twelve miles northeast of Charleston. Participants in the rally were asked to come unarmed, but men from both camps fired pistols over the water as they traveled up the river by steamboat.[41]

A crowd of about five hundred gathered around the speakers' stand. Both parties made a pretext of civility. St. Julien Jervey, a white Democrat, gave the first speech. Black Republican W. J. McKinlay followed. "Fellow citizens," McKinlay began, "hear what I got to say." Before he could continue, someone began beating a drum, a sound that had alarmed whites since the days when slaves had used drums to communicate between plantations. Several young white men ran out of a shed, holding shotguns and muskets that had been stashed there by blacks. An old black man walked up to one of the youths and said, "Gimme my gun." The boy fired into his chest.

Whites fled down the road with blacks in hot pursuit. Six people were killed outright and fifty-three were wounded, including a child who later died. President Ulysses S. Grant issued a proclamation ordering the rifle clubs to disperse and placing Cainhoy under military command until after the November election. About a thousand federal troops were sent to keep order in the state — but it was too little, too late. There would be no peace in South Carolina.

The Democrats had long complained that the Republican Party was hopelessly corrupt. But in the November 1876 election, it was the Democrats who stuffed ballot boxes, "lost" boxes, misreported the count, and ensured that most of their opponents were too frightened to go to the polls. As results trickled in the day after the election, crowds surrounded the bulletin board outside the *News and Courier* office. A white man slapped a Republican leader, and soon men were charging down Broad Street, shooting as they ran. A gun battle straight out of the Wild West raged in front of banks and offices. Frank Dawson rode on horseback into the thick of it. He caught a bullet in his calf and had to be carried home.[42]

The election results were so tight and the process for determining the winner so murky that the political turmoil continued for three months. During that time, both Daniel Chamberlain and Wade Hampton claimed to have been elected governor of South Carolina. Democrats and Republicans seated separate legislatures. The presidential race between Rutherford B. Hayes and Samuel Tilden was also too close to call. Finally, a compromise was struck early in 1877 in Washington, D.C. The governor's seat was granted to the Democratic candidate, Hampton, and South Carolina's electoral college votes in the presidential race were conferred on the Republican, Hayes, with the understanding that, in exchange, federal troops would be removed from the state. Frank Dawson traveled to the nation's capital to help broker the deal. Louisiana, the only other state that was still occupied, made the same agreement.[43] The outcome is now known as the Compromise of 1877.

By the end of America's centennial year, Reconstruction was in full retreat. In the words of historian Nicholas Lemann, Redemption was "the last battle of the Civil War." The white South had won.[44]

Having regained control of their state government, South Carolina whites set out to whittle away the remnants of black political power. Starting in 1882, black men who dared to show up at the polls were stymied by the eight-box rule, a complicated arrangement intended to confuse illiterate voters. Instead of marking a single ballot that included every office, voters had to fill out eight separate ballots and place each in a special box designated for that contest. A ballot inserted in the wrong box was automatically ruled invalid. The boxes were labeled, and the poll managers were required by law to read the signage out loud to anyone who asked, but the election officials were all Democrats, and a dishonest poll manager could easily misdirect people. The eight-box rule was meant to screen out black voters without running afoul of the election laws passed during Reconstruction, and for the most part it worked. It eliminated some white voters, too, but that was considered a small price to pay for the disfranchisement of virtually all blacks. Democrats also redrew the state's congressional districts to ensure white majorities in all but district 7 — known as the black district — around Beaufort.[45]

After that, the Democrats held almost total control of South Carolina's elections. And yet, as historian C. Vann Woodward has observed, "the era of stiff conformity and fanatical rigidity that was to come had not yet closed in and shut off all contact between the races, driven the Negroes from all public forums, silenced all white dissenters, put a stop to all rational discussion and exchange of views, and precluded all variety and experiment in types of interracial association."[46] It was ten minutes to midnight, the clock was ticking, but Jim Crow had not yet been written in stone.

Chapter Nine

"BURY THE DEAD AND
FEED THE LIVING"

T MIDNIGHT ON Saturday, September 4, Charleston mayor William Ashmead Courtenay sat in the saloon of the Cunard Line steamship *Etruria*. It was the last night of his vacation, and he looked forward with a mixture of dread and pleasure to the moment when the ship would clear quarantine and dock in New York City. It had left Liverpool the day before the earthquake. Although the *Etruria* was the fastest commercial passenger ship in the world, the transatlantic crossing still took at least six days. The wireless telegraph had not yet been invented, so until a ship put into port, the passengers received no news from the outside world. Courtenay expected to disembark quietly and board a train for Charleston. He had not seen his wife, his mother, or his children in more than three months.[1]

In the darkness off Sandy Hook, New Jersey, a tugboat pulled alongside the ship and handed off a large sack of mail. As Courtenay nursed his final drink, an officer strode into the saloon. "These are for you, Sir," he said.

On top was a sheaf of telegrams. Courtenay flicked through the stack.

"Sept. 1, Charleston, SC — Disastrous earthquake here last night."

"Sept. 3, Charleston, SC — Your family all safe and uninjured by earthquake. Your residence badly damaged — F. W. Dawson."

"Sept. 3, Charleston, SC — Property [damage] estimated three millions about forty persons killed."[2]

Courtenay was bewildered. Charleston had experienced a few tremors over the years, but a major destructive earthquake? He dug down into the sack and pulled out a letter. "Dear Mr. Courtenay: You have probably before this heard of the dreadful calamity which has befallen your noble City." There were hundreds more such letters and telegrams. Buried beneath them lay a batch of New York newspapers. "Shattered Charleston," read the headlines. "The Fair City In Ruins And Its People Panic Stricken. Public Buildings and Churches Wrecked and Thousands Homeless."[3] Courtenay shouldered the heavy bag and retired to his stateroom. The New York papers, especially the *Herald*, reported that city government had collapsed. Looting was rampant and the police force had given up trying to keep order.

The *Etruria* touched the pier at the foot of Clarkson Street in Manhattan at seven on Sunday morning. Courtenay ran down to the baggage compartment and buttonholed two customs officers. Trailed by reporters, he rummaged through the stacks of luggage, found his bags, and was passed through customs. An old friend met him and drove him to the New York Hotel.

"I know all," Courtenay telegraphed his wife, Julia. "Thank God for your wonderful preservation. You have acted bravely. Don't despair. Am coming first train."[4]

"Do not be disheartened," he wired Dawson. "Let's meet our great disaster bravely. . . . We own the land our city is built on and we have our heritage there."[5]

Reporters clamored for a statement, and Courtenay tried to oblige. "I don't know what to say," he began. "The news is almost incredible. I am overwhelmed with anxiety." Based on what he had read in the papers, Courtenay estimated that full recovery might take years. Without knowing exactly what they had done, he defended the officials he had left in charge — they "had their hands full." Acting Mayor Huger had waited days before asking for help, but Mayor Courtenay was much more decisive. He used the reporters thronging around him to call on the country to send relief — tents and food first and money later, to be used for repair and rebuilding.[6]

Someone asked him why so many blacks had been killed and injured, and so few whites. "It is inexplicable to me," he answered, "as there is no such thing as any distinctive colored district in Charleston. The colored people there are scattered all over the city." This answer, of course, evaded the reporter's point: blacks lived in substandard housing, no matter what the neighborhood. The question put Courtenay on notice: the North was watching Charleston, looking for evidence that unreconstructed Confederates were still mistreating blacks.[7]

At 4:30 that same afternoon, the mayor boarded a train heading south.

NO ONE LOOKED forward to Courtenay's return more than Frank Dawson. "Thank God for one thing," he wrote Sarah on Sunday. "Courtenay will be back the day after tomorrow morning and we shall have some brains and courage at the helm."[8]

Courtenay faced a problem he had confronted just the year before, after the hurricane: helping his city recover from a near-fatal blow. But he was no stranger to crisis. When South Carolina seceded from the Union, Courtenay enlisted as a private and fought in four of the bloodiest battles of the Civil War: First Bull Run, Fredericksburg, Gettysburg, and Chickamauga. He was captured near Winchester, Virginia, and for ten months lived at Johnson's Island, a prison camp for Confederate officers near Sandusky, Ohio, where winter temperatures sometimes fell to −20 degrees Fahrenheit.[9]

On the two-day train ride home to Charleston in 1886, Courtenay had plenty of time to think about how to proceed, and no doubt he drew on his wide reading and knowledge of history. Government officials reacted to disasters in many different ways, and Courtenay hoped to model himself on the best. Perhaps he thought about the king of Portugal surveying the ruined city of Lisbon in 1755: "What should we do?" Joseph I is said to have asked. "Bury the dead and feed the living," replied his trusted advisor. Charleston's dead had been buried, but the living were still hungry.[10]

Or perhaps Courtenay pondered a more recent urban calamity, the great Chicago fire of 1871. The enormous relief effort after the fire had passed into legend. The methodical, fiscally prudent Courtenay would have been impressed by the efforts of the Chicago Relief and Aid Society, which set up a system to screen requests and make sure that while those in need were assisted, none of the money would be spent on people able to provide for themselves.[11]

As soon as his train pulled into Charleston on Tuesday morning, September 7, even before he kissed his wife and checked on his mother, Courtenay headed to City Hall to meet with the relief committee. On the steps he met the French consul, who handed him a check for $100.[12]

Courtenay set about his huge task with vigor. His first official act was to set up a finance committee consisting of Councilman Francis S. Rodgers, the chairman of the city's ways and means committee and the councilman who directed the firefighting efforts after the quake, and W. W. Taft, a wholesaler, with the city treasurer handling the money. These men would be in charge of accepting donations.[13]

The mayor thanked his "fellow citizens" for their "moral courage and heroism." He praised the firemen, the policemen, the hospital workers, the telegraph operators, Acting Mayor William Huger, and the relief committee — everyone who had come in for criticism — and announced that the *New York Herald*'s report of chaos was "the worst slander I ever read." He congratulated blacks for their "exemplary conduct" and pointed out that they had resorted to prayer and song as a way to reach out to God. It was a generous speech and a brilliant stroke of public relations, since it encouraged all these groups to cooperate in the future. Certainly it generated better feelings than Dawson's curt dismissal of all idle men as "lazy." Courtenay closed by urging everyone to "escape" the perils of living "under thin shelter and on the open ground." He set an example by moving his wife and children back into his own brick house on Ashley Avenue. They had been living on a lawn on Montague Street.[14]

The mayor's positive attitude was contagious — people began to believe that the disaster could be managed. "A thousand welcomes, my dear Mayor Courtenay," wrote one Charlestonian. "We all feel better that you are at the head of affairs again."[15]

The recovery shifted into high gear. At daybreak on Wednesday, September 8, two hundred black women and children were standing in the streets around the commissary. By the time the doors opened at seven, five hundred more had joined them. That first day, everybody who stood in line was given one day's food, with no questions asked. Those who said they were sick received vouchers for prescription drugs and special groceries. But the relief committee, spooked by the size of the turnout and flooded with complaints about freeloading, soon stipulated that anyone who wanted food had to apply to a minister or public official. The applicants were asked to present a marriage certificate, a local address, a letter of reference, and proof that they did not have incomes large enough to support their families. Those who were deemed worthy were given tickets to exchange for a week's rations.[16]

The allowance for one person for one week was two pounds of sugar, three pounds of bacon, one and a half quarts of rice, two quarts of grist (ground corn), a pound of coffee, a half pint of salt, a loaf of bread, and a pound of biscuits. By the end of the first day, seven thousand packets of food had been claimed by hungry Charlestonians. The distribution center stayed open from seven to three, seven days a week. Twenty-one thousand packages went out the door in four days, all but five hundred of them to blacks. In other words, one in every three of the city's black residents received rations, while only one in every forty-two white residents showed up to claim food. The *News and Courier* did not point out that the city's black population was far poorer than whites to begin with, and far less likely to have savings or well-stocked pantries to rely on during the emergency.[17]

The soup kitchen across the street from the commissary opened at 3 o'clock that first day, with delicious odors wafting toward Washington Park, two blocks away. The *News and Courier* was especially impressed that the head chef had once cooked for Governor Francis W. Pickens and "had often prepared soup for John C. Calhoun," for whom a monument was still under construction eight blocks away. One old man was so excited by the smell of hot food that he was "paralyzed with indecision." Finally someone took the kettle he had brought and filled it with a steaming dollop of vegetable soup. Seeing a pan of bones that had been extracted from the soup, the old man begged, "Gib de old man one ob dem lean bone."[18]

Every day except Sunday, the cooks at the soup kitchen prepared a thousand gallons of soup. Women and children were always directed to the front of the line. If any soup were left over, men and "half-grown boys" would be served. A policeman was assigned to keep order, admitting six people at a time. The committee announced repeatedly that those "who are able-bodied and can have work for the asking will not, of course, receive rations." The *New York World* claimed that many of the applicants carried brand-new tin kettles, supposedly purchased especially for collecting large quantities of free soup. A reporter for the *News and Courier* noted, however, that most of the people in line were children carrying "pots, pans, broken pitchers and old porcelain teapots." Each child was given a pint of soup and a piece of meat.[19]

By September 9, having walked the streets and assessed the situation firsthand for two days, Courtenay was ready to move forward with a reorganization plan. He reappointed Huger's committee, though the members had offered to step aside so the mayor would be free to name other men if he saw fit. He asked Colonel Yates to continue as chairman, but Yates declined, citing the demands of his phosphate company. General Huguenin wanted to resume his duties as the city's superintendent of streets. So, after carefully informing the public that the old committee had done an excellent job, and that the only reason he was appointing more men was that there was so much important work still to be done, Courtenay asked new members — all white businessmen — to serve on the relief committee. Frank Dawson was the only member of the first group who agreed to stay on.[20]

This new team would be called the Executive Relief Committee, and it was empowered to make all major decisions and oversee the work of the subcommittees. The group agreed that the plans already made should be carried out: more wooden booths would be constructed, the commissary on Cumberland Street would continue to distribute rations, and the soup kitchen would go on providing cooked food. Dawson was put in charge of a subcommittee on immediate relief, which had the authority to pass out small sums so people could replace clothes, bedding, and other necessities.[21]

Many Charlestonians decided to leave town, and the South Carolina Railway offered free transportation to anyone who wanted to flee the city. Five hundred people applied for passes on the first day. Whites lined up to "refugee," just as they had during the war, though the *News and Courier* reported that blacks who joined them were using the passes for "excursions." Demand was so brisk that Mayor Courtenay imposed a new rule: anybody who wanted a free pass must present a letter from a physician or clergyman certifying need. A day later, no doubt responding to criticism, he revised the rule: everyone, no matter how poor, should pay at least one cent a mile (a trip to Columbia or Savannah under this system cost about a dollar). Courtenay did not accuse anyone of cheating. He simply laid down the law in a firm, calm way.[22]

ALL OF CHARLESTON seemed to draw strength from the mayor's return. A man who lived on Market Street found his favorite chicken "fit and lively" though it had been buried under the ruins of his house for eight days. Even some inanimate objects started working again. For over a week the hands of the clock on St. Michael's steeple had remained frozen at 9:54. On Wednesday morning, the sexton went up into the tower to tinker with the mechanism. At two that afternoon the hands began to turn, a sign, according to the *News and Courier*, that "Charleston lives in spite of the terrible calamity which has visited her."[23]

Engineers and architects from Atlanta were hired to decide which buildings should be pulled down and which could be safely repaired. Although there was plenty of bad news, people began to realize that with enough time and money most structures could be repaired. For example, the board of engineers reported three days after the earthquake that the post office building at the foot of Broad Street (now known as the Old Exchange Building) was unstable and would have to be torn down. On closer inspection they decided that the edifice could be safely used if the walls were reinforced. A crew climbed the steeple at St. Philip's Church and came down to say that the damage was not nearly as serious as it had appeared from the ground. The structure could be saved. The unfinished granite base of the Calhoun Monument had not been damaged, and, in spite of the emergency, masons continued laying stones amid a sea of campers.[24]

THE NATION's fascination with the earthquake was equaled by its philanthropy. The relief fund was swelling fast, and in Mayor Courtenay's absence, donations totaling more than $20,000 were sent directly to Frank Dawson. New York City raised $100,000 in less than a week, including $5,000 from millionaire J. P. Morgan. Baltimore and Philadelphia sent large sums, more than $20,000 apiece. The citizens of Richmond, Virginia, promised to raise $5,000, but upped its offer to $10,000 when someone pointed out that the city had sent that much to Chicago after the great fire in 1871. Augusta, Georgia, raised $1,000, although it too had been hit hard by the quake and people there were still sleeping in the streets.[25]

The list of contributors was soon a sort of social register, including four Vanderbilts, John Jacob Astor, William Astor, railroad tycoon Jay Gould, and former President Martin T. Van Buren. In New York City, stores on Broadway placed collection boxes on the sidewalk. Contributions came from businesses and organizations all over the country. The publisher Harper and Brothers sent $500. Joseph Pulitzer of the New York World wired $1,000, then followed up with other donations, including $10.17 from John Kenyon, the New Jersey principal who had led the campaign to raise money from schoolchildren to build a base for the Statue of Liberty. A bale of cotton from Georgia, the first of the season, was auctioned for the relief of the "Charleston sufferers."[26]

The Associated Press sent $500 for Dawson to divide among his reporters, in recognition of their faithful service. Dawson used his own money to reward three other employees who also stood by him on the night of the earthquake. These large cash payments were much publicized and served to chastise the "quakers" as well as to honor the men who had stayed at their posts.[27]

Employees of the South Carolina Lunatic Asylum donated $22.20. The Mystic Sisterhood of Pendleton, a ladies' club from the South Carolina Up-country, gave $16.25. A nine-year-old girl who found $5.00 sent it in to the relief fund. Aid also came in the form of goods. People and businesses sent building materials, food, medicine, and "$100 worth of black stiff hats."[28]

No matter how great or small the donation, Mayor Courtenay took the trouble to send each donor a gracious thank-you. The *News and Courier* printed a list of contributions each day, so many that the names and amounts took up much of a page.

The contributions that poured from the North took on symbolic importance. Charleston was still widely regarded as a nest of hotheaded slave-holding aristocrats who had led the secession movement and started the Civil War, a place that deserved punishment. Now, the *Boston Herald* instructed its readers "How to Wipe Out the Past" by giving generously to the relief fund. "We were her bitterest enemy a quarter of a century ago: let us be her most earnest friends now," said an officer of the Grand Army of the Republic (GAR), a national organization for Union veterans. The *New York World* was blunter: "The people of the North made a frantic effort some years ago to wipe out the City of Charleston. Now the charitable throughout the country have an opportunity to join in the more pleasing task of wiping it up. Let the bombardment with silver dollars from the mortars of generosity proceed."[29]

One GAR post offered to send its Civil War veterans to guard the streets of Charleston. City officials acknowledged this offer as "thoughtful" but speedily declined, remembering the ten bitter years after the war when the city was occupied by federal troops. Another GAR post in Brooklyn rallied its members to action: "Comrades!" read its resolution. "A sister city of the Union and its inhabitants are in dire distress!" A "one-armed soldier of the Union Army" contributed $1.00 for relief and wished he could send a thousand. The abolitionist John Greenleaf Whittier, some of whose most famous poems pictured antebellum Charleston as the heart of darkness, sent $10.00 to the relief fund. He urged every town and city in New England to take up a subscription: "New England in this matter knows no North and no South, and if . . . any old jealousies and resentments remain they should be swept away in the flood of practical sympathy for our afflicted fellow-countrymen." The *News and Courier* was quick to report that Edwin Booth, the brother of President Lincoln's assassin, John Wilkes Booth, but a loyal Unionist during the war, had sent $1,000 to "a dear friend in this city." Even the son of John Brown, the militant martyr of the abolitionist movement who was hanged for leading a raid on the federal arsenal at Harpers Ferry, sent a contribution.[30]

Francis Warrington Dawson, 1840–89. A native of England, Dawson crossed the Atlantic to fight for the Confederacy, yet he did not share white South Carolina's conviction that racial inequality was a higher law. As editor of the *Charleston News and Courier*, he became one of the most powerful figures in the postwar South. (Francis Warrington Dawson Family Papers, Rare Book, Manuscript, and Special Collections Library, Duke University)

Sarah Morgan Dawson, 1842–1909. The Civil War diarist married Francis Dawson in 1874. She and their two children were traveling in Europe at the time of the earthquake. (Francis Warrington Dawson Family Papers, Rare Book, Manuscript, and Special Collections Library, Duke University)

Eastern U.S. Isoseismal Map, August 31, 1886. As of December 2010, the 1886
earthquake was the most powerful seismic event in recorded history to strike
the East Coast. The roman numerals on the map correspond to the magnitude
levels of the Modified Mercalli Scale. Based on Stover and Coffman, *Seismicity
of the United States, 1568–1989*, rev. ed. (Washington, D.C.: U.S. Geological
Survey, 1993). Map by Paul F. Rossmann.

"The Night of the Earthquake in Charleston, August 31, 1886." Supplement to *Harper's Weekly*, September 11, 1886. (Authors' collection)

Hibernian Hall, Meeting Street, with St. Michael's Church in the background.
(Charleston County Public Library)

(*Top*) The Medical College of the State of South Carolina. (Charleston Library Society, Charleston, S.C.)

(*Bottom*) Brick wall of the city jail on Magazine Street, fissured by the earthquake. The night of the quake forty-three of the sixty-four prisoners escaped. (U.S. Geological Survey, Department of the Interior/USGS. USGS credits this photograph to J. K. Hillers; however, new evidence suggests that it was actually taken by C. C. Jones.)

Aftermath of the fire on King Street near Broad. A kerosene lamp overturned by the earthquake tremors ignited this blaze, the largest of several conflagrations that followed the first shock. (Waring Historical Library, Medical University of South Carolina)

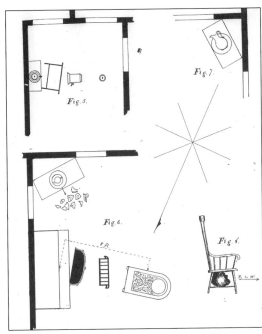

Diagram of displacement. Railroad cashier Frank Fisher made detailed drawings of how his furniture was thrown around a room during the earthquake. Like many other well-educated men, he seized on the rituals of scientific method as a way to exert some psychological control over the terrifying forces of geological upheaval. (Special Collections, Marlene and Nathan Addlestone Library, College of Charleston)

(*Above*) "Encampment on Capt. Dawson's Lawn." After the earthquake, Dawson camped in his backyard with friends, family, and servants under a tent fashioned from the sail of a boat. (Francis Warrington Dawson Family Papers, Rare Book, Manuscript, and Special Collections Library, Duke University)

(*Facing page, top*) "A Sudden Conversion. The Demi-Monde of Charleston, S.C. are temporarily converted from their wicked ways by the recent earthquake." *National Police Gazette: New York*, September 25, 1886. (Collection of Harlan Greene)

(*Facing page, bottom*) "The Inhabitants Taking Refuge in Washington Park. Ministering to the Wounded and Dying." *Frank Leslie's Illustrated Newspaper*, September 11, 1886. (Charleston County Public Library)

(*Left*) "Scene on Marion Square, Opposite The Citadel — A City of Tents." *Charleston As It Is After the Earthquake Shock of August 31, 1886.* (Charleston County Public Library)

(*Facing page, bottom*) "Camping Out in the Streets." *New York Graphic.* (Charleston County Public Library)

(*Below*) Tent city at Washington Square Park showing makeshift shelters. Whites and blacks alike took refuge here after the earthquake, but whites soon deserted the camp because of loud preaching. (Waring Historical Library, Medical University of South Carolina)

HARPER'S WEEKLY.

JOURNAL OF CIVILIZATION.

Vol. XXX.—No. 1551.
Copyright, 1886, by Harper & Brothers.   NEW YORK, SATURDAY, SEPTEMBER 11, 1886.   TEN CENTS A COPY.
WITH A SUPPLEMENT.

"The Earthquake — A Street Scene in Charleston." *Harper's Weekly,*
September 11, 1886. (Authors' collection)

"Scene in the Garden of a Residence on Society Street — A Shock at Breakfast-Time." *Frank Leslie's Illustrated Newspaper*, September 18, 1886. (Authors' collection)

William John McGee of the U.S. Geological Survey inspecting a fissure near a wrecked brick house on Tradd Street. A cardboard focimeter is propped against the telephone pole, with a map of Charleston nearby. (U.S. Geological Survey, Department of the Interior/USGS)

Turkey vultures. Known as "Charleston eagles," these birds were protected in the city because they cleaned up scraps at the City Market. After the earthquake, northern journalists depicted them as haunting symbols of death and destruction. *Harper's Weekly*, September 11, 1886. (Authors' collection)

(*Facing page*) Workers making repairs at Fire Station 5. (South Caroliniana Library, University of South Carolina)

Looking for a sleeping place.

Found insensible in the hospital.

Camp in the old cathedral grounds.

Getting out of the hotel.

Waiting for the tidal wave.

An ear of corn.

Thumbnail sketches by Walt McDougall in the *New York World*. McDougall was served an almost-bald ear of corn in Summerville after the quake. When he complained, his waiter scolded that he shouldn't be so particular. "Dis de bes' we kin do, and de Laud have mercy on our souls. It's 'nuff to wait on de table, when we ought to be in de meetin' prayin', sah, widout bein' 'bused fo' bringin' dat kine ob' coun." (Authors' collection)

(*Left*) William Ashmead Courtenay, 1831–1908. The dynamic mayor of Charleston was returning from a vacation in Europe when the earthquake struck. He quickly took charge of relief and recovery efforts. Though he worked closely with Dawson in 1886, he soon felt betrayed by him. (South Caroliniana Library, University of South Carolina)

(*Below*) "Generous Rivalry in a Good Cause." *Puck*, September 15, 1886. Groups around the world scrambled to send funds to the relief effort, until city leaders told them to stop. (Collection of Harlan Greene)

Rev. William Henry Harrison Heard, 1850–1937. This African Methodist Episcopal minister, who had been born a slave in Georgia, organized the Colored Clergy, which challenged the city's relief policies. *New York Freeman*, May 7, 1887. (Authors' collection)

(*Facing page, top*) "Subsistence Committee." *Harper's Weekly*, September 18, 1886. A firehouse was used as a commissary to distribute uncooked foods. (Authors' collection)

(*Facing page, bottom*) "Relief Committee." *Harper's Weekly*, September 18, 1886. Wagons carried tents to those who needed shelter. (Authors' collection)

Interior of the Dawson house after the cracked plaster walls had been patched. (Francis Warrington Dawson Family Papers, Rare Book, Manuscript, and Special Collections Library, Duke University)

(*Below*) In November 1886 this ornate silver tea set was presented to Frank Dawson by city leaders in gratitude for his service to the city. (Francis Warrington Dawson Family Papers, Rare Book, Manuscript, and Special Collections Library, Duke University)

Gala Week. In the fall of 1887 the city put on this grand weeklong festival to celebrate its recovery from the earthquake. For the first time since the end of the Civil War, U.S. flags flew everywhere. *Frank Leslie's Illustrated Magazine*, November 12, 1887. (Authors' collection)

Benjamin Tillman, 1847–1918. The farmers' advocate denounced Dawson from the steps of Charleston City Hall. "Dawsonism," he charged, "is the domination of that old, effete aristocratic element that clings to power like an octopus." Tillman went on to become governor of South Carolina and a U.S. senator. (South Caroliniana Library, University of South Carolina)

Marie Hélène Burdayron. Born in Switzerland, she moved to Charleston with Sarah Morgan Dawson and her children in 1887 to serve as an au pair. The world came to know her as the "French maid" during the trial of Dawson's killer. (Francis Warrington Dawson Family Papers, Rare Book, Manuscript, and Special Collections Library, Duke University)

Dr. Arthur B. McDow. The Dawsons' neighbor began to pursue Hélène in February 1889. On March 12 he shot Frank Dawson to death after Dawson tried to stop the affair and attempted to hide the body under the floor of a closet in his office. (Authors' collection, from the *Charleston World*)

The northern impulse to help wounded Charleston was part of a national trend that had begun not long after the war and was peaking in the mid-1880s. Both Courtenay and Dawson were early advocates of North-South reunion and had attended some of the first joint gatherings of Union and Confederate veterans. At first their motives had been largely commercial, an attempt to rebuild business relationships severed by the war. But, as historian David Blight points out in *Race and Reunion*, the push for reconciliation also required white men on both sides of the conflict to politely disregard their differences over slavery and emancipation. By 1886, old soldiers North and South had settled into a public compromise that allowed them to embrace each other: everyone was brave. For black Americans, however, this attitude meant that the nation was moving in a dangerous direction, away from its commitment to enforcing civil rights in the former Confederacy.[31]

BETWEEN SEPTEMBER 3 and September 11, fourteen names were added to Charleston's list of earthquake-related deaths. Twelve succumbed to "exposure," although doctors listed an additional disease aggravated by living outdoors. Two had measles, one gastritis, another epilepsy. Two suffered from scrofula, a form of tuberculosis. One young child's death was said to have been caused by "dentition"— teething. The committee set out to get people under cover before the fall rains — and hurricanes — came.[32]

Every possible enclosure was turned into housing. The Enterprise Railroad allowed people to sleep in its streetcars. The railroads donated one hundred boxcars for use as temporary homes. The owner of a newly constructed stable on King Street put down mattresses in the stalls for 150 people, including Charleston Chapman, the "earthquake baby" born in Washington Square on the night of the earthquake. The *Amethyst*, a huge iron steamship, arrived expecting to take on a cargo of cotton and found the city in ruins; though the captain reserved the right to "exclude all objectionable persons," he announced that the ship could provide sanctuary for up to two hundred refugees. His crew whitewashed an empty compartment and covered the floors with canvas. A U.S. lighthouse buoy tender, the *Wistaria*, took in refugees. Schooners, tugboats, pilot boats, fishing smacks, and steamships also welcomed the homeless. All Italian vessels in port were ordered by the Italian consul to accept refugees.[33]

So many people huddled together presented another problem. Mayor Courtenay had estimated before the earthquake, when he was trying to push the city into building a sewer system, that "at least 100,000 pounds of excreta, solid and fluid, is deposited [in Charleston] every twenty-four hours. The multiplication into the aggregate for a week! A month! A year!" he exclaimed. No sewer system had been built, and now, rather than being deposited neatly in vaults that could be emptied regularly, feces were lying in the streets and the sidewalks reeked of urine. The relief committee built "sanitary closets" at Marion Square, but elsewhere people relieved themselves wherever nature called.[34]

Each camp was assigned a supervisor with orders to keep things clean and neat and to pay special attention to sanitation. Hydrants were installed in Marion Square to provide fresh water. In some camps, chloride of lime was sprinkled liberally on what were euphemistically described as "nuisances." The Linguard Street washerwomen's encampment came in for special criticism — the area was heavily populated, and children were spotted running barefoot through piles of excrement.[35]

Washington Square was ignored yet again — it had no supervisor, no wooden shelters, no latrines, and no fresh water. One white man who lived nearby on Chalmers Street threatened to shoot campers if they kept dumping the contents of their chamber pots in the street. He bought lime at his own expense and sprinkled it around the square. Dawson published the man's complaints, and soon carts and men were sent by the city to "clean out" the camp. Apparently they hauled off tents and possessions along with garbage and sewage, and by the next day there was a "marked decrease" in the number of campers.[36]

Less than two weeks after the quake, the city's focus shifted away from providing temporary shelter and toward getting people out of the streets and back inside their houses. As long as the weather held, few were willing to follow Mayor Courtenay's lead in returning to their homes. However, when a storm blew up on September 12, panic erupted among the tenters. Rain poured through the roofs of the temporary structures. The rumor spread that a tornado had been sighted. Hundreds ran back to their damaged houses and slammed the shutters, huddling in darkness amid fallen plaster while the rain pounded down. There was no tornado, but many campers were convinced to try moving back home.[37]

Stung by attacks in out-of-town newspapers that said he was stabling his horses in a tent while thousands of poor people went without shelter, Francis Rodgers resigned from the finance subcommittee. Although the reports did not call Rodgers by name, they identified him in such a way that anyone who knew Charleston would figure out who was meant: what other city alderman, one of the richest men in the city, had just completed a "palatial" new house at a cost of more than $150,000? Dawson defended Rodgers, praising his devotion to duty while fighting the earthquake fires, but the damage had been done. Normally, Dawson or Courtenay might have been able to sit down with Rodgers and smooth over the offense. But there were far more pressing matters claiming their attention, so the usual gestures of politesse were forgotten and feelings were hurt.[38]

Someone who signed himself "Vigilance" sent a letter to the *News and Courier* predicting a rise in crime. "I understand very well that it will take Mayor Courtenay (God bless him!) some days to get into the traces, but let us beg him to increase the police force," he wrote. Half-a-dozen white vagrants had been spotted on King Street, and Vigilance was sure that in a week or two the city would be full of predatory strangers: "Every house is at the mercy of thieves, and there should be a policeman on every square in the city." Some merchants went out of their way to ramp up the city's anxiety: "No Jail! Stationhouse in Ruins! City Crowded with Rascally Tramps" read an ad in the *News and Courier*. "A fine stock of PISTOLS just received and for sale at low-down prices."[39]

Courtenay authorized the police department to hire fifty extra men, and plans were made to build a stockade where the prisoners displaced from the damaged jail could be housed. Whites all over the city still complained about black religious meetings in the parks, so Courtenay quietly sent for Col. Alfred Rhett, who had commanded Fort Sumter during the Civil War and who had served as chief of police. Courtenay asked Rhett to find some way to stop the noise. Rhett said that if the city would provide a mount and appoint a uniformed policeman to escort him, he would see what he could do. Colonel Rhett and his bodyguard rode from camp to camp, calling to the exhorters, "This thing must be stopped by ten o'clock to-night. You know who I am, don't you? I represent the city and I am coming round here to-night to see that you have stopped." Every evening he repeated his warnings, and the preachers soon kept earlier hours.[40]

AFFLUENT WHITES insisted that providing free food and shelter to the poor would lead to a moral breakdown. Rev. A. Toomer Porter, the white minister who had threatened to beat a hymn-singing black woman with his cane, warned that no one should "give help to a fellow who can clean bricks, or roll a wheelbarrow, white or black, or you will have a repetition of the Freedmen's Bureau business." Porter's comments offer a dramatic illustration of how the sparks of old conflicts often ignite after a disaster, rather than disappearing amid the sentimental declarations of solidarity. "Work, fellow-citizens," he urged, though he mainly meant blacks. "Don't take a dollar without doing something to earn it. The demoralization to you will do more harm to your character than the money will do good to your material wants." Porter also wrote a public letter to Rev. William Heard and the Colored Clergy urging them to use their "powerful influence" to encourage those living in the camps to move back home and thereby save the city and themselves from serious epidemics. "Break up those camps on Washington Square, and even those wooden sheds on Marion Square," he scolded, just days after the shelters were erected. "If all the thin plastering from low ceilings was to fall it would not hurt a baby. . . . Discourage this going for ration business." He encouraged black ministers to put a stop to the loud, emotional religious demonstrations that kept people stirred up. Such outbursts angered whites and could cause support from the North to dry up. Once again, Porter acted on the assumption that blacks respected him because of his service to St. Mark's. Though he probably did have more credibility than most other white ministers, his condescending, hectoring tone must have irritated Heard and the other black ministers.[41]

Stories about goldbricking ran rampant. One woman complained to her sister that household help was impossible to keep: "The trouble I suspect is that the husbands, brothers & c are getting exorbitant wages and rations have been distributed, so they have no need to work. Mr. Frost says that the stream of people with parcels in King Street last night reminded him of Christmas, and when I went to shut the windows, I saw a woman passing with so many bundles that she had to hold them on with her chin." The News and Courier agreed, claiming that "the promiscuous issuance of rations" had devastated the labor pool: "Servant girls have left their employers [and] washerwomen have refused to wash clothes." The paper indignantly reported that in spite of attempts to screen applicants, a black man rode into town on a morning train, collected a basket of provisions, got drunk, and rode out again.[42]

Nonetheless, in the pages of the News and Courier Dr. Arthur B. Rose defended the work of his subsistence subcommittee: "If we relieve five hundred persons who need relief, and at the same time give food to one thousand persons who do not deserve help, the fact remains that we have done something to afford relief, and that is what we are trying to do." Although he raged against those who would not work, Dawson agreed with Rose. There were thousands of worthy people in Charleston, he wrote the next day, who could "no longer earn their daily bread." Whatever the cost, they "must be given sustenance."[43]

Warnings and criticism also came from other parts of the country. The conservative New York Times disapproved of relief as a matter of principle: "The opening of soup kitchens on a great scale is always to be deprecated." A man from Baltimore wrote Mayor Courtenay about his experience helping to raise money for victims of the great Chicago fire. A number of French artists had donated paintings, and he had been in charge of selling them to raise funds. The effort was a huge success, but before the sale could be completed, the mayor of Chicago asked him to stop sending money. Laborers had stopped rebuilding the city when they no longer had to work for food and shelter.[44]

Word spread to the countryside that Charleston was the place to be, so black farm workers set out for it on foot and by boat. Hundreds arrived from Johns Island, James Island, Wadmalaw Island, and Cainhoy—an "invasion," claimed the News and Courier. Blacks seeking relief in Savannah were told to go to Charleston. Men began to congregate there at the corner of Broad and Meeting streets, clutching hatchets. A local black man told a reporter that these people had come from the islands to get rations, and that if they couldn't get free food, they intended to use their tools to clean bricks. The reporter thought they looked like "an assemblage of dusky George Washingtons."[45]

Hands abandoned the Santee and Pee Dee river rice fields, according to one planter, because they had heard reports that large sums of money were being sent to Charleston by "friends at the North." There was "dire hunger" in these regions. A legislator from Georgetown, sixty miles north of Charleston on the coast, admitted that the "only hope" for most farm laborers in his district was to leave home for other areas where work and food could be found. Many of those who came to Charleston had been starving for months on end as a result of spring floods and crop failures — they were the same Santee and Pee Dee "sufferers" to whom Congress had refused to send aid, and whose cause Heard had taken up in the pages of the *New York Freeman*. It took an earthquake to bring them relief.[46]

By September 10 the crowds at the commissary had grown so large they overwhelmed the clerks. The *News and Courier* announced that the problem was the "injudicious" distribution of ration tickets — presumably a state of affairs created by soft-hearted, easily duped ministers. And so the committee changed course again. Following procedures set up after the Civil War, Dr. Rose's subsistence subcommittee hired twelve "canvassers," one per ward. Each was trained to inspect houses, make inquiries, and otherwise assess applicants to make sure they were "absolutely in need." Then delivery wagons were dispatched with packages addressed to specific individuals. Clerks and canvassers were paid $2.00 for an eleven-hour day, and the committee tried to hire "hardworking and industrious" men who were themselves in need of charity. The subsistence subcommittee reported that about two-thirds of the people they had helped were black, so the canvassers were specifically told to seek out destitute whites and to examine all black applicants carefully to make sure they were not able to work. The *New York Herald* hailed this development as "Repressing Bummerism."[47]

Mayor Courtenay directed the subsistence subcommittee to hire six black canvassers and to ask Rev. William Heard and the Colored Clergy to recommend trustworthy men. Appeased for the moment, Heard backed off. His committee even followed Rev. A. Toomer Porter's condescending advice and sent a letter to the *News and Courier*, signed by Rev. John Dart, urging blacks to move back home: "What we all need is rest, the calmness of home-life and settling down to routine duties." But Heard was not so conciliatory when writing for the black press. "Colored people are the greatest sufferers. All money is in the hands of white people," he reported to the *New York Freeman*. Charleston's black community had to look to other blacks for aid. "Is there a sympathetic heart in the colored people of these United States?" Heard asked. He provided his own address and Rev. George Rowe's for those who wanted to send money.[48]

By mid-September the relief committee had doubled the number of canvassers to twenty-four, twelve white and twelve black. The expanded force turned in so many names that the delivery wagons could not keep up. By September 19 there were nine wagons, and six more were temporarily engaged to catch up with the work.[49]

EARTHQUAKE DAMAGE, of course, spread far beyond Charleston, so nearby communities demanded a portion of the relief money. A week after the quake, five men from Knightsville, a tiny settlement three miles from Summerville, wrote the *News and Courier* to beg that "while such a golden shower is falling on Charleston a few drops might reach us." Tents and sails had been sent to Summerville, but homeless people continued to arrive from the countryside with pitiful tales of houses wrecked and burned. Weeks after the earthquake, women and children were "nearly naked, and entirely destitute of provisions." A member of the Summerville Town Council formally petitioned the relief committee to send a portion of the relief fund to his town. Mt. Pleasant, across the Cooper River, also asked for money, as did Berkeley County and the town of Adams Run. The committee agreed to share its resources, so long as these other districts designated responsible men to preside over distribution.[50]

In Charleston, officials assumed that all such "responsible men" would be white. But the eight-person team appointed in Summerville included two black men, both ministers.[51] Charleston never appointed a black member to any committee. Nor would a representative of the labor unions be asked to serve.

FRANK DAWSON dominated the Charleston relief meetings, but he also acted as the city's cheerleader with a relentlessly positive message. "Courage! Hope! Work!" he urged in the pages of the *News and Courier*. "With these, and with time, we can overcome our every difficulty, as our brothers and fathers overcame the ravages of fire and the desolation of war." Charleston would soon renew itself, he believed, and "dispel" the "dark pall."[52]

But it was the dark pall that fascinated the world and attracted more donations. In a series of huge, melodramatic engravings, the September 11 issue of *Harper's Weekly* depicted Charleston as a city of death. Terrified people ran down a street as telephone poles snapped and stones hurtled toward them. A black cook presided over an outdoor cookstove while two white children watched. In the most haunting image of all, a vulture gazed over the forlorn skyline while other vultures circled.[53]

There really were vultures sitting on the rooftops of Charleston, but they weren't waiting to feast on earthquake victims. A flock patrolled the streets around the City Market buildings, protected from harm by a city ordinance because they kept the streets clean. The locals called them "buzzards" or

"Charleston eagles." No doubt the buzzards went hungry the week after the quake, since the market was filled with refugees instead of butchers' scraps and carcasses. Truck crops like beans, okra, and tomatoes, which were ripe and plentiful in the countryside, were not being brought into the city. Even the fishing fleet was idle, its sails serving as tents.[54]

The commercial slump was soft-pedaled by the *News and Courier*. Since the night of the quake, Dawson had been especially concerned that the city's business should continue with as little interruption as possible, or at least that the rest of the country should believe that this was the case. He sent his reporters to check on how local firms were doing. Most businessmen parroted the legend that Dawson had been actively promoting — commerce was thriving. A wholesale liquor and cigar dealer claimed he had "kept open from the day of the first shock and [was] not much hurt." Even James Robson, whose son Ainsley had been killed, put on a brave front: his wholesale grocery business was "going on just the same." And "while it is a pretty dear one," he added, "the earthquake is the greatest advertisement Charleston could have."[55]

Meanwhile, at the Dawson household, tensions continued to run high. Frank warned his sister-in-law Miriam not to talk about earthquakes or sickness or the danger that a hurricane might come or, most of all, "the threatening aspect of the negroes." Mollie Glidden was nervous, he explained, and they must do everything possible to keep up her spirits. Miriam seethed at Frank's deference to a woman who, in her view at least, was silly, self-centered, and all but useless. The Gliddens, Miriam complained to her sister Sarah, had not "spent one dollar [of their own] except for candy and soda water." Mollie drove around town in Sarah's carriage and had a servant button her boots. Miriam saw it as "a cool case of sponging on Frank."[56]

Frank couldn't care less. He was glad that Sarah and the children were safely away, and he clearly enjoyed having the Gliddens to talk to when he got home after a long day. Frank seems to have taken it for granted that Miriam would like having another woman around. But the more he deferred to "dear Mollie," the more Miriam fumed. She complained to Sarah, perhaps hoping that her sister would get jealous and see to it that Mollie was banished. Frank made light of the tensions. He wrote Sarah that Miriam was so skittish that she still slept with her boots on. He was counting the days until September 15, when Miriam and Lucile were scheduled to leave for Cincinnati and Lucile's music school. When Miriam expressed her desire to stay in Charleston an extra week, to pack up the family silver and take care of Frank, he told her she needed to go on and help her daughter get settled.[57]

In fact, despite her complaints about Mollie, Miriam herself was "sponging on Frank" and had been for some time. Only days after the earthquake, she hired a seamstress to make three new dresses, one for herself and two for Lucile. The cost came to more than $40.00, and Miriam had no income. Frank footed the bill. He would also pay for their train tickets, and for Lucile's expenses at the Cincinnati College of Music. If Miriam could not find a job, he would end up supporting them. Miriam was convinced that Lucile was a prodigy — she had played Mozart sonatas on the piano at age four — and that her talent would eventually prove the investment worthwhile.[58]

Frank was enjoying his new status as a hero. "I have made lots of reputation out of this thing," he wrote Sarah. "Will send you some evidence." He enclosed an editorial from the *New York Mail and Express* that called him "heroic." With Dawson's "zeal, his devotion, his unselfishness, his knowledge of the people and his boundless energy and fertility of expedients," the paper gushed, he was "the man of men in whom the people of this country will naturally trust."[59]

DAWSON'S OBSESSION with business as usual began to show up everywhere, even in the pulpit. Most of the white preachers in town adopted his encouraging "can-do" tone, as if they were his lieutenants in the campaign to rebuild Charleston. On the second Sunday after the quake, most white church services were still being held under the open sky. Having had more than a week to think about whether God had meant to punish Charleston, many white ministers now asserted that he had not. Flatly contradicting a sermon he had preached after the hurricane a year before, when he warned that the storm was a message from God to sinners, Rev. A. Toomer Porter announced that to believe "the earthquake was the direct act of God as a visitation for sins was not only unscientific, but unreasonable." To be sure, Charleston had had more than its share of disasters. But God had also given the city mild winters, rich phosphate deposits, and the ability to grow cotton.[61]

Rev. Robert Wilson of St. Luke's Lutheran Church, whose scientific explanation of the earthquake had calmed some fears the week before, talked about how desolate the Apostles had felt when Jesus ascended into heaven. An angel appeared and told them to put their minds on practical duties.

This, he said, was exactly what Charlestonians should do — return to their regular routines. It was a religious doctrine that Dawson could embrace. "The orderly government of society is entrusted to us," Wilson announced. People should pay their debts, be honest in reporting their losses, and work hard. Then, if Judgment Day came, the Lord would discover them doing their duty, and he would be pleased. If Judgment Day did not come, well, at least their chimneys would be fireproof.[62]

Chapter Ten

THE COMFORTS OF SCIENCE

SEISMOLOGY OFFERED a reassuring alternative to visions of the apocalypse. Like many Charlestonians, Edward Wells's little daughter sobbed in terror when the first shock hit. Then she heard someone explain the earthquake in scientific terms. "Papa," she exclaimed, "if I had known it was an *earthquake*, I wouldn't have cried!" Two days later Wells found her reading about seismic phenomena in Charles Lyell's *Principles of Geology.*[1]

Vast impersonal geophysical forces were, for many people, far less frightening than the idea of God's wrath. Science held out the possibility that men could understand exactly what had happened and so predict or even prevent future earthquakes. But none of the government investigators had been in Charleston the night of the quake, so they set out to collect firsthand reports from reliable witnesses. One of the best was provided by Gabriel Manigault, a professor of natural history and geology at the College of Charleston and the unpaid curator of the Charleston Museum. On the night of the earthquake Manigault was playing chess on the ground floor of his house, which had been built on the edge of made ground near the Ashley River. When the shock hit, he and his friend ran out into the garden and saw earth waves rolling across the yard like breakers on the beach. The men had to spread their legs to stay on their feet. Several fissures opened on the lawn, and a crater spouted next door.[2]

Another member of the college faculty, a professor of mathematics, astronomy, and chemistry named Lewis Gibbes, conducted his own scientific studies, following, as William McGee had done, the example of Robert Mallet. Gibbes walked through the eight major graveyards for whites in Charleston, including the vast expanse of Magnolia, looking for twisted tombstones and fallen urns. The previous year's hurricane had also damaged the monuments, so Gibbes had to consult the keepers of the cemeteries to distinguish the damage of one calamity from the other. He was not much interested in buildings, since he thought it was impossible to see all sides of the "cracks, rents, and other injuries."[3]

Gibbes believed that the center of the earthquake was near Ten Mile Hill and that the slippage had probably occurred from eleven to fifteen miles underground. He calculated these numbers according to equations developed by Mallet some thirty years before, the simplest of which held that the radius of the circle of greatest disturbance is equal to the depth of the quake. Gibbes contended that the most powerful shocks had moved *toward* the focus, which would confirm Mallet's theory — later proved correct — that earth waves, like sound waves, can be deflected and reflected so that they arrive from various directions.

Some of the most precise records of what happened during the earthquake came from an amateur scientist and inventor named Frank Fisher who worked as a cashier for the South Carolina Railway. When the earthquake hit, Fisher was sitting in a rocking chair on the piazza of his house on Wentworth Street. He took careful notes on the movement of his chair and the exact way it lurched as his floor twisted and bent. One rocker rose five inches off the floor when the piazza pulled away from the house and rotated on one of its columns. His chair had spun around so that it faced the southwest. Carefully counting off seconds, he recorded that the first shock lasted half a minute. And he later made a set of drawings, like a house plan, using arrows to show how clocks, china, and furniture had flown around his bedroom.[4]

Some may find it hard to believe that Fisher could have counted while the whole world, in his own words, appeared to be "falling to pieces." But he truly seems to have kept his head and realized, even as the house bucked under him like an unbroken horse, that everything he was seeing and feeling would be important in a scientific investigation. "Under such circumstances the greatest exertion of will is requisite to maintain self-possession," he dryly noted.

Counting and measuring creates an illusion of order amid the chaos. As James Penick observed in his book on the New Madrid earthquakes, "if Americans are suddenly introduced into a situation in which the ground shakes for weeks and months on end and all nature seems about to come undone, the first impulse of many is to count, make lists, and sort."[5]

In his brilliant book, *Acts of God: The Unnatural History of Natural Disasters in America*, Ted Steinberg notes that business leaders in the late nineteenth century "tried to normalize events such as earthquakes by draining them, as best they could, of any larger meaning." The message could not have been clearer: "Natural disasters simply happened, and wallowing in the spectacle of life turned upside down or prostrating oneself before God only prolonged the agony." This was Frank Dawson's attitude, and also Ashmead Courtenay's.[6]

In order to convince people that the earthquake was not a message from God, men like Dawson and Courtenay needed scientific facts the public could understand. Almost before the plaster dust settled, the newspapers were filled with scientific-sounding pronouncements. The most popular theory, though hardly the most current in professional circles, was the one Professor James C. Mendenhall had cited, the idea that the earth resembled an apple drying in its skin. As the pulpy flesh shrank, the smooth surface began to wrinkle and crack, causing earthquakes. This mundane image was based on the work of an Austrian geologist, Edward Seuss, and it had the tremendous advantage of making earthquakes seem comprehensible. The president of the British Geological Association compared the earth to a peach, with a hard center, a dense layer of flesh, and a thin skin. He said the mountains along the eastern seaboard marked places where the skin had been folded and creased by shrinking, swelling, and "oozing."[7]

Frank Dawson was openly delighted by the remarks of Professor Cleveland Abbe, head of the National Weather Bureau, who said that earthquakes relieve geological strain and announced with great conviction that the whole country was "now entitled to a period of rest" from quakes. He even went so far as to claim that the hiatus would probably last from fifty-eight to seventy-five years, based on the intervals between the Boston quake of 1755, the New Madrid quakes of 1811, and the Charleston earthquake; therefore the nation could expect to be spared from seismic events until at least 1944.[8] (No doubt he was shocked when San Francisco was rocked by a massive quake in 1906, just twenty years after his pronouncement.)

Science magazine rushed to print an account of the earthquake in its September 10 issue, along with a U.S. map that purported to show the origin of the shock and its intensity in various areas. The article located the epicenter in central North Carolina and identified a "line of weakness in the earth's crust" stretching from Troy, New York, south through Baltimore, Washington, and Richmond. *Science* urged its readers to send their observations of the earthquake to the U.S. Geological Survey, Division of Volcanic

Geology, "while they are still fresh in the memory," and to respond to a long series of specific questions that started with the exact time and location and ended with suggestions to jog people's memories about phenomena they might have considered too trivial to write down: "Mention any unusual condition of the atmosphere; any strange effects on animals. . . . If a clock was stopped, give the time it indicated, and some idea as to how fast or how slow it was, its position, the direction in which it was standing or facing, and the approximate height and length of the pendulum. . . . If pictures swung. . . . if doors were closed or opened. . . . All such little facts, if only noticed, remembered, and recorded, are of great value."[9]

Nonscientists were eager to suggest causes for the shock, many of which betrayed anxiety about the environmental impact of modern technology. Theories dating back to the eighteenth century were often trotted out as fact, and it was hard for the average person to sort out the new from the old. Sarah Dawson met a woman in Lausanne who was sure that the quake had been caused by the proliferation of telegraph wires, and Frank perpetuated her notions in print. One man sent the relief committee advice about preventing further earthquake damage along with his donation of ten cents: city officials should set up a cannon, and whenever the roar of an aftershock was detected, someone should fire it. "If you destroy the sound you destroy the earthquake effects," the writer assured them. He added, as an afterthought, "Don't shoot anybody."[10]

The agency most interested in the earthquake was the U.S. Geological Survey (USGS), which had sent McGee and Mendenhall to investigate. Formed in 1879 to catalog the agricultural and mineral resources of the country, its mission had expanded by 1886 to measuring and describing the U.S. landscape. Just a week before the earthquake, USGS explorers under the command of Captain Clarence E. Dutton were surveying Oregon's Crater Lake, then thought to be the deepest body of fresh water on the continent.[11]

Until August 1886 earthquakes had not ranked high on the list of USGS priorities, partly because tremors were so infrequent. The New Madrid earthquakes had struck a sparsely populated frontier containing few large manmade structures and no urban areas. The eighteenth-century New England earthquakes, scary as they were, did not cause massive property damage or kill anyone. In 1812, forty Native Americans near what is now Los Angeles died as the result of a quake, but that disaster was long forgotten. A temblor shook the western end of Long Island in 1884, causing minor damage. But earthquakes had never threatened a U.S. city in any meaningful way.[12]

Charleston changed everything. Large earthquakes clearly *were* a threat to the United States, and the government felt obligated to make sense of this one. Before McGee and Mendenhall departed from Charleston, they appointed a "special agent" to continue their fieldwork. Twenty-eight-year-old Earle Sloan was a native Charlestonian who had been working as a mining consultant in Colorado and Alabama. He was on the same train as Anna Robson when the earthquake hit, sitting with his friend Sam Stoney, the Berkeley County planter. Sloan and Stoney got off the train and walked down the tracks toward Ridgeville, hoping to find a working telegraph. The lines were dead there, too. Then they trudged back to Summerville, miserably aware, as Stoney wrote his mother, that death was facing them "above[,] around and below." They had hoped to catch a train into the city, but "after four hours of terrible suspense" they gave up and started walking to Charleston. About halfway there they met a construction train that took them the rest of the way. Stoney reported to his mother that what he saw that night aged him ten years and turned his hair gray. Sloan sought out McGee and Mendenhall and tried his hand at cataloging evidence of the earthquake.[13]

Sloan had studied geology and chemistry at the University of Virginia, but when it came to investigating the earthquake, his youth and love of vigorous outdoor sports may have been even more valuable than his academic credentials. One of his first duties was to go out on a handcar along the line of the Charleston and Savannah Railway, looking for damage. Near the twenty-five-mile post he discovered a fissure more than two thousand feet long, the largest yet noted. In Charleston, he inspected sites ranging from warehouses to gravestones. Sometimes the evidence he found was dramatic: an enormous guano shed at a wharf on the Cooper River had shifted more than eight feet along with its contents, 1,500 tons of fertilizer. A buried brick reservoir at the gas works had moved eight inches. Between Charleston and Goose Creek, Sloan found many fissures, one 600 feet long and 125 feet wide. A nearby railroad trestle had shifted seven feet.[14]

Sloan also recorded a wealth of tiny, homely details. In a dairy near Ravenel, for instance, thirty miles west of Charleston, a bowl of butter had tilted southwest so that its contents overhung the rim. Near Wadmalaw Island, thirty miles southwest of Charleston, the water in a well was so "violently agitated" that the owner believed a calf must have fallen in. Along the line of the South Carolina Railway resin captured in turpentine boxes had been thrown southeast and northwest.[15]

Sloan inspected over a thousand monuments, scrutinized innumerable buildings and chimneys, measured and plotted countless fissures and craters, described the condition of scores of wells, compared the times recorded by dozens of stopped clocks, interviewed hundreds of people, performed an impressive series of mathematical calculations, and concluded that the main quake had really been two nearly simultaneous shocks originating about fourteen miles from Charleston. He noted an "elbow" in the line of disturbance about 8.5 miles southeast of Summerville. By mid-September he grew convinced that some of McGee's conclusions were incorrect and politely wrote him to suggest that there had been a second epicenter to the southwest of Summerville, near Middleton Place plantation, about fifteen miles outside Charleston. On the night of the quake, the manmade butterfly lakes there had been drained. By the time he completed his fieldwork, Sloan would identify three epicenters, an idea rejected by the USGS as contrary to accepted scientific theory. However, present-day geologists confirm that Sloan was right.[16]

EARLE SLOAN'S careful fieldwork was part of a worldwide revolution in seismology. The first scientific society devoted to the study of earthquakes, the Seismological Society of Japan, had been established in 1880 by John Milne, a British scientist teaching at the Imperial College of Engineering in Tokyo. Milne and his colleagues James Ewing and Thomas Gray were designing instruments capable of measuring and recording earthquake waves. Together the three expatriate Englishmen were responsible for many breakthroughs in the 1880s, including the development of a reliable device to record the time and strength of earthquakes.[17]

For thousands of years, ordinary people living in seismic zones have used common objects to register shocks, such as liquid-filled bowls and dangling objects. William McGee looked at the knife swinging from his bedpost in Washington, D.C., to measure the first tremors of the quake. Later, in Charleston, a judge would half-fill a glass jar with water covered with a mixture of oil and lampblack. Aftershocks jostled the water, leaving a trail of oil on the sides of the jar that could be read and interpreted hours later. Dr. Charles Shepard, who lived on Meeting Street, constructed an apparatus using a shallow concave glass dish with eight radiating funnel-shaped paper spouts attached to the rim. He filled the dish to the brim with mercury, set it in a stand, and put a beaker under each spout, hoping that any aftershocks would spill the mercury into the beakers. The device registered two of the largest shocks, but Shepard was disappointed to realize that heavy footsteps were more likely to spill the mercury than small tremors. Shepard also suspended a pencil over a piece of paper, but this device was even less successful. These improvised instruments were crude seismoscopes — or, as they were sometimes called in 1886, seismographs. Both terms were still so unfamiliar that whenever they appeared in the *News and Courier*, the article usually defined the instrument as an "earthquake shock indicator." Today the term *seismograph* refers to an apparatus that can record both the motion and the time of an earthquake, though scientists prefer the term *seismometer*. A *seismoscope* is a simple instrument — it indicates only that ground motion has occurred.[18]

Until just two weeks before the Charleston earthquake, a seismoscope had been mounted on top of the Washington Monument in Washington, D.C. It was the only instrument of its kind in the eastern United States, and the quake should have provided the perfect opportunity to see what it could do. But it had just been removed for repair and lay, dismantled and useless, in a laboratory across town.[19]

The first known seismoscope was devised in China in 132 AD. It was a large jar about six feet in diameter, with eight dragon heads on the outside facing the eight directions of the compass. Below each one was a ceramic frog with open jaws. Each dragon held a ball in its mouth, and when an earthquake moved the jar, one of the eight would drop its ball, to be caught by the frog below. (Dr. Shepard's experiment with the mercury was similar.) The mechanism involved an inverted pendulum.[20]

The first Western scientific instruments to measure and record earth tremors also incorporated pendulums. An Italian scientist built a crude pendulum-based seismoscope in 1731. Twenty years later another Italian thought to suspend a similar mechanism above a bed of fine sand with a pointer attached, so that the tip would drag through the sand and leave marks. A series of strong earthquakes in 1783 that shook Calabria, the toe of Italy's boot, inspired more scientists to work on the problem.

Not surprisingly, advances in scientific knowledge often came just after major shocks, too late to document the initial quake. Immediately following the first Calabrian quake, in February 1783, an Italian clockmaker constructed a pendulum tipped with a brush, which used slow-drying ink to sketch on an ivory slab. The device was rigged to ring a bell when the oscillations were large. A series of earthquakes that hit Scotland in 1839 inspired a number of new instruments, including one that recorded tremors with a pencil on a paper-lined dome. Six of these seismographs were set up in the earthquake-prone region. Hopes ran high, but the invention did not perform as expected.

By the middle of the nineteenth century, scientists were trying to measure several features of earthquakes, including how long the tremors lasted, the horizontal motion of the earth, vertical motion, magnitude, and intensity. It was hoped that seismographs could someday be used to predict damaging shocks by alerting scientists to the small tremors thought to precede major quakes. In the ten years before Charleston's earthquake, a number of prototype instruments were built in Italy and Japan. But it was the combined efforts of John Milne, James Ewing, and Thomas Gray that led to a true functioning seismograph. Ewing's earliest effort, completed in 1879, placed a revolving smoked-glass plate under a pendulum, where a moving bob would scratch lines whenever the earth trembled. His results were published in *Nature* in 1884.

In the years just before the Charleston earthquake, Milne, Ewing, and Gray had been experimenting with earth waves produced by explosions. They would start their instruments and set off dynamite, measuring how quickly the waves moved and how much they disturbed the earth's surface. In 1886, Ermanno Brassart of Rome constructed a seismograph that captured the movements of a pendulum on smoked paper. The instrument was successfully tested in 1893. After that, improvements were frequent and many, but they came too late to study the Charleston earthquake.

Imperfect as seismic instruments were in 1886, one would expect Mendenhall, McGee, and their colleagues to try to round up as many as possible in order to measure Charleston's aftershocks. They did not, although Mendenhall did point out to his colleagues that "nothing short of the use of well-constructed seismographs can furnish satisfactory measures" of seismic disturbances. Nor did those who were experimenting with the devices hurry to Charleston to test them. One professor at the Yale Observatory attempted to construct a seismoscope, a long pendulum suspended from his ceiling. He also balanced a ball on a box and filled a cup with ink, hoping that these simple devices would register any seismic waves that reached as far as Connecticut. A researcher at the Paris Observatory suggested starting a network of seismographic observation posts in the United States, modeled on those in Italy and Japan, but his idea would not be carried out for many years. The dismembered instrument from atop the Washington Monument was "dusted off and put together," but it received little attention. By October 24, Earle Sloan was trying to use some type of device to measure aftershocks, but it apparently did not work.[21]

Today, earthquakes are measured by two standards: intensity and magnitude. Intensity is evaluated by observation, the impact of the shaking on people and buildings. Magnitude is computed with instruments that calculate the amount of seismic energy released at the hypocenter of the quake — the point directly beneath the surface where the rupture begins. Only one of these two standards, intensity, was used in 1886. Then as now, the lowest rankings were based mainly on human reactions, such as "felt indoors by a few." The highest were gauged by the appearance of features such as fissures, landslides, and surface faulting. The middle range was based mainly on the degree of damage to manmade structures.[22]

The Richter magnitude scale, the numerical measurement most Americans think of as the benchmark of earthquake strength, was invented in 1935, almost fifty years after the Charleston quake, for use in southern California. Some researchers have suggested that the Charleston earthquake would have measured between 6.6 and 7.3 on the Richter scale.[23]

Scientists prefer moment magnitude, a scale devised in the 1980s, because the computation is more precise. Just as a car's speedometer goes up to 120 miles per hour and cannot register any higher speed even if the car goes much faster, other magnitude scales become saturated at 6–7 and do not give correct values for large earthquakes. Like all such scales, the moment magnitude scale is logarithmic — that is, each unit on the scale corresponds to a thirty-two-fold increase in the total energy released. Ratings are based on an analysis of instrumental recordings. Scientists have inferred that the Charleston quake would have registered at least 7.3 on the moment magnitude scale, stronger than the 1989 San Francisco earthquake that collapsed a freeway in Oakland and the 2010 earthquake that killed hundreds of thousands in Haiti. Increased magnitude does not signify that a quake is more intense or will last longer, but it does mean that severe shaking will be felt over a wider area.[24]

The scale scientists now use to describe intensity is called the Modified Mercalli Scale, which was adopted by the international community in 1931. Because the Modified Mercalli Scale assigns a number based on observed effects, it is possible to rank earlier quakes according to its twelve-point system, rendered in Roman numerals. I represents "not felt except by a very few under especially favorable conditions" and XII equals "damage total." Between are carefully calibrated levels of destruction, including such visible results as the fall of chimneys, factory stacks, columns, monuments, and walls. Other evidence includes heavy furniture overturned, buildings shifted off their foundations, and bridges destroyed. On this scale, the three New Madrid quakes each score XII and the 1906 San Francisco earthquake XI. The Charleston quake is rated X: "Some well-built wooden structures destroyed; most masonry and frame structures destroyed with foundations. Rails bent."[25]

WHAT CAUSED THE Charleston earthquake? Today's geologists offer an explanation based on plate tectonics. One hundred eighty million years ago, when the global land mass was one huge unbroken continent surrounded by the sea, a rift opened and the jaws of the Atlantic began to open, stretching until the gap grew to thousands of miles. Each coast carries the imprint of the long-departed other. If sea floor spreading were to reverse itself and swing the halves back together again, the swelling bosom of western Africa would nestle into the slim waist between North and South America.[26]

Most large earthquakes occur at the edges of tectonic plates, where one mass is pushing its way under the edge of another. The east coast of North America is far from the edge of a tectonic plate, but the rift in the seafloor is still spreading, and seismologists surmise that in 1886 pressure from a long ridge of undersea volcanoes at the eastern edge of the North American Plate, in the middle of the Atlantic Ocean, may have caused a sudden slip on a fault near Charleston, thousands of miles away. That impact apparently triggered slips on intersecting faults.

The rocks beneath Charleston are webbed with ancient fault lines. Unlike the highly visible surface breaks that reveal the path of the San Andreas Fault through coastal California, these fissures resemble cracks in a cake covered by a thick coat of frosting. Geologists call them blind faults, since even now their tracks can be mapped only through informed guesswork.

The Atlantic Coastal Plain is a wedge of mud that thickens from a feather edge at the fall line near Columbia, South Carolina, along the border of the mountainous Piedmont region, to a slab almost three-quarters of a mile thick where the ocean laps the shore. The west coast of North America has folds and fractured rock foundations that absorb a lot of energy, so that western quakes tend to be localized, while the hard rock deposits beneath the sediments in the eastern two-thirds of the United States can transmit seismic waves for hundreds and even thousands of miles. Because of a phenomenon called wave amplification, structures built on soft deep soils, like the sediments along Charleston's Ashley and Cooper rivers or the "made ground" in downtown Charleston, often suffer more damage than structures built on rigid rock. The soft soil can intensify the shaking by four times or more.[27]

In the last two decades of the twentieth century, paleoseismologists discovered evidence of many prehistoric sandblows in the ground around Charleston, signs that the soil had liquefied in response to severe shaking. Their work in South Carolina suggests that cataclysmic earthquakes strike the area at roughly five-hundred-year intervals, which means, of course, that the one just previous to 1886 probably occurred before Europeans and Africans reached the New World.[28]

The Woodstock fault runs from the present-day towns of Hollywood and Ravenel, South Carolina, northeast through the city of Summerville. At some time in the distant past, the fault was more or less straight. But seismic activity broke the line between the sites we know now as old Fort Dorchester and Middleton Place plantation, and there are two distinct sections of the Woodstock fault, connected by a dogleg called Sawmill Branch that follows the course of the Ashley River for about four miles. At Fort Dorchester, now a state park, the river narrows drastically, like a rubber tube pinched off between a giant thumb and finger (in 1886, sections of a century-old church tower there were thrown thirty-five feet). The major waterways of South Carolina all mirror the Ashley's shape, having been pushed by some mighty seismic upheaval into matching curves. Middleton Place is now pinpointed as the spot where the Sawmill Branch, Ashley River, and Woodstock faults intersect.[29]

Geologists studying the area around Summerville have discovered a cluster of magnetized underground anomalies, called plutons, sometimes associated with severe earthquakes. Using global-positioning technology, they have determined that the earth's surface is squeezing toward Middleton Place from the north and south at the rate of half an inch per year. The Sawmill Branch area is now recognized as a seismic hot spot, where small quakes are common.

Dr. Pradeep Talwani, a professor of geology at the University of South Carolina, led the research on prehistoric sandblows and has studied the Woodstock fault for more than thirty years. He does not doubt that the region will again be rocked by destructive shocks, although of course no one can say when. A "five-hundred-year interval" means the next major earthquake can be expected in 2386 — or anytime before then. In terms of prediction, modern science has made few advances.

But when, as in 1886, hundreds of thousands of people beg to be told what will happen next, someone is always willing to oblige. On September 6, 1886, a week after the quake, Professor E. P. Hammond declared that "terrific cyclones, earthquakes, and tornadoes" would devastate the United States on September 26, 27, and 28. Hammond's predictions were echoed by Professor Andrew Jackson Devoe, an eighty-seven-year-old "self-taught meteorologist" who believed that "atmospheric disturbances" caused earthquakes. Devoe claimed that a series of shocks would begin on or about September 25, 1886, centered in the Pacific Northwest but so strong that they would be felt across the continent in New Jersey. Devoe had some credibility among attentive readers of the *News and Courier*, since he had successfully foretold the previous year's hurricane, down to the very day, a month before the storm.[30]

Now Dawson ridiculed Devoe, whose forecast could cause delays in Charleston's reconstruction. "The mainstay of Prof. Devoe's earthquake theory is the moon. He swears by the moon. The moon lifts the tides, therefore the moon lifts the air, and therefore, we would suggest to the Professor, we should have earthquakes every twelve hours. But we do not. . . . Go to! Professor Devoe. The moon is doubtless always directly overhead for you, as you are evidently a lunatic."[31]

Professor Devoe failed to capture the public's attention, but on September 21 the *New York Herald* published a small article that would set off a wave of panic across the United States. A self-styled Canadian "weather prophet" named Ezekiel Stone Wiggins claimed that because of the confluence of the planets and the combined influence of "invisible moons" he had discovered, a series of devastating earthquakes and storms would strike the southern United States on September 29.[32]

Dawson, who had turned down an offer to publish the prediction himself, branded Wiggins "the earthquake and cataclysm manufacturer for the Northern newspaper trade." Yet even Frank Dawson could not keep people from talking. Not only did Wiggins's prediction sound scientific, but he had chosen the very day appointed for the apocalypse by the "prophetess" of Liberty County, Georgia, who had allegedly risen from her coffin during the earthquake. For once, science and religion seemed to agree: something terrible was going to happen on September 29. Newspapers dubbed it Wiggins Day.[33]

Chapter Eleven

RELIEF

WITH AFTERSHOCKS rattling houses and Wiggins Day imminent, drugstores did a booming business. "I cannot live without my powders," a schoolteacher confessed. "I sleep very little at night and am very nerveless in the morning." A physician wrote to a colleague that his whole family was still in "a terrible condition of mind" and apologized for his shaky script: "I can scarcely write as my mind is not clear enough from the Mental perturbation which I has pass through."[1]

One woman lost most of her hair, which fell out in clumps. Her doctor diagnosed "paralysis of the scalp" caused by fright. A Savannah man asked his pharmacist for a sedative. "Between my wife and my mother and two ladies who are visiting at my house," he complained, "I have not averaged ten minutes sleep a night since the earth first quaked. . . . They insist on sitting in the hall from the time it gets dark until breakfast, and every time a hack or carriage comes within a block of the house they imagine it as a shock, and have hysterics. I'll put laudanum or morphine in their coffee next time!"[2]

Violent quarrels erupted in the camps. A woman named Molsey Edwards was "shaking down her bed" in a tent on Linguard Street when two other women came in and accused her of stealing a blanket. Edwards denied the theft and beat them up. Two men got into a fight when one hired the other to move his possessions out of a "rackety, rickety, tumble-down, jumble-up house." The owner of the wagon, improbably enough, hit his customer with a baby carriage and was hauled off to jail. A man who had been out of town returned to find his wife sharing her rations with another fellow. The outraged husband burst into her tent with a pistol, a hatchet, and a razor. A fish seller hawked strings of porgy in Marion Square for twice the usual price; a crowd of women retaliated by confiscating his merchandise.[3]

On Sullivan's Island, an enterprising black woman named Hattie Haines stole sheets, tablecloths, and other household goods from an unoccupied house. She built a tent on the back beach and set up a kind of boardinghouse for other homeless women. Whites spread the word that blacks were camping to avoid paying rent. The police arrested Haines and took her to jail.[4]

Despite these incidents, the official camps were now generally in good order, with fresh water and clean latrines. The soup kitchen on Cumberland Street was operating with businesslike efficiency, its fourteen kettles bubbling away. The extra wagons had speeded up deliveries at the commissary.[5]

With the most pressing immediate needs met, the relief committee turned to the problem of repairing thousands of houses. Should they attempt to restore all the losses, whether or not the property owner could afford to make repairs? Or should they aid the indigent, at least those who were unable to work, and leave the better-off to fend for themselves? Dawson calculated that the city would need ten times the money already received just to cover the losses of people who could not pay for repairs.[6] The obvious model for disaster recovery came from the Chicago fire of 1871, when a massive relief effort begun by city government was soon turned over to a private group, the Chicago Relief and Aid Society. Dawson and his colleagues seem to have adopted many of the Chicago group's policies. They checked carefully to make sure that applicants for relief were truly needy and set up a two-tiered system where the poor got food and the better-off got money, an arrangement designed to preserve the status quo. The groups in both cities issued railroad passes and then quickly stopped, for fear that the city's labor force would flee. There were major differences, however: Chicago's weekly rations seem stingy in comparison to Charleston's, while Chicago was far more generous with tools and long-term housing.[7]

THE EXECUTIVE RELIEF COMMITTEE decided that its first step toward repairing houses was to figure out how much money would be necessary to fill every request. Less than three weeks after the earthquake the committee had application forms printed and ran advertisements in the *News and Courier* specifying where and when to pick them up. The one-page form included questions about how much property the applicant owned and how much he earned. Twelve hundred copies were sent out, and pastors were given batches to distribute at church.[8]

"Relief is confined to loss by earthquake," the fine print warned. "If every blank . . . is not filled up, the application will be returned." Many of those who needed help were unable to read and write, and even those who were literate found the unfamiliar task daunting. Ministers helped their parishioners complete the forms, but the News and Courier soon reported that many contained "fatal irregularities" that would disqualify the applicants.[9]

Dawson proposed that the city hire inspectors to make sure that homeowners and workmen were truthful. A letter was sent to local contractors, asking them to bid on the job of repairing all the houses for which applications were submitted. Many refused outright — they had too much to do as it was. Some offered to work part-time, a few hours here and there. Realizing that local men would likely favor their friends and relatives, someone suggested hiring a contractor from out of town who would "have no prejudices in any way, [who] had no friends to offend and who would be perfectly independent in any judgment he might pass on any piece of property that came under his examination." The proposal made sense, but in the end the committee voted to hire Charleston men.[10]

Finally a process was worked out: once the completed application was received from the homeowner, the inspectors would assess the damage and verify the costs of repair. A clerk would check the tax rolls to confirm that the applicant really owned the property in question and that it had not been seized for back taxes. The committee would then issue vouchers to workmen to repair the approved houses. Chimney repairs were a top priority because of the danger of fire, whereas plastering could wait until later. Fees for plastering were high, and the committee believed that they would come down over time.[11]

The committee was proud of its safeguards against cheats and double dippers. But the very idea of revealing personal information on the form was enough to put some people off. "In the history of the world there never has been a more prohibitory system of 'red tape,' " one Charlestonian complained to the New York Herald. "There are thousands of my fellow-citizens, men and women, who, rather than go through the ordeal of filling up these forms and having them made public, would prefer to have their shattered homes forever remain a mass of ruins."[12]

The faultfinding infuriated Dawson. Those in charge of the money had to make sure that all the recipients were "worthy," he snapped in the pages of the News and Courier. Perhaps the anonymous complainer might prefer to move to "some other community where there is to be a big relief fund to be liberally dispensed." It was "outrageous to suppose" that the applications would be published, and the forms were no more "inquisitorial" than property tax papers. The committee expected criticism, he wrote, and actually invited it. "They have no other purpose in the world than to distribute to the best advantage the means which the noble generosity of the American people has placed at their command."[13]

However, one man's notion of the "best advantage" seemed like favoritism to another. For example, the application form clearly stated that married women "must not apply if their husbands are still alive." This rule was in accordance with South Carolina law: all assets possessed by married women were controlled by their husbands. Then someone pointed out that this restriction would "exclude a very needy class of ladies who will be left to suffer." In response, the Executive Relief Committee modified the rule: if a woman's husband had deserted her, she could fill out an application, and in such cases the committee would be even more sympathetic to her claim.[14]

There were more guidelines: requests for less than $200 would be evaluated first, and "no loss of any person owning more than one house [would] be considered." By September 22 about 750 applications had been returned, requesting sums from $15 to $5,000. The News and Courier reported that some people who owned several buildings had put in claims on all of them, though "of course claims of this kind [would] be considered last." This stipulation, meant to screen out wealthier applicants, virtually insured that landlords would be slow to repair their rental property, leaving thousands of people to subsist in damaged quarters. And many "deserving widows" who owned houses had, before the earthquake, rented them out. They depended on the income to put food on the table and had lost their only means of support. "Their future seems very dark and hopeless," observed a letter from a Charlestonian to the head of the New York Chamber of Commerce printed in the New York Tribune.[15]

Far from ignoring these women, many of whom had lost their husbands in the Civil War, the committee decided to fast-track the claims of single women and widows. In the case of ladies who could not "attend to their own repairs," the committee would contract directly with workmen and purchase materials. About two-thirds of the applications came from working people whose houses were worth from $1,000 to $1,500. But some outrageous petitions arrived, one asking for $5,800 to repair a house that had been assessed at $4,000.[16]

On September 23, the inspectors started in the upper wards, where the damage was comparatively light and the residents had lower incomes, and worked their way down the peninsula toward higher-income neighbor-hoods, completing printed inspection forms for about fifty dwellings every day. Soon they speeded up to seventy-five houses a day. Several people grumbled that even this pace was too slow — they expected work vouchers to be issued right away. "These people," Dawson scoffed, "belong to the class who imagine that the filing of their application should be immediately followed by a shower of bricks from the nearest brickyard, or an avalanche of tongue-and-grooved boards from over the way." The Executive Relief Committee refused to be rushed, though their pace seems astonishingly speedy by today's standards; they voted not to approve any claim before it had "laid on the table twenty-four hours at least." Most applications were considered within a day or two of receipt.[17]

AS THE CLEANUP progressed, Charlestonians had to face some dismay-ing revelations about the physical integrity of their city. Stripping used brick should be a difficult task: good mortar bonds with the brick and has to be pounded with mallets and chisels to break its stony grip. But workers found that in many cases the old mortar had loosened to the point where it needed only a tap. Sometimes most of the bricks in a heap of debris would be clean already, because the mortar had turned to dust when they crashed to the earth.

In the first week after the earthquake, a New York architect inspecting piles of rubble noticed that the mortar seemed to contain almost no lime or cement. Shortly afterward the supervising architect of the U.S. Treasury Department, W. E. Spier, pointed out that the mortar in many damaged buildings was made of fine sand and clay that became dry and crumbly over time — a mixture with no binding power. Moreover, repairs were being made "with the same worthless mortar that has been the chief factor in their destruction." Spier was indignant: "We have a society for the prevention of cruelty to animals," he said, "and yet neglect to take the necessary precau-tions to secure our own personal safety."[18]

As almost everybody knew, bad mortar had recently proved itself capable of murder. A little over a year before, in New York City, eight five-story tene-ment houses had collapsed without warning. The buildings were still under construction, and dozens of workers and passersby were thought to lie bur-ied in the wreckage. The rescue effort went on for days, covered in front-page stories by all the major New York papers, though excavators turned up only one corpse, the body of a carpenter who had been working inside.

Investigators discovered that the mortar in the building was little more than mud. The owner, Charles Buddensiek, was notorious for this kind of skullduggery. Ten years before, tenants in several of his buildings had fallen desperately ill. A health inspector discovered that the indoor toilets had never been connected to a sewer, and the buildup of human waste had resulted in a health crisis. Buddensiek was never charged with having caused the epidemic, but when his tenements collapsed he was arrested for murder, tried, and sentenced to six years in the notorious Sing Sing prison in Upstate New York. Buddensiek's name became synonymous with poor construction, and New York City undertook a massive revision of its building code. "We Want No More Buddensieck Mortar," Dawson declared, misspelling the name.[19]

The oldest buildings in Charleston were constructed of handmade gray bricks held together by mortar containing lime from burned oyster shells. Early masons used two methods of laying bricks, both of which produced walls that were thick and strong. English bond used uninterrupted courses of longways bricks alternating with rows of crossways bricks, so that the face of a building showed lines of rectangles and squares. Flemish bond, which was even stronger, created interlocking rows by alternating longwise and crosswise bricks.[20]

After Charleston's great fire of 1838, bricklayers arrived from northern cities, bringing with them a new method called common bond. These newcomers laid five rows of lengthwise bricks for every crosswise row, which took less time and less brick. Unscrupulous workmen made even quicker progress by scrimping on the crosswise bricks, the element that strengthened the walls. They also used cheaper limes that produced a softer mortar.[21]

Most structures fabricated in Flemish bond withstood the shaking. The oldest portion of the main building at the College of Charleston, built in the 1820s, was laid in Flemish bond. This part of the building, which was three feet thick at the base, survived the earthquake in good shape. But the east and west wings had been constructed in the common bond style in 1850, with five courses and a header. The walls were so badly damaged that they had to be torn down and rebuilt. The oldest part of the Unitarian Church, built in 1787, survived the shaking nearly intact, but newer additions dating from the 1850s crumbled.[22]

Though city officials were slow to take up the issue, Dawson embarked on a personal crusade against careless brick masons. "Death in the Mortar!" he warned. A contractor displayed a "model" wall in front of the newspaper office to demonstrate the right way to lay brick.[23]

The danger was real enough — even now, in the twenty-first century, Charleston officials have to deal with the consequences of shoddy repairs from the 1886 earthquake, and some of the worst cases of plastering over cracks without correcting structural damage have surfaced at the former post office (the Old Exchange Building) and City Hall. Yet just beneath the surface of Dawson's diatribes lay another message: bricklayers could not be trusted.

The fifty-cent raise mandated by the Knights of Labor on September 6 had not lasted long. In order to round up enough workers to carry out several large repair jobs, one well-heeled contractor had offered much higher wages to anyone who could wield a trowel. The incentive succeeded, and soon most bricklayers were demanding $5.00 a day. The International Bricklayers' Union — not a part of the KOL — backed them up.[24]

On September 15 a meeting of Bricklayers' Union Number One was held, attended by thirty white men and "a few colored laborers." The president, D. J. Flynn, headed off a reporter who was trying to get inside, assuring him that there was "nothing at all of an alarming nature in the fact of the meeting of the bricklayers." His men simply wanted to make sure that all bricklayers, union and nonunion, were charging $5.00 a day. And, no, he did not consider that an exorbitant rate, since northern workers had been getting that much for some time now. Flynn noted that all the black men who were present at the meeting were "members of the Union and first-rate workmen."[25]

Flynn knew that the very idea of a mixed-race union was threatening to white Charlestonians. Black and white laborers had always competed for work, and well-to-do whites had exploited the antagonism between the two groups to keep wages low. What would happen if black and white workers banded together as they were doing in many KOL locals?

D. J. Flynn protested that the bricklayers had no intention of striking. Why strike when people were throwing money at them every day? But other construction workers did walk off the job, raising fears that balky laborers could bring repairs to a halt. On the morning of September 14 twenty black workers were tearing down the damaged part of Military Hall on Wentworth Street. At noon they stopped the demolition and asked for a fifty-cent raise. When the contractor refused, all twenty men quit. The contractor brought in twenty more men who agreed to work for the original rate of $1.00 a day. But the strikers formed a cordon around the site and threatened to beat the "rats." Extra policemen arrived, the ringleader was arrested, and violence was averted. Everybody went home and the trouble seemed to pass. The next day, the contractor hired fifteen new workmen, but by lunchtime eight had gone over to the strikers.[26]

The need was great, the workmen were available, but either they wouldn't agree to make repairs or they demanded wages that customers considered exorbitant. Homeowners and businessmen were sure that the problem stemmed from free food. If the subsistence subcommittee would just stop handing out supplies, the men would return to work at reasonable prices because they would have no alternative. Hunger would force them to take up their tools. Bowing to pressure, the Executive Relief Committee voted to shut down both of the food distribution systems, the commissary and the soup kitchen, claiming that after two weeks the emergency was over.[27]

Dr. Arthur B. Rose, the chairman of the subsistence subcommittee, objected that the city must continue to distribute food until "the fears of the community subside." In addition to its vital role in preventing outright hunger, the food distribution effort provided employment for twenty clerks, twenty-four canvassers, four porters, two clerks and two helpers for the soup kitchen, one night watchman, and nine wagon drivers. To shut down rationing would eliminate more than sixty jobs. But Rose's pleas fell on deaf ears, and on September 19 he was forced to discharge twenty employees. Three days later his canvassers were also let go, since the city now felt it had a record of everybody in need of assistance, and two delivery wagons were laid off. "All Bills Against the Subsistence Committee must be rendered at Phoenix Engine House . . . on or before Thursday, Sept. 30" read an announcement in the News and Courier.[28]

There was far less opposition to the soup kitchen than to the distribution of raw rations, perhaps because those who received cooked food could not easily hoard or resell it. The kitchen was still "doling out soup" on September 29 to about eight hundred people a day. Prodded by Dawson and Rose, the Executive Relief Committee reluctantly agreed to keep the kitchen open as long as there was a demand.[29]

The subcommittee on shelter also faced pressure to close up shop. Many of the "booths" the city had erected now stood empty, since the residents had either returned home or left town. Others had been floored and weatherized, as if the occupants meant to stay for a long time, and a clothing store and a groundnut (peanut) cake stand had been set up in the shelters at Marion Square. Many of the donated tents were abandoned, though a visitor from out of town observed people sleeping on benches at the Battery. Those who had found other shelter were asked to notify the subcommittee so the tents could be collected and returned to their owners. People still living in the wooden structures were told to leave by September 30. To ensure that the settlements did not become permanent, and to recoup some of the money spent on temporary shelter, an auction was scheduled to resell the lumber.[30]

Overseeing relief was time consuming, and the committee members were anxious to get back to their own businesses. Moreover, in their view, every dollar spent on rations and camps could be better used to repair and rebuild the city.

FREE FOOD or no free food, even those who had no skills now held out for higher wages. On September 21 a white man approached a large group of black men who were standing on the corner of Broad and Meeting streets. "Any of you men want work?" he inquired. They asked how much he was paying.[31]

"Dollar an' a half. Come along, eight of you."

The contractor turned to walk away, and not one man followed.

That same day several men were hired to plaster walls at the Citadel for $4.50 a day. When they heard that other plasterers were making double that amount, they went to the school's board of visitors and asked for a raise. The board refused, fired them, and hired replacements. "Work, or Go to Jail," the *News and Courier* declared. Idle men should be arrested under the vagrancy laws and sentenced to hard labor at the penitentiary.[32]

Intent on bringing down "earthquake prices," Dawson also plotted to bring in bricklayers and plasterers from other places. This was "indispensable to the safety, the health and comfort" of the people, he said. Word went out all over the country that skilled construction workers could find jobs and good wages in Charleston. On September 22 fifty skilled bricklayers and plasterers arrived from New York City, raising hopes that prices would soon drop. A group of "prominent citizens" resolved to let their houses go unplastered until they did. The city set up a labor bureau in the basement of City Hall to match workmen and jobs, and by September 28 eighty-five men had signed up, including tinners, upholsterers, and carpenters. The *News and Courier* estimated that hundreds if not thousands of bricklayers and plasterers could find well-paid work in the city. However, no bricklayers or plasterers signed the list.[33]

FRANK DAWSON had been the powerhouse of the Executive Relief Committee, and under his leadership the subcommittee on immediate relief took on more and more responsibility. Originally, the plan had been to give people no more than $10.00 at a time to replace lost items like clothes and bedding. Soon, however, cases came up that fit none of the usual categories. On September 21 the men decided to raise the official limit to $25.00, and in "extreme cases" they granted $50.00, as they did to Charles Chin Sang, a Chinese American grocer. Shortly thereafter, they voted to buy $75.00 worth of tools for a locksmith. From then on, the limit was ignored and claims were assessed on an individual basis. When one woman asked for fifty cents, the committee, after reviewing her case, decided to give her $50.00. They awarded $500 to a dealer in hay, grain, and groceries, to pay for lost inventory, and $500 to a saloonkeeper, presumably to replace bottles of liquor that had shattered during the quake.[34]

The largest payment went to Mrs. J. O. Goutevenier, whose husband was the fireman who suffered a stroke while working on the night of the earthquake. The committee awarded her $1,060 for mortgage payments and living expenses, and asked that the family house and lot on Savage Street be put in her name. It was a highly unusual request. But the executive committee voted unanimously to authorize the subcommittee to "do whatever they need to do" to secure the title of the property for Mrs. Goutevenier and her children.[35]

As much as he wanted to close the books and be done with relief by the end of September, Dawson knew that many people who had already been helped—especially women like Mrs. Goutevenier—would need assistance "again and again before they [became] self-supporting." When the original appropriation was used up, the subcommittee on immediate relief asked for and received $3,000 more from the executive committee.[36]

Fortunately, donations continued to arrive as September turned to October. "Mr. Mayor, will you be so kind as to give this $5 to the very needy Africans," wrote one anonymous donor. Americans living in China collected

$630. Some "very poor" lacemakers from Ireland contributed two lace collars and a bodice front, to be sold in New York for the benefit of the Charleston sufferers. The women said they were thankful for U.S. assistance during the potato famine and wanted to return the favor. Mrs. Phoebe Canfield invited a group of little girls to blow soap bubbles at a benefit entertainment in Georgetown, South Carolina, and collected $2.00 for relief.[37]

Dozens of groups around the country staged benefit performances in September to raise more funds. The New Orleans Amateur Opera Company staged a production of *The Mikado*. Elsa Von Blumen challenged Buffalo Bill's troupe to a hundred-mile race, with the cowboys riding ponies while she pedaled a bicycle. At a sanitarium in Oswego, New York, two teams calling themselves the Corpulents and the Consumptives played a benefit baseball game.[38]

At the other end of the spectrum were scores of professional events. A performance at Ford's Grand Opera House in Baltimore raised $5,000, boosted by the efforts of city policemen who sold the tickets "aggressively." The Nashville Grand Opera House and the Philadelphia Academy of Music put on benefits, and the Cunard steamer *Umbria*, which had sheltered Charleston refugees after the quake, sponsored an on-board concert. Opera and theater companies across the country got into the act.[39]

Atlanta still seemed strangely unsympathetic, and Dawson blamed Henry Grady. After his return from Charleston on September 3, Grady had flaunted Atlanta's supposed immunity to earthquakes as much as he mourned Charleston's loss. Atlanta was built on "the solid Piedmont escarpment," he pointed out at every opportunity. And unlike poor benighted Charleston, Atlanta had invested in new ideas and modern machinery. Atlanta collected some money for relief, but not nearly as much as other cities its size, north or south.[40]

The *Greenville (S.C.) News*, whose editor had once worked for Dawson, accused Grady of "gloating" over Charleston's misfortune, and of trying to steal business away from the shaken city. One Charlestonian echoed this charge in a letter to his fiancée, who had been evacuated to Atlanta. "I wish very much I was with you," he wrote, "altho' I should not care particularly about being in Atlanta." The *Atlanta Constitution* had "endeavored to chill the interest that her citizens . . . were beginning to evince in the ruined old City. As a community, I am sorry to say, Atlanta is the only one in the South and one of the very few in the whole country which has expressed no sympathy . . . nor made any sign."[41]

Dawson branded Atlanta "The Meanest City in America." He reprinted an article from the *Augusta Chronicle* headlined "A Good Place to Avoid," which claimed that the climate of Atlanta caused a whole host of ailments, including but not limited to "miasma and malaria, chills and fever, torpidity of the liver, barber's itch, boils, ring-worms, pimples, coughs, neuralgia, rheumatism, gout, carbuncles, sore throat, milk leg, snake- and dog-bites."[42]

WHILE CHARLESTON and Atlanta traded insults, the earthquake city was being enriched by a new industry — disaster tourism. The first visitors, including a Delaware group that arrived by train on September 11, claimed to have come for humanitarian reasons. They stopped at Ten Mile Hill and spent an hour marveling at the fissures. Then they took the ferry to Sullivan's Island, where they viewed small craters and enjoyed the beach. That evening they returned to the city for a "moonlight ramble" including a visit to the Orphan House, where two hundred children still camped in the yard. The leader of the group, Job H. Jackson, visited Graham's Stable, where Rev. John Johnson, rector of St. Philip's Church, was living with his family. He caught sight of Charleston Chapman, the famous earthquake baby, and compared him to the infant Jesus lying in the manger. Next came a visit to the Broad Street law office of former South Carolina governor Andrew G. McGrath, which was "almost buried in bricks and fallen boards." Jackson climbed in through a rear window. The visitors declared themselves "solemnly impressed" and returned home expressing their determination to raise funds for the victims.[43]

The railroads scrambled to repair the tracks and clean up after the wrecks. Soon several companies were advertising excursions, with half the proceeds to be donated to the relief fund. At first, visitors shunned the hotels. When the steamship *City of Atlanta* docked a week after the quake, the sixty passengers walked up to the Charleston Hotel, took a look at the damage, and refused to enter, even to eat dinner. But on September 12, fifteen hundred visitors arrived from Georgia and Florida, four hundred of whom stopped to have dinner in the big hotels. Most got back on the train and left before dusk. A few brave souls spent the night.[44]

The Atlantic Coastline Railroad planned special excursions that brought visitors from as far away as Boston to see the ruins. Ticket sales fell off a few days before the trains were due to leave, when a rumor spread that another huge shock had hit Charleston, causing a tidal wave, but they picked up again when the rumor proved false. In early October three trains within

twenty-four hours brought more than a thousand visitors. All three big hotels were open for business, and the *News and Courier* declared that "no one
need be deterred from taking advantage of the excursion through fear that
he will not be properly cared for." The expeditions swelled the relief fund:
a "monster" Atlantic Coastline trip raised $3,706.[45]

Just as some pastors claimed that the earthquake itself had been caused
by people indulging in Sunday entertainments, one Presbyterian minister
was upset that "in the very face of our appalling calamity the railroads of
our state [are] running Sunday excursions in defiance of the law of God,
offering special encouragement to men to sin." But most people couldn't
have cared less, and September was a "phenomenal" month for the damaged
hotels, which the *News and Courier* reported drew at least 20 percent more
guests than usual.[46]

Many of those visitors bought disaster souvenirs. Colorful "earthquake
sand" sold for as much as fifty cents a bottle. When the supply of real sand
was exhausted, enterprising children filled glass tubes with red pepper and
ground coffee. Just as a year before they had hawked "cyclonic cigars" and
"cyclonic shakes," stores offered "earthquake beer" made by Charleston's
own Palmetto Brewery "from the purest ingredients." Vendors sold pictures
of the city, "before and after the earthquake." Several businesses produced
booklets of photographs showing earthquake damage.[47]

To meet the demand for "earthquake relics," one antique dealer ran an
advertisement seeking andirons, fenders, door knockers, shovels, tongs,
and candlesticks that had survived the quake for sale to "Northern parties." Agents for the dime museums were said to be in town seeking "earthquake babies" as special exhibits. These attractions were really traveling
freak shows, including such human curiosities as hermaphrodites and
sword swallowers. In theory, a genuine earthquake baby was one born on
the night of the quake. Charleston Chapman was still in the city, and there
was also a pair of earthquake twins, jokingly nicknamed Earth and Quake.
But the scouts, in the grand tradition of P. T. Barnum, who invented the
dime museum, didn't care much about authenticity. According to the *News
and Courier*, one found a single baby and another located twins. Then the
first scout discovered black triplets, who weren't really "earthquake vintage"
but seemed close enough.[48]

JUST WHEN people appeared to be putting the earthquake behind them,
the ground moved again. At 5:15 a.m. on September 21 a powerful aftershock

rocked the city, the strongest since the quake on August 31. It felt, one terrified resident said, like a thousand pounds of dynamite exploding underground. People jumped up in their nightclothes and ran outside. Some fled to Adger's Wharf on the Cooper River near the foot of Tradd Street, where the steamship *City of Monticello* lay at anchor. They asked to come on board, but the purser, unlike his counterparts the night of the big earthquake, refused. "It would have been a little thing to have given shelter to those who were afraid to stay at home," scolded the *News and Courier*. Thousands of dead fish washed up on the beach in Bulls Bay, north of the city, a man was injured by a falling wall, and part of the medical college collapsed. Dawson cabled Sarah, still in Europe, to say that he was safe.[49]

Upsetting as it was to the locals, the aftershock did not deter visitors from coming to see the ruins. In the *News and Courier*, a jovial dispatch from Spartanburg spoofed the jargon of the geologists: "You may expect some excursionists from the 'Piedmont Escarpment' to go down to examine 'the coastal plane' to-day. Take good care of them while they are there, and if you shake them a little let it be gentle."[50]

Dawson urged everyone to get ready for an influx of tourists, especially the "hotel men" and the owners of boardinghouses. The plaster must be dry and the furniture mended, he wrote, so that sightseers could be treated like royalty. Walking through the ruins with a journalist from Atlanta, he pointed to a broken column and mused, "Truly that is typical of the life and the death of some men. That exquisite carving in stone, broken in twain and brought down to mingle with the ruin and desolation." Two and a half years later, when Dawson was dead, the man would remember these words and wonder if the editor had seen in the earthquake a premonition of his own end.[51]

AMONG THOSE who toured the city was Clara Barton, founder of the American Association of the Red Cross. Barton arrived in Charleston on September 27. "The Red Cross to the Rescue," crowed the *News and Courier*. Barton apologized for not coming earlier — she had been traveling in the West. "If I had been at home in Washington when this thing happened we should have been here within twenty-four hours," she said. Her organization was so new that the *News and Courier* felt obliged to explain that it was not "a secret society." Though the European Red Cross had been active for many years, the U.S. organization had been founded just five years before and had not yet made its mark on the nation. The European societies were strictly wartime operations and had repeatedly rejected attempts to broaden their mission. But Barton had set up the U.S. branch specifically to aid victims of natural disasters.[52]

The Red Cross had no endowment and relied on newspaper appeals to bring in money for each emergency. When forest fires broke out in Michigan in 1881, leaving hundreds homeless, the Red Cross raised more than $80,000. Two years later, when the Ohio and Mississippi rivers flooded, the Red Cross took on the huge relief task; Barton herself traveled up and down the river for nearly four months, distributing food and supplies.[53]

The Chicago chapter of the American Red Cross had already sent $2,000 to Charleston, and Clara Barton brought assurances that more would come if it were needed. She was on a fact-finding mission, inspecting the damage and assessing the city's self-created system of relief. Barton felt that the Red Cross should intervene only when the disaster was "so great as to be beyond the means of local charity and recognized by the public as a national calamity." In the 1880s its role was often simply to certify the need for aid. Mayor Courtenay escorted Barton wherever she wanted to go, pronouncing her an official "guest of the city."[54]

Barton had been to the area before, though certainly not as an honoree. During the federal siege of Charleston in 1863, she worked as a nurse for Union troops who were shelling the city. Many Union supporters were horrified by the very idea of a woman behind the lines. The criticism heated up when Barton began to keep company with a married officer named John J. Elwell, chief quartermaster of the Department of the South. The two were seen riding horses, picking blackberries, and chasing sea turtles. Most inflammatory of all, Barton and Elwell were spotted visiting each other's tents late at night. When Elwell was wounded and another man took over his duties, Barton's two tents were confiscated by the Union Army. She contracted acute dysentery and had to go home.[55]

This story was not repeated on her return to Charleston in 1886. At age sixty-five, Clara Barton was dignified and dressed in black, with a gold watch and chain and a red ribbon "entertwined among the buttons of her basque." Barton gave the mayor several checks, to be presented as "remembrances" of her visit to the city: $100 each to the Confederate Home, the City Hospital, the Old Folks Home, the Charleston Orphan House, and the House of Rest. Some hospital patients were given a silver dollar apiece. After visiting the various branches of the relief committee, she pronounced the city's needs "fully covered."[56]

When Barton left for Washington on September 29, the *News and Courier* speculated that the Red Cross would put new resources at the disposal of the city. But as it turned out, $500 was all the group had to give, a sum equaled by such tiny towns as Blackville, South Carolina, and Key West, Florida. Barton wrote the mayor of Chicago that she had never seen a city so shattered, not even Atlanta after Sherman's march. A bit more money came in from Chicago as a result of her endorsement, but the city made no move to transfer the fire fund or to mount a new fund-raising effort. The Philadelphia branch collected clothes and other items, an effort Barton praised extravagantly.[57]

The earthquake was a turning point in Clara Barton's career. She recognized that her own efforts had come too late, and that the American Red Cross lacked the resources to address large natural disasters. Barton retooled the organization so that, in the future, it would be better prepared to act quickly in emergencies. After the Johnstown flood in Pennsylvania in 1889 and the Sea Islands hurricane on the South Carolina and Georgia coasts in 1893, the Red Cross would take more responsibility for sheltering and feeding the victims. But it couldn't do much for Charleston.

For Dawson and the other men serving on the relief committees, Barton's departure was a clear sign that they were on their own. Money would continue to arrive from outside, but no agency, private or public, was going to step up to take charge of the recovery. The former Confederate officers who ran the relief effort could do as they pleased. They were confident they could push aside the objections of black preachers and laborers. But they failed to realize how seriously people all over the country would take the predictions of the "Canadian weather prophet."

Chapter Twelve

WAITING FOR THE APOCALYPSE

ACCORDING TO THE New York newspapers, Ezekiel Stone Wiggins was growing "daily more positive in his prediction" that an even more destructive earthquake would occur in late September. He pinpointed the exact time: two p.m. on Wednesday, September 29. New Orleans, Macon, and Mobile would be ruined, and Atlanta, Jacksonville, Baton Rouge, Houston, San Antonio, and Galveston would suffer catastrophic damage. The earth's center of gravity was shifting, Wiggins explained, the result of a conjunction of Jupiter, Saturn, Mars, and the moon, plus another invisible moon that he had recently discovered. This analysis was confirmed by the president of the Astronomical Meteorological Association of Canada, who added that the quake would be accompanied by heavy storms across the continent.[1]

Wiggins had a way with newspapers. His announcements increased circulation, whether or not they were true. In 1876 he had grabbed headlines by claiming that dinosaurs still roamed the bottom of the oceans. Seven years later, in 1883, he had forecast a great storm that would sweep the North Atlantic. The tempest would be so huge and destructive that no vessel smaller than an ocean liner could survive it, and "all the low lands on the Atlantic [would] be submerged." The warning was picked up by the Associated Press and published in scores of newspapers. An ad for a grocery store urged in verse,

> Wiggins' Storm is drawing nigh,
> 5 lbs. of Tea you had better buy,
> Go to Stroud's without delay,
> For perhaps your money may blow away.

Fishermen docked their boats for days before the fateful date and lost thousands of dollars in revenue. Rain fell on parts of New England on March 9, but there was no doomsday gale.[2]

Afterward, the *New York Times* ridiculed "Wiggins's Storm" and the man himself. Wiggins, it claimed, was "impossible to believe in," if only because of his name: "no child [named] Wiggins could possibly reach maturity. Such a name would crush all ambition and interest in life out of a boy." Having searched the scientific record in vain for the existence of an astronomer named Wiggins, the reporter concluded that he was probably really "a faro-dealer or cornet player." In fact, Wiggins worked for the Canadian Finance Department. He held degrees in both law and medicine, but not in any field that would equip him to predict storms or earthquakes.[3]

When Wiggins announced his new prophecy, the papers were quick to call him a quack and remind their readers that "the fishermen of the New England coast were looking for him with a view of choking, hanging, drowning, boiling, or otherwise disposing of his prophetship." Within days, his name popped up in every headline, and Charleston, almost a month after the earthquake, again became the center of journalistic interest.[4]

Trying to foster the illusion that nothing could slow or stop the city's miraculous recovery, Dawson treated the Wiggins scare with breezy scorn. "A City Full of Scaffolds," crowed the *News and Courier*. "Not Built to Hang Wiggins, But Would Be Glad if So Used." "The People Cheerful, Coura-geous and Hopeful and They Don't Care a Button for Wiggins," read an-other. Dawson asked the U.S. Signal Corps, the agency in charge of meteo-rological forecasts, to give predictions for September 26 through 29, "to be a set-off against the lugubrious and lying [fantasies] of Prophet-of-Evil Wiggins." "Charleston would have been herself again," he lamented, "but for the Wiggins prediction." The prospect of future earthquakes made people reluctant to rebuild and undermined the spirit of hope that Dawson was trying to foster.[5]

From New York to San Francisco, panic spread. In Galveston, fear was epidemic. "The Poor People Rendered Nearly Frantic by the Folly of Wig-gins," ran the *News and Courier* headline. New Orleans, too, was affected: country folk put off going to town to buy supplies. Two traveling salesmen caused a panic in the South Carolina upstate by announcing to their cus-tomers that the world was coming to an end.[6]

Dire predictions seemed to pop up everywhere. In the Lowcountry of South Carolina and Georgia, farm laborers halted work. Five hundred people gathered near the home of the Liberty County prophetess, whose earlier proclamation gained credibility thanks to Wiggins. Physicians were treating a huge number of nervous disorders, and some were "indignant enough ... to give Wiggins an old-fashioned coat of tar and feathers."[7]

In Charleston, the *News and Courier* reported, "thousands of negroes" were convinced that Judgment Day would arrive on September 29, though Wiggins had not mentioned Charleston in his forecast. The streets were full of talk about prophecies and predictions, "narrated," as the paper put it, "by street preachers and seers."[8]

In Savannah, many blacks quit work and refused to make commitments past the twenty-ninth. Revivals at two white Methodist churches there brought in many new members, and hundreds of black convicts were baptized in the Ogeechee Canal. Ministers all over the city were "reaping a rich harvest" of new members. One preacher boasted that every tremor was "good for fifty souls."[9]

It was not only poor folk who worried about the predictions. Augustine Smythe, one of the pillars of Old Charleston society, fretted that his wife was anxious "about that miserable prophecy." Another member of the upper crust, Sam Stoney, noted that Wiggins had "disturbed the rest of many people with his absurd predictions" and expected the twenty-ninth to be a "most trying and torturing day."[10]

Dawson wired every expert he could locate, especially his two favorite geologists, soliciting rebuttals for publication in the *News and Courier*. James C. Mendenhall reiterated that "there may ... not be another severe earthquake in Charleston for centuries." William McGee agreed: "No attention whatsoever should be paid to Wiggins's predictions."[11]

An astronomer at the U.S. Naval Observatory in Washington, D.C., debunked Wiggins's predictions as "absurd, if they were not cruel and criminal," and pointed out in no uncertain terms that "the planets which [Wiggins] says will be in conjunction will not be, and even if they were this would not affect the earth as he predicts." In a letter to a St. Louis newspaper, an English astronomer dismissed Wiggins as "half-educated and wholly unscientific."[12]

The Charleston officers of the U.S. Signal Corps appealed to their superiors in Washington for "some official contradiction" of Wiggins's "wildcat-earthquake-cyclone theory," and were rewarded with a dry little wire: "There are at present no indications of any severe atmospheric disturbance between now and the 30th. Timely notice will be given you should any change appear." The Canadian government ordered Wiggins to stop issuing prophecies, but fears could not be quelled.[13]

An excursion from Atlanta to Charleston planned for September 25 found few takers. A railroad official was sure it would have been full if not for "the Wiggins prediction." Reporters collected anecdotes that whipped up the excitement. As Wiggins Day approached, a visitor fresh off the steamer from New York stopped to ask a policeman for directions. All of a sudden the ship let off a loud rush of steam. The policeman yelped and trembled "like an aspen leaf." Another man ran for a block after hearing a strange sound that later proved to be "the step of a man on the turn-table of the street railway." Merchants grabbed attention by playing on the anxiety: "Professor Mendenhall says there will be a recurrence of earthquake unless you send your discarded furniture to W. K. Darby's Auction Room," read an advertisement in the *News and Courier*.[14]

Wiggins tried to dampen the hysteria. He pointed out that he had never exactly said there would be earthquakes on September 29, only that enormous forces would be at work. In fact, he now wished to alert people to the fact that they were *escaping* "the greatest earthquake force that would appear in America in 1886." He claimed that the "earthquake wave" had moved eastward. "There is absolutely no danger from earthquake in the latitude of Atlanta east of the Rocky Mountains except Wednesday next," he wrote, again pointing to September 29. "The greatest danger is to Central America, South America, and California."[15]

"Wiggins Says He Didn't," gloated the *News and Courier* on the eve of Wiggins Day. "It is to be hoped that he will lecture and come down this way. There would be a chance for grocers to unload their stocks of stale eggs."[16]

There were so many wild reports that it was hard to tell the difference between what Wiggins had really said and what the newspapers had invented. Fact and rumor were woven together with abandon. Off the coast of New York, a Loch Ness–type "sea serpent" was reported by several different ships. Before long, Wiggins was said to have announced that the recent convulsions of the earth had caused the bottom of the sea to open up and release hundreds of amphibious monsters. When a large wormlike creature squirmed out of a faucet in a Savannah soda fountain, startling a young man who was rinsing tumblers, a reporter wrote it up as "One of Wiggins's Wrigglers." He pronounced it not yet fully grown, with a head like a water moccasin and a mane of bristles along its back. "There is nothing very ornamental about the animal," he concluded, "and it would never be likely to become a household pet." A crowd soon gathered, and one man said the creature was only an eel. He was hooted down, so "the thing will go on record as a veritable serpent," added the amused reporter. "There is some talk of sending it to Wiggins."[17]

Sea serpents. Aftershocks. Armageddon. People needed a break. And as if on cue, the *News and Courier* announced the ultimate distraction: "Barnum Will Come to Charleston in Spite of Wiggins." An advance agent had been sent to Charleston to find out whether a visit from the famous circus would be "ill-timed" or "acceptable." Though the itinerary was already planned and canceling would cost the operation two days' work, the agent said that Barnum didn't want to annoy people who already had so much trouble.[18]

Ill-timed? Dawson was delighted. He sent his reporters around the city asking people what they thought, and the consensus was that the circus would be very welcome. The streets buzzed at the prospect of cavorting elephants and acrobats.

AS "WIGGINS'S JUDGMENT DAY" drew near, the details of his prediction were forgotten and people throughout the United States began to prepare for the end of the world. An old black man went to the bank in Savannah, the largest city near Liberty County, and withdrew his life savings, saying it would be of no further use to him and his church had better have it. A Baptist minister in the same city wept when he told a reporter that the Lord was going to let the devil come and "carry his beautiful chillen down to de land of fire."[19]

The black churches filled with praying citizens. Services were held behind closed doors and drawn blinds, and some people wore "ascension robes" to bed. A roving reporter found plenty of people who dismissed it all as nonsense: "Wiggings, Wiggings. Let's see," said one man. "Dat's somefin like what old Mr. Scott's been awearin' on his hade fo' de pas' fo'ty yea's." Another conceded that Wiggins was "a big tater hill 'mongst the 'stronomers," but said he wasn't fooled. "White folks better take Wiggins outten hitch 'im to a tree, and if er quake don' cum along jes pull him up like white folks sometimes do wid nigger what ben killin' somebody."[20]

In Wilkes County, Georgia, near Atlanta, four more prophets predicted earthquakes on September 29. In Jacksonville, Florida, people were so terrified that they planned to stay outdoors all day praying. One woman made flowing garments for herself and her children so they would be appropriately dressed when they went to heaven. Another packed baskets of provisions to take along on the journey. A family of four in Hillman, Michigan, far from the places where Wiggins had predicted problems, built a platform and huddled on top, dressed in their best clothes. They expected blue flames to erupt from fissures and destroy the world. In Charleston, several black churches held revival services, and whites complained "bitterly" about loud preaching that disturbed the peace every night in the neighborhood of Old Bethel Church. Wiggins told the *New York Times* that he had hoped to visit Charleston on the big day but found — to no one's surprise — that he could not get away.[21]

At a little after five p.m. on September 27, Charleston was rattled by a small shock. True to form, Dawson rushed to reassure people that this was a good thing: "These shocks," he wrote, invoking the pronouncements of Cleveland Abbe, "are guarantees of our security against any further serious disturbance." The next day, Wiggins Eve, another seismic wave rippled through. This one was only a "Baby Quake . . . Lost in the Streets," Dawson wrote, though Summerville experienced three separate shocks and many people were terrified. According to the *News and Courier*, the inevitable aftershocks were "drawing to a close" and should be completely over in about six weeks.[22]

When Wiggins Day finally arrived, a crowd gathered outside St. Michael's in Charleston to watch the hands of the clock approach two in the afternoon. People attending a trial in nearby Orangeburg made jokes about Wiggins, but a court reporter noted uneasiness as the fateful hour approached.[23]

In the end, nothing happened.

As the big hand of St. Michael's clock pointed straight up to mark the hour and then swept onward, the crowd waiting below heaved an audible sigh. Many of them "breathed easily for the first time since the lunatic astrologer's predictions," as the *News and Courier* put it. "When the time passed," noted the Orangeburg reporter, "everybody seemed more cheerful and self-composed." Even in Summerville, where aftershocks were still an almost-daily occurrence, there were "no shocks, no reverberations, no nothing." One disgruntled Summervillean remarked that "Wiggins was a liar at 2 o'clock, and was getting to be a bigger liar every minute thereafter."[24]

But those who had looked forward to Judgment Day were slow to give up hope. "It mayn't be too late yet," an old woman told a Savannah reporter as she made her way home from church that evening. The family on the platform in Michigan had to be coaxed down by some of their neighbors.

Nerves were raw across the country. When a dynamite factory exploded the next day near Nyack, New York, a family ran from their home crying "Wiggins! Wiggins!"[25]

At first only the *New York Times* acknowledged that Wiggins had been partially right. On September 23 a powerful hurricane blew in between Matamoros, Mexico, and Brownsville, Texas, with winds reaching a hundred miles an hour. The storm leveled more than five hundred homes and inundated the countryside. At Galveston, Harbor Island was under water. On the Pacific coast of Mexico, the Colima volcano began belching steam and was soon in the throes of a massive eruption.[26]

Wiggins issued an indignant statement. He claimed that he had actually predicted only that the earth would be under great strain, and what the press had said about him was nothing but "a tissue of lies." A great storm had indeed swept the coast of the United States. Earthquakes and volcanic eruptions had struck Mexico, and there were, in all probability, "a score of mountains in action" in Central America at that very moment. Why did people persist in ridiculing him, when one of his ancestors had served as the governor of Massachusetts? He undermined his credibility a bit by reminding reporters that it was he who had discovered dinosaurs roaming the bottom of the sea.[27]

AS THE SUN ROSE on September 30, an evil spell seemed to have lifted. Thousands of scaffolds swarmed with workmen, and people went about their business with a lighter step. The statue of Charity on top of the Orphan House was restored to her upright position. Hoping to corner the market on temporary shelters, a company from Grand Rapids, Michigan, erected a prototype "portable house" in Washington Square, complete with glass windows and shutters, but most people were more interested in moving back into their nonportable houses. Two small shocks rattled Summerville that afternoon, but no one paid much attention. The *News and Courier* reported that there had been thirty tremors since August 27, not counting the almost-constant, barely perceptible quivers. And yet there had been no shocks on Wiggins Day proper. Dawson insisted that most Charlestonians had not feared September 29, but admitted that it would not be "historical truth to say that [they had] built their faith and hopes solely on the kindly utterances of responsible scientists."[28]

Now that the threat had passed, Wiggins and his astrological theories became the butt of jokes. "Wiggins says he is descended from a Pilgrim Father," quipped the *New York World*. "His descent is very pronounced." Charleston restaurants sold "Wiggins soup," the contents of which, sadly enough, reporters failed to disclose.[29]

Even Mark Twain could not resist Wiggins, a character who might have stepped from the pages of his recently published *Huckleberry Finn*. The Wiggins frenzy was, for him, familiar comic territory. Twain had experienced an earthquake in San Francisco on October 8, 1865. His "Earthquake Almanac" pretended to forecast what each day would bring in the month after a quake. Two weeks after the first shock, people would experience "occasional shakes, followed by light showers of bricks and plaster." Three weeks later, there would be "spasmodic but exhilarating earthquakes, accompanied by occasional showers of rain, and churches and things." After that, the end would be near. The later entries are a to-do list for those getting ready for Judgment Day:

Nov. 3 — Make your will.
Nov. 4 — Sell out.
Nov. 5 — Select your "last words."
Nov. 6 — Prepare to shed this mortal coil.

The entry for November 7 reads simply, "Shed." In 1886, as Wiggins Day faded into history, Twain issued a prediction of his own: a giant meteor would swoop down on Canada, "take the prophet Wiggins right in the seat of his inspiration, . . . lift him straight up into the back yard of the planet Mars and leave him permanently there in an inconceivably mashed and unpleasant condition."[30]

FRANK DAWSON was not on Broad Street to see the hands of the clock pass two o'clock. He spent Wiggins Day on the steamship *City of Columbia*, bound for New York. Mollie Glidden and her children were on the same ship, Charles Glidden having left for Florida to start his new job with a phosphate company. At least one Charleston family was also on board: Edward Wells, who had earlier worried about how to move his wife and children away from the phantom volcano, now sent them all off to New York to avoid Wiggins Day.[31]

Dawson was worn out, and he knew he would not be able to rest in Charleston. His private secretary had just resigned, and he was feeling overwhelmed by relief work on top of his job at the newspaper. On September 27 he asked the Executive Relief Committee for a week off. Banker Morris Israel took over as chair of the subcommittee on immediate relief.[32]

Sarah, reading the newspapers and her husband's letters as they arrived in her hotel room at Lausanne, could not stop worrying that the family would run out of money. She offered to cut back on expenses, but Dawson said there was no need, though repairs to their home would run about $5,000. One wall was badly cracked, and sections of brickwork would have to be taken out and relaid. Long iron bolts were being installed to hold the house together, as they were in many other damaged buildings. He sent word to his nervous son Warrington, with Sarah in Lausanne, that these would make the cracked house "absolutely secure." To Sarah, he explained that the rods were anchored by iron end pieces, and that they were tightened by a "swivel" in the middle of the rods.[33]

As co-owner of the newspaper, Dawson also had to find the money to rebuild the structures that housed the *News and Courier*. As it turned out, the balky typesetters, the "quakers," had been right — inspectors declared their work space unsafe. Dawson admitted to Sarah that the structure was in "desperate condition," and that the annex on Elliott Street would have to be torn down. The front of the main building facing Broad needed extensive repairs.[34]

However, the most irksome drain on Dawson's finances came from Sarah's family. Having made up his mind to support Miriam and Lucile for another year, he was now caught in another family drama. Sarah's brother Jimmy Morgan was in Australia, serving as ambassador, and he asked Frank to book passage to Melbourne from the United States for his teenage daughter, Emmie. Jimmy, always a bit of a moocher, had not sent money for her ticket. Frank worked with a family friend to find his niece a suitable escort, but they had no success. Finally, they bought the girl a ticket and asked the shipping line to make sure she was well looked after. Frank's outlay came to more than $500. He grumbled but wired the money to New York City, hoping, though probably without much optimism, that Jimmy eventually would see fit to pay him back.[35]

Though Dawson dismissed his wife's concerns about the family finances, he knew that he would somehow have to raise additional funds. He had recently invested in a new invention that promised to change the world, or at least the world of the South. Crops like wheat and corn already could be harvested by machine, sharply reducing the need for farm labor, but countless human hands were still needed to pull cotton fibers from the plant. Though the Mason Cotton Harvester was still under development, Dawson had seen enough to believe it would work. He planned to contact potential investors in New York and create a buzz. If the equipment caught on, he stood to make a fortune, rather like Cyrus McCormick, inventor of the mechanical reaper. Moreover, a mechanical cotton picker would clear the way for South Carolina to move large numbers of black agricultural workers out of state, and the last three weeks had convinced Dawson that black labor was not to be trusted.[36]

But Dawson's industrial schemes were not what New York reporters wanted to talk about. Charleston was the earthquake city, and he was the earthquake man. A reporter from the *New York World* met him at the dock. How was Charleston doing? The money already pledged should be enough to cover relief, Dawson said. The reporter asked if he meant that everything was taken care of. Far from it, he replied. Charlestonians needed low-interest loans in order to rebuild. The government should boost the economy by building jetties at the mouth of the harbor to create a deeper shipping channel.[37]

Then the reporter posed a loaded question: "Has there been much indignation in Charleston over the President's failure to express his sympathy?"

Dawson hedged. "I do not like to talk about that," he said. But talk he did. After telling the reporter that his remarks were off the record, he said things that were bound to get him in trouble. "I have been very close to the President," he began, "and have held him in high esteem. It certainly seemed, considering the fearful calamity which had befallen a city, that the proper thing for the President of the United States to do was to go at once to Washington and say to the suffering people: 'I am here at the post of duty. What can I do for you?'" But Cleveland had ignored the whole thing, even though Charleston had just sent him an expensive wedding present. Nor, Dawson continued (inaccurately, as it turned out), had there been any word from either of South Carolina's senators, Matthew C. Butler and Wade Hampton. True, Butler was traveling in Europe, but at least he could have sent a telegram.[38]

Before Dawson could turn around, these indiscreet comments were printed in the *World*, a national newspaper that Cleveland was sure to read. Word flew back from Washington that the president was "really mad." General Hampton, Dawson wrote Sarah, was also "on the warpath."[39]

"I hardly know what to do," he admitted in a letter to Sarah. Aware that he had made a serious blunder, Dawson turned for advice to Hugh S. Thompson, the former governor of South Carolina now serving as Cleveland's assistant secretary of the navy. Thompson asked the president for a private conference, bracing himself for an angry diatribe. Instead, Cleveland listened quietly and seemed fairly calm. The president told Thompson that he was most distressed that Dawson had spouted off to a newspaper known to be hostile to the Cleveland administration. And, of course, Dawson *should* have known better. He was an editor himself, and the *News and Courier* respected few confidences when news was at stake. His slip may have been a sign of how stress was affecting his judgment. He was offending people unnecessarily, losing allies, and isolating himself. Cleveland was especially annoyed by Dawson's mercenary and ungracious reference to the wedding present. Thompson made excuses for Dawson and conveyed his humble apologies. He left convinced that the president would not bear a grudge, but Cleveland's attitude toward Dawson chilled perceptibly.[40]

Dawson wrote President Cleveland that he was "pained beyond measure" to have caused him any annoyance. The *World's* reporter, he said, had violated his confidence, and he had never made any remarks about the wedding present. Yet he admitted that in other ways the report was not far off the mark. "No one really doubted your sympathy," Dawson wrote, "but everybody longed for an exhibition of it. While the Queen of England could speak, 'our President' was silent." He hoped that "no cloud" would come between them and that Cleveland would still allow him to call himself "your friend and servant."[41]

Dawson followed up with a letter to the *New York World* in which he admitted having criticized Cleveland but repeated that he had not meant these remarks for public consumption. Soon after Dawson apologized, the president sent $20.00 to the Confederate Home, a haven for white widows and orphans which was sacred to Charleston's elite, and $10.00 to a black church, Emanuel AME. No letter of sympathy ever arrived.[42]

Contrary to what the *New York World* quoted Dawson as saying, in fact General Hampton had contributed $148 for relief, and Senator Butler had sent $50.00. (Hampton's check had gotten lost in the shuffle, and Butler's had just arrived from Europe.) Dawson apologized for having caused them annoyance. A few weeks later, Butler wrote Dawson that he had seen the interview and "did not get the least mad. Life is entirely too short to worry about such things." Butler could not really afford to get angry at his old friend, however, since just before the earthquake Dawson had lent him a large sum of money.[43]

And then, as Dawson had suggested, less than three weeks after Mayor Ashmead Courtenay pleaded to the nation for funds, the Executive Relief Committee informed the city council that enough money had already come in to take care of the *"actual loss of needy sufferers"* (original emphasis). Grateful as they were for the help, the members of the committee preferred to err, if err they must, "by limiting the estimate rather than [by] placing it too high."[44]

The city council authorized the mayor to withdraw his request for aid, and a telegram was sent to newspapers all over the country. The city was "Too Grateful to be Greedy," Dawson wrote, praising his own committee for its selfless actions. The city should not "stand, hat in hand, on the public highway seeking alms . . . when the crisis which made such assistance necessary and most welcome has plainly passed." Most national newspapers applauded the move, though a few felt it was premature. Even Dawson acknowledged that the announcement was misleading. Many institutions, especially churches, still needed thousands of dollars for repairs.[45]

The soup kitchen closed on October 9, and the kettles and other utensils were sold at auction. Most people who read the papers assumed this meant that the crisis was over. But Rev. William Heard wrote the *New York Freeman* that poor, black earthquake victims were still "standing around the place of distribution, shivering and crying for something." Dawson, of course, knew that, but he believed that he had to stop the labor battles from holding back Charleston's reconstruction. The committee was taking action on Rev. A. Toomer Porter's earlier claim that farm laborers and railroad hands would not work until rations were cut off. And so Heard's lament was drowned out by the city's announcement that the crisis was over. Heard and seven of his colleagues could not even convince the city council to declare a day of "fasting, humiliation and prayer," as the city had in 1812. Without free shelter and food, Charleston laborers would be forced to work for more reasonable wages. Just as the mayor of Chicago had said "no more" to fund-raisers after the fire, Dawson decided that a little suffering among the laboring classes might be beneficial to his city. Rather than "bring[ing] our people nearer and closer together," as he had hoped, the earthquake and the relief effort were driving them apart.[46]

Chapter Thirteen

RISING FROM THE RUINS

THREE HARD SHOCKS jarred Charleston on October 9. Knowing that they would be reported around the world, Dawson cabled Sarah that all was well, though he admitted in a follow-up letter that he could now rock the whole house just by standing on the balls of his feet and raising and lowering his heels. He estimated that a hundred cartloads of fallen brick still lay scattered around the yard, but the most recent series of shocks made him reluctant to continue repairs. Even Dawson was beginning to lose heart after five weeks of shaking.[1]

For one thing, hiring someone to lay bricks in Charleston was no longer a simple transaction. The Bricklayers' Union made the rules, and their membership had swelled to astonishing numbers. At a meeting on October 12, 175 old members welcomed thirty-five new recruits. The union authorized their president, D. J. Flynn, to visit jobsites around the city and check for compliance. Whenever he discovered a nonunion bricklayer, the man would be invited to join up. If he refused, Flynn was to inform the employer that all the union men working for him would have to quit if the nonmember was not fired. Dawson considered this practice disgraceful. "How the Charleston Bricklayers' Union Boycotts American Citizens" read a headline on October 15.[2]

Strikes, boycotts, and labor unions dominated the national headlines, too. While Charleston was pressuring its workforce to rebuild the city at reduced rates, the National Assembly of the Knights of Labor, the group that had first pushed for wage hikes after the earthquake, convened in Richmond, Virginia, for their annual meeting. The *New York Herald* predicted that this would be "the most important labor meeting ever held in this country." The Knights were expanding beyond traditional economic concerns to take a stand on that most divisive of issues, race.[3]

"No human eye can detect a difference between the article manufactured by the black mechanic and that manufactured by the white mechanic,"

Grand Master Workman Terence Powderly declared. "Both claim an equal share of the protection afforded to American labor." This attitude, almost unheard of in the late nineteenth-century United States, had attracted thousands of black workmen to join the KOL, and as the annual meeting drew near, the nation was watching to see if the Knights would stand by their principles. It was no accident that they had chosen to meet in the former Confederate capital, where racial separation and inequality were the rule. Dawson would cover each day's events on his front page, as would most major U.S. papers.[4]

Sure enough, even before the assembly convened, the Knights challenged the color line. The delegation from New York City's district 49 included one black man, James Ferrell. In mid-September, a hotel in Richmond had refused to accept his reservation. Ferrell's fellow delegates declined to stay in a place where their colleague was unwelcome.

Virginia Governor Fitzhugh Lee, Frank Dawson's friend and Civil War commander, had been asked to address the delegates on opening day. The men from district 49 wrote to Powderly and asked that James Ferrell be invited to introduce the governor. Powderly knew such a gesture would be taken as a terrible insult by Virginia whites — not only was Lee the governor, he was a nephew of Gen. Robert E. Lee. And yet to refuse would betray the philosophy of the KOL. Powderly came up with a compromise — Ferrell could introduce Powderly, who would then introduce Lee. Thus the governor would not have to share the stage with a black man, but the Knights could still take a stand for racial equality. Lukewarm as it seems today, the proposal thrilled black workers. A black newspaper in Philadelphia declared that Powderly and the delegates of district 49 had "immortalized themselves," and another black newspaper was sure that thousands would be inspired to join the KOL.

Meanwhile, Ferrell's fellow Knights decided to attend a performance of *Hamlet* at the Academy of Music in downtown Richmond. In a move that predated the lunch-counter sit-ins of the 1960s by more than seventy years, they paid for eighty tickets and took their seats. A few people noticed Ferrell in the audience and complained to the manager, but the Knights were not asked to leave. The next day, however, rumors spread that the Knights planned to take Ferrell to another theater and force his admission. The theater owner announced that she would not be intimidated, and that this time Ferrell would have to sit in a gallery reserved for his race. She asked the police chief for protection. That night, thirty-five police officers stood guard at the theater. Thousands of people crowded the streets, looking for a fight, but Ferrell did not appear.

Richmond was choked with tension. Groups of heavily armed white men haunted the hotel where Powderly and the other officials were staying, threatening to kill or maim them. KOL officers were told that the building where the convention was being held would be attacked the following night. Powderly decided to ignore the threats and issued a statement taking responsibility for the trouble. It was his idea to put Ferrell on stage, he said, and he had not heard an argument since that would have made him behave differently.

These were fighting words in 1886. For whites and blacks to sit in an audience together in the South was out of the question, even for Dawson. He was willing to allow blacks to hold spots on the police force, yet now he editorialized that Powderly must be insane to encourage racial mixing. "Social equality means miscegenation. The general mixing of the two races would destroy the best qualities of whites and blacks alike, and leave the Southern country in possession of a nation of mongrels and hybrids." This statement played directly to the fears and prejudices of most of his white readers. The Knights of Labor seemed to provide an easy target, a way to declare his sympathy with white southerners. Race mixing did not threaten other parts of the United States, he wrote, where the black population was small: "A single drop of ink produces very little effect on a bucket of water. . . . But when there is more ink than water, there is no mistaking the effect or denying the defilement."[5]

ON OCTOBER 16 Charleston was invaded — not by radical labor organizers but by elephants and acrobats. Showman Phineas T. Barnum was despised in the white South. Just two years before, he had warned that if Grover Cleveland, Dawson's candidate, won the presidency, the South would "establish free trade, get [compensation] for its slaves, and obtain pensions for all rebel soldiers." Yet his spectacular circus was hard to resist, and even where Barnum's politics were most reviled, huge crowds turned up and paid the price of admission. In North Carolina earlier that fall, the Raleigh News and Observer had charged that the troupe currently touring was just a fraction of Barnum's full extravaganza, another slap at the South.[6]

Dawson refused to join the chorus of abuse. As Charleston's circus day drew near, the *News and Courier* reported that this show dwarfed all of the famous impresario's previous productions. Every paper was filled with free publicity. Dawson must have hoped for a huge crowd, if only to make people forget their difficulties.[7]

Barnum's "monster parade" started near the railroad station. The head chariot, carrying the band, passed the corner of Broad and Meeting streets just as the bells of St. Michael's Church tolled twelve noon. People crowded the sidewalks and hung from every window. A "cavalcade of forty horsemen" led the procession. Cages of lions, leopards, tigers, and panthers rolled past the scaffolded, shored-up walls of the post office and City Hall. Elephants, polar bears, and sea lions accompanied a herd of ponies. The circus parade marched in all its glory back up the spine of the peninsula to Line Street, where twenty-eight tents had been pitched at the baseball park. Every streetcar in the city was put on the "circus route," the line that served the baseball park, but even so, many people had to walk. The magnificent sight that met their eyes made the long journey worthwhile.[8]

The menagerie tent alone was so large that it took up most of the park, with space for twelve elephants, thirty-two camels, five hundred draft horses, two hundred and twenty-five horses and ponies, lions, tigers, monkeys, and bears. The big top covered ten acres and could seat twenty thousand, a third of the city's population. One of Barnum's most popular attractions was a "museum" tent filled with "giants, midgets, dwarfs, skeletons, fat people, armless and legless people, [and] bearded women." The "Congress of Giants" featured people from "every country on earth," and sixty-five cages held "rare birds, beasts, and sinewy reptiles."

Most exciting of all — and most advertised — was the skeleton of Jumbo the elephant, "the history of whose pathetic death is still fresh in the minds of the public." Everybody knew, or thought they knew, what had happened to Jumbo. Brought to the United States from the London Zoo in 1882, Jumbo was so large that a deck had to be removed from the ship that carried him so that he could stand upright. Barnum billed him as the "Largest Living Quadruped on Earth."[9] For three years the elephant was Barnum's star attraction, a gargantuan draw at the box office. Stores sold Jumbo brands of almost everything, from peanut butter to cigars. Jumbo was exhibited alongside a pygmy elephant named Tom Thumb, making him look even bigger than he was. But almost exactly a year before the earthquake, on September 12, 1885, Jumbo and Tom Thumb were walking along the tracks of the aptly named Grand Trunk Line railway in Ontario, Canada, when a train came barreling along the track. Tom Thumb was thrown clear, though one of his legs was broken. Jumbo was hit by the oncoming train and slammed into another train standing on an adjacent track. His tusks were rammed into his brain.

It took more than two hundred men to move Jumbo's corpse. Barnum rushed a noted taxidermist to the scene and hired six butchers to dissect the cadaver. The heart alone weighed forty-six pounds. Three tons of bones were shipped to New York in a railroad car emblazoned with the words: "In this car are the mortal remains of the immortal Jumbo."

Barnum intended to display Jumbo in a museum, but his shrewd wife suggested that the elephant's remains could still travel with the circus. To add a further note of poignancy, Barnum purchased a female elephant named Alice from the London Zoo, had her dressed in black crepe and jet beads, and billed her as Jumbo's widow.

Charleston loved Alice, Jumbo's bones, and everything else about the circus. More than five thousand people attended the matinee, mostly women and children, and the evening performance drew almost fifteen thousand. In short, concluded the *News and Courier*, "Barnum has created almost as great a sensation in Charleston as the recent seismic disturbances. It is doubtful there were as many people on the streets on the memorable morning of September 1."[10]

The *New York World* reported that Barnum's circus had taken in $14,000 in Charleston in one day. For a city still welcoming donations for relief, said the *World*, Charleston seemed strangely willing to throw away money on frivolity. Dawson was annoyed at the criticism. It was natural for people recovering from disaster to crave entertainment, and word had gone out that this would be Barnum's last appearance in Charleston. Moreover, many of the circus-goers were not even residents of Charleston, but visitors from other parts of the state.[11]

In reality, the well-heeled had never stopped seeking entertainment. The Academy of Music, which was not badly damaged, started its season less than three weeks after the earthquake with a benefit performance of *A Flash of Light*, starring Marion Booth, who was married to the brother of Lincoln's assassin. The theater manager had earlier offered the building as a hospital for the disabled or a "refuge for the homeless," but apparently no one took him up on it. In the four months after the earthquake, the theater presented twenty-seven different shows, from comedy to grand opera.[12]

JUST AS THE CIRCUS was rolling into town, Dawson attempted to resign permanently from the subcommittee on immediate relief. Again the members of the Executive Relief Committee begged him not to. After all, the work would soon be done. Urgent requests continued to pour in, and cases they had turned down earlier were now being reconsidered. They needed Dawson's help to finish the job.[13]

But Dawson's mind was on a new task: wringing disaster aid from the South Carolina legislature. No funds could be allocated for relief without an amendment to the state constitution, which prohibited the use of tax money for private purposes. State Representative William H. Brawley of Charleston wrote the governor, begging him to convene a special session to consider the question. "Now is the hour for action," Dawson wrote on October 8, the same day he published and praised Mayor Courtenay's proclamation that no more private relief funds should be sent to Charleston. "It is absolutely necessary to amend the Constitution so as to permit this aid."[14]

Time was running out. The General Assembly would have to vote to place the question on the ballot, and if a special session wasn't called, the measure couldn't be decided until November 1888, two years away. Representative Brawley's plan was to ask the state to finance low-interest loans. Dawson suggested that the state could fund the loans by using its phosphate royalties — money collected as a tax on minerals mined from the Lowcountry and used to manufacture fertilizer. Although the idea seems reasonable today, in 1886 it was a shocking expansion of government responsibility. Dawson berated Mayor Courtenay and most of the city council members who, he claimed, were opposed to the idea, though they had never announced their positions. The poor were already provided for through the relief fund, Dawson explained. Loans would allow the middle and upper classes to rebuild within a year, rather than dragging out the work over ten years, "*or even a century*" (original emphasis).[15]

People in towns and cities across the state saw things differently. Disaster or no disaster, Charleston was rich and the rest of the state was poor. "Our people cannot afford [disaster aid]," declared the *Georgetown Enquirer*, "nor does Charleston need it. She has within her own limits capital enough to rebuild and repair nearly all the damaged private residences and stores." Farmers who had lost crops in the spring floods considered their misfortune as much an act of God as the destruction of houses. Charleston could take care of herself. The *News and Courier's* correspondent in Spartanburg summed up the general attitude: when disaster struck, people should cut expenses, not ask for help. "Last winter's suits have to be darned ... and hash has to take the place of porter-house steak."[16]

The governor privately consulted friends about whether he should call a special session. One, an attorney, worried that the bill might fail, in which case the people of Charleston would wind up paying for the fruitless assembly with taxes they could ill afford.[17]

Finally, Brawley suggested that since the idea of state funding was going nowhere, perhaps all the rich men in Charleston should get together and form a private company to lend money for repairs. No such company was ever formed.[18]

Nor did South Carolina's senators Butler and Hampton make any move toward asking Congress for federal assistance. Hampton did urge President Cleveland to visit Charleston: "Coming of your own accord, to visit your fellow citizens who have suffered so greatly, would gratify them more than if you came on a formal invitation," he said. Cleveland did not respond.[19]

LOANS OR NO LOANS, hundreds of buildings were being torn down, repaired, altered, and rebuilt. Charlestonians were putting the earthquake behind them, as Dawson had encouraged them to do. An "earthquake proof store" went up opposite the Charleston Hotel, its walls and ceiling finished with wood instead of plaster. At Citadel Square Baptist Church, the fractured steeple, which had collapsed in the cyclone of 1885, was torn down to the sanctuary roofline, and the Bagging Factory was partly demolished. The stone parapet and cornices on the chamber of commerce building were replaced with wood trim, which was less likely to kill people if it fell off and hit them. At Circular Church, the congregation voted to remove the ruins left by the 1861 fire and build a modern sanctuary. Reverend William Heard received $250 from a group of prominent men in New York to repair the Mt. Zion AME sanctuary. The money was funneled through the Executive Relief Committee's books, probably to avoid the appearance of a separate fund for blacks. Letters between the major donor, William E. Dodge of the New York Chamber of Commerce, and Mayor Courtenay suggest that the money was intended to pacify Heard so he would stop criticizing the city.[20]

School officials scrambled to put their buildings in usable shape. The Citadel and the College of Charleston reopened on October 4, right on schedule, though both wings of the college's main building had been razed. The medical college convened on October 15, holding classes in the old U.S.

Marine Hospital, with "clinicals" at the Agricultural Hall. Avery Institute, a private black academy just down the street from Dawson's house, was so badly damaged that it would not reopen until after the first of the year. The sponsor of the school, the American Missionary Association, had to raise repair money on its own. The city's relief fund would not pitch in. The white high school was in relatively good shape despite its stint as a temporary police station, and classes resumed by November 1. A. Toomer Porter allowed the Memminger School to use one of the buildings at Porter Academy, and arrangements were made to hold classes in various churches, storerooms, hotels, and meeting halls all over the city.[21]

"A new city is being built on the ruins of the old," Dawson observed. Yet despite the incessant warnings that appeared in the *News and Courier*, many masons were still using inferior mortar to repair homes and businesses. Dawson urged the city council to appoint a building commission to supervise repairs and new construction. The insurance inspectors agreed. An architect from Atlanta sounded the alarm: "We have inspected several buildings in which women and children are living, that should have immediate attention, or I fear we will soon read of some of them being buried alive." The very next day, the city council moved to elect an official inspector of buildings.[22]

The city was preoccupied with rebuilding, but not so much that racial politics were entirely forgotten. Local Republicans complained that Democrats were disfranchising thousands of black voters, and the upstate farmer's advocate Ben Tillman chose this moment to launch an assault on the laws that protected black civil rights. "Why do we cling to our Radical constitution and the expensive and cumbersome county government left us by our Yankee masters?" he demanded. "[It] was fashioned by scalawags and negroes to rob and oppress taxpayers." Tillman's call for a new constitution would soon electrify the state, but less than three months after the earthquake, most Charlestonians were too busy to pay attention.[23]

ON TOP OF everything else, the city was suffering from drought. Many cisterns had run dry, and the water level in the wells was alarmingly low. On October 19 a windstorm whipped up, raising hopes of a shower, but all it did was stir up dust so that everybody who ventured outside was whitewashed "from head to foot with pulverized reminiscences of the earthquake." Other areas of the country were not so parched. A hurricane formed off Havana in the second week of October, veering to the west and strafing the Gulf Coast from Pensacola to New Orleans. On October 15 the storm roared ashore at Sabine Pass, Texas, pushing a wall of water so high that fifty-foot waves broke over the lighthouse. At least ninety people drowned in the same area that had been hit by another hurricane just three weeks earlier.[24]

Reports from Sabine Pass were heartrending. One woman floated for twenty-five miles on a feather bed, trying to hold onto a small child suffering from convulsions. Two men blistered their hands fighting off thousands of water moccasins. "Every vestige of property" was swept away. Dawson collected contributions for the Sabine Pass victims. "The sufferers [in Texas] will not receive more sincere sympathy from any source, we are sure, than from the people of Charleston," he wrote the day after the storm, but little money was contributed. The nation was faced with a new disaster and a new call for relief funds. Just six weeks after the earthquake, Charleston's plight had faded into history for everyone who did not live there.[25]

CHARLESTON WAS STILL subject to severe jolts. Early in the morning on Friday, October 22, another strong tremor startled the city. That afternoon, a priest was reading the Catholic funeral service for the captain of a Spanish steamer. "And the earth shall open and give up her dead," he intoned. All at once the mourners heard a roar, and the coffin lurched and swayed so that the corpse seemed to come back to life. Stones crashed from the ruins of the cathedral, and cracks as wide as a man's hand opened at the Custom House. Workmen jumped and fell from scaffolds. Dry wells filled with up to thirty-four feet of water and an oily fluid spouted from the ground. At least seventy-five newly repaired chimneys cracked or collapsed. One woman admitted to a friend that "there are times when I feel an almost irresistible desire to rush away from the ever present terror." She found it difficult to sleep and was always "waiting." She and her husband argued about whether they should stay and rebuild or move to New York City. Finally, they agreed to stay. The woman wrote her daughter, "Here we are and here unless the Earthquake ends all things we shall be."[26]

Some people built new makeshift shelters or returned to old ones that were still standing. Many went back to sleeping in their clothes. Summerville officials met and voted to discontinue repairs, especially to brick and plasterwork. Rev. William Heard wrote the *New York Freeman* that many blacks were leaving the area because they were frightened. "Some one is being killed or injured every day," he reported. Fevers afflicted one out of every two people, and "there are many who are suffering and many who are sick."[27]

The shock jarred people as far away as Columbus, Ohio; Louisville, Kentucky; and Jacksonville, Florida. Dawson's sister-in-law Miriam DuPré felt the earth tremble in Cincinnati. "I shudder even now when I enter a house," she wrote her sister Sarah with her usual histrionics. "I watch every exit, count every chance, and my heart stops beating at every rumble, even the deep note of the organ sent a thrill of terror through me at Communion last Sunday." Miriam had managed to find a job as a stenographer. It paid by the word, and she was slow, but "if it will only lift one load from poor Frank I will be grateful." Dawson, she said, had rallied Charleston almost single-handedly. "Certainly [the city] would have remained in her ruins for fifty years to come but for his heroism."[28]

Dawson did his best to convince people that the repeated shocks did not mean his city was still at risk. The cause lay "far to the west," he wrote, and despite the continuing tremors there was no reason to believe that Charleston was "peculiarly exposed to danger." This absurd spin was sent out over the wires. The *Springfield Republican* in Massachusetts was not persuaded, remarking that "this is indeed sucking honey out of a pretty dry stalk" and providing a new version of an old prayer:

Rocked in the cradle of the quake
I lay me down in fear to shake.
Alarmed I rest upon the crest;
For only Heaven knows the rest.[29]

Publicly, Dawson continued to assert that Charleston was invincible. But he admitted to Sarah that the new shocks had pushed people to the brink. Emma, his cook, was so frightened that she had gone back to sleeping on the lawn. "We are not in as good condition to stand the strain as we were two months ago," he confessed. "Had you been here you would have been dead, or in a lunatic asylum."[30]

Chapter Fourteen

THE OLD JOY OF COMBAT

PEOPLE WHO HAVE experienced the unthinkable become conditioned to expect the worst. After a month of living in the ruins and feeling the ground shiver under their feet, the residents of Charleston were so traumatized that even chalk marks seemed like harbingers of doom. In early October "certain cabalistic signs" began appearing on sidewalks, curbs, and walls. The marks looked like "a cross between an Algebraic formula and an example in short division." Whites wondered if this mysterious graffiti might be a way for blacks to broadcast plans for an insurrection. One of Dawson's reporters asked around to find out what the scrawls meant, and a member of the Knights of Labor told him, "I don't know as there's any secret about it. It's the way we summon the Knights to a Lodge meeting." He explained how to read the formula, which included the number of the lodge, the date, and the time. The answer calmed no one.[1]

Union membership in Charleston had been growing by leaps and bounds, and as the city struggled to clean up and rebuild, workers could command double or even triple wages. The Bricklayers' Union wordlessly demonstrated its new strength by marching through the heart of the city on November 3. The News and Courier pointed out that a "remarkable" percentage of the two hundred members were black, and that the parade drew a large and enthusiastic crowd of black spectators.[2]

AS IF TO ENSURE that the earthquake was not forgotten, another aftershock hit just after noon on Sunday, November 5. At Jedburg, where the shock was strongest, chimneys that had withstood the August 31 quake were "torn to pieces." In Charleston, 150 black parents stormed the Shaw School and refused to leave without their children. The News and Courier reported that both the students and their teachers had remained calm, but the New York Freeman countered that several children were seriously injured when they scrambled for the doors. There was talk of instituting "earthquake drills" so that students could practice what to do when buildings started shaking. The black-owned *Charleston Recorder* saw the tremor as retribution: "Charleston seems to be doomed. And why not there is so much election frauds?"[3]

In the midst of all this turmoil, Dawson took time to reflect in the pages of the *News and Courier* on his twenty years in Charleston. He remembered arriving on November 10, 1866, nineteen months after the end of the Civil War, to a burned-out wasteland where the streets were paved with rotted planks. The ladies wore no color but black, and the young women never seemed to "chirp" or "chatter" as modern girls did. The long, fond, good-natured piece ended on a note of triumph. "Charleston lives," Dawson declared, even after the earthquake.[4]

He would not be the only one to remember the anniversary. Early on the morning of November 10, a large, heavy wooden chest was delivered to his house on Bull Street. Inside was a solid-silver tea service, ornate and clearly expensive. A card was tucked inside: "Dear Sir: It is, today, exactly twenty years since you first came to Charleston, and cast in your lot with its citizens. In that period have happened, in quick succession, events which will be always counted as among the most momentous in the history of Charleston. In the narrative of all these events your name will appear as one of the chiefest actors, and always in the part of one striving for the weal of our city and its citizens." The note was signed by twenty-six of the most prominent white men in Charleston. Mayor Courtenay had initiated the gesture and made the largest contribution. The presentation certified that Frank Dawson, so often out of step with native southerners, had been accepted as one of their own.[5]

The gift delighted Dawson. He described every feature of the tea set to Sarah and promised not to use it until she came home. Thanking the men who signed the letter, he wrote them that except for their kind gesture, November 10 would have passed as a sad day for him. He had been dwelling on things he had left undone rather than on what he had accomplished. But because of their confidence and friendship, he said, he was "pledged anew to the service of a city which is all the dearer to me for the misfortunes to which it has been subjected."[6]

His efforts had been appreciated, his life's work applauded. Determined to spend his political capital, Dawson started taking on new crusades. Some

would not be controversial, but others would put him on the opposite side
from most of his subscribers and would alienate even those who admired
him most. Dawson's self-confidence had always been one of his greatest assets, whether he was wooing Sarah or encouraging the victims of the earthquake. Eventually, it would also be his undoing.

DAWSON'S FIRST new campaign had nothing to do with politics — he set
out to persuade Charleston to adopt standard time, a system that had been
implemented by the railroads three years before. Most cities still used their
own local times, set according to the position of the sun as determined by
a sundial. Town and church clocks like the one at St. Michael's established
a local standard. Some jewelers paid to have time signals telegraphed from
the Harvard Observatory in Massachusetts and set the clocks in their windows to reflect standard time. But the great majority of Americans saw no
need for outside regulation, and in fact regarded standard time as artificial
at best. At worst, they feared that man was tampering with the laws of God
and nature.[7]

Scientists used time differently, and many were impatient with the lack
of a standard. The U.S. Army Signal Corps, which coordinated information from many sources in order to make weather predictions, had been
especially frustrated by the discrepancies. Meteorologists like Cleveland
Abbe had joined forces with scientists, map makers, and mathematicians in
an attempt to abolish local times. In 1883 the railroad companies agreed —
standard time was essential if the trains were to run on schedule. Frank
Dawson sided with the scientists.

Like most U.S. cities, Charleston had pretty much ignored the push for
standard time. But after the earthquake, there was a new reason to care
about minutes and seconds when the scientists started trying to figure out
where the main shock had originated and how long the earth waves took to
reach various localities. In theory, the calculations were easy, but they de-
pended on knowing exact times, down to a fraction of a second. Every town
and city in the country operated on a different system, so the first reports of
the quake varied by up to half an hour.

Finally it was determined that the earthquake had occurred at 51 minutes and 48 seconds after nine o'clock, the time as observed by the train
master on the Regulator clock at the South Carolina Railway office. The

U.S. Geological Service ran a series of conversions to translate all reports of the shock from local times to standard time. Another twelve months would pass before Charleston adopted standard time, but on October 30, 1887, even the clock at St. Michael's Church would be adjusted to the modern world.[8]

THREE MONTHS AFTER the earthquake, the relief effort was winding down. On November 30 Frank Dawson's committee on immediate relief closed its books, having spent almost $26,000 to replace personal property like clothes, furniture, and sewing machines. On December 14 the Executive Relief Committee presented its final report to the city council. More than $800,000 had been donated, though certainly more would have been sent had the city council not discouraged contributions after October 6. The report listed the names of more than two thousand applicants, along with the assessed values of their property, the number of people dependent on them for support, the amount applied for, and the amount awarded.[9]

The committee had turned away almost everyone who owned property assessed at more than $15,000. None of the successful individual applicants were wealthy or prominent. Sixty-seven people were awarded $1,000 or more, most of them single women and widows. No applicant had been given more than $1,250, because contractors had estimated that a comfortable new four-room house with a kitchen could be erected for that much. The committee moved to table additional applications. Dawson alone voted that they should remain open to new claims. Though he continued telling the rest of the country that Charleston was almost back to normal, he recognized that the city was still in the midst of a crisis.[10]

A fund had been reserved to cover plastering, which had been excluded from the first round of allotments, and $100,000 was presented to the city to repair or replace public buildings, including the hospitals, the City Almshouse, the public schools, the Orphan House, and the Old Folks Home. People who had lost arms or legs to the earthquake were given money to purchase prosthetic limbs.

Dawson did not hesitate to pat his own committee on the back: "The task was gigantic," he wrote, and no one outside the group could have "more than a faint idea of the complicated and delicate character of the relief work." He admitted that at first the task had seemed "appalling," and that at times the men in charge had been "groping in the dark." And yet, he said, the relief fund "could not have been committed to clearer heads or to cleaner hands," including his own.[11]

One of the aldermen wrote a flowery official thank-you note and the city printed twenty thousand copies. A clerk was given the daunting task of addressing an envelope to every donor.[12]

EVEN WHILE the city was closing the books on private donations, it was lobbying hard for public funds to finish the job of rebuilding. On the fourth Tuesday in November, the state legislature had convened for its regular session. Finally Charleston had a chance to make its case for emergency assistance, though it had become abundantly clear that the prospect of low-interest loans was dead. A new "earthquake bill" called for the state to reassess all property in the three counties worst hit by the quake, Charleston, Colleton, and Berkeley, and to reduce or refund taxes on all damaged structures. Even this modest proposal provoked cries of outrage.[13]

Dawson argued that the reassessment was only fair: the people simply asked that they not have to pay taxes on "property which they no longer possess." The sponsor, Rep. William Brawley, could not believe that his fellow legislators were so hostile to the bill. "Could Carolinians speak about short crops and freshets and the low price of cotton in comparison with this awful calamity?" he asked. They could and they did, at great length. One Charleston legislator wrote his wife, "We had a hard day yesterday over the bill to afford relief to Charleston. The fight was severe but we carried our measure by one vote. It comes up again to-day." The state senate finally passed the weakened earthquake bill on December 1.[14]

WHILE DAWSON was struggling with local matters like repairs, relief, and the earthquake bill, his nemesis Henry Grady was taking the nation by storm. Partly because his earthquake reporting had made such a splash, Grady was invited to appear before the New England Society, a prestigious club that included such industrialist millionaires as J. P. Morgan, Henry Flagler, Seth Thomas, and Russell Sage. He was the first southerner ever to address the organization.[15]

On December 22 Grady delivered a speech that would define a new era. All 360 seats in Delmonico's Restaurant in New York City were filled with movers and shakers, and Gen. William T. Sherman, whose army had torched Grady's beloved Atlanta in 1864, was conspicuous among them. Grady begged his listeners to bear with him while he talked about the defeated Confederate soldier. He painted a tragic picture of what that man had found at the end of the war — "his house in ruins, his farm devastated; his slaves free; his stock killed; his barns empty; his trade destroyed; his money worthless; his social system, feudal in its magnificence, swept away; his people without law or legal status; his comrades slain; and the burdens of others heavy on his shoulders." The typical southern soldier, he said, did not give up, but "stepped from the trenches into the furrow" and tried to make a crop.

"I want to say to General Sherman," he added, "who is considered an able man in our hearts, though some people think he is a kind of careless man about fire — that from the ashes he left us in 1864 we have raised a brave and beautiful city." The South had learned that "the free negro counts more than he did as a slave." Grady even went so far as to praise Abraham Lincoln, who was still regarded by many southerners as the devil himself. Lincoln, Grady said, was the quintessential American who concentrated in his homely body "the vast and thrilling forces of his ideal government" and "charg[ed] it with . . . tremendous meaning."

Grady understood his audience, both the men in the restaurant and the northern investors who would read the speech later. "But what of the negro?" he asked. "Have we solved the problem he presents or progressed in honor and equity towards the solution?" The South, he said, was trying. "We understand that when Lincoln signed the Emancipation Proclamation, your victory was assured; for he then committed you to the cause of human liberty, against which the arms of man cannot prevail." Those who linked the Confederacy to slavery had pledged the South to a cause "that reason could not defend." Grady flattered his audience, declaring, "I am glad God held the balance of battle in His Almighty hand, and that human slavery was swept from American soil." The audience drowned his words with applause.

The *Chicago Tribune* hailed this oration as "the speech of the year." Grady had laid claim to a phrase that would be used by historians and business leaders alike for more than a century — "the New South." The idea and the epithet were old, as Grady himself acknowledged, yet he made them seem fresh and exciting.[16] The speech was discussed and reprinted everywhere. In the blink of an eye, Henry Grady became a celebrity, the spokesman for a region.

Or at least for part of a region. The *New York Freeman* sniffed that Grady should have called his speech "The White South." Grady, it charged, should "count the graves of the colored men, women and children that have been tortured, burned, hanged, murdered, butchered, and worked to death on the chain gang."[17]

White newspapers loved Grady, and many printed the full text of his speech. However, to Dawson, Henry Grady had obviously sold out, and he could hardly believe that his fellow southerners would embrace a man who joked with General Sherman. In fact, Grady's attitudes were typical of Atlanta, and Dawson's were characteristic of Charleston. After the Civil War, white Charleston had felt sorry for itself, mourning the Lost Cause. Charleston still had its handsome houses and public buildings, its ruins, as a heritage; Atlanta, having lost almost everything to Sherman's torch, made a clean sweep. It simply got busy and — as Dawson himself would have said — it boomed. In 1886 Atlanta was a city on the make, where money was valued far above genealogy and manners. Dawson was trying his best to push Charleston in the same direction, yet he resented Grady for scooping him and for using the earthquake — Dawson's earthquake — as a springboard to fame. In the end, their feud came down to personal rivalry. Stung by Grady's runaway success and determined to compete, Dawson resolved to accept invitations to speak whenever they were offered, though he did not enjoy "orating" and knew he was not good at it.[18]

Henry Grady added insult to injury by poking fun at Dawson. Calling him "The Star-Eyed Beauty of the Coastal Plain," Grady clowned in the pages of the *Constitution* that the editor of the *News and Courier* was "one of the most beautiful persons in existence, regardless of sex." Even Dawson's socks were fair game — according to Grady, they cost an outrageous $1.50 a pair — a day's wages for some readers.[19]

STILL SEETHING over Grady's triumph, Dawson prepared to endure a lonely Christmas. When Sarah wrote that she was getting heavy, mainly around the hips, he wrote, "I should be delighted to see you fat, just there, for once." On an impulse that would eventually prove fatal, he suggested that if Sarah found "a model governess" she should bring the woman home.[20]

The holidays unleashed a new surge of earthquake giving. Dawson was sent large donations to be used for Christmas cheer from two unexpected sources, Whitelaw Reid of the *New York Tribune*, a high-profile Republican, and Flora Payne Whitney, wife of Secretary of the Navy William Whitney. Dawson was delighted to have a sum he could distribute to those he considered worthy without any red tape. He divided most of the money between eleven white churches in Charleston. A box of oranges, a barrel of apples, a bunch of bananas, some cigars, and two large fruitcakes went to the City Almshouse, "where the white people in distress are quartered," and a "similar allotment" was sent to the Old Folks Home, "where the colored poor are taken care of." Presents were delivered to each of the orphans cared for by the Sisters of Mercy, and a "Christmas tree for the poor" was set up at the Confederate Home.[21]

Dawson bought many gifts for his friends and employees. He gave carefully selected books to the children of Carlyle McKinley and two other *News and Courier* employees. Emma, his cook, got a dress and some gloves. To his own children he sent a rattlesnake rattle, some "Indian money," books, and copies of *St. Nicholas* magazine. For Sarah he purchased an expensive book.[22]

Frank spent most of Christmas Eve at the newspaper office, filling in for an employee whose daughter was sick. On Christmas Day he went to early Mass and came home feeling that it was "the dreariest day of [my] life." He did not even go to the cemetery to put flowers on his son's grave. A telegram from Sarah arrived just before noon, and he cheered up a bit, reminding himself that in the spring he would go to Europe and see her.[23]

Dawson was not so sad, however, that he would back away from an inflammatory news story, especially one that had to do with how the local government spent its money. The city had completed a reassessment on the day the earthquake hit, and their recommendations had gotten buried in the confusion. Now Dawson heard rumors that the assessor had been told to keep the new numbers a secret until it was too late for taxpayers to protest. He went down to City Hall and demanded to see the figures. In general, the assessed value of property seemed to have risen by an astronomical 20 to 25 percent, and in some cases the valuations had more than doubled. His own house and office fell into this category, which probably accounts, at least in part, for the vehemence of his response. Dawson printed a scathing article, and indignant citizens stormed City Hall demanding to see their tax bills.

"The long sought for cause of the earthquake has been found at last," he sniped on December 29. "It was the increase in the assessment of property in Charleston, which was completed on August 31. No wonder that every house in the city trembled and kicked, and that the very ground got up and bucked."[24]

Now, of course, many buildings were worth a good deal less than they had been on August 30. A group of prominent citizens suggested that the city should follow the state earthquake reassessment with a reassessment of its own. Dawson supported the idea. "There is no room for much argument on the subject," he wrote. "The people . . . cannot pay as much as they have paid hitherto and keep body and soul together." Therefore, it was "absolutely necessary . . . that the usual expenditures of the City Government shall be curtailed and put on an earthquake basis." Sounding exactly like the Upcountry journalists who had opposed the earthquake bill, Dawson advocated shrinking the police department, halting all work on the streets and parks, and reducing the salaries of city officers.[25]

Mayor Ashmead Courtenay, his old ally, was furious. "I am *mortified* at the articles in the *News and Courier* this morning," he scrawled in a note to Dawson. "The figures [were] *penciled* in [the] assessor's book. These are *not* figures for taxation and were never intended to be" (original emphasis). Courtenay was especially upset that Councilman Francis Rodgers had been criticized for trying to raise taxes, when in reality he was the one member of the ways and means committee who had argued for cutting them. "All these newspaper Bombs and Rockets are altogether unnecessary," Courtenay scolded. "Give a dog a bad name and he will carry it right along."[26]

Courtenay called a special meeting of the city council to try to repair the damage Dawson had caused. Francis Rodgers began the discussion by saying that the committee had already been planning to cut expenses. The figures Dawson quoted in the newspaper were tentative ones, never meant to be final. The ways and means committee had intended all along to let taxpayers deduct damages from the earthquake. In fact, they had unanimously decided that the total assessment should be capped at the minimum amount needed to run the city, and that individual tax bills should be revised to reflect this reduction.[27]

Nonetheless, Dawson claimed victory: "The City Council Steps Down." He lambasted the mayor's "tone," and accused him of displaying "bad taste" by suggesting that those who questioned the assessment had "unworthy motives." But all this, he said, was beside the point. "Expenses must come down. . . . Salaries must be cut. Improvements must stop. Rebuilding must be postponed." Dawson urged that all of Mayor Courtenay's pet projects be put on the chopping block — the new police station, the new city hospital, the new fire stations, the board of health, even routine repairs to the streets and parks. "This is no time for building new engine houses, or new anything else," he ranted. "So long as the present houses will not actually tumble down, and are water-tight, they will serve the purpose in this earthquake time."[28]

Ashmead Courtenay could not understand why his old ally would print such an inflammatory story without consulting him. The warm feelings embodied by the silver tea set flew out the window. Courtenay stopped his friendly visits to the News and Courier office, and he would never forgive Dawson or trust him again. Soon he would begin laying plans to break Dawson's hold on city politics.[29]

Far from being sorry for having started the flap, Dawson was elated. "We shall win," he wrote Sarah, "because I am determined to. I have not so had the old . . . joy of combat [in] many days."[30]

Chapter Fifteen

WRAPPED IN THE STARS AND STRIPES

A S THE NEW year of 1887 dawned, Frank had not seen his family in more than eight months. Sarah wrote that she was feeling better than she had since Ethel was born — but she was lying. On February 1, Dr. Amos Bellinger, the man who had killed Stephney Riley in 1885, showed Dawson a letter from Sarah confessing that she was seriously ill and asking him for help. On the advice of her Swiss doctor, she was drinking asses' milk, a remedy Dawson and Bellinger both regarded as worthless.

Frank left for Europe at the end of February. By March 7 he was in Lausanne, Switzerland, marveling at how his children had grown. The family visited Paris, Bologna, Verona, Lake Geneva, and Berne. At the end of April Frank left Sarah and the children in Lausanne, making Warrington and Ethel promise not to worry their mother "through temper or disobedience." On the way home he intended to stop in England to visit relatives, including his brother Joe, a Catholic priest. While he was waiting to cross the English Channel, a telegram arrived with the news that Sarah was gravely ill. Frank could not decide whether to rush to her side or continue as planned. Sarah urged him to carry on, and he did. In London he shopped for new clothes, from underwear to an overcoat.

When the ship sailed for New York, Frank was on it, though he later told Sarah that he had been "paralyzed" by worry and indecision. "I thought I could stand . . . anything but I know now that I can't," he wrote. "I know now, as never before, what you suffered during those horrible hours when you thought me dead" after the earthquake.

He arrived back in Charleston on May 5 to find a cheerful cable from Sarah, which said her health was improving.[1]

Sarah, Ethel, and Warrington finally returned home in August 1887, almost exactly a year after the earthquake, to the damp, enervating heat of a Charleston summer. With them came Marie Hélène Burdayron, a voluptuous young Swiss woman hired to watch the children. From the day she arrived, the Dawsons' new employee cultivated a double identity. Inside the household she was called Hélène; everywhere else, she introduced herself as Marie. Some people thought the young woman was a guest, others that she was a governess, depending on what she was doing and wearing when they saw her. Sometimes she dressed in a cap and apron that marked her as a servant, but not always. The children were enrolled in Mrs. Isabel Smith's school, and one of Hélène's duties was to escort them there every morning. She spoke French to the children and made a good salad, a skill foreign to most Charleston cooks. And as everybody but Sarah noticed, Hélène turned heads whenever she walked down the street. Hélène knew how to play on Sarah's need for attention, how to flatter and cajole her. It was soon apparent to the other servants that Hélène had a special hold over her mistress. Sarah installed her in a room adjoining the children's bedrooms.[2]

Frank was relieved to have his family back, yet perhaps he was also a bit sorry to give up the life of a work-obsessed bachelor. The mansion changed overnight from a second newspaper office into a lively home. Sarah soon hired a new set of servants: a cook named Celia Riels; a chambermaid, Jane Jackson; and a butler, Isaac Heyward, who doubled as a carriage driver.

Every morning Sarah and Frank ate breakfast together while Hélène took the children to school, either in the carriage or on foot. Then Sarah rode with Frank to work and drove herself home. Occasionally she stopped to shop. As Frank Dawson's wife, all she had to do was pull up outside a store and the clerks ran out with a selection of goods to choose from. Most days, Frank arrived on the streetcar for dinner at four. Around six, Sarah drove him back to the office, and between ten and eleven in the evening he would return home.[3]

Dawson adored his wife, but living with her could be trying. She had a weakness for astrologers and fortune-tellers and claimed that she had telepathic powers. Somewhere in the house on Bull Street, sewed into linen wrappings and hidden in a trunk, lay the journals Sarah had kept during the Civil War, when she was a teenager. With them was a scrapbook of the *News and Courier* essays on women's rights that she had written while being courted by Frank. Sarah had long since given up writing anything but letters. She was lonely, left to herself by Frank and the children for all but a few hours of every day. Frank was under so much pressure at work that they seldom invited people to dinner or hosted parties as they had just a few years before. Hélène Burdayron soon made herself indispensable. She was always there to soothe Sarah's nervous fits and shield her from the children.[4]

Ethel, now in her early teens, was unhappy at school, convinced that she didn't fit in with her Charleston classmates and that she could do nothing to win her teacher's praise. Eleven-year-old Warrington observed the dramas unfolding around him and dreamed of becoming a writer.[5]

Warrington studied his father constantly, trying to understand this near stranger and make sense of his contradictions. Frank, he would later confide to a biographer, could shift from blazing anger to bland courtesy in the blink of an eye. Once, not long after their return from Europe, he watched as his mother and father came down to dinner, descending the narrow, curving stairway arm in arm. The carpet had just been taken up for cleaning, and Frank lost his balance. He tried to grab the banister, but it was no use — as Warrington later remembered, Frank and Sarah "cannoned" to the bottom, bumping along on their backs. Frank jumped up, checked to make sure that Sarah was not "dead or crippled for life," and then turned back to the stairway. He raised his arm and cursed each step individually, from the first at the bottom of the flight to the twenty-second at the top. Then he started down again, shouting profanities at each step. As soon as he reached the last stair, Frank recovered his self-control. "Well!" he said in a gentle voice. "Now we'll go in and have dinner!"[6]

After almost a year and a half of separation, during which Sarah and the children never stayed in one place long enough to accumulate many friends, possessions, or pets, the reunited Dawsons started rebuilding their domestic life. Frank's new secretary presented the family with a Newfoundland puppy, and the children named him Bruno in honor of a famous St. Bernard whose stuffed head they had seen in Switzerland. Bruno was crazy about Dawson and kept watch for him at the gate every night. He recognized his master's step and pressed his body against the ironwork until Frank appeared.[7]

The Charleston that Sarah and the children returned to was very different from the city they had left in the spring of 1886. The *New York Times* reported that a year after the earthquake the walls were still "cracked and tumbling, streets torn, monuments scarred and broken."[7] Frank was different, too — unwilling to compromise, impatient with the needs of others, and far less likely than he had been to give people in the lower ranks of society the benefit of the doubt. Living in the aftermath of disaster had hardened his heart.

The aftershocks had finally subsided, and most people acknowledged that perhaps the world would not soon end. A reporter noted that "no white religious meetings were held" to mark the first anniversary. But a black couple in Summerville had predicted in March that another earthquake would strike the area on August 31, 1887. Fifty black men and women performed a passion play based on the Oberammergau, a Bavarian tradition that originated as a gesture of gratitude after a plague ended in 1633. The Summervilleans hoped the ritual would prevent a recurrence of the shock.[9]

In the year since the earthquake, between five thousand and six thousand buildings had been restored, and 271 new homes and businesses had been built. Even the long-delayed plastering jobs were mostly completed. Debris from the earthquake had been hauled to low-lying areas, so that dozens of "water lots" along the Ashley River had been converted into dry land. Despite what everyone had observed after the earthquake about the vulnerability of houses that sat on made ground, contractors eagerly set to work building on this fresh slice of urban real estate. The new City Hospital rose on reclaimed marshland along the banks of the Ashley, and no one pointed out that if another large earthquake hit, this location would be just as treacherous as the unstable filled creek beds that had torn apart the old hospitals, the jail, and the medical college. In the rush to rebuild, the most obvious lessons of the disaster were ignored.[10]

John C. Calhoun now towered over Marion Square, Charleston's answer to the Statue of Liberty, which had just been dedicated in New York Harbor. On April 26, 1887, while Dawson was in Europe visiting his family, Calhoun's enormous glaring head had been ceremoniously uncovered by a team of thirty-two young women and six "baby unveilers," most of whom were direct descendents of John C. Calhoun. At forty-eight feet high, the monument could be seen for several blocks. The celebration drew thousands of spectators and included a lavish parade. The base of the monument was meant to include four allegorical figures, representing Truth, Justice, the Constitution, and History, but so far only one had been completed and installed, a woman clad in a diaphanous toga who seemed to kneel at Calhoun's feet. Not long after the dedication ceremony, an old black man nicknamed the monument "Calhoun and 'e wife." To the dismay of worshipful whites, the name stuck. Teenagers lobbed rocks and brickbats at the figure of Calhoun, trying to knock off his nose.[11]

In spite of Dawson's tirades against spending city money and the city council's pledge to hold down expenses, electric lights had been installed at

Marion and Washington squares, and the trampled lawns and flower beds in the parks had been replanted. The medical college had been rebuilt to modern specifications, with steam heat, a ventilator, a large amphitheater, a museum, a dissecting room, and even an elevator for moving cadavers to the upper stories. The Guard House at Meeting and Broad streets was slated for demolition, to be replaced by a modern post office paid for by the federal government. A restaurant and barber shop had been built on the former earthquake campground at Robb's Lot. Most of the historic churches had been sufficiently repaired for services to have moved back into their sanctuaries. The city had removed one of the most brutal and egregious symbols of slavery, the Workhouse, where slaves were once whipped and yoked like mules to walk endless circles on a treadmill, an instrument of torture also used to grind corn.[12]

The heart of the city was shifting north near the Calhoun Monument, and in the spring of 1888 the *News and Courier* opened an "uptown office" there. A new Central Police Station went up at the edge of Marion Square, in a castellated style designed to match its next-door neighbor, the Citadel. The station included dorm rooms for more than 250 men, along with modern bathrooms. While they were at it, the city fathers invested in a new fire alarm and a police telegraph service.[13]

But the disaster that had necessitated all this rebuilding was still fresh enough in most people's minds that anything out of the ordinary was still blamed on the earthquake. A fox that attacked a pack of dogs was christened the "earthquake fox." When domestic hens laid extra eggs or wild huckleberry bushes produced a bumper crop, or rattlesnakes grew scarce, or a herd of milk cows ran dry, the aberrations were attributed to the earthquake.[14]

To publicize the city's recovery, Dawson proposed a "monster excursion" to lure tourists from all over the region. The event would give local businesses a boost and would show, as he had been insisting since the night of the quake, that Charleston was "back at the old stand." City merchants loved the idea. As Captain F. W. Wagener put it, "Every visitor that comes to Charleston is as valuable to the city's trade as a bale of cotton." Soon the event acquired a name —"Gala Week"— and a date, the first week of November 1887.[15]

The merchants exchange and the city council invited President and Mrs. Cleveland to attend, overruling the objections of the contentious alderman A. W. Eckel, who pointed out that Cleveland had done nothing to help the city recover from the earthquake. But the president was much in demand. Atlanta's Piedmont Exposition was also set to open that fall, and in early August Henry Grady hand-delivered an invitation to the Clevelands. Engraved on a gold tablet, it was sandwiched between portraits of the president and Mrs. Cleveland inside a book covered in leaves of Georgia gold, bound with clasps of Georgia silver, set with Georgia diamonds, and enclosed in a mosaic box made of sixty-eight types of Georgia wood embedded in a slab of Georgia marble. Charleston printed its invitation on paper. Needless to say, Cleveland said yes to Atlanta and no to Charleston. Grady had upstaged Dawson once again.[16]

The city was undaunted by the snub. There were soon large, energetic Gala Week committees on yacht racing, decorations, horse and donkey racing, "illuminations," music, baseball, "glass ball shooting," "pyrotechnics," and "aquatic sports." Plans were made for a "trades display" to showcase local businesses, and for a "fantastic parade" whose nature was left vague. It was all a lighthearted mirror image of the deadly serious relief bureaucracy of the past year. Frank Dawson emphasized that young men should take the lead, yet he agreed to serve as vice president of the Gala Week Committee.[17]

The plans grew more ambitious with every day that passed. The railroads were asked to offer special rates of one cent a mile, just as they had after the earthquake when people were fleeing the city. Those who lived in houses on South Battery and East Bay Street were more or less ordered to illuminate them for the week using candles, lanterns, gas lamps, or electric bulbs. An electrical circuit was installed around Colonial Lake. Eleven new arc lights brightened the South Carolina Railway Station, and incoming trains were supplied with twice the usual number of coaches. Before each train arrived at the station on the northern edge of the city, the railroads telegraphed the streetcar lines with the number of passengers, so that enough cars were always waiting to whisk visitors downtown. A special tourist guidebook was issued. Hotels and boardinghouses advertised discount rates, and cots filled the second floor of the Academy of Music. Restaurant windows displayed pyramids of oysters, haunches of venison, doves, porgy, pompano, and shrimp. Huge cargoes of bananas and coconuts were unloaded at the wharves.[18]

The event took on a patriotic flavor, part of Dawson's plan to attract national attention. The bells of St. Michael's Church were rung, playing such patriotic (and unsouthern) airs as "Yankee Doodle," "The Star-Spangled Banner," and "Hail, Columbia." From the Battery to Marion Square, U.S. flags draped every building. "The Cradle of Secession," Dawson crowed, was "Wrapped in the Stars and Stripes."[19]

No matter how many years had passed since the war or how much money northerners had donated for earthquake relief, most white Charlestonians still regarded the U.S. flag as a galling symbol of defeat and occupation. Blacks celebrated Independence Day on July 4, while whites ignored it and went all out for Confederate Memorial Day on May 10, established to honor those who died defending the "Lost Cause." Southern businessmen like Dawson, however, hoped that waving the Stars and Stripes would pay major dividends in northern investment, so the News and Courier almost demanded the display of the once-hated flag. As Gala Week approached, all of Charleston seemed to contract patriotic fever.[20]

Fifty thousand U.S. flags were sold in less than a week. "Everything on two wheels, four wheels, and one wheel was decorated with flags, and even the pedestrians wore flags in their overcoats," reported the News and Courier. Steamers waiting in port were swathed in bunting. It became "quite the thing" for ladies to wear a miniature flag pinned on one shoulder. Shoe stores tucked tiny flags into every slipper and boot. Even the pies and cakes in bakeries sported Old Glory. As Dawson put it, "Charleston means to emphasize the fact that she is in the Union and in the Union to stay." Some businesses tried for an international look. The Charleston Tea Pot, a King Street emporium that specialized in fancy groceries and high-quality teas, flew the Chinese and Japanese colors. On King Street between Society and Calhoun, where many recent immigrants operated shops, German, Irish, and French flags flew.[21]

Only one flag was off-limits — the Confederate. A small example of the Stars and Bars, the first flag of the Confederacy, "full of bullet holes, as well as moth holes," was exhibited on King Street. "The display of this one relic of the old Confederacy among fifty thousand national flags is not intended as any disrespect to the flag of our common country," Dawson announced, with an eye toward northern readers. "Charleston is loyal — how could she be otherwise, after the help which the people of the North sent her in her hour of distress?" Jefferson Davis, president of the defeated Confederacy, was then making a tour of the South. He was pointedly not asked to come to Charleston, and the New York Times approved: "A Celebration in the South at which Jeff Davis Has Not Been Invited to Appear" read the headline.[22]

However, people found indirect ways to declare their loyalties. Witcofsky's grocery proudly displayed the "large gilded rooster" that had been carried in Wade Hampton's victory parade in 1876 when he was elected governor. A banner at King and Society streets, near the German Rifle Club Hall, home to one of the white militias, featured "the closing scene of a cockfight," showing one of the combatants lying on the ground with its legs in the air. The winner was described by the *News and Courier* as a "Democratic game chicken, indulging in the usual crow which began in 1884," the year of Grover Cleveland's victory. Outsiders might take this as a depiction of the unofficial state sport, but any South Carolinian would have understood the political message. The vanquished rooster represented black power, while the winner stood for Wade Hampton's Redshirts, the men who restored white supremacy.[23]

The first day of Gala Week, Monday, October 31, 1887, dawned cold and misty. Homeowners and shopkeepers were out early, struggling to put up flags, bunting, garlands, arches of evergreen, flowers, and streamers. Japanese paper lanterns sold almost as fast as flags, to be hung on everything from boats and buggies to stores and houses. Dawson was kept busy meeting dignitaries at the train station and escorting them to their hotels.[24]

The opening ceremony took place on the banks of Colonial Lake, where a bandstand had been erected. That afternoon, "day fireworks" floated out over the water — balloonlike paper contraptions in the shape of various animals, pushed aloft by hot air generated by candles. Many of them turned out to be defective, and the first event of Gala Week got off to a sputtering start. One paper elephant lurched away toward James Island. Another caught fire and flamed out near Broad Street. A fish plunged into the water amid a cloud of smoke. Boats hung with hundreds of Chinese lanterns paraded around the lake while their occupants shot off fireworks.

That night the whole city was alight, "from the Ashley to the Cooper [rivers] and from the suburbs to White Point Garden." The glare made the familiar streets seem strange and surreal. A street vendor who sold fish and shrimp told a reporter he couldn't believe that he was standing in downtown Charleston. Even the shrimp had "lanterns een dey eyes an' flag on dey tail." The climax of the evening was a reenactment of the Battle of Fort Sumter, with two "monitors" bombarding a model of the fort with Roman candles, flaming projectiles, and eggs.

Swinton Baynard, Dawson's cashier, took charge of decorating the *News and Courier* office. He swathed the front in red, white, and blue cambric, lit by a row of "twenty-five pendant, pear-shaped electric lights, swinging immediately over the sign board." Chinese colored lanterns hung in every window, and a mammoth U.S. flag completed the picture. Unable to resist giving itself a plug, the paper reported that "there was not in all the city a more tasteful and striking illumination."[25]

Gala Week was at heart an advertising campaign, aimed at luring potential customers to the recovered city. To promote his line of flour, one store owner offered free pancakes to "ladies and housekeepers"—though not to "loafers and idlers." Another establishment ran a "baking school for the ladies" designed to sell Fleischmann's yeast.[26]

The Trades Display parade Tuesday night was a rolling commercial for Charleston business. It formed under a full moon at Marion Square, where the Citadel was lighted like a fairy-tale castle. John C. Calhoun towered over the unruly throng, his stern "bronze features . . . clearly outlined in the magnificent illumination." There were, in all, eleven bands, 171 floats, and six hundred horses and mules. Many businesses spent small fortunes to construct their magnificent displays. Walker, Evans, and Cogswell, the city's largest purveyor of printed materials and office supplies, created a float in the shape of a book, crowned with a "monster bottle" of ink and two gold pens, "large enough for a Brobdingnagian." The Charleston Tea Pot fashioned a huge replica of its famous teapot sign, with real steam billowing from the spout. A sausage maker displayed stuffed pigs and raw haunches of beef. A cigar factory put the proprietor's children on a wagon stripping tobacco and shaping it into cigars. A blacksmith shop on wheels featured smiths pounding iron beside red-hot forges. A "realistic steam locomotive" was tugged along by a hundred employees of the South Carolina Railway. One float carried a cottage "built entirely of South Carolina grain." Merchants threw sweets into the crowd and passed out apples and bananas. Workers on the Von Santen's float gave away ice cream. The Palmetto Brewery provided free samples of beer. "Showers of . . . stars" lit up the night as the crowd shot Roman candles at the distinguished guests and the highly inflammable floats. As Dawson's carriage passed in front of the News and Courier office, it was pelted with "balls of flame." A reporter nervously noted that the nearby float for a gunpowder factory was loaded with stacks of powder cans — empty, he hoped.[27]

"The People Went Wild" ran a cheerful headline in the News and Courier the next day. "Verily it was an earthquake on wheels, with all Charleston as an audience." The very word "earthquake," once so terrifying, was transformed into a synonym for fun and games. A rowing match in the harbor was won by Mayor Courtenay's wayward son Campbell. Three baseball games featured two major league teams, the Chicago Giants and the St. Louis Browns, with more than four thousand people in attendance at the ballpark where just a year before P. T. Barnum's elephants had pranced. Each night a different opera was performed at the Academy of Music.[28]

Word had spread across the state that Charleston was the place to be. By midweek the city was so crowded that hotels put people to bed on top of billiards tables. A headquarters was set up to find lodging for latecomers, with an attendant who consulted a list of private homes willing to take in paying guests. Dawson announced that anyone who failed to find a bed should simply knock on the nearest door and "there would be a place there for him to sleep." Surely Sarah Dawson would not have greeted an unannounced stranger so warmly.[29]

When the weather cleared on Wednesday, the executive committee begged the schools to let their students out early for a balloon launch at Washington Square, the spot once used as a refugee camp. Finally, officials agreed. The "inflation" began around nine that morning, when an oilskin hose was run from a gas main. Slowly the pile of fabric began to lift, until at last it tugged against fifty sandbags attached to the balloon by ropes. The owner, gray-bearded Professor King, studied the wind vane atop St. Michael's. At a little after two, when the balloon stood high and taut, the hose was detached. Professor King climbed into the basket, stroked his beard, and asked if anyone would like to go up with him. No one said a word. A little boy shouted, "Good-bye, old gentleman!" and King tossed out several sandbags. As he rose into the air, thousands of voices shouted "God Speed!" The balloon sailed toward the Battery and landed safely across the harbor on James Island.[30]

For most of the week, the celebration was dignified, but the atmosphere turned boisterous with the Fantastic Parade on Wednesday. Defying a city ordinance that prohibited cross-dressing, men in drag (called "homemade women") roamed the streets, flaunting gargantuan false breasts and buttocks. The Carolina Rifles and the Sumter Guards wore "red and white Mother Hubbards and bonnets" while the German Fusiliers donned chintz gowns. Students from the medical college put on fancy dresses and drove carriages topped by skeletons posed atop a coffin. Employees of the Wando

Phosphate Company sported burlap-bag dresses. The Pinkusohn Brothers' tobacco factory deployed a squad of men in skirts to hand out samples of their newest product, Calhoun Monument–brand cigars. A group of young men riding a grocery cart sang minstrel songs loudly and off-key. White men played at being black and female, trying on roles that were forbidden in daily life. This drunken procession, said the *News and Courier,* was like a "dress parade of all the baboons in the forests of Ceylon." The event turned into a bacchanal, an uninhibited parody of the dignified Trades Display the day before. "Doubtless some of the old fashioned saints in the churchyards hereabout will turn over in their coffins," smirked the *New York Times.* And yet it was probably the best loved of all the Gala Week festivities.[31]

As the cavalcade passed the bend of King Street, a ball of fire from a Roman candle ignited a huge flag-draped arch, and at least a dozen U.S. flags went up in flames. A black man scurried up a ladder and quickly put them out. At the firm of F. W. Wagener and Company on East Bay, an elaborate display of lanterns and draperies caught fire, and the building was "wrapped in flame." The fire department was able to extinguish the blaze quickly.

According to Dawson, Gala Week marked the beginning of a new era in Charleston, one in which "war, pestilence, cyclone, fire, war and earthquake" would "have no place except as memories." But the gap between Dawson's pronouncements and reality began to seem like a chasm. The hallowed bones of the dead had been turned into props for drunken medical students. In the hands of a new generation, chivalry was dead, sexual repression was giving way to libertine behavior, slavery had been replaced by a doctrine of racial inferiority, and white women, once protected and idealized, were rudely caricatured. The city had rejoined the national mainstream, but not in the way Dawson had hoped.[32]

Chapter Sixteen

FAULT LINES

AS THE PATRIOTIC glow of Gala Week died away, Dawson's star reporter, Carlyle McKinley, began writing a book about America's problem with race, one that reflected the growing aggression of white attitudes. McKinley complained that every year the authorities assured people that "*now* the Union is certainly restored, and sectionalism is no more" (original emphasis). He was tired of hearing the old line that there was "no North, no South," which Dawson had repeated over and over as donations rolled in after the earthquake. Each new assertion, McKinley said, showed "how little of truth there was in the last." The North and the South would never be reunited while there were black people in the United States — any black people — of that he was certain.[1]

In a manuscript that would later be published as a book, McKinley proposed a "radical solution." The nation should pay to deport every black woman of childbearing age to Africa, and to equip each with a cabin and household furniture. He was sure that most of them would be glad to accept this offer. Though the eventual cost might reach a million dollars, he predicted that by the year 2000 not a single black person would remain in the United States. Bizarre and repulsive as McKinley's manifesto seems today, it reflects the drastic changes that had been sweeping South Carolina and the country since the earthquake. Whites were determined to turn back the clock on racial progress.[2]

About the time Dawson left for Europe in early 1887, a former member of the Knights of Labor, Hiram Hoover, began organizing farm workers in the South Carolina upstate. His goal was not to unionize or strike, but simply to form cooperative stores that would help sharecroppers and tenant farmers avoid paying their white landlords extortionate prices for supplies. The groups, nicknamed Hoover Clubs, often met in secret, fueling white fears that something subversive must be afoot. Blacks were said to be making plans to "take possession of the State as their rightful inheritance."

Rumors spread that they planned to "exterminate" elderly whites, enslave young white men, and "take young [white] women for their wives." These rumors, of course, reflected a terror of slave revolts that persisted long after emancipation and a heritage of racist stereotypes that cast all assertive black males as bloodthirsty predators bent on raping white women. Bands of armed white men rounded up black farm workers and interrogated them at gunpoint. The terrified captives insisted that they were only interested in lower prices and higher wages.[3]

Around the same time, black ministers, doctors, and educators began to protest the growing tendency to segregate public transportation. And just as he had after the earthquake, Rev. William Henry Heard led the way. In January 1887 Heard and two colleagues bought first-class railway tickets to Charleston from Cincinnati. All went well until the train pulled into Atlanta, where the brakeman told the three to move to a crowded, smoky, smelly car reserved for blacks. A boisterous gang of railroad hands got on, and at every stop more rowdy people crammed in, along with their chickens and dogs.[4]

As soon as he got home, Heard filed suit with the newly established Interstate Commerce Commission. The Georgia Railroad Company, he said, had accepted his first-class fare and then forced him to ride in a "Jim Crow" car. The railroad countered that there was no such thing as a Jim Crow car, though it admitted that it maintained separate cars for blacks. The cars for blacks and whites, according to the railroad, were exactly alike, with identical amenities like upholstered seats, iced water for drinking, and clean floors.

In his challenge to the Georgia Railroad, Heard was almost certainly inspired by a similar lawsuit filed by journalist Ida B. Wells, and by Booker T. Washington's effort in 1885 to organize protests against discriminatory treatment. Wells won her case plus $500 damages, but her victory was short lived — the railroad appealed and the verdict was overturned. She filed another discrimination suit later the same year, and again she won but lost on appeal. Wells was mocked and belittled by the white press, and the railroad launched a smear campaign to destroy her reputation.[5]

Heard's legal action triggered similar attacks. The *New York Times* dismissed the minister as "an indignant . . . short-legged, pigeon-toed, colored man of ginger-bread hue." The *Atlanta Constitution* charged that he had been an "offensive politician" during Reconstruction. But because of their

many encounters after the earthquake, Frank Dawson had learned to respect and admire Heard, who was articulate, tastefully dressed, and well
mannered. The *Times'* description fit Heard no more than it would have fit
Dawson himself. Taking Heard's side of the question, as most of the *News
and Courier's* readers would not, Dawson suggested in his newspaper that
the Georgia Railroad switch the cars for a week, so that white passengers
would have to ride in the cars once assigned to blacks. Then they would not
be so ready to believe that the amenities were identical.[6]

Soon another black man, William S. Councill, the president of the Alabama Agricultural and Mechanical College, filed a complaint against the
Western and Atlantic Railroad. While Heard had simply been ordered to
move, Councill was brutally assaulted. In court, an employee of the railroad
readily confessed: "I grabbed him by the collar and struck him over the
head with [a] lantern, . . . knocked him out of his seat and pulled him out of
the car." When Councill tried to get up, "I let him have it again with the lantern. I hit him several times before I conquered him, and then rushed him
right . . . to the darkies' car. He was willing to go by the time I got through
with him." The railroad was adamant: it had the legal right to enforce segregation. Like Heard, Councill charged that the railroad had not given him
what he had paid for.[7]

To the shock of his readers, Dawson, staunch capitalist that he was,
agreed with Heard and Councill. "Equal accommodation for equal payment is all that is required," he concluded, articulating the philosophy — if
not the practice — that would soon dominate southern race relations. In
doing so, he challenged the official white view of the case and, just as he
had done in 1876, risked the wrath of his subscribers and advertisers. In
Alabama, Booker T. Washington was making the same argument — equal
accommodation for equal payment was only fair, and did not amount to the
"social equality" dreaded by whites.[8]

In May 1887 the Interstate Commerce Commission agreed with Dawson.
It ruled that the duty of the railroad was "to furnish to passengers paying the
same fare equal accommodations and protection without discrimination on
account of color." The Georgia Railroad was ordered to "cease and desist
from subjecting colored passengers to undue and unreasonable prejudice
and disadvantage." Heard had won his battle, as would Councill, but the rul-
ings moved the U.S. government one step closer to endorsing segregation
— the railroads retained the right to separate passengers by race.[9]

In South Carolina even the churches were writing new rules meant to keep blacks in submission. In Charleston, lay delegates "seceded" from the Episcopal diocese when a group of clergymen pushed to seat a black minister at their annual convention. One man fumed in his diary, "The sooner we are rid of a nigger-loving bishop the better." After a bitter struggle that alienated church members on both sides of the racial divide, the Episcopalians demoted black congregations to "missionary" status, making them wards of the church instead of equal partners. The black minister was grudgingly admitted as a representative for these congregations, but as a northern newspaper observed, "The one black Christian will probably be furnished with a seat close to the door — possibly there will be a wire cage built around him — and the White Christians will get as far away from him as they can, and console themselves with the reflection that no more niggers can get in."[10]

The state legislature joined in by debating a series of bills that would reduce blacks, especially farmworkers, to a condition resembling slavery. The News and Courier was filled with stories about groups of black agricultural laborers leaving South Carolina to settle in the western states, South America, and Africa. Some would-be emigrants were so eager to depart that they sold their farms at a loss and left cane and cotton unharvested in the fields.[11]

Carlyle McKinley was telling the truth when he wrote that many blacks would gladly leave the United States if only they had the means. It was not just their livelihoods that were in jeopardy — it was their very lives. In 1886, for the first time since records had been kept, more blacks than whites were victims of lynching, a record that surpassed even the bloody deeds of 1876. The right to lynch lawbreakers, especially blacks accused of "the usual crime"— raping or attempting to rape white women — was widely regarded as God-given. In South Carolina, lynchers might occasionally be arrested, but they were never convicted, much less punished. Just as Dawson had flouted South Carolina's sacred traditions by calling for legislation to ban dueling and concealed weapons, he would now argue that the state should treat lynching like any other murder.[12]

On the day after Christmas 1887 fate offered him an unusual opportunity to make this point. Near the town of Pickens, in the South Carolina upstate, a white man named Manse Waldrop brutally raped a fourteen-year-old black girl, Lula Sherman, who died two days later of her injuries. Her father, four other black men, and one white man abducted Waldrop as he was being transported to jail and killed him by the side of the road. It was, as historian Bruce E. Baker points out, "an anomaly in the history of lynching," one of only four known incidents in this period where black men lynched a white man. The "Pickens lynchers" became a cause célèbre far from the scene of the crime. In Charleston, Rev. William Heard and his fellow activists demanded "a full and thorough investigation in this case." Using language very similar to Dawson's words about the Matilda McKnight murder case in 1885, they declared, "The civilization of the age demands it; the peace and good will of both races call for it." Heard's committee sent a letter to every black minister in South Carolina, calling for donations to defend the prisoners.[13]

The case raised a question most whites did not want to confront: was lynching justified if it meant that blacks could kill whites? Many were willing to let these black killers go, rather than risk undermining the traditional tolerance for white lynchers. Frank Dawson abhorred South Carolina's eagerness to resort to vigilante justice, and he knew that, because all but one of the aggressors in this case were black, it might be possible for the courts to convict a lyncher and set a legal precedent. As he saw it, whether Manse Waldrop was guilty of rape or not, he had been murdered, and the question was how his murderers should be punished. Dawson was taking a courageous stand, one that would antagonize most South Carolinians, white and black. The case would come back to haunt his memory.[14]

BY THE END of 1887, things looked so bleak for South Carolina blacks that even Rev. William Heard, who had led so many fights for equal rights, had more or less given up hope. Blacks living anywhere in the United States might as well be slaves, he now said. They would never get a fair shake in the country that had once held them in bondage. One lesson Heard had learned from the aftermath of the earthquake was that life improved dramatically for black people when there were fewer workers than jobs. If a large number of laborers left an area, the ones who stayed could command higher wages. "The whites will not go," he preached, "for they have the advantage; therefore let the colored people go anywhere to better their condition." Now that earthquake repairs were mostly finished, there were "two thousand too many laborers" in the city of Charleston alone. Black emigration made sense.[15]

Although Heard was frustrated, he hadn't given up. Along with Crum,

Dart, and Rowe, all of whom had cut their political teeth on earthquake protests, he was trying to organize black voters to chip away at white control of the city government, and the numbers were in his favor. If just a handful of white voters defected to the Republicans or to an independent slate (and if the elections were not rigged), the Republicans might be able to win at least one seat on the city council. When the city held local elections in December 1887, Dr. Crum ran for alderman in ward 8, while Rowe and Dart ran for seats on the school commission.[16]

The mayor's office was also up for grabs. Mayor Courtenay had refused to run for a third term, despite cries that the city could not do without him. Regardless of his differences with the mayor, Dawson knew that Courtenay's shoes would be hard to fill. Many men were suggested as candidates for mayor, but most declined to run. By the time Gala Week was over, three candidates remained: Aldermen Edward F. Sweegan and A. W. Eckel, both of whom were antagonistic to Dawson, and Captain George D. Bryan, an attorney who served as corporate counsel to the city. The race would be a test of Dawson's power to dictate city politics.[17]

A year before, Dawson's authority was unchallenged. In the fall of 1886, Dawson and the Democratic candidates he supported had won the general election so easily that the editor called the result "A Democratic Walk-Over." However, northern newspapers charged that the Democrats had stolen the election. Republicans in the so-called black district reported that they had been threatened and intimidated if they dared try to vote. The district included four times as many potential black voters as white, yet white Democrat William Elliott was declared the winner over black Republican Robert Smalls, the incumbent, by five hundred votes. He had been one of only two black congressmen still serving after the end of Reconstruction, and the other, James E. O'Hara of North Carolina, also lost the election. Smalls filed an official challenge, but without any black legislators left in power there was no one to take up his cause.[18]

SWEEGAN AND ECKEL ran for mayor mostly on their opposition to a new business-license law, which required anyone who ran a retail operation in Charleston to pay an annual fee. More than sixty protesters sued the city, arguing that the charges were unfair and illegal. Among them were jeweler John McElree, two druggists, a basket manufacturer, and a man who sold crockery. Most were small businessmen who felt they were being squeezed while men who made big money, like shippers, bankers, and manufacturers, got a free ride.[19]

Bryan defended the licenses as an appropriate way to raise money to run the city, certainly preferable to higher property taxes. "If you repeal the license law you must put a tax on the thousands of homesteads that the people of this country sent money here to rebuild," he warned at a political meeting. Dawson praised Bryan in the *News and Courier* and suggested that the other candidates were untrustworthy. Sweegan and Eckel dropped out before the election, leaving Bryan the only Democratic candidate for mayor.[20]

Dawson announced that the new slate of candidates would run on the record of the past eight years, emphasizing "the power and efficiency of the Democratic government" during the aftermath of the earthquake. Courtenay was nominated for school commissioner in ward 3. Conspicuously absent from the list was the name of William E. Huger, the man who had presided over the postearthquake chaos as acting mayor. Dawson and his political allies, who had lost confidence in Huger, had quietly arranged to support someone else for alderman of the first ward. No one who opposed the license law had been allowed a slot, and even hard-core Democrats grumbled about the "one-sidedness" of this ticket.[21]

In contrast, the newly formed United Labor Party, headed by Knights of Labor official W. P. Russell, took the remarkable step of joining with the Republicans to endorse a ticket that included both white and black men, including Dr. William Crum, Rev. George Rowe, and Rev. John Dart. Dawson scoffed at what the *News and Courier* derisively called a "mermaid party," made up of elements as wildly mismatched as a human with a fish's tail. In the lower wards of Charleston, where well-to-do whites formed a majority, there was not much prospect of victory. But in the upper wards, north of Marion Square, blacks and working-class whites could realistically hope to win.[22] The black vote had not been suppressed inside the city, and in the upper wards whites were outnumbered.

The biggest shock came when the full United Labor ticket was announced. For alderman in ward 1, the "mermaid party" nominated former acting mayor William E. Huger, who had been snubbed by Dawson's Democrats. In ward 2, they listed blue-blooded J. Adger Smyth, and for school commissioner, in addition to Rowe and Dart, they endorsed Mayor William Ashmead Courtenay. Dawson knew he couldn't dismiss this ticket out of hand. Instead, he claimed that many of the candidates listed on this "bolters and revolters" slate had been drafted without their consent, and that they were actually "loyal supporters of the Democratic ticket." Huger, he insisted, was not really a candidate. But when the polls opened on December 13, Huger's name remained on the ballot, and in the morning he seemed to be winning ward 1 as a large number of black voters turned out to vote for him. In ward 8, the northernmost ward, black Republicans came out in force for Crum and Rowe.[23]

Yet when the votes were counted, the *News and Courier* announced that Crum, Rowe, and Huger had lost to Democratic candidates. Suspicious as the results seemed, there was no way for the losing candidates to contest them. The United Labor Party had earlier demanded that one of their representatives be allowed to observe the final count and threatened to "blow up the managers of the Election with dynamite" if they were denied. Their request was firmly refused. Frank Dawson had won again.[24]

AFTER THE 1887 elections, those in Charleston who hoped to topple the newspaper editor must have sensed blood in the water. Just three months later, his enemies, led by Courtenay, launched a rival newspaper, the *Charleston World*. The president of the new newspaper company was former city councilman Francis Rodgers, who felt that Dawson had smeared his reputation during the postearthquake property-tax flap, and one of the principal investors was William E. Huger.[25]

Several Charleston businesses tried to buy large blocks of advertising space in the *News and Courier*, announcing the publication of this new paper. Dawson refused to run the ads but couldn't prevent the news from spreading by word of mouth. The price of the *World* was just three cents an issue, undercutting the *News and Courier*'s nickel price tag, and on its very first day, the *World* sold 6,400 copies. It soon started referring to itself as "The People's Paper."[26]

From the beginning it was clear that the *World*'s overriding mission was to bring down Dawson. In a typical taunt, it charged that the *News and Courier* "shields the criminal" and "hushes up crimes." The *World* took credit — and probably deserved it — for pushing Dawson to print more illustrations and for goading him to install telegraph lines inside the newspaper office instead of sending a man to the telegraph office down the street to pick up incoming wires.[27]

Over the years Dawson had experimented with many tactics to build circulation and advertising, from starting a lost-and-found section to publishing on Sundays, an innovation that drew fire for violating the Sabbath. Now he mounted a circulation drive headlined by a raffle that offered fabulous prizes for new subscribers, including a grand piano. More importantly, the *News and Courier* started running engravings, cartoons, human-interest stories, and other popular features that Dawson had once scorned as vulgar. A newspaper war was under way, and Dawson's power was at stake.[28]

The *World's* first scoop came in early March, when it broke a grisly story about people who dug up corpses in Potter's Field and used them to file false claims for life insurance. The first case — and the most notorious — was that of Mary Dudley, who took out a policy on her husband Joseph from the grand-sounding Royal Templars of Temperance, a company that only insured teetotallers. No one who knew Mrs. Dudley in Charleston had ever seen her husband. Then one day she appeared in tears and told a neighbor that he had come home but had fallen down the stairs and hit his head. Now he was dead. And what a pity, she said — after being estranged for years, they were just getting back together. She invited the neighbor in to see his body laid out in the parlor. The woman later testified that the odor of the corpse "was very offensive." But a doctor signed the death certificate, and the insurance company paid the widow $2,000.[29]

Eventually the insurance companies grew suspicious and brought in a team of Pinkerton men to investigate. No less than fifteen "fraudulent funerals" were discovered, and several local doctors were charged with signing spurious death certificates. The *News and Courier* was not far behind in reporting the "Corpse Trust" story, but on March 8 the *World* gloated that its superiority was now "beyond question." "We showed [the *News and Courier*] how to run a first-class, live newspaper, a thing of which they were profoundly ignorant until after our advent here." The "grave-yard robbers" eventually pled guilty, but the investigation was far from over, and detectives continued watching other suspects who were thought to have played a part. Among them was Dawson's new neighbor, Dr. Thomas B. McDow.[30]

McDow, his wife Katie, and their six-year-old daughter Gladys had just moved to 75 Rutledge Street, around the corner from the Dawsons' house and in sight of their back porch. But Frank and Sarah gave them a wide berth. The McDows were not people they chose to acknowledge. Katie McDow's father was a wealthy wholesale grocer, but she was chubby and disheveled, not the kind of wife a man would choose to show off socially.

DAWSON WORRIED about the *Charleston World* and what it might do to his business, but he had weathered such challenges before. He was more concerned with bigger issues, like how to pump up Charleston's faltering economy. It was a topic that he and many other city leaders had tried to address for years, without much success. The city had never developed enough profitable new enterprises to replace the plantation economy after the Civil War. Textile manufacturing was mostly an upstate industry; phosphate mining had once seemed like the answer to the city's prayers, but now the rock was being harvested more cheaply in Florida. Big ships had a hard time maneuvering through the shallow channels to Charleston's docks, so the port had lost much of its traditional business to cities with deeper harbors.

For several years Dawson had been watching Henry Flagler, one of the richest men in the world, who had made a fortune in the oil industry and used it to develop railroads and tourist hotels. Flagler's Ponce de Leon Hotel, which opened in St. Augustine, Florida, in January 1888, had cost $2.5 million to build, a huge sum to spend in a tiny city with no major attractions but the ocean, yet it was already becoming known as the most elegant resort in the country.[31]

Dawson reasoned that if Florida could lure swarms of tourists, then surely Charleston, with its many historic and natural charms, could entice those same people to stop on their way south. But the city's main accommodation, the Charleston Hotel, was almost fifty years old, and Dawson knew that affluent visitors wanted more opulence, more service, and better views than the venerable structure in the heart of downtown could offer. With the triumph of the great "earthquake carnival" behind him, he called on Charleston businessmen to build a new hotel. On May 31, 1888, the movers and shakers met at the German Artillery Hall. The atmosphere was electric, evangelistic, and full of hope for the future. George Walton Williams, the wealthiest man in town, pledged $50,000. Dawson guaranteed $1,000, more than he could afford. Other pledges followed. "What Florida has done, Charleston can do," Dawson exhorted the crowd. "We can do it, and we must." At the end of the rally, pledges of $117,000 had been recorded, a good start toward the estimated cost of one million dollars.[32]

For weeks Dawson made the hotel campaign his lead story, endlessly trumpeting its potential. He proposed calling the hotel the Eden, a nod to the old Charleston story that the city had been built on the original site of Paradise. Possible locations were discussed, and the company applied for a charter. In order to qualify, the corporation had to have raised one-fifth of the money, but by mid-July only about half of those who had agreed to invest money had come through. Members of the canvassing committee went door to door, reminding men of their vows. But the initial fervor was wearing off, and pledges made in the heat of the moment now looked like gambles. The committee cut its goal of a million dollars in half. The canvassing committee also started pressuring men who had not yet subscribed money. Dawson had originally discouraged outside investors, wanting the hotel to be a homegrown product, but as it became clear that local businessmen would not back up their pledges, the committee began courting northerners. By late July, enough money had been raised to hire an architect.[33]

Then disaster struck in the form of yellow fever, a terrifying viral infection that causes its victims to bleed from every orifice and often leads to kidney failure, liver failure, and death. One of the greatest fears after the earthquake had been that camping out might spark an epidemic of yellow fever, but that threat came to nothing. Unfortunately for Dawson's project, however, yellow fever now broke out in a resort hotel in Jacksonville, Florida. The hotel was condemned and burned to the ground. The entire city was quarantined, and thousands of people were evacuated to refugee camps in the countryside.[34]

Both the *Charleston World* and the *News and Courier* collected money for the Jacksonville "sufferers," and Charleston sent seven trained nurses to treat patients. Dawson helped organize a benefit concert, the first entertainment ever presented in a new theater that had taken over Agricultural Hall after the earthquake hospital moved out. But the take was only $400, less than a third of what the committee had hoped for. Charleston's black churches took up collections for relief. As a black Charlestonian wrote to the *New York Age* (formerly the *New York Freeman*), "We know from experience that the real sufferers, in this part of the country, in such calamities, are the negroes. We know too, that what is sent by the generous North, is given to us in the stingiest manner; and it does seem, that the liars who have so much fault to find with the colored folks, begrudge them even that."[35]

As the fever spread up the eastern Florida coast to Fernandina and down to St. Augustine, other southern states began to panic. Fearing that outbreaks could shut down commerce for months and discourage investments, many communities — including Charleston — adopted strong-arm tactics to limit the spread of the disease. On August 11 the City of Charleston Board of Health published an official notice that anyone arriving in the city from the fever district would be quarantined for two weeks. The *News and Courier* played down the city's actions, but the *World* reported that detectives were "scouring the city day and night" and using citizens to spy on each other. One man who arrived to nurse his sick father was promptly thrown in jail. His father died while he was still in quarantine.[36]

By the end of September, rail transportation was shut down over much of the Southeast. Congress voted $100,000 to aid the areas affected by the disaster, something it had refused to do after the earthquake. A few optimistic souls dared to hope that Jacksonville's loss would be Charleston's gain — that tourists afraid to visit Florida might come to South Carolina instead — but the epidemic brought no good news. Putting money into southern resorts suddenly seemed like a very bad idea, and more prospective hotel investors developed cold feet. Epidemic or not, Dawson continued to argue that Charlestonians should step up and cover the full cost of the new hotel. After all, he wrote, "the cyclone and earthquake taught the people . . . what they could accomplish, without ruining themselves or robbing themselves of bread and butter." The Jacksonville epidemic sputtered out in early December, when colder temperatures arrived, but all hope of building a new hotel in Charleston vanished along with the fever. Dawson took it as a personal defeat.[37]

More challenges to his authority loomed on the horizon. The new year, 1888, was a presidential election year, and Dawson was a delegate to the national Democratic convention in St. Louis that June. As expected, President Grover Cleveland was nominated to run for a second term, and Dawson, who was slowly making his way back into Cleveland's good graces, was given the honor of seconding the nomination of former Ohio senator Allen G. Thurman for vice president. Yet many Democrats, including Dawson, had major reservations about Cleveland, and the seventy-five-year-old Thurman, more than three decades older than the president, hardly strengthened the ticket.[38]

Two weeks later in Chicago, the Republicans nominated Benjamin Harrison, the grandson of President William Henry Harrison. The candidate, a Union veteran, firmly believed that the mission of the Republican Party was to "bring freedom and equal rights" to southern blacks. During the presidential campaign of 1884, he had flayed southern Democrats for preventing blacks from voting and had declared that he would not rest until "the humble cabin of the negro is made safe against the midnight assaults of barbarian Democrats." Black Charlestonians were thrilled at Harrison's nomination, and Rev. William Henry Harrison Heard must have been especially pleased, since he was named for Harrison's grandfather.[39]

But Harrison was not likely to win the election on the strength of his personal attractions. The short, dour, unassuming nominee looked, as Theodore Roosevelt later remarked, "like a pig blinking in a strong wind." "If we can't beat Harrison, we can't beat anybody," declared South Carolina senator Matthew C. Butler. But Harrison seemed like a godsend to those who feared that slavery would be revived, especially southern blacks. Republicans held stump meetings across South Carolina to rally black voters. At a gathering in Sumter on September 30, a crowd of more than two thousand carried banners that read, "We Already Feel Their Chains . . . Tightening Around Our Necks."[40]

At a noisy mass meeting on Charleston's Hampstead Mall, Henry M. "Barber" Morris, president of the Republican Protective Union, called on Republicans to unite. He was joined by Knights of Labor leader W. P. Russell. Fifes, drums, and lifted voices rang out over the city. "De other party is weakenin'," Morris announced, "an' dey sick ob dey ticket." The *News and Courier* made Morris seem ridiculous by quoting him in dialect, but the man had put his finger on Frank Dawson's biggest problem. The Democrats were indeed weakening; many were tired of being ruled by the editor and his handpicked followers. Soon they would find a leader to give voice to their frustrations.[41]

Chapter Seventeen

STANDING OVER A VOLCANO

THE MAN WHIPPING up most of the discontent among Democrats was Dawson's one-time ally Ben Tillman. Using a metaphor all too familiar to those who had suffered through the aftermath of the earthquake, Tillman told delegates to the state Democratic convention: "We are standing over a volcano, gentlemen." Though he held no office, Tillman controlled one of the most discontented constituencies in the state — farmers. His great crusade was to establish a state agricultural college, a project that took on new life in the spring of 1888, when John C. Calhoun's son-in-law, Thomas Clemson, died and left a large endowment for that purpose.[1]

Tillman had worked closely with Dawson in the past and was indebted to the *News and Courier* for much of his present fame. Now Dawson became the target of his scorn. On July 20 Tillman addressed a crowd in Abbeville County, in the northwest corner of the state. Dawson, he sneered, was nothing but an old buzzard who had escaped from the market building in Charleston to "spew his slime" through the pages of the *News and Courier*. Denouncing "ring rule," he urged his party to give ordinary men a chance to pick their leaders in primaries, rather than allowing a few powerful men — a ring — to choose candidates in smoke-filled rooms. Such a move would strip Dawson of at least half his influence.[2]

To Tillman and to his followers, mostly Upcountry farmers and small businessmen, Charleston was a vampire that sucked prosperity from the rest of the state. Nobody but the wealthy and privileged could hope to share in the spoils. On August 3, 1888, while Dawson's hotel scheme was sputtering out, Tillman arrived in the city itching for a fight. His supporters marched down Meeting Street by torchlight, following a brass band and an illuminated silhouette of a blood-red gamecock, the well-known local symbol of white supremacy. The parade ended at City Hall, where a crowd of several thousand waited. Dawson, who had rushed home from New York when he heard that Tillman was coming, stood on the brightly lighted portico under a huge U.S. flag.[3]

Tillman strode to the railing and the throng went wild. "You vote, it is true," he taunted them, "but it is all fixed at the Convention." Suddenly a bass drum boomed and panic erupted. As the *News and Courier* put it, "many faces paled as the dread whisper 'Earthquake' passed through the crowd." Everybody scattered. The *World* reported that "men rushed pell-mell in every direction and many leaped wildly over the high iron fence enclosing Washington Square. . . . The crowd seemed mad with terror." A man who had been carrying a sack of peaches found himself holding an empty paper bag, relieved of his hat, his stick, and his umbrella, and wearing only the rags of a coat. Ben Tillman surveyed the chaos and stood his ground. When the confusion and noise died away and the crowd reassembled, somebody pounded the drum again and people fled in all directions. Tillman attempted to continue, but there was too much noise.

In the midst of the tumult, Frank Dawson stepped to the railing and started talking. His voice was drowned out by cries of "Tillman! Tillman!" Dawson appealed to the crowd to listen. If Tillman were unable to finish his speech, he said, he himself would hire the largest hall in Charleston and give his foe a chance to speak for as long as he wanted. The crowd cheered, then quieted.

Tillman again took up his diatribe. Charleston, he said, was tied hand and foot by the *News and Courier*. He had noticed — and here he cut his one eye toward Dawson — that when "the big dog down the street barked, all the little [mutts] throughout the State took up the yelp." He continued in this folksy vein for some time, alternately attacking Dawson and making fun of Charleston. The crowd ate it up. When Tillman finally stepped down, the lieutenant governor and the comptroller general gave dry, droning, traditional speeches. By the time they finished talking, it was after midnight. Some in the crowd called out for Dawson, but he had already left.

Soon a petition was making the rounds, begging Tillman to return to Charleston and "purify the Democratic Party." It accused the *News and Courier* of distorting facts and suppressing information. Another rally was planned for August 28.[4]

Inspired by Tillman, the *World* stepped up its attacks on Dawson. Filler lines started to appear in the *World* wherever there was an inch of space: "*Charlestonians are becoming heartily disgusted with Ring Rule*" and "*Ring-*

Rule Must Go" (original emphasis). Editorials called Dawson "The Lord High Executioner." Jeweler John McElree, one of the organizers of the rally, predicted that a huge crowd would turn out to hear Tillman "tell us how to get rid of the incubus."[5]

On August 28 Tillman again appeared on the steps of City Hall. Black clouds darkened the sky north of the city. A band played "Dixie" and "Wait Till the Clouds Roll By, Jenny." But the clouds did not roll by, and a clap of thunder accompanied Tillman's entrance like a drum roll. A crowd of 3,500 braved the weather to witness the performance. Hoping to avoid a repetition of the earlier "panic," the police sent the bass drum to the rear.[6]

Tillman rose. "I am not here to take any part in any family fight among you," he began. "I'm not here to help a set of greedy and fat officeholders on the outside turn out a set of greedy and fat officeholders on the inside. If that was the case I don't know but what you hadn't better let the fat ones alone, because now that they are fat they won't gouge you so much." Tillman was a master showman who knew exactly how to make the city his stage. "The ring fixes up its little slates," he jeered, "and a few of their lackeys go and do its will, and I can only say, God have mercy on your pusillanimous souls if you submit to it any longer. . . . If a law were passed by the Legislature disfranchising you, a rebellion would be raised, and a revolution would follow such as the country never saw, but when you disfranchise yourselves by your own inactivity how can you expect to prosper?"

Up to this point, Tillman seemed to be asking his fellow citizens to let every voice be heard. But now, standing defiantly on the balcony, he called for a new law, one that would disfranchise more than half the male population of Charleston. "Let the only qualification for voting be that the voters are white men!" he shouted. "For eight long years you were ground in the mire of political despair by negro domination. That lesson should be written upon your hearts in indelible ink. But you are now submitting to a tyranny more degrading."

Tillman soon made it clear that the tyrant was Frank Dawson. "You are here cringing," he taunted the crowd, "binding yourselves down in the mire because you are afraid of that newspaper down the street. Its editor bestrides the State like a Colossus. One foot on Georgetown and the other on Beaufort, while we poor petty men, whose boots he ain't fit to lick, are crawling under him, seeking dishonored graves."[7]

A voice cried, "Trot him out!" People muttered that the crowd ought to march down to the *News and Courier* office, lynch Dawson, and burn the building.

Tillman said he had gone to the archives of the South Carolina College and looked at issues of the *News and Courier* published during the 1870s. Dawson had donated these papers just three years before, believing that they would serve as a proud record of all he had done for the state. Tillman presented them now as evidence in his indictment of the editor. "Dawson's domination in South Carolina is drawing to an end," Tillman thundered. Then he started reading from the papers in his hand, and Dawson's brave condemnation of the 1876 killings at Hamburg rang out over Broad Street: "'We find no excuse for the cowardly killing of the seven negro prisoners who were shot down like rabbits long after they had surrendered. . . . The killing . . . was barbarous in the extreme. We have no words strong enough to express our condemnation of such a crime.'"

Tillman's voice dripped with scorn, mocking Dawson's British lilt. "'Hamburg, it must be remembered, is inhabited almost exclusively by negroes. In what way did the defiant attitude of the militia, in that town, threaten the security of the good people of Edgefield? . . . [The dead men's] offense is, we fear, in being negroes.'" Tillman, of course, had been part of that mob, one of the butchers. "I proclaim aloud that I was one of the Hamburg rioters who dared even the devil to save the state," he roared. "What did you people in Charleston do for it? You sent a score of men over to your Cainhoy over there, and let them be shot down; and you never even killed a nigger for it!"

At that moment, Dawson appeared, taking the steps at a run. When the roar of the crowd died away, he stepped forward. "Mr. Chairman," he said, addressing former alderman A. W. Eckel, "I have just been informed that this gentleman, in his remarks, has been making attacks on my personal character."

Someone cried out, "Yes, that's so!" The crowd hissed and cheered.

"I came here, sir, to meet his attacks face to face and to court the verdict of my fellow citizens," Dawson said. He took a seat on the platform, in full view of the crowd.

"I want to wind up now," Tillman said, "by contrasting Tillmanism with Dawsonism. Dawsonism is ring rule. Dawsonism is the domination of that old, effete aristocratic element that clings to power like an octopus." With the editor sitting just a few feet away, he proclaimed that Dawson was betraying his race.

"What about the Convention?" someone yelled.

"I'll tell you this," Tillman shot back. "If you've got a thimbleful of brains in your head . . . you'll organize between now and next Wednesday and sweep your convention system into the Cooper River."

Tillman had given a great performance, and Frank Dawson knew it. He himself had made a mockery of his fine words after Hamburg by later accepting the white men's story that they had acted in self-defense. What could he say now that would not make him look worse? Yet he could see no way out of the situation except to make a speech, something he did rather badly under the best of circumstances. He stood up, looked down at the crowd, and apologized that his voice was not strong. Then he launched into a long, dry self-justification. After Tillman's barnyard hell-raising, Dawson came across as devious, hairsplitting, and effete, just as Tillman had charged. "Not only was I there fighting with my pen [in 1876]," Dawson said, "but not an hundred yards from where I am standing, I was shot by a band of negro rowdies . . . and that bullet I carry in my body to this day. Does that sound like flinching or deserting the cause of South Carolina?"

Being shot by black men, of course, was not the same thing as shooting them, a fact so obvious to everyone in the crowd that Tillman did not bother to comment. But Dawson had succeeded in pointing out that he had shed blood in the battle for the South's "Redemption." Perhaps he should have stopped there, but he went on to beg the crowd for understanding and forgiveness. "Will you not allow me to count in my favor the years I have lived in Charleston, meeting my obligations, paying my debts and looking my fellow citizens squarely in the face every day?" he pleaded. "If I have sometimes made mistakes, which were mistakes of judgment and nothing else, they ought, at all events, when I shall pass from the scene of my work, to be regarded as honest errors." He hoped that when his life was over, Charlestonians would at least grant that he had done his duty "to my State and my people." How very soon that day would come, Dawson had no way of knowing, but the thought of his own impending death rendered him speechless. Overcome with emotion, he turned and left the stand.

THE NEXT NIGHT, according to the *News and Courier*, Dawson was working late in his office when he heard a band outside playing "Dixie." Several hundred men crowded Broad Street, cheering and calling his name. He put his head out the window and addressed the crowd. Tillman's attack, he said, was far more than a personal vendetta against him. The man was trying to "degrade" and "destroy" all that Charleston held dear.[8]

Dawson was preaching to the choir, of course, but he was in much better form now that he was among friends. He recited his own version of the Cainhoy massacre, "when our white people, a handful in number, went up there without any arms . . . and the negro militia . . . shot them down." Tillman thought he deserved respect because he was "the murderer of defenseless negroes." Was it fair, Dawson asked, for such a man to brand Charlestonians as cowards when they were "taken by surprise and shot down in ambush?"

And what about the riots in Charleston, when white men were assaulted within sight of the Guard House? Whites could easily have gathered their young men and "swept the city from one end to the other." And yet, when the blood of their kinsmen was spilled, they held back. Why? Because Wade Hampton had warned that "any act of retaliation, any act of aggression, even any act of self-defense in Charleston would destroy the chances of freeing South Carolina" from federal occupation. Charlestonians had acted, as they always did, in the best interests of the state.

Just as he had immediately after the Hamburg and Cainhoy shootings, Dawson appealed to reason and urged respect for the rule of law. The men around him nodded and cheered, assuring him that he was right. But at least some of them must have known that Tillman was winning. It was after midnight when the procession made its noisy way back uptown. The men stopped in front of John McElree's house, where the band played several tunes and the men gave three cheers for Dawson. They went home to bed, satisfied that they had made their point, defended Dawson's control of the Democratic Party, and annoyed at least one of his adversaries.

Anyone who read the *News and Courier*'s account the next morning would have believed that the rally was spontaneous and that Dawson's fine speech was impromptu. However, the *World* reported that the whole production had been staged. Instead of "hundreds" of men cheering Dawson, there had been just seventy-three. Dawson's speech had been set in type hours before the serenade, and "a copious supply of punch" had been delivered to the newspaper office that afternoon.

Energized by Tillman's triumph, Dawson's enemies launched an even more virulent attack. "For fourteen years," the *World* declared, "the people of South Carolina have been under a thumb-screw manipulated by a newspaper whose greed for gain . . . has rankled in the breasts of the people. . . . The *Charleston News and Courier* does not represent South Carolina in the remotest degree, either her people or the progress of that people. It is the embodiment of Self."[9]

The *World* was sure that Dawson's empire was about to be smashed. "Never in the history of political parties in South Carolina," blustered the paper, "has there been such a prodigious popular upheaval imminent in this state as there is to-day, and in the near future it will shake the state . . . with a national force as powerful as that of the [earthquake]."[10]

August 31, 1888, was the second anniversary of the quake, but Dawson was preoccupied with Ben Tillman, who, he said, was as dangerous as "war, pestilence, fire, plague, [and] cyclone." Few men had ever faced a situation as awful as that which confronted every Charlestonian on the night of August 31, 1886. And yet the city had recovered quickly and peacefully. "In two years," he declared, co-opting Tillman's racist language, "the city has been rebuilt without even 'killing one nigger.' "[11]

Tillman's attack had upset Dawson more than he wanted to admit. He had been played for a fool and had lost his hometown crowd to a vulgar, strutting rube. As Sarah would later write, "on that fateful night he realized that twenty-two years of singular devotion and enthusiasm had been vainly lavished on an altar of cold, hard, insensible stone." He instructed his staff to avoid printing Tillman's name whenever possible, using what he called "the editorial snuffers" to blunt the force of the enemy. It was no use.[12]

The *World* had tasted blood, and it now had an informant — probably cashier Swinton Baynard — inside the *News and Courier* offices. On September 1 it had scornfully predicted the gist of the next Thomas Nast political cartoon that Dawson would publish, complete with the caption. This cartoon, it said, had already run in many other newspapers, and the *News and Courier* was pitifully behind. It printed a note, purportedly from Dawson, asking his cartoon supplier to please be more punctual. On September 11 there was another bulletin in the *World* predicting the contents of the next cartoon, followed by another leaked (or possibly invented) letter from Dawson, who was in New York. Sure enough, the cartoon as described ran in the *News and Courier* on September 13.[13]

In the third week of September Swinton Baynard defected to the *World*. The assistant bookkeeper soon followed. Both were given jobs with grander titles than those they had held at the *News and Courier*. Baynard's brother

Henry stayed with Dawson's paper, managing advertising and circulation. But Hemphill and reporter Yates Snowden began looking for other employment, and Snowden soon went to work for the *World*. The *News and Courier* lost six hundred subscribers in a single day.[14]

Dawson frantically tried to raise money to keep his paper afloat. He appealed to his business partner, Rudolph Siegling, who was on vacation. Siegling laconically suggested in a letter that the company could save money by cutting the number of pages by half. To Frank, this was tantamount to giving up. The paper had already gone back to its eight-page format. He telegraphed Siegling to come to Charleston and then walked the floor for three nights, "in the extremity of horror and distress." When Siegling finally appeared, he laughed and said he must have sent the letter when he was drunk, since he didn't remember writing it. Finally he agreed to help Dawson bail out the paper, though he put in far less money than Frank.[15]

WHILE EVERYONE in town was arguing about politics, shopkeepers and entrepreneurs alike looked back on the previous year's Gala Week as a time free from petty bickering, when the city's focus was on commerce. They decided to bring back the "great earthquake carnival," hoping that the magic could be conjured up a second time. A date was set, and a new batch of committees was formed. But this year Dawson's attention stayed focused on politics. In the fall of 1888, two high-stakes contests would be held — a primary for city offices on October 5 and state and national elections on November 6.

Unfortunately for Dawson, Charleston Democrats were doing exactly what Tillman had told them to — organizing to sweep the convention system into the Cooper River. In the city contest, Dawson's name as usual was at the head of the delegation ticket for ward 4. But just after Tillman's second visit, eighty-eight men in ward 4 proposed an alternative slate of delegates, including Dawson's enemy Francis Rodgers, who was president of the *World*. The system, they said, was "rotten," and they must find a way to choose delegates "unpledged to any candidate."[16]

Dawson saw this rebellion as treason. But there was another newspaper in town now, one that could put a different spin on the situation: "Have the Democratic citizens of Charleston a right to name a ticket in Ward Four," asked the *World*, "which has not upon it the name of their self-appointed guardian [Frank Dawson]? Turn it, twist it as you please, that is the issue, and to represent it under any other form is misleading and vicious." The Reformers, as they came to be known, appointed a committee to watch the polls on Election Day and stay until all the votes were counted. Discontented voters in ward 1 followed their lead. At 6:30 p.m. on October 5, just as the primary polls were about to close, the Reformers submitted a letter to the poll managers asking that one man from each side be allowed to witness the count. The poll managers refused.[17]

According to the managers, Dawson's ticket won in ward 4, with 628 votes to the reform ticket's 369. But then the Reformers pointed out that all the winning candidates received the same number of votes despite the fact that many men had refused to vote a straight ticket. The poll managers admitted that instead of taking the time to count every name on every ballot, they had agreed to call the election for Dawson's team, since they were so far ahead that nothing could change the result. They were tired, they wanted to go home, and it would have taken another hour to tally all the split tickets. Dawson was embarrassed. It would have been far better to have won with fewer votes and no hint of fraud. He had always smoked ten or twelve cigars a day; now, trying to cope with the stress, he puffed his way through twenty-three every twenty-four hours.[18]

When Dawson turned his attention to the November state and federal elections, he encountered more critics. Though Rev. William Heard had moved to Philadelphia to lead Allen Temple, the legendary mother church of the African Methodist Episcopal denomination, the black men who had allied themselves with him after the earthquake —John Dart, William Crum, and George Rowe —managed to create such a buzz among Charleston Republicans that Dawson resorted to scare tactics. If the Republicans won, he wrote, all the federal jobs in the post office, the Internal Revenue Service, and the Custom Houses would be back in the hands of "ignorant, dishonest, and spiteful Republicans who would then be out to annoy, insult, inconvenience and persecute the Democratic voters of South Carolina."[19]

As Election Day drew near, Dawson's exhortations grew hysterical and openly racist. "A dollar apiece and the prospect of a good dinner" would "bring out Republican voters by the hundred," and unless Democrats turned out in force, united, the state would be ruled by "flippant negroes." Democrats could not afford to quarrel among themselves; to support Tillman was to hand over the election to the Republican Party. Dawson did not promote his own ticket so much as he incited white men to defend their homes and families, just as they had in 1876. In his desperation to hold onto power, he was sounding more and more like Ben Tillman.[20]

"Speak with your boys," he urged all white men, "who before long will have to take your places at the polls, and with the kiss of your wives on your lips and the eyes of your daughters looking up into yours, and with the loving touch of little fingers on your arms, determine that on next Tuesday week it will be your first charge, reverently, and trustfully, to go to the polls and vote . . . for Democratic candidates, for in voting for them you are not voting for men but for your houses, your altars, your firesides — for all that is most sacred and precious."[21]

"Vote Often and Early," urged the headline, referring, only partly in jest, to one of the battle cries of the 1876 campaign for white supremacy.[22]

The Democrats called a mass meeting of the upper wards at Hampstead Mall, a traditional gathering place for black Charlestonians. Dawson delivered a speech about the tariff, hardly a subject calculated to thrill working-class voters. The *News and Courier* claimed that a huge crowd had supported Dawson, but the *World* scoffed that in reality only thirty people had turned up. Dawson had called the meeting to demonstrate that he was still in command, the *World* jeered, but what the incident really proved was that he had been abandoned. "It's just come to this," the *World* gloated: Dawson "changes or leaves out what he don't approve of, and cheats the public by pretending to give full reports." The tactics that had once worked so well were revealed as smoke and mirrors.[23]

Resentment still festered among the city shopkeepers who had sued the city after the earthquake, challenging its right to make them pay for business licenses. On the eve of the election, three men were sent to jail for refusing to buy a permit after the South Carolina Supreme Court ruled that the city did have the right to collect these fees. Among the protesters was jeweler John McElree, who had led the movement to embarrass Dawson by bringing Ben Tillman to Charleston. McElree refused to pay his fine, and on November 1, five days before the election, deputies were sent to arrest him. Before long, twenty-eight arrest warrants were served; five men settled up, but the others went to jail. McElree was sentenced to 120 days for four violations, but he and his allies received special treatment and much public support. The jailer put the businessmen in a separate building without a guard, where they enjoyed the contents of gift baskets that included champagne and fine cigars. The imprisoned men retained former governor

Andrew G. McGrath to represent them. The city council struggled to find a way to save face and set the men free without compromising the city's right to collect license fees.[24]

On Election Day, Dawson buttoned his naturalization papers into his inner breast pocket before he headed for the office. He had been a U.S. citizen since 1867, but his enemies now claimed that he was an alien who for years had been voting under false pretenses.[25]

The newspaper war prompted a revolution in election-night coverage: battling stereopticons. In the past, the *News and Courier* had posted telegraphic reports on outside bulletin boards. Now the returns would also be projected from the second-story window of the newspaper office onto a canvas screen across Broad Street. In the intervals between reports, there would be "brilliant and magnificent views of countries and places and people" bound to "tickle the voters down to the very soles of their feet." The *World* countered with its own stereopticon extravaganza at the Charleston Hotel. And instead of showing picturesque scenes as filler, the *World* would project political cartoons — "none of your little, two-for-a-cent, pen and ink sketches," but "a flaming Aurora borealis, Puck style of cartoon."[26]

As evening fell on Election Day, both newspaper offices drew huge crowds. At seven o'clock, an image materialized on Dawson's canvas screen: billowing clouds "in rainbow hues" against a clear blue sky. Black letters flashed the words, "How's Grover Cleveland?"[27]

"Oh, he's all right!" yelled the crowd, and a towering image of the portly president lit up the night. Then came pictures of Benjamin Harrison, Mrs. Harrison, and Mrs. Cleveland, along with shots of the flag and the U.S. Capitol.

The results, as they trickled in, did not bode well for the incumbent. At midnight, well before the election was settled, the *News and Courier*'s screen went dark. Many of the spectators pushed their way up to the *World*'s show, where results were still coming in. The *World* claimed that more than twenty thousand people, a third of the city's population, swarmed the streets around the Charleston Hotel. Bulletins were "thrown so expeditiously on the great stretch of canvas that the insects did not have time to light." Black Republicans paraded through the streets carrying a banner that read "Dead! Dead! Funeral of Fourth March. Harrison is President."[28]

At 2:30 the morning after the election the *World* declared Benjamin Harrison the winner. "Defeat," read that day's headline. "The Result No Longer

Up in the Air." Dawson, on the other hand, insisted that the election results were still inconclusive. Broad Street overflowed with Harrison's supporters. A policeman was sent to move them along "so that white men and better men might see how the record stood." The Republicans had been routed in South Carolina, even in the black district, but the national race looked ominous for Cleveland.[29]

As the second day of counting drew to a close and the results continued to favor Harrison, Cleveland refused to concede the election. That night, election coverage resumed. At 9:30 on Wednesday, Chief Joseph Golden rode up to some black teenagers who were blocking the beam of the *News and Courier*'s projector. He ordered them to be quiet, and the boys broke and ran. While scenes from the life of Napoleon Bonaparte flashed incongruously on the big screen, the crowd surged outward and spilled into the *News and Courier* office, through it, out the back doors, and down the adjacent streets and alleys.[30]

The Republicans organized a victory parade, taunting Democrats as they took over the streets:

Cleveland in de butcher pen,
Scrapin' out de tripe,
Harrison in de parlor
Smokin' wid he pipe.[31]

At midnight, a final message appeared on Dawson's screen: "The Country is Safe Whoever is President! Union and Unity. Good Night!"

Cleveland won the popular vote but Harrison carried New York State and so won the electoral college. For the first time since 1874, Republicans controlled not only the White House but both branches of Congress.[32]

The *World* warned that the Republicans planned to enforce fair elections in the South, and everyone knew that white supremacy could never survive that. Dawson urged his allies to try to work with the new administration, suggesting that maybe it wouldn't be as harsh as he had earlier claimed. The *World* charged that Dawson was "preparing to go over horse, foot and dragoon" to the victorious Republicans, pointing out that two of Sarah's brothers-in-law were prominent in the party. It was an outrageous charge — Dawson had staked his whole career on the Democratic Party — but there was no longer any middle ground in southern politics. "It Is About Time For You, Captain Dawson, To Sit Down!" a huge headline

216 | CHAPTER SEVENTEEN

blared. A newspaper in the Midwest offered Dawson a job, but he told Sarah that he would not leave as long as Charleston needed him — and he was sure that his adopted city needed him now, more than ever.[33]

Despite the election results, word went out that Gala Week would go on as planned. "Certainly earthquakes and Republican national victories cannot subdue" the spirit of Charleston, wrote Dawson, who was beginning to feel sharp pains in his gut, the first symptoms of an ulcer. The flags went up, the lanterns were hung, and crowds of visitors arrived, but the heavens opened and rain poured down all week long. Professor King again launched his hot-air balloon, only to get caught in a lightning storm as he scudded across the harbor. The *World* offered a stereopticon show every night in front of the Charleston Hotel, "Free, Gratis, and for Nothing," but most people stayed home or attended indoor events, including a program about earthquake damage presented by the U.S. Geological Survey. With so much rain pounding the city, parades and fireworks were out of the question. The city tried to salvage the celebration by extending it for another seven days, but most visitors gave up and headed home. The *World* pronounced Gala Week 1888 "a failure."[34]

WHITE CHARLESTONIANS may have felt defeated by Benjamin Harrison, but their black neighbors also found little to celebrate. On the first of January 1889, black Charlestonians gathered to remember the twenty-fifth anniversary of the official end of slavery. In spite of a persistent drizzle, a parade formed at Calhoun Street and made its way around the city, ending at Hampstead Mall, on the northeast edge of town, in an area with many black residents. Dr. William Crum read the Emancipation Proclamation, and Rev. George Rowe recalled what it was like to be packed into a slave ship and sold on the auction block. He invoked the patron saints of abolition, from Nat Turner and John Brown to William Lloyd Garrison. But the black man's prospects in the United States, he said, were now very bleak.[35]

"On this New Year's Day," he urged, "turn your attention to Africa, the home of your fathers, and see how eagerly your brethren [are] calling you to come and join with them in the march of progress toward a higher civilization!" Only twenty-five years after the death of slavery, the idea that blacks could find liberty in America had almost withered away.

Chapter Eighteen

KILLING CAPTAIN DAWSON

O N THE FIRST DAY of February 1889, a new crisis started unfolding inside the Dawson household when Celia Riels, Sarah's new cook, brought her sick baby to work. She knew that Dr. Thomas McDow's home and office were just around the corner, and she sent word to ask if he would be willing to make a house call. McDow came over right away. He was a short, dark, intense man who spoke with great animation.

Hélène Burdayron carried the infant into the room. When she left, McDow bombarded Celia with questions. Who was this girl, where was she from, how old was she? Did she live in the main house or in the servants' quarters out back? Celia shrugged him off. The baby was treated, McDow went home, and the incident seemed to be over.

But it quickly became evident to the servants in the Dawson household that Dr. McDow was obsessed. The next day, he loitered near the street when Hélène passed in the Dawsons' carriage. Soon he was lurking in his garden every morning, waiting for her to go by with the children on their way to school. As Hélène later recalled, it was only a matter of time before McDow grew bolder. Late one evening as Hélène got off the streetcar, he called her over. How was Celia's baby getting along? Did Hélène like living in Charleston? That was the end of the small talk: McDow proposed marriage. Though he was already married, and divorce was illegal in South Carolina, he promised to file the papers in North Carolina.

Hélène thought McDow must be drunk. She scolded him for saying such things and darted inside the gate. McDow followed her into the yard, begging to see her again. He was miserable with his wife, he said, and had only married her for her money. The next evening McDow met Hélène at the gate and handed her a bouquet of flowers. Again he asked her to marry him.

Whenever Hélène left the house, Dr. McDow followed. Every evening the two huddled in the garden for several hours. The servants knew exactly what was going on, but Sarah and Frank apparently never looked out their windows. A willing participant in this dangerous game, Hélène may or may not have known that McDow already had one lover, his wife's best friend, a twenty-two-year-old widow named Julia Smith who rented rooms in a nearby boardinghouse. Smith often stayed overnight with the McDows. On the very day he met Hélène for the first time, McDow had asked his brother Arthur, who was visiting from out of town, to murder his father-in-law, retired wholesale-grocer Charles D. Ahrens, and to make it appear to be a random killing.[1]

A little more than a week later, while Thomas McDow was pursuing Hélène with flowers and promises by day, Arthur eavesdropped on his brother one night as he climbed into bed with Julia in a guest room of his own house. "I will get rid of Katie and marry you," Thomas said, "a few drops will do all, and people know Katie is in bad health. No one will suspect anything wrong."

This was certainly reckless behavior, but everything might have gone as planned, leaving Thomas McDow with no wife, a sizeable fortune, and the tantalizing problem of which young woman to marry, Julia or Hélène. However, a few days later, Charles Ahrens somehow got wind that Arthur and Thomas were planning to kill him. He had recently moved out of Thomas and Katie's house and was living at the Waverly Hotel downtown. Ahrens asked the police for protection. He wanted to warn his daughter that her life was in danger, but he feared that if he did, his son-in-law might kill them both. Officer M. J. McManus was dispatched to the hotel, where he intercepted Arthur McDow and disarmed him. Then he presided over a painful series of confessions. Arthur revealed the murder plot to Ahrens and urged him to take his daughter and granddaughter to another state. Katie and her daughter Gladys did move to the hotel for a while, but sometime before March 12 they came back home. Dr. McDow continued having sex with Julia Smith and stalking Hélène.

Around the first of March, Sarah left for Washington, D.C., to visit her sister. While she was out of town and Frank was at work, McDow walked up to their house and rang the front doorbell. Hélène let him in. The two went into the library, closed the door, and stayed there for over an hour. The next day McDow showed up again, and he and Hélène shut themselves into the children's room. McDow gave Hélène a watch engraved with her initials.

As the week wore on, they continued to meet, closeting themselves in the music room and in one of the outbuildings where the other servants slept. Hélène offered McDow a book from Dawson's library, a novel about a single girl who falls in love with a married man. Celia warned Hélène that the Dawsons would be furious if they found out she was letting a strange man into the house. Hélène paid no attention, and the meetings continued.

Earlier that year Dawson had told a friend in New York that some "worthless fellows" had been pestering Hélène because she was so pretty. Such men ought to be horsewhipped, he said, though he apparently took no immediate steps to discover who they were.[2] In fact, he did nothing until March 5, when he received an anonymous letter that claimed Hélène had taken up with someone "unsuitable."

Dawson sat Hélène down and asked point-blank what she was up to. Hélène said that her friendships were none of his business. Dawson insisted that he had every right to question her behavior. After all, she had been entrusted with the care of his children. Hélène boasted to the other servants that she had stood up to Captain Dawson. They threatened to tell on her, but Hélène warned that if they did, she would use her special hold over Sarah to have them all fired.

Frank picked Sarah up at the station on her return from Washington on Friday, March 8. On the way home he seemed preoccupied, and when they passed Captain Joseph Golden, the chief of police, he halted the carriage and called Golden over. Frank asked the chief to meet him at the office that night. Golden politely wondered if the next morning would be soon enough. "Tomorrow will be fine," Frank replied. "I only want you to look into something for me."

Meanwhile, his newspaper was teetering on the brink of bankruptcy. Rudolph Siegling, the president of the board, refused to invest more money, so Dawson had applied for a loan using his own News and Courier stock as collateral, assuring potential lenders that the paper was on a firm footing despite the "sharpness of the competition." He had just been turned down for full life insurance coverage because of his health, and between his ulcer and several other nagging ailments, he had been feeling tired. He joked with a friend that it was absurd to insure his life, since "he could not afford to die and had no intention of dying." Nevertheless, he accepted the company's offer to provide partial coverage. He had recently invested more money in the Mason Cotton Harvester Company, which now advertised a new machine capable of picking a ton of cotton a day. If the *News and Courier* went belly-up, he hoped to have a source of steady income to fall back on.[3]

ON SATURDAY the weather turned chilly. Frank took the day off, something he almost never did. He helped Ethel and Warrington rig a rope and pulley to transport letters from their upstairs gallery to the Lafittes' house next door, where a little girl named Marie Lewis, a relative of his first wife, was staying. They named the mechanism a "telephore." Frank laughed and joked with the children while Hélène hovered in the background, uncharacteristically silent. Sarah stood on the back stoop watching her family. When she happened to glance across the yard she saw a strange man staring toward their house.[4]

Later that day, Dawson met with Chief Golden, and on Monday morning a patrolman was detailed to follow Hélène. It was, of course, unusual for the police to intervene in domestic affairs. But Frank Dawson had asked a favor, and no questions were asked.

Around nine o'clock on Monday morning, Hélène dropped the children off at school and walked home by a meandering route. Plainclothes officer John P. Dunn followed her. Hélène walked along for several blocks with another young woman, stopping to browse in a shoe store. Then she strolled up Rutledge Avenue. But instead of going straight home she continued walking north to a house on Nunan Street, where she went inside and stayed for about ten minutes. When she emerged, she made her way to the Dawsons'. Sergeant Dunn took notes. At the end of his report, he remarked, "She does attract a great deal of attention on the street on account of her dress."

THE FOLLOWING MORNING, March 12, Ethel appeared at Sarah's bedside in tears, unable to find her schoolbooks. Sarah told her to ask Hélène to help her look for them. Frank woke up in his bedroom next door but drifted back to sleep. An hour later he leaped out of bed, terrified by a nightmare. In the dream, he was wrestling with a stranger on the brink of a cliff. The man had a pistol and was attempting to shoot him. Dawson tried to wrest the gun away, but it went off. He grabbed the man's ankle as he hurtled over the edge. Then Frank woke up.

"Tell me what my dream means!" he begged Sarah. "Do you believe my life is in danger?"

Sarah hesitated. "No more than usual," she replied.

"Do you believe anyone would murder me? I know no one who wants to kill me — just now!"

Sarah could think of several possibilities, but she did not say so. Instead, she told him that she, too, had had a terrible nightmare. In it she and Frank were walking barefoot while a veiled woman spread burning coals under their feet. "What does that mean?" she asked.

"It means that a woman will make trouble for us," Frank replied, "trouble which you and I must bear alone."

Frank plopped down in his usual chair to put on his socks. He heard something crunch. Underneath the seat cushion he found his large triple shaving mirror, with all three panels shattered. The mirror had been removed from its hook on the wall, folded flat, and hidden where he would be sure to sit on it. Breaking a mirror was bad luck. Had someone tried to hex him? Frank shook off the idea and continued dressing.

The children left for school with Hélène, and Frank and Sarah sat down to an uneasy breakfast. Frank tried to lighten the mood. He asked his wife if she would like to have an oil portrait of him. This was her last chance, he teased. Sarah would have preferred a dignified marble bust like the one of Mayor Courtenay that now stood in City Hall. "But this artist is here now," Frank insisted. "If you can be at the office at three o'clock, and make me leave, no matter what business pressure I plead, you will have that first sitting. Then we can come home to an early dinner. I want you to have this portrait. Don't let me put it off."

While Frank and Sarah were discussing Frank's portrait, Hélène was climbing onto a streetcar at the corner of Broad and Meeting streets. Sergeant Dunn got on with her. Thomas McDow boarded the car at a stop near his house. Charleston was much too small a town for real undercover work: Dr. McDow recognized Dunn and struck up a conversation. When the car stopped at Bee Street, he and Hélène got out. Dunn stayed on the car.

The minute he had Hélène alone, McDow took up his old refrain: he would divorce his wife and marry her. The couple ended up in front of a small house in a poor area of town not far from Potter's Field. McDow left Hélène standing in the garden and stepped onto the porch. An old black woman came out to meet him. McDow asked if he and his friend could borrow a room. The woman refused. A buggy rumbled past on the street and McDow glimpsed Sergeant Dunn inside. He hustled Hélène back to the streetcar stop and had her home by ten. Sarah scolded her for being late, but Hélène apologized and played with the ribbons of Sarah's bonnet until she was forgiven.

Soon Hélène's guilty secret was revealed. Captain Golden went to Dawson's office and gave him a copy of Sergeant Dunn's report. When Dawson learned that Hélène was seeing McDow, he flew into a rage, but the police refused to do anything more since no crime had been committed. Golden warned Dawson that McDow was dangerous. He was about to be charged with signing false death certificates in the life insurance scandal, and he was likely to be even more volatile than usual because he now knew he was under surveillance. Under no circumstances should Dawson try to confront the man on his own. But Dawson was notorious for taking matters into his own hands, so just in case trouble started, Golden sent an officer to patrol the neighborhood.

Dawson turned back to his work. The black men from Pickens who had lynched a white man had just gone back to court for a second trial, the first having ended in a mistrial. In the last editorial he would ever write, Dawson declared that "there are and will be black lynchers if there shall continue to be white lynchers." Lynching did not prevent rape, he wrote, refuting one of the sacred beliefs of white southerners. The state must do everything possible to halt vigilante killings. Dawson understood what historian Bruce E. Baker observed more than a century later: "Had Lula Sherman been white, there would probably have been no debate over whether she was an innocent victim and whether her attacker deserved to be shot and hanged by the side of the road." Most whites felt that lynching was justified by "the genuine sense of uncontrollable outrage white men feel when a black man rapes a white woman." Dawson was echoing upstate editors when he closed with an inflammatory statement: "it cannot be pretended, for a moment, that any such horror attaches to [rape] when the aggressor is a white man and the object is a colored woman." Dawson had learned the hard way that if he moved too far ahead of his peers he would be a leader with no followers. Or perhaps he was just acknowledging widespread public attitudes, as he often did when commenting on controversial subjects, but many people understood him to mean that rape was not really a crime at all when a white man did it to a black woman. His black readers were outraged. The man who had opposed segregation and lynching seemed to be turning into a bigot.[5]

To Dawson, it was just another editorial, no more or less important than thousands of others he had written in the last twenty years. And had he lived to fight another day, the piece might have caused no more than a momentary uproar. But Frank Dawson was about to confront his final adversary.

Sarah called Frank at his office a couple of times around noon, though apparently they both forgot his promise to sit for a portrait. She spent the early afternoon overseeing her yardman as he planted shrubs, replacing vegetation that had been lost to the hurricane and the earthquake. Dinner waited on the stove, ready to be whisked to the table the minute her husband walked in the door.

A LETTER LAY on Dawson's desk, already set in type. It was a lengthy discourse on the benefits of cremation, signed "T.B.M." Corpses gave off poisonous fumes that could make the living sick, the writer warned, even when they were properly buried. Burning was a far more sanitary method of dealing with human bodies. Cremation was a hot topic nationwide, and the *Charleston World* had recently printed several articles about it. But Dawson was not about to hand free publicity to the very man who had been causing turmoil inside his household: Thomas Ballard McDow. In a final flourish of his blue editorial pencil, Dawson exercised the power that had made him the "Czar of South Carolina"— the power to silence his enemies. Across the sheet he scrawled, "Kill this."[6]

At a little past three o'clock that Tuesday afternoon, Frank Dawson grabbed his cane and went out to catch a streetcar. As the horse-drawn trolley clattered up Rutledge, he chatted pleasantly with acquaintances. When it reached his corner, he stepped off and headed for McDow's office. Ethel happened to be standing at her bedroom window with Hélène. "There he is!" she cried out. "That's my Papa!"

"It cannot be," snapped Hélène.

AT THE MCDOW HOUSE across the way, Katie McDow and Julia Smith were sitting upstairs in the family quarters, apparently as close as ever despite Julia's liaison with Thomas. Katie and Thomas had just quarreled, and Thomas had stormed downstairs to his office. Their black servants, Emma Drayton, the cook, and Moses Johnson, the coachman, were eating lunch in the kitchen. Suddenly a shot rang out. Katie was paralyzed, sure that her husband had committed suicide. Julia Smith ran downstairs and nearly tripped over Frank, who was sprawled on the floor. "For God's sake, bring me some water," he moaned.

Unlike the Dawson home, which was set back from the street on a spacious lawn, McDow's home and office fronted directly on the sidewalk. A street vendor carrying a tray of peanut cakes tried to see in the office window, which was made of ground glass. "Oh God, somebody's murdered!" she cried. McDow slammed the shutters. Having regained her wits, Katie McDow hustled outside with her little daughter, heading for her father's rooms at the Waverly Hotel. Emma Drayton also went outside and stood by the gate, rolling her hands in her apron.

A coachman named George Harper hailed Private Samuel Gordon, the patrolman who had been detailed to watch Dawson's neighborhood. "Someone is being murdered over there," he said. Gordon walked over and asked Emma Drayton if she had heard a shot. She evaded the question. He approached McDow's door and rang the bell. The doctor peeped out through a crack. "Is anything wrong?" Gordon asked. McDow said no. But Gordon, turning to leave, heard an odd noise that sounded like a sack of corn being dragged over a carpet. Another officer might have insisted on coming inside, but Gordon was black, one of the few African Americans left on the force after years of Democratic purges, and his authority when dealing with whites was strictly limited. He backed off the porch and sent a boy to alert Chief Golden, who was waiting nearby. The chief evidently felt he did not have enough evidence to enter McDow's home by force. He asked Mayor Bryan for permission to investigate further.[7]

SARAH WAS BESIDE HERSELF with worry. Since the day she had met Frank, sixteen years before, she had been waiting for his corpse to be carried home. Unsigned threats arrived in the mail almost every day, and twice since they were married he had been assaulted, once on their own porch. At a little after four o'clock, Hélène rushed up the stairs, burst into Sarah's bedroom, and threw herself on the floor. Thinking that she must be ill, Warrington ran after her. Hélène turned on the boy in a fury, sprang to her feet, and swiped him out of her way. She bolted into her own room and latched the door behind her.[8]

THOMAS MCDOW, in his office, stared down at Frank Dawson's body. There was no blood on the fine gray suit and no blood on the floor. Yet McDow could see the belly bulging, which he knew indicated that blood was pooling in the abdomen. Snatching up Dawson's hat and cane, he headed for the back yard, yanked open the door to the privy, and heaved both into the stink. He stopped by the stables and grabbed a shovel. Then he ducked back into the house and pried off the cover to a small storage space concealed under the stairs to the private part of the house. The opening was so low that he bumped his head. McDow set to work ripping up the board floor. It was too dark to see well, and there were no candles in the house. He put on his hat and went back to squint into the tiny closet, where the sand under the floor was exposed.

Finally, he set out for the shop on the corner, where he bought candles and fruit. Trying to look nonchalant, he munched an apple while strolling home. Private Gordon and Chief Golden watched him pass, his clothing dusty and disheveled. The crown of his hat was dented and smudged with whitewash. "He looks like he has had a fracas," the chief remarked.

McDow's neighbor, Edward Lafitte, called out, "Doctor, look at your hat!" McDow brushed at his bowler and hurried back to his office.

The candles helped — at least he could see — but there was a layer of clay under the sand, packed very hard. McDow sweated, gasped for air, but eventually carved out a shallow hole he hoped would accommodate the body. It was an act of desperation, especially for someone who, only the day before, had tried to warn the public that deadly toxins were released by decaying corpses. Dawson was a big man, an athlete run to fat since the earthquake, and McDow had a hard time dragging his body into the closet. When the head caught on a board McDow forced it downward, scraping the face. At last he gave up, hauled out the corpse, and pulled it back into the office. He fished the cane out of the privy, wiped it, and laid it on the lounge. Then he put his pistol in a drawer and tidied up the office.

WHEN THE DAWSONS' clock struck five, Sarah realized that Ethel and Warrington were late for dance class. The children gulped down a few bites of cold dinner before running out the door with Hélène. Sarah was left alone. A vision of Frank doubled up in a corner flashed in front of her eyes. Trying to shake off her terror, she walked out on the front porch. At the gate was a slender, dirty, rumpled-looking man glaring at her through the latticework. Though he looked vaguely familiar, Sarah decided that he must be a tramp, and she hurried inside.

The man Sarah saw lurking in her yard was Thomas McDow, who waited until she had disappeared and then knocked on the kitchen door to ask for Hélène. The butler said she had taken the children to their dancing lesson but refused to tell him where the classes took place. McDow ran to the boardinghouse where Julia Smith lived. He pulled on the bell and his girl-friend appeared at the top of the stairs. "Come down to the door," McDow begged. "I have killed Captain Dawson."

This was not news to Julia Smith, who had stumbled over the dying man before fleeing to her own apartment. "But why?" she asked. It was all because of the girl, McDow explained, the one who worked for the Dawsons. Captain Dawson had forbidden him to speak to her, and threatened, if he ever came near her, to "publish him in the papers." McDow said he intended to turn himself in and asked Julia Smith to go back to his house and wait for his wife to return home. At a little after six he jumped into his buggy and started up the street. When he spotted a patrolman, he pulled over. "What's the trouble?" the policeman asked.

"I have killed Captain Dawson."

FOR AN HOUR and a half after McDow appeared in her yard, Sarah waited. At six thirty, she called Frank's office, hoping he would answer. Instead a secretary came on the line. Sarah was too embarrassed to admit the real reason for her call. "Were the wood and coal ordered for me today?" she asked. The secretary did not know. Someone would have to be sent downstairs to find the answer.

"Oh! No matter!" Sarah said, trying to sound nonchalant. "Is Captain Dawson there?"

"No, ma'am," replied the tinny voice. "He has not yet returned."

Sarah stared out the window, imagining the worst. The telephone rang. "Did you get the wood and coal?" asked James LaCoste, the newspaper's business manager.

"No. But — "

"Is Captain Dawson there?"

"No!" Sarah exclaimed. "Mr. LaCoste! I believe he has been waylaid and murdered!" It was the first time she had let herself say the words. The phone line went dead.

Sarah was angry at being cut off, sure that all the men in the newspaper office had dismissed her as a hysterical woman. She called back. This time James Armstrong, the business editor, answered. "What are you afraid of?" he asked. "Captain Dawson is in perfect health."

"I believe he has been waylaid and murdered!" Sarah shouted. Armstrong was taken aback. Frank was in a committee meeting, he said. Sarah begged him to go to the meeting and tell Frank she could not rest until she received a message from him. Finally, Armstrong promised that he would find his boss and escort him home.

By now Hélène and the children had returned from their dance lesson. Ethel threw her arms around Sarah as she turned away from the phone. "Why are you so upset about Papa?" she asked.

Sarah ordered Celia to rewarm the dinner and serve it as supper. "Make his salad," she snapped at Hélène. "Hurry. Hurry!"

Meanwhile, Private Gordon was driving McDow toward the Central Police Station. McDow asked him to stop by the home of lawyer Andrew G. McGrath, and, when he found that McGrath was not at home, directed Gordon to the residence of attorney Julian Mitchell. He, too, was unavailable. At the station, McDow was handcuffed, put in a police wagon, and transported to the new jail. By then, the news was out: Captain Dawson was dead.

The *News and Courier*, of course, had reporters all over town. Within minutes the men in the office knew what Sarah only suspected. Henry Baynard, Dawson's advertising and circulation manager, appeared at Sarah's door. Under the crimson-shaded gaslight, Baynard sank to his knees, sobbing. Sarah stared at him, grasping at straws. Maybe Frank had killed Henry's brother Swinton, she thought. He had seemed angry enough to do it when Swinton went over to the *World*. Or maybe he had shot Ashmead Courtenay, as he had lately been threatening to do. "Has he killed some-one?" she gasped.

"He has killed no one!" cried Baynard. "He would hurt no one! He is quite, quite well." He had come to help break the news, but he could not face telling Sarah the truth without his colleagues.

Sarah heard feet running up the stairs. For a wild moment she let herself hope that they belonged to her husband. But the door burst open to reveal James Hemphill and John Weber from the newspaper office. Sarah searched Weber's grim face. "Is my husband dead?"

"Yes," Weber answered.

PALE, TREMBLING, and soaked with sweat, McDow arrived at the jail. A doctor examined the top of his head and discovered a small scrape. Strange as it seems today, prominent men who shot each other were often treated with great deference, perhaps because they were viewed as having acted within the southern tradition of honor killings, which Dawson had vehemently opposed. McDow spotted Officer McManus, the policeman who had investigated his plan to kill Katie and her father. Pulling some money from his pocket, McDow ordered McManus to go out and buy him some cigars. The officer took the money and left, but he brought back the wrong brand. Still acting like a free man, McDow insisted that he return them. Finally, McManus came back with the right type of cigars. McDow smoked and paced, pausing to eat a tray of dinner brought in from a nearby restaurant. The police allowed him to talk with reporters, and with no lawyer present to save him from himself, the prisoner freely admitted that he had shot Dawson. He claimed that the editor had hit him with his fist and struck him on the forehead with his cane. "I am addicted to running after women," he added, seemingly out of the blue. At midnight he was locked in a cell on the third floor of the jail.

Several men standing on a street corner vowed to kill McDow, but then one of them remembered Dawson's crusade against lynching. The group disbanded.[9]

A policeman knocked on the door of Charles Ahrens's hotel room and asked to see Katie McDow and Julia Smith, both of whom were there. Ahrens produced a note from a doctor saying that his daughter was too distraught to testify. Julia Smith was taken to the police station for questioning.

A raucous throng collected in front of McDow's house. When the coroner arrived, Dawson's body was lifted from the floor onto a cloth stretcher. Several spectators, including George Walton Williams, were enlisted to serve on the coroner's jury.

At a little before eight, Dr. Middleton Michel arrived to perform an autopsy in McDow's office. A large tub was trundled in to catch the blood.

Michel noticed some odd scratches on Dawson's forehead. He removed the dead man's clothes, carefully putting each item aside to be preserved as evidence. Sand fell out of the overcoat, and Michel observed that the waistcoat was stained with clay. The trousers, one glove, and one shoe were smudged with whitewash.[10]

Finally, Frank Dawson's body lay naked on the stretcher in the room where he had been killed. A neat hole about the size of a half-dollar pierced his side. Michel sliced the swollen belly and peered into the cavity. There was so much clotted gore that he had to scoop it out by handfuls.

While Michel searched for the bullet, up to his elbows in blood, Lt. James Fordham, another of the few black policemen in the city, roamed around the office. He noticed a little door under the stairs, set into a whitewashed wall. On the facing was a bloody fingerprint. Pulling out some nails that looked freshly driven, Fordham held his lantern high. Inside he spotted the freshly dug hole and several drops of blood.

The crime scene abruptly took on a whole new dimension. Every man who went into the closet emerged with a splotch of whitewash on his head or hat. The sand and clay on the floor matched the stains on Dawson's coat. Someone noticed that Dawson's hat was missing; a lantern was tied to a clothesline and lowered into the privy to look for it. Lieutenant Fordham opened the door to a back room and discovered a shovel caked with damp clay and a wet, bloodstained towel wrapped around a candle.

A cold rain began to fall. At the stroke of midnight, Dawson's body was carried out of the McDow house, borne around the corner of Rutledge Avenue, and laid out in the Dawsons' drawing room.

Chapter Nineteen

THE TRIAL

DEAD! DEAD!!" EXCLAIMED the *News and Courier* the morning after the murder. "His chair is vacant. His pen is still. His work is done."[1]

Former President Grover Cleveland sent Sarah a brief telegram of "heartfelt sympathy and condolence." Newspapers across the country remembered Dawson as a "fearless spirit" who "when the ground of Charleston was heaving . . . held his post and with his devoted band toiled through the night and brought . . . to wretched thousands the blessing of news."[2]

Thomas McDow sat in a jail cell muttering, "bad, bad, bad!" Reporters asked him about the grave in his closet, and he said that he often buried "chips of flesh" removed during surgery there. News spread that two sets of footprints had been found, and the *Charleston World* speculated that the smaller set must belong to a woman who had helped McDow move the body. At noon, Dawson's hat turned up in the privy. By then, however, McDow had hired two of the city's most respected attorneys, Andrew McGrath and Asher Cohen, who ordered him to stop talking to the press.[3]

McGrath was seventy-six years old, white haired, and venerable. His associate, Cohen, was fifty-one, Jewish, and descended from an old family that had owned plantations and slaves. Both men were former Confederates — McGrath served as a judge, Cohen as a soldier — with sterling credentials among Charleston's gentry. In hiring them to manage his defense, McDow ensured that both expertise and respectability were on his side.[4]

A BODY THAT has been disemboweled quickly grows unfit for public display, and Dawson did not have a refrigerated coffin like Stephney Riley, the wealthy black man whose killing had almost caused a riot four years before. The funeral service was set for four o'clock that Wednesday afternoon, just twenty-four hours after the murder. There was no way for Sarah's sisters and brothers to make it to Charleston in time.[5]

As rain poured down outside, mourners filed through the Dawsons' parlor where Frank lay "coffined and cold." Sarah sat beside the handsome black casket gazing at his face. The ribbon he had been given by the pope for his opposition to dueling was prominently displayed in his buttonhole, now an ironic reminder of his long campaign against bloodshed. Remembering all the times his citizenship had been questioned, Sarah slipped her husband's naturalization papers into the inside pocket of his coat.[6]

Just after three, the coffin was closed and carried down the front steps. Sarah followed, supported on the arm of her minister. The whole city, reported the *Charleston Daily Sun*, was like a "troubled human sea, not a sea which is storm-whipped and noisy, but a sea whose muffled murmurs are the prophets of the storm." Silent spectators lined the route to St. Finbar's Cathedral Chapel, behind the ruins of the cathedral, their heads bowed against a driving rain. Flags flew at half mast. Every store and office on Broad Street was shuttered, and the *News and Courier* office was draped in black crepe.

A soprano sang "Raise Me, Jesus" as the "deep sobs of the great organ" filled the church. Seven priests and two bishops presided over the service. Roman Catholic bishop H. P. Northrop gave the eulogy, calling Dawson a "gallant and knightly gentleman, and a true Christian man." But, inexplicably, Northrop went on to tell a vague story that would set off a new round of gossip. Dawson, the bishop said, believed in God and was loyal to the church, but "he shared with you and me in the frailties of a common nature." Several months before, he said, Dawson had been accused of misconduct by one of his political opponents. Bishop Northrop had called Dawson in and begged him never to give anyone cause to say such things again. Dawson promised that he wouldn't. But about a month before the murder, he had come back to confess his sins and ask the bishop if he should resign from the vestry. Northrop had said no.

The mourners were left confused. What kind of "misconduct" had made Dawson offer to resign? Had he been unfaithful to Sarah? Was Hélène involved? Dawson's former business partner Bartholomew R. Riordan, now a real-estate developer, assured the *New York Times* that Dawson's home life was happy and that "insinuations to the contrary were utterly without foundation." But the rumors would not die.

The *Times* praised Dawson as a "power for good," a man who "counseled the people of the South to bury dead things and take hold of living opportunities." However, the black newspaper the *New York Age* recalled a different Dawson, a man who had defended "the outrages and murders committed upon the colored citizens of South Carolina." Instead of remembering him as the man who had risked his career by condemning the Hamburg murders, the paper called attention to the way he later backed down. Dawson's death proved that "those who live by violence shall die by violence," and the pope should have "snatched back" his knighthood and "spewed" him out of the church.[7] Firmly planted in the center when it came to racial politics, since the earthquake Dawson had lost the respect of people on both ends of the spectrum. He was buried next to his baby son at St. Lawrence Cemetery.

THE NEXT MORNING, March 14, the coroner's jury convened to hold a formal inquest. Spectators packed the basement of the Fireproof Building, trying to catch a glimpse of Thomas McDow, who was guarded by four policemen and three deputy sheriffs. The *New York Times* claimed that only the pouring rain prevented the prisoner from being lynched.[8]

Responding to questions from the solicitor, and by now well coached by his attorneys, McDow claimed that he had shot in self-defense, after Dawson hit him once with his cane and was about to strike him again. He was charged with murder and denied bail. His coachman Moses Johnson was charged with being an "accessory before the fact"—he was said to have carried notes from McDow to both Hélène Burdayron and Julia Smith. Johnson and McDow's cook were both jailed, though the cook was freed on bail after one day. Julia Smith was also released. Moses Johnson was held in seclusion, while McDow welcomed visitors "at his pleasure."[9] A sofa was brought to his cell, and instead of eating prison fare he had fine meals delivered.

DAWSON'S DOG BRUNO, the Newfoundland, took up his usual post at the gate every evening to watch for his master's return. When Dawson failed to appear, he began to howl. After enduring several sleepless nights, the neighbors threatened to poison him. Finally, Sarah took Bruno upstairs to Dawson's room, where he wriggled under the bed and came out with an old pair of slippers. After that, the dog seemed to understand that Frank was gone. He stopped howling, but he also stopped eating. Finally, he collapsed and died, a clear case, Warrington later claimed, of "animal suicide."[10]

AT THE END OF March, Katie McDow moved back into her house with her daughter and her father. A stream of poor people paid their respects, telling reporters from the *World* that Dr. McDow had often helped them without demanding payment.[11]

Andrew McGrath and Asher Cohen knew that McDow had a bad reputation. He had been blackballed by the local medical society, and one South Carolina newspaper reported that he was "known in almost every bawdy house in the city." There was no telling when his name might be publicly linked to the grave-robbing scandal, and one of the key witnesses to the murder, Julia Smith, was also his mistress. McDow had tried to bribe his brother to kill his wife and father-in-law, and there were police reports to prove it. And one of his patients, a Mrs. Fair, offered to testify that Dawson had not inflicted the wound on his forehead. At 1:30 on the afternoon of the murder, she said, McDow had come to her home and "insulted her grossly." She had a pistol handy and pulled it out to defend her honor. McDow turned to flee and banged his head on the doorframe. If the prosecution could find a way to introduce this information in court, they could paint a picture of the killer as a menace to society.[12]

The man who would take charge of making the case against McDow was William St. Julien Jervey, solicitor of the first circuit. Jervey brought in two attorneys to assist him, Henry Augustus Middleton Smith and Julian Mitchell. Smith, Dawson's personal lawyer and now the administrator of his estate, was descended from a signer of the Declaration of Independence, a distinction that set him apart even in a room full of bluebloods. His partner, Julian Mitchell, was one of the lawyers McDow had tried to reach the night of the murder. Both were at least a decade younger than the defense attorneys.[13]

As Smith prepared for the trial, Sarah Dawson badgered him with advice and exhortations. He must not under any circumstances admit that Dawson might have struck McDow. He must make sure that Hélène did not try to pass herself off as the children's governess; Hélène, she said, was "a maid for my children and their playmate and trusted companion"— an au pair, as we would say today. That, she told Smith, would "sufficiently explain why a man like Captain Dawson who would have protected the vilest of women who claimed protection, was doubly bound to save a foolish girl from the consequences of her own indiscretion, and in so doing, protect his innocent children from a lawless beast."[14]

"I trust [Hélène] has been sent away," one of Sarah's sisters wrote to another. "It is too horrible to think of her sheltered by the roof her vileness has made desolate — and there is great danger of its giving rise to the belief that the creature has [Sarah] in her power some way, and that she dare not discharge her." But Sarah was convinced that Hélène was innocent, the victim of a predatory man, and she needed someone to care for the children more than ever. Hélène continued to live in the Dawson household.[15]

As the date of McDow's trial approached, Sarah grew nearly deranged. She was sure McDow had been hired to kill her husband. When Isaac Heyward told her he wanted to quit his job as butler, she decided that he must have been bribed to leave so that her enemies could plant a spy in his place. She preferred to keep Isaac with her and, as she put it, "intimidate him into silence." One evening she drove out to the cemetery to put flowers on Frank's grave. Several black men were working nearby. "She is fixing that old devil again," one remarked, and the others chuckled loudly. The idea that black laborers felt free to mock her and her dead husband upset Sarah so much that she reported it to H. A. M. Smith.[16]

"May God bless and inspire you and Mr. Mitchell," Sarah wrote Smith the Friday before the trial. "It is not only my husband's name you are striving to save from assassins of body as well as fame. It is the honor of South Carolina." She added, "Dear friend, I am not meddling! I am only too wretched for silence."[17]

MCDOW'S TRIAL began on Monday, June 24, 1889, as gusts of rain swept the streets. At the county courthouse, men jammed the stairways from the first floor to the third, while those still outside pushed to get in. The bailiff and his deputies struggled to keep a passageway clear. Inside, the courtroom was a sea of human flesh. Hundreds of sweaty bodies pushed against the railings that separated spectators from participants.[18]

At a little before ten o'clock, McDow was led to the dock. He paused before sitting to flick the dust from his chair with a white silk handkerchief. Before the first words were spoken, the trial took on a symbolic meaning far removed from the original quarrel. The question to be decided, of course, was not whether Thomas B. McDow had killed Francis Dawson. After all, McDow had confessed. The question was why he had pulled the trigger and whether he had acted in self-defense. The genteel and well-to-do saw the trial as a tournament between two teams of clever lawyers. Working people saw it differently. Frank Dawson might be dead, yet everything he stood for was on trial. But what, exactly, did he stand for?

As soon as McDow was seated, Judge Joseph Brevard Kershaw called the court to order and jury selection began.[19] There were seventeen blacks and nineteen whites in the pool of potential jurors. By law, all were men — women would not be allowed to serve as jurors in South Carolina state courts until 1969. To the amusement of the out-of-town press, a barefoot boy drew the names from a battered cigar box. Local people saw this process as anything but funny. Earlier that month, when jurors had been selected to serve in the current term of the South Carolina Court of General Sessions, the black jury commissioner, William Ingliss, had been accused of tampering with the box. One newspaper reported that the container had not been shaken as required by law, and that Ingliss had taken all of the slips from one corner, presumably because he had planted the names of black men there. Like the late Stephney Riley, Ingliss, a barber at the Charleston Hotel, was dependent on white patronage. After the earthquake, he had pleased white officials by opposing a separate relief fund for black victims. On the first day of McDow's trial, Ingliss was called to the witness stand to swear again that he had pulled the names at random. Cohen settled the matter by declaring that he saw Ingliss stir the ballots with his hand and that "he thought the jury fairly drawn."

In fact, Cohen must have been delighted by the large number of black and working-class men in the pool, since his defense strategy rested on picking twelve jurors who were likely to be sympathetic to McDow. He and McGrath rejected six whites and two blacks by peremptory challenge. One white man admitted under questioning by the prosecution that he had publicly expressed support for McDow. He was excused for cause. In the end, seven black men and five white were called to serve. They included a bricklayer, three carpenters, a fisherman, and a drayman — all black — two blacksmiths, one white and one black, and four other white men. A white insurance agent was elected foreman.[20]

The very existence of that mixed-race, mostly working-class jury was considered by many whites to be a threat to the social order. But for blacks and to a lesser extent for poor whites, the jury represented democracy in action, a rare occurrence in their part of the world. Though the state of South Carolina still operated under a constitution written during Radical Reconstruction and the U.S. Supreme Court had ruled in 1880 that blacks could not be excluded from juries solely on the basis of race, southern states routinely dodged the law. It was not unusual to find a token black man serving on a jury, as had been the case at Dr. Amos Bellinger's first trial in 1885 for the murder of Stephney Riley, or no black men at all, as at Bellinger's second trial that year. It was also fairly common for mixed juries to rule on cases of black-on-black crime. But for a majority-black jury to sit in judgment of a respected white man was unprecedented in South Carolina.

The trial was also sure to raise another set of troubling questions: Did a servant have a right to live her own life? Should she be free to love any man she chose? "Ladies" were entitled by tradition to male deference — but was chivalry owed to a menial employee? And more than that, the trial was a judgment on the complicated legacy of Frank Dawson himself — the public servant and the ruler of the ring, the man who condemned separate and unequal railroad cars yet was thought to have said that rape wasn't rape when a white man did it to a black woman.

HIS EYEGLASSES dangling from a hook on his lapel, prosecutor William St. Julien Jervey opened the trial by calling witnesses to reconstruct the day of the murder. Policeman Samuel Gordon described the moment George Harper drove up to him and shouted that someone had been killed. Jervey tried to get Gordon to explain why he was in the neighborhood. At first he would only say that he had been on some vague "special duty." Jervey demanded that he reveal the nature of his assignment, and the judge ruled that he must. Using crude words not often heard in polite society, Gordon said that he was looking for a man who had been flashing his penis at passing women.

Gordon's revelation made the spectators sit up and listen, but the first real sensation of the trial came from Dr. Middleton Michel, who had autopsied Dawson's body. Michel reached into a bag and, like a magician producing a rabbit, pulled out a headless, armless, legless human torso. The dismembered corpse, a specimen from the medical school, had been preserved by drying. It was essentially human jerky, having been hung up to desiccate like so much salted beef. Doctors and medical students were accustomed to seeing these grotesque artifacts, but the general public was not. Michel explained that dye had been injected into the blood vessels: red for arteries and blue for veins. Jabbing his finger at a nondescript lump, he said, "This is a dried, shriveled kidney." The bottom of Dawson's right kidney had been "grooved" by the bullet.

Michel pointed out the aorta and the vena cava. If the ball had come from the front, he told the jury, it would have opened both of these large blood vessels. Instead, it had cut only the vena cava, the "great vein which returns the blood to the heart from all parts of the body." It would take about half a minute for such an injury to cause death. A torn vena cava could empty the body in just a few seconds — "gurgle, gurgle, gurgle." Michel admitted that he had stopped searching for the ball as soon as he saw the condition of these two blood vessels. They told him everything he needed to know: Dawson had been shot in the back.

Dr. Michel had practiced medicine for thirty-five years, and, he told the court, he had examined many dead bodies. But he may have felt squeamish about dissecting Dawson's corpse, the remains of a friend with whom he had spoken just hours before the murder. Whatever the reason, Michel had closed Dawson's body before conducting a thorough examination, and the fact that he did not find the ball would score a major point for the defense.

Lt. James Fordham, the black police officer who had discovered McDow's attempt to bury the body, was called to the stand. The black men in the courtroom, both jurors and spectators, watched closely to see how this dignified witness would be treated by both sets of lawyers. Jervey, who hoped to paint a picture of McDow as a cold-blooded killer, simply asked questions that would serve to draw out ghoulish details about the grave in the closet. But cross-examination was a minefield for the defense. With a majority-black jury, Asher Cohen could not afford to cast doubt on Fordham's honesty and intelligence. He asked a few easy questions and Fordham was dismissed.

And on this anticlimactic note, court adjourned for the day. McDow shook dozens of hands before he was led away to a carriage at the rear of the building. Ordinarily the jury would have been sequestered in such an important case. Cots would have been brought in and set up in the courthouse. But this jury included both blacks and whites, and there was no convenient way to house them separately. After much debate, the jurors were all sent home.

ON TUESDAY MORNING, the crowds were so thick that the police used clubs to clear a path into the courtroom. At ten sharp the constables "rammed their staffs upon the floor" and shouted, "Silence in the Court." For two hours both sides droned on, quibbling about the mundane facts of the case, but at noon, there was a flurry at the back of the courtroom. "The Governess!" spectators cried. "The French maid!"

Hélène Burdayron squeezed through a narrow opening cleared by the constable. Her black dress was demure, with white lace at the cuffs, but as more than one reporter noted, it was also snug enough to reveal "a bust fit for a Venus." Dr. McDow stared, tipping back in his chair. Their eyes met and held.

Hélène was handed a ragged Bible tied up with string. "Kiss the book," demanded the clerk. Hélène looked bewildered. The prosecution offered to call in an interpreter. McGrath and Cohen objected. Hélène could speak English, they said, and a translator would "break the force of the cross-examination." "Kiss the book," repeated the constable. The witness did not move.

"Kiss the book," urged H. A. M. Smith. Finally, the constable raised the book to his own lips, and Hélène's eyes lit up. She took the Bible and kissed it.

"What is your name?" asked Smith.

"Marie Burdayron," she answered.

"What?" barked the court stenographer. Hélène calmly spelled her name. The crowd inched forward "like the walls of a glacier."

Playing to a room full of rapt men, Hélène told her story. She had met Dr. McDow on the first of February and he had asked her to run away with him. She replied that she wouldn't leave Mrs. Dawson "for anything in the world." The next day she encountered him in the street, near the Dawsons' gate. After that he always followed when she walked the children to school. He claimed he could no longer bear to live with his wife. Hélène swore that she had told McDow to "get patience." She reminded him that he was married and "not the only man in Charleston who was unhappy with his wife." Sitting on the edge of his chair, Dr. McDow leaned toward the witness-box.

On the day before the murder, Hélène said, McDow had told her that they were being tailed by a detective. "McDow," she claimed to have said, "you are ruining my reputation. My duty is to be in Captain Dawson's house, not running in the street with a married man and father."

"I don't give a snap for what Charleston thinks," McDow replied, according to Hélène.

On cross-examination, McGrath asked Hélène if she loved McDow. Hélène responded that she "felt for his misfortunes."

McGrath bore down: did she believe that McDow would support her if she "gave herself" to him? "I never gave myself to him," Hélène shot back.

"I said if you had consented to give yourself to him, did you have any doubt that he would have supported you?"

"As he was talking to me I had a right to believe it."

Jervey stood up to protest that Hélène had not understood the question. He asked again for an interpreter. "I think her answers are very pertinent, comprehensive, and well-expressed," Judge Kershaw answered. The interrogation continued.

McGrath asked Hélène why, if she knew it was wrong, she had continued to listen to McDow. "I don't know," she replied. Did she believe that McDow was in love with her? "No."

"You say that with so much emphasis that I am inclined to believe you mean yes," McGrath taunted.

"I am not accustomed to say lies," Hélène shot back, "and I tell you no!"

Hélène Marie Burdayron refused to bow to Charleston's notion of how a virtuous girl should behave. She would not even pay lip service to South Carolina's sacred principles: divorce was wrong, adultery was unthinkable, and no respectable woman would encourage a married man. Watching her give as good as she got, the spectators and the jury must have wondered whether Dawson himself had succumbed to her charms. After all, she had been living in his house for eighteen months.

McGrath handed Hélène a portrait of herself and asked how Dr. McDow had come to possess it. She had not *given* the photograph to McDow, Hélène said — she *showed* it to him, at his request, and he had snatched it from her hand. Several times she asked him to give it back, and he refused. How hard had she tried to get the picture back? "I did not fall on my knees and beg for it."

How many times had McDow kissed her? Hélène didn't know.

"How many times?" McGrath pressed.

"Two times, and two times too much." The crowd began to titter.

"Only twice?"

"Yes, only twice. You want some more?" The courtroom erupted in laughter.

"You let him kiss you?"

"I scratched his face."

What had she scratched him with?

"My hat pin."

"You let a man's hand rest on your shoulder without reproving him?"
"Yes."

"He can put his hand on your shoulder whenever he pleases?"
"Not when he pleases."

"When it pleases you?"
"Yes."

"When you don't make him take it away it is because it pleases you that it should be there?"

"Of course," Hélène replied, as if the answer were obvious.

Frustrated by Hélène's saucy obstinacy, McGrath turned to the police reports found in Dawson's pocket. He asked what had happened between her and McDow at the house on Bee Street. McDow, Hélène said, took her by the arm "softly and sweetly" and tried to lead her inside the gate. She had refused to follow him. McGrath attempted to get Hélène to say that McDow wanted her to go into the house and have sex with him. Hélène swore she had no idea what he was up to. "Did you suppose that he wanted you to go and play croquet with him?" McGrath quipped.

"I did not suppose so," she answered.

Again McGrath asked for a translator, and again Judge Kershaw replied that Hélène's answers were perfectly intelligible. "If you think that it is so easy to explain yourself in a strange language suppose you speak French to me," Hélène told Judge Kershaw.

"You would twist me around your finger just like this," the judge replied, openly flirting with the witness. "You are young and I am old and my only safety is in English."

As one reporter observed, Hélène was simply "too much for Judge McGrath, old stager that he is."

For more than two hours, the lawyers kept Hélène on the stand. At the end of her testimony, H. A. M. Smith offered his arm and escorted her out. Smiling, McDow moved his chair aside to let them pass. The prosecution had presented its evidence against him, and he had come off as a vulnerable, unhappy man who had lost his head over a beautiful woman. Could he be convicted for that?

ON DAY THREE, Wednesday, the courtroom was again full to bursting. All "the available standing, sitting, and breathing room" was fully occupied. To launch McDow's defense, Asher Cohen called George Washington Harper, who had been sitting in a buggy near the McDow house when the fatal shot was fired. Harper, the key witness in McDow's claim of self-defense, wore his best clothes: a long-tailed black coat, a pair of striped trousers, a white lace shirt with an oversized collar, and a multicolored tie. He recalled seeing Dawson get out of the streetcar on the afternoon of the murder and go into McDow's office. Four or five minutes later he heard a shot and what he described as a "surkling" groan. Someone exclaimed, "You said you would take my life and now I have taken yours."

The prosecution argued that Harper was too far away to have heard people talking inside the office, much less a "surkling groan." But the coachman stuck to his story, and the black men on the jury watched to see how the lawyers treated him. Prosecutors Smith and Jervey were condescending, defense attorneys Cohen and McGrath respectful.

Judge Kershaw called Dr. McDow to the stand. Spectators poured in from the lobby and the streets outside. Pale and agitated, the defendant asked for a glass of water. McGrath asked the questions. McDow said that around 3:40 p.m. on March 12, he heard his doorbell ring. The servants were all at dinner, so he went to answer it himself.

"Are you Dr. McDow?" asked his visitor. McDow said that he was.

"I am Captain Dawson."

McDow invited Dawson in. His neighbor stalked into the vestibule and announced, "Dr. McDow, I have just been informed of your ungentlemanly conduct toward one of my servants." Dawson's manner, McDow added, was "irritable" and "aggressive."

"I forbid you to speak to her," Dawson growled. McDow retorted that he would speak to Hélène whenever he pleased.

"I give you to understand that she is under my protection, and if you speak to her again I shall publish you in the paper."

"And if you do, you infernal scoundrel," shouted McDow, "I will hold you personally responsible. Get out of my office!"

McDow testified that Dawson raised his cane and smacked McDow on the head, knocking him onto the sofa. He lifted his hand to strike again, and as the enraged editor towered over him, McDow drew his pistol and "fired without taking aim."

Dawson groaned, "You have killed me."

McDow replied, "You have tried to take my life, sir, and I have taken yours." Dawson turned white, staggered toward the desk — and fell.

McDow leaned down and felt for a pulse. He thought of calling another doctor, or of trying to treat the wound himself, but he knew that Dawson was dying. "Under the appalling circumstances I lost all self-control," McDow admitted. He described hiding Dawson's hat and cane in the privy and attempting — without success — to conceal the body under the stairs. The doorbell rang, and McDow answered it to find Officer Gordon. When Gordon finally left, he said, he tried to move Dawson's body back out of the closet.

But he was exhausted, and he could barely see in the darkness under the stair. He went out to buy some candles, and when he got back, he managed to drag the body back into the office. By then he was "almost crazy with excitement." He saw that Dawson's face was scraped, so he dampened a towel and knelt down, "lovingly," to wipe off the blood.[21]

Cohen asked McDow if he felt regret. After a pregnant pause he answered, "I regretted the necessity of having to do this thing." The *New York Times* characterized McDow's attitude as "chipper." He had reason to feel pleased — when the prosecution attempted to bring up his past misdeeds, Judge Kershaw ruled that the character of the witness "could not be inquired into by the State unless [McDow] voluntarily put it at issue."

The rest of the afternoon was taken up with a series of lesser witnesses — the doctor who had examined the wound on McDow's head, an architect who had made a scale drawing of the closet, and two men who were brought in to testify to Dawson's reputation. Former mayor William W. Sale said Dawson was widely regarded as "violent and aggressive," a man "on the bulldog order" who "never let go." On cross-examination he admitted that he had quarreled with the editor, who, during an election campaign, had spread "a most malicious lie" about him through the *News and Courier*.

The defense rested. At the prosecutor's request, the court adjourned early.

ON THURSDAY, a pouring rain failed to disperse the crowds outside the courthouse. Inside, men jammed the steamy corridors. The heat was taking a toll on the defense lawyers. McGrath mopped his brow with a large bandanna and resorted frequently to the comfort of his snuffbox, a habit that shocked a New York reporter. Cohen was limping.

Dr. Michel was brought back to the stand to testify again about the path of the bullet. Then Dr. Robert A. Kinloch, a professor of clinical surgery at the medical college, was called to provide expert testimony. Kinloch was an important witness because, like Dr. Michel, he had examined Dawson's body on the night of the murder. He did not say outright that Dawson had been shot from the side, not the back, but he announced that it was impossible for soft tissue to deflect a bullet. He added that the notion of deflection was "an old one," dating to the days when gun barrels were smooth instead of rifled and bullets were generally round. Some surgeons still believed that soft tissue could change the path of a bullet. He did not.

Defense attorney Cohen asked what Kinloch would think of a man who said that a bullet could be diverted by soft tissue. "I should say that such a man had no knowledge of physiology, anatomy, surgery, or medical science," he declared. The dried torso was brought in again, and Kinloch used a pink cord to illustrate the path of the bullet.

Cohen dismissed Kinloch and called Dr. Michel back to the stand. Michel had not been in the courtroom during Kinloch's testimony, and Cohen tried to get him to say that the bullet that had killed Dawson might have been fired from the front. Michel refused. "Would you have any respect for the opinion of a man who said that [a bullet] could not be deflected except by a spinal column, a large bone, or a tough sinew?" asked Cohen, deliberately repeating the same phrases he had used with Dr. Kinloch.

"I should doubt his knowledge of anatomy, surgery, and medical science," replied Michel. The crowd, to his bewilderment, roared with laughter and could not be brought to order for some time. Confusion reigned, just as Cohen had hoped.

When Cohen finished discrediting Dr. Michel, St. Julien Jervey rose to face the jury and sum up the case for the prosecution. "My business here is . . . to ask you for justice," he announced. "Justice to the community." It was the responsibility of the jurors, he said, to "save society." This was not a competition between McDow and Dawson. "We are representing this State," he said, "its civilization and society; and what the State demands is that where crime has been committed it shall be punished."

In fact, what Jervey called "civilization" and "society" had not been kind to blacks. These words were well-known euphemisms for white rule, and they were frequently used as high-sounding excuses for butchery and oppression. Jervey himself, in fact, was a living reminder of the violent overthrow of black rights. He had helped organize the Carolina Rifle Club, he had been present at the Cainhoy massacre, and his very appointment as solicitor was the result of what most blacks considered outright thievery: in 1876, the year white supremacists overthrew Republican rule, Jervey had lost the election, but the Democrats had simply ousted the winner and appointed Jervey in his place. Interrupted frequently by Asher Cohen, whose objections often resulted in lengthy discussions with the judge, Jervey pontificated for more than three hours. George Harper, the coachman who had heard McDow say, "You have tried to take my life, Sir, and so I have taken yours," was the only witness who could corroborate the doctor's claim of self-defense. Jervey concentrated on undermining his credibility. Could Harper really have heard what was said inside McDow's office from where he was standing down the street? The solicitor sneered at the very idea. "You must make due allowance for a man like that. His mind was inflamed." And how likely was it that in the heat of a quarrel two men would use such formal language? Harper must be lying.

Then Jervey turned to another subject, Dawson's clothes. When he was killed, the editor had been wearing a pair of expensive dog-skin gloves. If he had anticipated a fight, wouldn't he have removed them? However, this strategy backfired. Very few of the jurors, white or black, had ever owned such fancy gloves, much less faced the problem of whether to remove them while picking a fight.

Was Hélène a servant, Jervey asked, or, as Sarah had insisted, almost a member of the family? The upper classes attached great importance to such distinctions, believing as they did that servants were not entitled to much respect. But because most of the jury came from walks of life where that notion was insulting, instead of suggesting that Dawson had acted out of chivalry, Jervey had managed to show that Dawson was not like them at all.

When Jervey finally concluded, Judge Kershaw announced that from this point on, the jury would be sequestered. Cots were brought in and set up in the courtroom, with sections cordoned off for blacks and whites. The jurors could determine a man's guilt or innocence together, but when relaxing they had to be separated.

At ten o'clock on Friday morning, Asher Cohen took the floor, remarkably spry for a man who just the day before had appeared exhausted and in pain. His summation would earn him an enduring place in Charleston's legal history. Abandoning the dispassionate pose he had maintained throughout the trial, he took up the attack-dog stance of the *Charleston*

World. Cohen led with an indictment of Dawson's newspaper, which he said had tried to poison the city and the nation against McDow. And yet, he declared, in a conscious echo of Ben Tillman's rhetoric, it could be said "to the glory of this old city, to the credit of the press and the glory and honor of religion there were some journals who by their independent course protested against this pre-judgment."

Playing to the jury's distrust of the system, he suggested that in this case the State itself was prejudiced, so that "the very source to which we look for safety and protection becomes a source of ruin." Cohen pointed out that McDow's office was a part of his home. Dawson had invaded the man's private sanctuary to assail him with words and blows. McDow had pulled the trigger only because he believed himself to be in mortal danger. The jurors, he said, should ask themselves if they would not have done the same thing.

White South Carolinians were almost always unwilling to convict someone who claimed he was acting in self-defense.[22] And for the seven black jurors, only a generation removed from slavery, the idea that a powerful man felt free to invade a private home was particularly offensive. To make sure they got the point, Cohen hammered it home: "When any one can ruthlessly enter your home after being told to retire," he roared, when someone "assails you in your own home, whether your home be a palace on your sea front or an honest cottage in your suburbs," society itself is "adrift upon an unknown, dark and dangerous sea." The spectators burst into applause.

Dawson, Cohen said, could surely have protected his family by simply discharging Hélène. Moreover, he could have found a way to do so quietly, without damaging her reputation. Instead, he went to McDow's office determined to "degrade," to "punish," and to "chastise" him. To demonstrate self-defense, a man did not have to prove that he had been "battered from head to foot." Indeed, the whole idea of self-defense was to prevent being battered.

Cohen said that God must have sent George Harper to the murder scene to make sure the truth would come out. "I want to put Harper before you in the light that his honesty and purpose entitle him to be put. He stands before you uncontradicted and unimpeachable."

Then he called for Dawson's underpants. He held up the knee-length linen garment, pointed to the bullet hole an inch in front of the seam, and suggested that as soon as the jury retired, the men should take off their own trousers and look at their underwear. Dawson's pants could never have twisted so that a bullet that was fired at his back would penetrate in front of the seam. "I don't know that there are any tailors on the jury, but I wish there was," Cohen said. "They all know that when pants are made . . . they should be made with the seam right on the hip."

Cohen conceded that McDow had been wrong to try to seduce Hélène. "But Gentlemen," he went on, "a man seldom makes the first advances. There is always something in the eye or manner that extends an invitation." The prosecution had depicted McDow as a sexual predator; now the defense was blaming Hélène for luring him into a trap.

Asher Cohen went on speaking for more than three hours. McDow, he said, had already paid a high price for his actions. "Send him to [his wife]," Cohen begged, "chastened by his trials, to be baptized in her and that little girl's tears of innocent joy and love to a better and, God grant, a happier life."

Compared to Cohen's spellbinding performance on Friday, Julian Mitchell's concluding remarks on Saturday were forgettable. After the dinner break that day, Judge Kershaw charged the jury to compare the definitions of justifiable homicide, felonious homicide, murder, and manslaughter. He talked about reasonable doubt, circumstantial evidence, and the difference between malice and provocation. Then he sent the men into seclusion to decide McDow's fate.

The talk on the street was that the black jurors would vote to acquit but that one or more of the white jurors would certainly hold out for conviction. The New York World predicted that McDow would walk free.

Inside the courthouse, there was no indecision. When the jury took an initial vote, the result was twelve to zero. Black and white, all the men agreed — McDow was not guilty. Although they were eager to go home and put the trial behind them, the jurors did not want to be criticized for making a hasty decision. The door to the conference room remained firmly shut.

About two that afternoon a deputy entered the jury room to collect orders for dinner. The foreman told him that the jury would need no dinner that day. At 2:45 the telephone rang at Judge Kershaw's house. The Charleston World reported that "a silence as gruesome as the stillness about a death-bed" fell inside the courthouse. Twelve stone-faced men filed in and took their seats in the jury box. Dr. McDow was led to his chair, grinning around a quid of tobacco.

"We find the defendant not guilty," the foreman declared.

A cheer rose from both sides of the aisle, from white spectators and black.

Charles Ahrens, of all people, rushed up to shake the hand of his son-in-law, the man who had tried to have him killed. "Mr. Sheriff!" shouted Judge Kershaw over the din. "Can't you arrest some one . . . for this violation of all decency?"

Thomas McDow strolled out of the courtroom. The little street behind the courthouse was so packed that there was barely room for his carriage to squeeze through. The owner of a livery stable, John Frazer, threw his hat in the air. "Hurrah for McDow!" he shouted. An answering yell went up from the mostly black crowd.

One man cried, "That settles it! The richest man in Charleston can't call me a nigger again."[23]

Frank Dawson, of course, was certainly rich and powerful, but in the post-Reconstruction world of the South he wasn't the enemy of the black man. Or at least he wasn't compared to the many people who were making plans to return blacks to near-slavery.

Tragically, Dawson was now remembered by black Charlestonians only for his last editorial and not for his long record of bucking white supremacy. He was remembered by white Charlestonians as a tyrant, a man who thought he knew better than they did.

In just thirty months, the hero of the earthquake had become an enemy of the people.

Epilogue

REBUILDING THE WALLS

THE VERDICT OUTRAGED newspaper editors from New York to San Francisco, spawning indignant editorials. The case was invoked not to honor Dawson's strong stands but as a reason to disfranchise blacks and bar them from serving on juries. The *Savannah Morning News* acknowledged that black jurors may "intend to do what is right, but in many instances they are not capable of discerning the right." Even some of the northern press, such as the *New York World*, warned that blacks "are not safely to be trusted with the function of jury-man in cases of a publicly exciting character."[1]

Letters appeared at the Charleston post office addressed to "The Murderer of Captain Dawson," and they were promptly delivered to Dr. McDow's door. One, signed "A Southern M.D.," cursed him with biblical vengeance: "May snakes spring up in your path; [may] earth's fruits turn to ashes in your mouth; . . . May the earth deny thee a home; the dust a grave; the sun its light, and heaven her God. . . . Your hell will surely burn within your own vile bosom."[2]

But the tone among those who knew both Dawson and McDow was decidedly different. In the room where Frank Dawson had died, Thomas McDow boasted to the press that he still had a good medical practice and no intention of leaving Charleston. "I have plenty of friends," he said, "and I know they will overlook this little indiscretion." Indeed, along with the letters attacking him, McDow received many baskets of flowers. At the Charleston Club, where Dawson had been a member, one man declared that killing the editor was the best piece of work Dr. McDow had ever done. Ashmead Courtenay wrote to congratulate attorney Asher Cohen, condemning Dawson and his allies as if they had been running a crime syndicate: "It is seldom one can be found bold enough to denounce a crowd that is hurling our old city down into the depths, and he who does it deserves the praise of all." A woman from Summerville put it even more bluntly: "It was a great thing for us Dawson being killed, he was trying to cultivate us up to being Yankees." An Alabama lawyer who had grown up in Charleston exclaimed, "What a sad commentary on Dawson's life that he should be killed with his name tacked to a servant girl, when there were so many other and nobler things to kill him for."[3]

Sarah, who had always been fragile, turned bitter and vindictive. When Frank's personal effects were returned after the trial, she found among them the bloody towel that McDow had used to wipe her husband's dead face. She shoved it in an envelope, addressed it "To the Murderer," and asked the coroner to hand deliver it to her neighbor.[4]

Shortly after the trial, novelist Grace King encountered Sarah at Blowing Rock, a resort in the mountains of North Carolina. The widow's hair had turned "snow white" and her face was "ghastly pale." "She had been sent to the mountains in search of health," King wrote, "but she did not seem to care if she lost or found it." Another vacationer reported that Sarah had brought Hélène along, and that a huge crowd gathered to gawk at the notorious "French Maid" when the train stopped in Asheville.[5]

Dawson left his family a sizeable fortune, but most of his assets were tied up in stocks and bonds. Sarah received dividends from his investments and a check for the insurance he had taken out shortly before his death, but she could no longer live in the grand style to which she had been accustomed. She became convinced that Rudolph Siegling had duped her into signing away most of Frank's shares in the *News and Courier*. "Shame! Shame!" she wrote James Hemphill a year after the murder. "May God's hand be stretched out to save my children's heritage from the brand of infamy in the unclean hands of a disreputable parasite!"[6]

Sarah occupied her lonely days by cutting out newspaper accounts of the murder and trial and pasting them into a scrapbook, annotating them in the margins. Her brother Jimmy tried his best to convince her to move away. "Your dead husband had no friends in Charleston, neither have you or your children," he wrote in a letter that must have cut her to the quick. "Better far that you and yours should leave the accursed country and let God Almighty annihilate them with his earthquakes, storms, and fires."[7]

Hélène continued to live with the family, though Sarah insisted that she be examined by a doctor to determine whether she was still a virgin. (The doctor concluded that she was.) A little more than a year after Dawson's murder, Hélène walked into Warrington's bedroom and saw him sprawled on the floor, writing in his diary. She glanced over his shoulder and spied a reference to "the French maid," the phrase that had so often been used to cast doubt on her morals. Grabbing the book from Warrington's hands, she flung it into the fire. He wailed. Sarah ran to investigate and confronted Hélène. The argument quickly escalated.[8]

"I am glad your husband is dead! It serves you right!" Hélène hissed. "I knew in advance that he was going to be killed and *I let him be killed*" (original emphasis).

For a moment Sarah simply stared. Then she spat, "You will return immediately to Europe."

Attorney H. A. M. Smith advised Sarah to give Hélène some money and send her away, telling no one what she had said. Sarah followed this advice to the letter and asked her sister Miriam, who had moved to New York, to meet Hélène at the train station and make sure she boarded a ship. When Hélène complained that Sarah had failed to give her a reference, Miriam wrote a glowing letter herself. At five in the morning on April 19, 1890, Hélène Marie Burdayron sailed out of the Dawsons' lives. By 1891 Sarah felt that her life was "a daily crucifixion." For a time she hoped that her relatives and Frank's would pay back the money he had lent them, but those hopes were dashed. She harangued them all until her brother Jimmy refused to deal with her except through an attorney.[9]

Ethel married a lawyer and set up housekeeping in New Jersey. Warrington moved to Paris and eventually Sarah joined him there, leaving behind, as Grace King observed, "a country that had become loathsome to her." She was sure that her son was destined to become one of the world's great writers, worthy of all the sacrifices she had made to finance his education. When she died in 1909, her body was returned to Charleston and buried next to Frank's in the Catholic cemetery.[10]

WARRINGTON NEVER quite lived up to his mother's faith in his genius. His one real contribution to literature was to convince Sarah not to burn the journals she had kept during the Civil War. Published in 1913 as *A Confederate Girl's Diary* and republished in 1991 as *The Civil War Diary of Sarah Morgan*, they have won a place alongside Mary Chesnut's diaries as one of the greatest autobiographical works of the era.[11]

Henry Grady died of pneumonia just eight months after Dawson, and a statue of him was unveiled in Atlanta in 1891. "What Georgia has done for Grady[,] South Carolina should do for Dawson," declared an article in *The State*, a newspaper in Columbia founded by one of Dawson's former reporters.[12] But aside from his gravestone — a five-foot granite cross — no memorial to Frank Dawson was ever erected. No street or building bears his name. Only the newspaper he edited for twenty-two turbulent years, now called the *Post and Courier*, stands as a lasting tribute to his energy, his aspirations, and his tragic flaws.

Without Dawson to fight against, the *Charleston World* soon folded, and the *News and Courier* was again unchallenged as the city's premier newspaper.

THOMAS MCDOW killed himself in July 1904. He, his wife Katie, and her father, Charles Ahrens, lie buried side by side in Magnolia Cemetery, a stark testament to the ties that bind even the unhappiest of families.[13]

After the murder, according to Sarah, McDow's daughter Gladys "stopped growing and shriveled into a monkey-like dwarf." To the end of her life Sarah believed that the child had been "marked" by the sight of her father trying to hide Frank's dead body. Gladys eventually married, however, and published a book of sentimental verse.[14]

THE LADIES' Calhoun Monument Association was unhappy with the Calhoun Monument from the day it was erected. In 1896, less than ten years after it was built, the monument was pulled down and replaced by a larger figure on a taller pedestal. The new structure was ninety-six feet high, raising both Calhoun's nose and white supremacy to a height that would protect them from brickbats. The allegorical figures that had been planned for the original monument — Truth, Justice, the Constitution, and History — were nowhere in sight. The first statue was evidently melted down and sold for scrap, except for a single crooked finger that is now on display at the Charleston Museum.

The 1886 earthquake continues to play an important role in the lives of Charleston residents. In 2010 all of the older public schools on the peninsula and on Sullivan's Island were declared inadequate to withstand tremors comparable to those that shook Charleston on the sweltering night of August 31. Parents, teachers, and administrators debated what to do about the danger. What were the odds that such a quake would happen soon? They were small, but thousands of lives could be at risk. What would be the cost of repairing or rebuilding all those schools? It was high, and the school district didn't have the money. In the midst of the debate, Haiti was devastated by a quake less powerful than Charleston's. Photos of destroyed buildings and dead bodies filled the news. All of the suspect schools in Charleston County were closed and thousands of schoolchildren were bused to facilities miles away while education officials sought the funds to replace or retrofit their old institutions. Meanwhile, school-board officials made plans to test the other schools in the county, including those much closer to the 1886 epicenters than those downtown.

IN THE AFTERMATH of the earthquake, Charleston did not build a progressive new city on the ruins of the old, as Dawson had predicted. Instead, it joined the rest of the South in forging a social order that would oppress blacks almost as totally as had slavery. In 1885 a New York attorney who had grown up in antebellum Charleston was astonished to see black laborers riding the streetcars side by side with whites and sitting on the benches in Washington Square. Just five years later, the concept of equal treatment would be almost dead.[15]

Carlyle McKinley's scheme to rid the United States of all black people was published in September 1889 as An Appeal to Pharaoh. The famous explorer Henry M. Stanley promoted the plan, and Congress seriously debated deporting every black man, woman, and child in the nation. Even some black leaders supported the idea of emigration because they could see no prospect of a better life for their people in the United States.[16]

Just as the News and Courier and the Charleston World had predicted, President Benjamin Harrison pushed for legislation to protect voting rights and prosecute those who violated the election laws. "When and under what conditions is the black man to have a free ballot?" he asked. "When is he in fact to have those full civil rights which have so long been his in law?"[17] But the Democrats fought election reform tooth and nail, and it soon became a dead issue as white Americans across the country moved to reunite by agreeing to forget the cause of the Civil War.

The New York Age dared to hope in May 1889 that "respectable colored persons" would never again be forced, "at the mouth of the revolver," to accept shabby treatment by the railroads.[18] But the Age had it backward: southern railroads that did not discriminate would soon fall into line with those that did, and on Christmas Eve 1889, less than a year after Dawson's death, South Carolina state legislators repudiated the section of the state constitution that protected civil rights.

Their position would soon be officially endorsed by the Supreme Court of the United States. On June 7, 1892, a shoemaker named Homer Plessy boarded a train in New Orleans and deliberately sat down in a compartment reserved for whites. Plessy was very light skinned and could have passed for white, but when the conductor asked his race, he said that he was colored. When the conductor told him to move to a car reserved for blacks, Plessy refused. A detective arrested him and threw him in jail. In 1896 the U.S. Supreme Court's decision in *Plessy v. Ferguson* would give the states permission to maintain "separate but equal" public facilities.[19]

WITH DAWSON no longer standing in his way, Ben Tillman was elected governor of South Carolina in 1890 and called a convention to draft a new state constitution, one that systematically undid everything the Reconstruction government had stood for. It mandated separate schools for whites and blacks, banned interracial marriage, and stripped most blacks of the right to vote. Robert Smalls, the former U.S. congressman who had seen his own political power shrink to almost nothing, warned the federal government that the convention had been called "for no other purpose than the disfranchisement of the negro." His words fell on deaf ears. Tillman moved on to the U.S. Senate in 1894, where he proudly announced to his colleagues that South Carolina had done its "level best" to prevent blacks from voting. "We stuffed ballot boxes. We shot them," he boasted. And "we are not ashamed of it." Thus, in the words of W. E. B. Du Bois, "the slave went free; stood a brief moment in the sun; then moved back again toward slavery."[20]

THE BLACK MEN who struggled for equal treatment after the earthquake went on to fight other battles. Rev. George Rowe stayed in Charleston and continued to serve as minister to Plymouth Congregational Church. In 1897 he resigned to take over the Battery Congregational Church on Tradd Street, which was established as a "mission." He edited a newspaper called the *Charleston Enquirer* from 1892 to 1901. Rev. John Dart remained in Charleston, operating a print shop and editing a newspaper in addition to his ministerial duties. Dart tried to cooperate with the new regime, promising Governor Tillman the help of "the better class of colored people in up-holding law and order." Tillman frostily replied that "the negro must remain subordinate or be exterminated."[21]

Rev. William Henry Harrison Heard often said that his travels after the earthquake to raise funds from northern donors "opened up a whole new world." Heard worked tirelessly on behalf of the AME Church, the largest black denomination in the country, and served as U.S. minister and consul general to Liberia from 1895 to 1899. He died in 1937, seventy-two years after he was freed from slavery. Shortly before his death, he was denied a hotel room in Edinburgh, Scotland, because the proprietor was afraid that a black guest would repel U.S. tourists.[22]

The career of Dr. William D. Crum epitomizes the uphill battles await-ing black men of his generation. When Benjamin Harrison won the White House in 1888, Charleston Republicans expected Crum to be appointed postmaster of the city or collector of the Custom House in Charleston. Both positions went to whites. In 1892 President Harrison did appoint Crum postmaster, but whites protested and he quickly withdrew the offer. Crum ran for the U.S. Senate against Ben Tillman that year but lost by a landslide.[23]

In 1902 President Theodore Roosevelt appointed Crum as Charleston's collector of customs, a post that would give him authority over white men. A storm of controversy erupted, and the fight over his confirmation became one of the most significant battles of Roosevelt's presidency. U.S. Senator Ben Tillman blustered, "we still have guns and ropes in the South." James C. Hemphill, Dawson's successor as editor of the News and Courier, wrote in the newspaper that Crum "is a colored man, and that in itself ought to bar him from office." Roosevelt resorted to a technicality, first to put Crum in office and then to keep him there — he made the appointment during a congressional recess, removing the need for Senate approval. He declared, "I cannot consent to take the position that the door of hope — the door of opportunity — is to be shut upon all men, no matter how worthy, purely on the grounds of color."[24]

But as soon as Roosevelt left the White House, the door of opportunity slammed. William Howard Taft became president in 1909, and he refused to reappoint Crum as collector of the customs. Instead, Taft proposed that Crum be made consul general to Liberia, a position traditionally given to a black politician and the one held earlier by Rev. William Heard. Crum accepted the job and moved to Monrovia with his wife. He had always been interested in infectious diseases, and he treated some of his colleagues for "African fever." In September 1912 Dr. Crum himself contracted African fever and returned to the United States, where he could get better medical care. Shortly after he reached Charleston, Dr. Crum died, a sacrifice, as one northern newspaper put it, "upon the altar of . . . Southern prejudice."[25]

NATURAL DISASTERS give people an opportunity to shake things up, to change the way society works and build for the future. But in the wake of the 1886 earthquake, Charleston, like other southern communities, grew ever more determined to preserve the remnants of its past. As the twentieth century dawned, Charleston continued to struggle with two conundrums: how to develop new industries and how to deal with the color line. In 1901 off-and-on experiments with Gala Week morphed into a more ambitious attempt to bring tourists and investors to Charleston: the South Carolina Inter-State and West Indian Exposition. An imitation of similar fairs in Atlanta, Nashville, and elsewhere, it included a "Negro Department," headed by Booker T. Washington and Dr. William D. Crum, which was intended to showcase black achievements since emancipation. The white board of directors commissioned a sculpture that depicted a woman carrying cotton in a basket on her head, a man strumming a banjo, and another man with one hand on an anvil and the other on a plow. Black Charlestonians protested that the statue was demeaning and succeeded in having it moved but not banished from the fair. As historian Don Doyle observes, "the incident set the tone for an exposition that, though intended to display a new appreciation for blacks in Charleston's future, became yet another discouraging testament to the alienation between the races."[26]

In the 1920s a renewed reverence for the values of the Old South found expression in a literary and artistic movement now called the Charleston Renaissance. DuBose Heyward, who had narrowly escaped death on his first birthday when the earthquake shook down a chimney near his crib, would go on to write the novel *Porgy*, the inspiration for George and Ira Gershwin's folk opera *Porgy and Bess*. Alice Ravenel Huger Smith, the little girl who saw her world turned upside down when she camped under carpets after the earthquake, grew up to paint transcendently beautiful watercolor images of Lowcountry life before the Civil War, many of which glamorize slavery and the drudgery of the rice fields. With her father, D. E. Huger

Smith, she produced *The Dwelling Houses of Charleston*, a volume that helped launch the historic-preservation movement and laid the groundwork for Charleston's modern tourist industry.[27]

Novelist Josephine Pinckney, a generation younger than Smith and steeped in Freudian psychology, pictured the earthquake in her 1948 novel *Great Mischief* as the moment when Charleston's demons rose from the depths. Smothered by the demands of family and tradition, the protagonist sets his own house on fire, killing his obnoxious sister and her lover, a disabled Confederate veteran who embodies the unending burdens of the war. When the earth cracks open to reveal the depths of Hell, he leaps out into the abyss to join the devil.[28]

But if there was evil in Charleston after the earthquake, it resided not in Satan's imps but in man's worst instincts. Even as Frank Dawson lay dying on Thomas McDow's office floor, a raging river of racial hatred was carrying the nation toward seventy years of segregation and discrimination. Dawson himself could not have stopped it, and perhaps he would not have tried. He had learned that when it came to race, his fellow citizens were intransigent.

ACKNOWLEDGMENTS

To observe and record the effects of the Earthquake
require much journeying and patience.
—Lewis R. Gibbes, *Proceedings of the Elliott Society*, 1887

We are deeply grateful to the many friends, relatives, and colleagues who have patiently assisted us in our journeying.

Pradeep Talwani of the University of South Carolina educated us about earthquake science and the faults that lie under Charleston, both by showing us the great earthquake's marks on the landscape and by commenting on the manuscript.

Nancy Grayson believed in this story from the beginning and went to extraordinary lengths to acquire it for the University of Georgia Press.

Celia Patterson, Ted Rosengarten, Harlan Greene, Suzanne Galloway, Billy Dinwiddie, Jane Dupuis, and Cathy Woods read and commented on the manuscript in its many forms. We could not have asked for better historians, better writers, or better friends to help us shape a complex story.

Without the help of skilled archivists, historians would be paralyzed. We are especially grateful to Nic Butler and the rest of the staff at the South Carolina Room of the Charleston County Public Library; to Harlan Greene, Gene Waddell, and Marie Ferrara in Special Collections, Marlene and Nathan Addlestone Library, College of Charleston; to Allen Stokes and Beth Bilderback at the South Caroliniana Library; to Elizabeth Dunn in the Rare Book, Manuscript, and Special Collections Library, Duke University; to Susan Hoffius at the Waring Historical Library, Medical University of South Carolina; to Jennifer Scheetz and Sharon Bennett at the Charleston Museum; and to the staffs of the South Carolina Historical Society, the Charleston Library Society, the Charleston Catholic Diocese Archives, the City of Charleston Archives (whose earthquake records are now in the holdings of the Charleston County Public Library), the South Carolina Department of Archives and History, the Georgia Historical Society, and the New York Historical Society.

Robin Kelsey generously shared his unpublished manuscript on U.S. Geological Survey photographers. Robert B. Cuthbert brought to our attention many relevant letters from the collections of the South Carolina Historical Society.

Darren Felty and Kim Taylor, chairs of the English Department, Tim Brown, dean of the Division of Humanities and Social Sciences, and Mary Thornley, president of Trident Technical College, made it possible for Susan to carve out time for research and writing.

Most of all, we are grateful to our families for enduring twelve years of our shared obsession with sandblows, soup kitchens, Hoover Clubs, and Francis Warrington Dawson. When we started this project we each had children in grade school; now they are of an age to have graduated from college, and they wonder what on earth we've been doing while they've been growing up. Sometimes we do, too. But more often we're still excited by all these little stories and this big and very important one. We feel extremely lucky to have worked on it together.

NOTES

Throughout the notes, the following abbreviations and shortened citations are used:

AC	*Atlanta Constitution*
CCPL	Charleston County Public Library
BRT	Benjamin R. Tillman
CLS	Charleston Library Society
CDR	*Columbia (S.C.) Daily Register*
CW	*Charleston World*
ERC	Executive Relief Committee
FWD	Francis Warrington Dawson
FWD Family Papers	Francis Warrington Dawson Family Papers, Rare Book, Manuscript, and Special Collections Library, Duke University, Durham, N.C.
Hemphill Papers	Hemphill Family Papers, Rare Book, Manuscript, and Special Collections Library, Duke University, Durham, N.C.
KOL	Knights of Labor
Logan Papers	Frank Logan Papers (unprocessed), Rare Book, Manuscript, and Special Collections Library, Duke University, Durham, N.C.
N&C	*Charleston News and Courier*
N&O	*Raleigh News and Observer*
NYA	*New York Age*
NYF	*New York Freeman*
NYH	*New York Herald*
NYT	*New York Times*
NYW	*New York World*
RBMSCL, Duke	Rare Book, Manuscript, and Special Collections Library, Duke University, Durham, N.C.
RD	*Richmond (Va.) Dispatch*
Records of the ERC	Records of the Executive Relief Committee for the Earthquake of 1886, South Carolina Room, Charleston County Public Library

SCDAH	South Carolina Department of Archives and History, Columbia, S.C.
SCHM	*South Carolina Historical Magazine*
SCHS	South Carolina Historical Society, Charleston, S.C.
SCL	South Caroliniana Library, University of South Carolina, Columbia, S.C.
SMD	Sarah Morgan Dawson
SMD Scrapbook	Sarah Morgan Dawson Scrapbook, Francis Warrington Dawson Family Papers, Rare Book, Manuscript, and Special Collections Library, Duke University, Durham, N.C.
SMN	*Savannah (Ga.) Morning News*
WAC	William Ashmead Courtenay

Preface. Living with Disaster

1. "Czar of South Carolina": *Commercial Gazette* (Columbia, S.C.), December 2, 1883, qtd. in Dale B. J. Randall, *Joseph Conrad and Warrington Dawson: The Record of a Friendship* (Durham, N.C.: Duke University Press, 1968), 7.

2. C. Vann Woodward, *The Strange Career of Jim Crow* (1955; rpt., New York: Oxford University Press, 1974), 33.

Chapter One. The Great Shock

1. The "Speed of the Shocks" is discussed in Clarence Edward Dutton, *The Charleston Earthquake of August 31, 1886* (U.S. Geological Survey Ninth Annual Report, 1887–88; rpt., Arlington, Va.: U.S. Geological Survey, 1979), 355–89; Carl McKinley, "A Descriptive Narrative of the Earthquake of August 31, 1886," in *Year Book — 1886. Charleston, So. Ca.* (Charleston: Walker, Evans and Cogswell, n.d.), 428, claims the shocks traveled at three miles per second. Dutton details the effects of the earthquake throughout North America on pages 321–48, 410–528.

2. *NYW*, September 2, 1886, claimed the revival of the geyser at Yellowstone was caused by the Charleston earthquake. However, the *SMN* reported on September 1, 1886, that the Excelsior geyser at Yellowstone, "the most powerful geyser in the world," started spouting on Friday, August 27. Contemporary seismologists confirm that geysers can be triggered by large earthquakes far away. See S. Huysen et al., "Changes in Geyser Eruption Behavior and Remotely Triggered Seismicity in Yellowstone National Park Produced by the 2002 M7.9 Denali Fault Earthquake, Alaska," *Geology* 32, no. 6 (June 2004): 537–40. Cuba: Dutton, *Charleston Earthquake*, 527. Maine: *NYH*, September 1, 1886. N.C. mountains: *NYH*, September 5, 1886.

3. McGee in Washington, D.C.: *NYH*, September 2, 1886; *NYW*, September 2,

1886. McGee's grandfather at New Madrid: Emma P. McGee, *Life of W J McGee: Distinguished Geologist, Ethnologist, Anthropologist, Hydrologist, etc. in Service of United States Government* (Farley, Iowa: self-published, 1915).

4. *NYH*, September 1, 1886.

5. *RD*, September 1, 1886.

6. Terre Haute man, Louisville hotel, New Haven pool players: *NYH*, September 1, 1886. Savannah women: ibid., September 2, 1886. The woman without a child later died of her injuries (*SMN*, September 6, 1886).

7. *N&C*, September 4, 1886; McKinley, "Descriptive Narrative," 371.

8. *N&C*, September 3, 1886; McKinley, "Descriptive Narrative," 370.

9. *AC*, September 1, 1886. Henry Grady on August 31: Raymond B. Nixon, *Henry W. Grady: Spokesman of the New South* (New York: Alfred A. Knopf, 1943), 1, 3–4; Harold E. Davis, *Henry Grady's New South: Atlanta, a Brave and Beautiful City* (Tuscaloosa: University of Alabama Press, 1990), 50–51; *AC*, September 1, 1886.

10. *AC*, September 1, 1886.

Chapter Two. Seeds of Destruction

For general information on Charleston in the 1880s, see Don H. Doyle, *New Men, New Cities, New South: Atlanta, Nashville, Charleston, Mobile, 1865–1910* (Chapel Hill: University of North Carolina Press, 1990); and Arthur Mazyck and Gene Waddell, *Charleston in 1883* (Easley, S.C.: Southern Historical Press, 1983).

1. "Earthquakes Everywhere," *N&C*, August 29, 1886.

2. Earthquakes in Charleston history: T. R. Visvanathan, "Earthquakes in South Carolina 1698–1975," bulletin 40, South Carolina Geological Survey, 1980; *Charleston Courier*, January 8, 1812. The 1812 day of fasting is mentioned in *N&C*, October 3, 1886. Dozens of earthquakes shake the Charleston area every year, but most are too small to be felt.

3. "The Trade of the Year," *N&C*, September 1, 1886. For more on Charleston's economic struggles in the 1880s and before, see Don H. Doyle, *New Men, New Cities, New South: Atlanta, Nashville, Charleston, Mobile, 1865–1910* (Chapel Hill: University of North Carolina Press, 1990), and Blaine A. Brownell and David R. Goldfield, eds., *The City in Southern History: The Growth of Urban Civilization in the South* (Port Washington, N.Y.: Kennikat Press, 1977).

4. *N&C*, September 1, 1886; E. Culpepper Clark, *Francis Warrington Dawson and the Politics of Restoration: South Carolina, 1874–1889* (University: University of Alabama Press, 1980), 138–39; Miriam DuPré to SMD, September 1, 1886, FWD Family Papers, and Miriam DuPré to Mrs. J. C. Hemphill, September 27, 1886, Hemphill Papers.

5. FWD to SMD, August 6 and 10, 1886, FWD Family Papers.

6. E. Culpepper Clark, *Francis Warrington Dawson*, 10–26; Dumas Malone, ed., *Dictionary of American Biography* (New York: Scribners, 1933), 3:151–52.

7. "Most delightfully romantic": E. Culpepper Clark, *Francis Warrington Dawson*, 14.

8. SMD's scrapbook re FWD's death (f:5323), 13, FWD Family Papers.

9. Dale B. J. Randall, *Joseph Conrad and Warrington Dawson: The Record of a Friendship* (Durham, N.C.: Duke University Press, 1968), 9.

10. Qtd. in Carl R. Osthaus, *Partisans of the Southern Press: Editorial Spokesmen of the Nineteenth Century* (Lexington: University of Kentucky Press, 1994), 155.

11. Sarah's articles in the *N&C* are discussed in E. Culpepper Clark, "Sarah Morgan and Francis Dawson: Raising the Woman Question in Reconstruction South Carolina," *SCHM* 80 (January 1981): 8–23. Most of her articles are listed and some are reprinted in Giselle Roberts, ed., *The Correspondence of Sarah Morgan and Francis Warrington Dawson* (Athens: University of Georgia Press, 2004), "Young Couples" (*N&C*, March 29, 1873), 77.

12. E. Culpepper Clark, *Francis Warrington Dawson*, 123–28.

13. "Our New Dress," *N&C*, September 27, 1886.

14. One of Dawson's reporters, Narciso G. Gonzales, referred to him as a "tyrant" and described himself as "Dawson's darky." Qtd. in Osthaus, *Partisans of the Southern Press*, 157.

15. Martha Severens, ed., *Alice Ravenel Huger Smith: An Artist, a Place, and a Time* (Charleston: Carolina Art Association, Gibbes Museum of Art, 1993), 76–79. Smith later claimed that her mother used a wheelchair because she was "pale and weak from an anemic condition." Ibid., 73.

16. Severens, *Alice Ravenel Huger Smith*, 76–79. Death of Alice Smith's uncles: *Mason Smith Family Letters, 1860–68* (Columbia: University of South Carolina Press, 1950), 280–81.

17. The full hurricane rhyme goes: "June, too soon; July, stand by; August, come it must; September, remember; October, all over." Duncan Clinch Heyward, *Seed from Madagascar* (1937; rpt., Columbia: University of South Carolina Press, 1993), 222.

18. Citadel Square Baptist Church: *N&C*, August 26, 1885. French Huguenot Church pamphlet: "An American Time Capsule: Three Centuries of Broadsides and Other Printed Ephemera," Library of Congress: American Memory, http://memory.loc.gov (accessed September 24, 2010). St. Michael's steeple: *N&C*, August 26, 1885; George W. Williams, *St. Michael's Charleston 1751–1951 With Supplements 1951–2001* (Charleston: College of Charleston Library, 2001), 160. Battery railings reset: "Report of Superintendent of Streets," in *Year Book — 1886. Charleston, So. Ca.* (Charleston: Walker, Evans and Cogswell, n.d.), 40. Tree limbs col-

lected: Carl McKinley, "The August Cyclone," appendix to *Year Book — 1885. Charleston, So. Ca.* (Charleston: News and Courier Book Presses, n.d.), 379.

19. For a map on which "made ground" looked like a child's drawing of waves, see the maps in Andrew Robinson and Pradeep Talwani, "Building Damage at Charleston, South Carolina, Associated with the 1886 Earthquake," *Bulletin of the Seismological Society of America* 73, no. 2 (April 1983): 632–52. See also "Map of Charleston and its Vicinity Showing the Original Settlement of 1670 at Albemarle Point . . ." (1883), which appeared as the frontispiece of the *Year Book — 1883. Charleston, So. Ca.* (Charleston: News and Courier Book Presses, n.d.). It is overlaid on an 1849 grid of the city and shows the extent to which creeks and other bodies of water previously dominated the peninsula.

20. C. E. [Charlotte Elizabeth] Hayden to Sidney, September 2, 1886, 1886 Earthquake folder (30/29/1), SCHS.

21. "Late Dinners in Savannah: Six O' Clock Adopted as the Dinner Hour of Business Men" rpt. from the *SMN*, *N&C*, January 25, 1887. See also Barbara L. Bellows, intro. to *Three O'Clock Dinner* by Josephine Pinckney (1945; rpt., Columbia: University of South Carolina Press, 2001), xvii–xviii. The tradition continued in Charleston well past 1922 when poet Amy Lowell visited Charleston and, unaware of the late midday meal, was puzzled that no one invited her to dinner. Harlan Greene, *Mister Skylark: John Bennett and the Charleston Renaissance* (Athens: University of Georgia Press, 2001), 181.

22. *N&C*, August 31, 1886.

23. Achievements of Mayor WAC: "Capt. Wm. A. Courtenay Is Dead," *N&C*, March 18, 1908. Courtenay initiated the annual publication of the City of Charleston yearbook beginning in 1880, which detailed the income and expenses of every city department. Because of Courtenay's interest in history, each issue also included essays on various aspects of Charleston and South Carolina history.

24. Campbell Courtenay expelled from the Citadel: *N&C*, September 4, 1885; Official Registry of the South Carolina Military Academy, February 1885 and July 1885, 13; see also Minutes of the Board of Visitors, South Carolina Military Academy, August 5, 1885; transcription of a letter by WAC to Gen. Johnson Hagood, chairman of the Board of Visitors, all in Citadel Archives, Daniel Library, the Citadel, Charleston, S.C. The board's response is on the back of this letter. Letter to *N&C*, September 4, 1885; "Dude factory": E. Culpepper Clark, *Francis Warrington Dawson*, 169, 207.

25. "The Mayor's Resignation," in *Year Book — 1886. Charleston, So. Ca.* (Charleston: Walker, Evans and Cogswell, n.d.), 228–31, includes an account of Courtenay's resignations and the city council's responses. For an account of his movements at the end of August 1886, see WAC Scrapbooks, vol. 3, SCL. J. A. Riols's letters are pasted into this volume.

26. Osthaus, *Partisans of the Southern Press*, 69.

27. WAC Scrapbooks, vol. 3, SCL.

28. WAC's accounts of the 1861 fire were printed in the *Charleston Mercury*, "The Great Fire — Further Particulars," December 13, 1861, and "The Great Fire of 1861, Full List of the Losses," December 14, 1861. See also his obituary, "Capt. Wm. A. Courtenay is Dead," and Walter J. Fraser, *Charleston! Charleston! The History of a Southern City* (Columbia: University of South Carolina Press, 1989), 254.

29. Sidney Andrews, *The South Since the Civil War*, qtd. in Doyle, *New Men*, 56.

30. The *Charleston City Directory* for 1886 lists 27,605 whites and 32,540 blacks, for a total of 60,145.

31. Calhoun qtd. in David S. Reynolds, *John Brown, Abolitionist* (New York: Knopf, 2005), 115.

32. Robert Alexander: *N&C*, September 1, 2, 3, and 29, 1886; *NYH*, September 3 and 4, 1886. "Every foot of ground": Arthur Mazyck and Gene Waddell, *Charleston in 1883* (Easley, S.C.: Southern Historical Press, 1983), xv.

33. Miriam DuPré to SMD, September 1, 1886, FWD Family Papers, and Miriam DuPré to Mrs. J. C. Hemphill, September 27, 1886, Hemphill Papers.

34. Charles East, ed., *The Civil War Diary of Sarah Morgan* (Athens: University of Georgia Press, 1991), 353–60.

35. Miriam DuPré to SMD, September 1, 1886, FWD Family Papers; Frank Dawson: *N&C*, September 1, 1886; Carl McKinley, "A Descriptive Narrative of the Earthquake of August 31, 1886," in *Year Book — 1886. Charleston, So. Ca.* (Charleston: Walker, Evans and Cogswell, n.d.), 350.

36. "Balls in a ten-pin alley": *NYH*, September 6, 1886; "hogshead rolled through a warehouse": Frank Fisher, "June 1st, 1889: The Earthquake of August 1886" (unpublished), Frank R. Fisher Notes, 1882–1902, Special Collections, Marlene and Nathan Addlestone Library, College of Charleston; George Walton Williams: E. Merton Coulter, *George Walton Williams: The Life of a Southern Merchant and Banker 1820–1903* (Athens, Ga.: Hibriten Press, 1976), 231; Edward Wells: Edward Wells, "Mem. of the Charleston Earthquake of 1886" (11/521C/1), SCHS; Richmond visitor: *RD*, September 7, 1886; ship's captain (Capt. Joseph Jervey): McKinley, "Descriptive Narrative," 404.

37. McKinley, "Descriptive Narrative," 352.

Chapter Three. "The Earthquake Is upon Us!"

Unless otherwise noted, earthquake experiences are from Carl McKinley, "A Descriptive Narrative of the Earthquake of August 31, 1886," in *Year Book — 1886. Charleston, So. Ca.* (Charleston: Walker, Evans and Cogswell, n.d.), 343–441, and the *News and Courier*, September 1, 3, and 4, 1886.

1. FWD to SMD, September 2, 1886, FWD Family Papers.

2. Experiences of accountant (J. A. Riols): WAC Scrapbooks, vol. 3, SCL; George Walton Williams's experience: E. Merton Coulter, *George Walton Williams: The Life of a Southern Merchant and Banker, 1820–1903* (Athens, Ga.: Hibriten Press, 1976), 231.

3. Animals' reactions: *NYW*, September 9, 1886; church bells and doorbells: "A Woman's Account of the Earthquake," *N&C*, "Earthquake of 1886," n.d., vertical file, CCPL.

4. Adams Run and grandfather cut off by jet: *N&C*, September 14, 1886. Ravenel, S.C.: *NYW*, September 12, 1886. Edisto Island boy: Nick Lindsay, *And I'm Glad: An Oral History of Edisto Island* (Charleston: Tempus, 2000), 109.

5. Diary of Julius M. Bacot, 1886, Bacot-Huger Collection (11/57/4), SCHS.

6. Experiences in the northern wards, fires: *N&C*, September 5, 1886.

7. James C. Scott, *Domination and the Arts of Resistance* (New Haven, Conn.: Yale University Press, 1990) argues that the anger of oppressed groups (the "hidden transcript of indignation," 7), which is kept carefully under wraps in normal times, is often expressed openly at moments of extreme crisis.

Many scholars have noted that African Americans have historically viewed the story of Exodus differently from European Americans. Both groups saw themselves as a chosen people, but blacks identified whites with the Egyptian enslavers and used the idea of Moses leading his people to the Promised Land as a metaphor for the abolition of slavery. For more on this subject, see Albert J. Raboteau, "African-Americans, Exodus, and the American Israel," 17–36, *A Fire in the Bones: Reflections on African-American Religious History* (Boston: Beacon Press, 1995). Raboteau suggests that "No single story captures more clearly the distinctiveness of African-American Christianity than that of the Exodus" because it "contradicted the claim made by white Christians that God intended Africans to be slaves" (28, 32).

8. Owner of afternoon paper (Julian Selby) and "Grand wind-up": "Old Account of Charleston Earthquake Pictures Flames, Terror, Free Whiskey," *Charleston Evening Post*, July 4, 1951.

9. On primary and secondary waves, see Bruce A. Bolt, *Earthquakes and Geological Discovery* (New York: Scientific American Library, 1993), 38.

10. Frank Fisher, "June 1st, 1889: The Earthquake of August 1886" (unpublished), Frank R. Fisher Notes, 1882–1902, Special Collections, Marlene and Nathan Addlestone Library, College of Charleston.

11. According to the *N&C* on September 16, 1886, bookstore clerk Samuel Hammond jumped from the window of his third-floor residence. Later he explained that he had been cared for the night of the quake by John McCaffrey, "an entire stranger," who took him "from the street, where I was lying mangled

and with broken limbs and helpless" and remained with him through the night "when others refused to stay within the house." *N&C*, October 19, 1886.

12. *N&C*, October 13, 1886; *NYH*, September 4, 1886; *AC*, September 4, 1886. Alexander boarded with "Mrs. Campbell" in a house Huger owned on Meeting Street, but he was visiting Huger's own home at the time of the quake. *N&C*, September 29, 1886. The Caldwells' experiences are described in the *SMN*, September 15, 1886. The tablet in the steps of 34 Meeting Street honored Francis Kinloch Huger, who was locally famous for his failed scheme to free General Lafayette, a hero of the American Revolution, from his captors during the French Revolution: Alice R. Huger Smith and D. E. Huger Smith, *Dwelling Houses of Charleston* (1917; rpt., Diadem Books, 1974), 78–81. According to one account, Alexander's ghost still can be heard making tapping noises in front of 34 Meeting Street. Geordie Buxton and Ed Macy, *Haunted Harbor: Charleston's Maritime Ghosts and the Unexplained* (Charleston: History Press, 2005), 101–8.

13. Dorothy Walker to Mrs. W. Howell Taylor, October 7, 1886, H. P. Walker Papers (24/274/2), SCHS.

14. *N&C*, September 11 and 5, 1886.

15. Severens, *Alice Ravenel Huger Smith*, 76–79. On Huger Smith's walk to his mother-in-law's, see Edward Wells, "Mem. of the Charleston Earthquake of 1886," 8–9 (11/521C/1), SCHS.

16. Miriam DuPré to SMD, September 1, 1886, FWD Family Papers, and Miriam DuPré to Mrs. J. C. Hemphill, September 27, 1886, Hemphill Papers.

17. *N&C*, September 5 and 29, 1886.

18. The damage to the city's waterworks infrastructure is described in the minutes to the private waterworks' annual meeting, February 24, 1887. Dawson was one of the most active members of the board of directors. "Minutes of the City of Charleston Water Works Company from Feby 25th to [May 20, 1897]," Records Dept., Charleston Water System.

19. *N&C*, September 30, 1886.

20. "Shaken from the County Jail: The Prisoners Who Made Hay While the Earthquake Shook," *N&C*, September 7, 1886. See also *N&C*, September 5, 6, and 9, 1886. The *Atlanta Constitution* reported on September 4 that the cracks in the wall were big enough for prisoners to climb through.

21. Experiences at the medical college, Roper Hospital, and City Hospital: *N&C*, September 5, 1886. According to Richard H. Fitzgerald Jr., M.D., "Medical Consequences of the Earthquake of 1886," 160 patients were at Roper the night of the earthquake. *Southern Medical Journal* 78, no. 4 (April 1985): 458–62.

22. Dr. Thomas B. McDow: *N&C*, September 8, 1886; City of Charleston

Health Department, "Return of Deaths Within the City of Charleston, South Carolina," CCPL.

23. On May 1, 1889, the *N&C* reported that Charles Chapman of Savannah had visited town and told the story of his son Charleston's birth the night of the earthquake.

24. A list of the reporters and editors who stayed at their posts can be found in the *N&C*, September 18, 1886.

25. Keitt Walker: Dorothy Walker to Mrs. W. Howell Taylor, October 7, 1886 (24/274/2), SCHS. Tulane professor: *SMN*, September 15, 1886. Six-year-old girl (Rachel Ahrens): *NYH*, September 3, 1886; *New York Star*, September 2 and 3, 1886; Charleston Health Department, "Return of Deaths."

26. Ainsley Robson's death was mourned in a separate news item a week and a half after the quake: "One of the saddest incidents of the recent earthquake was the death of Ainsley H. Robson. . . . He will be sadly missed at the Exchange, on the Bay, and still more so in his own immediate circle of relatives and friends." *N&C*, September 11, 1886.

Chapter Four. A World Turned Upside Down

1. Shocks during the night: Carl McKinley, "A Descriptive Narrative of the Earthquake of August 31, 1886," in *Year Book — 1886. Charleston, So. Ca.* (Charleston: Walker, Evans and Cogswell, n.d.), 355.

2. "A sign of the shadow of death": *N&C*, November 14, 1886. Watches stopped: ibid., September 11, 1886. On the other hand, on October 22 a clock in Fairfield County, S.C., that had stopped was restarted by a tremor: ibid., October 26, 1886.

3. Glass shade: *N&C*, September 16 and 29, 1886; drugstore ceiling: ibid., September 29, 1886; force of gravity: "First Hand Observations of the Charleston Earthquake of August 31, 1886, and other Earthquake Materials, S.C. Geological Survey," 1986, qtd. in Bo Peterson, "I Was Taken Up into the Air," *Charleston Post and Courier*, December 2, 2000.

4. Experiences at medical institutions: *N&C*, September 4 and 5, 1886. List of injuries: *RD*, September 4, 1886.

5. The silver was tarnished by fumes of sulfur: Robert P. Stockton, *The Great Shock: The Effects of the 1886 Earthquake on the Built Environment of Charleston, South Carolina* (Easley, S.C.: Southern Historical Press, 1986), 28. Condition of Hayden house: C. E. [Charlotte Elizabeth] Hayden to Sidney, September 2, 1886 (30/29/1), SCHS.

6. Martha Severens, ed., *Alice Ravenel Huger Smith: An Artist, a Place, and a Time* (Charleston, S.C.: Carolina Art Association, Gibbes Museum of Art, 1993), 76–79.

7. Bakery's bread: *N&C*, September 16, 1886; *Charleston As It Is After the Earthquake Shock of August 31, 1886* (Charleston: n.p., 1886), 12. William Bird: *N&C*, September 8, 1886.

8. Old man (Henry A. Middleton) "meant to stay": *NYW*, September 9, 1886; *SMN*, September 13, 1886. Two days before the earthquake the *N&C* reported that "Mr. Middleton, probably the oldest living white person" in the city, "may be seen almost every day on Broad St. taking a walk." *N&C*, August 29, 1886. He died seven months later. *N&C*, March 12, 1887.

9. "Slow and quivering" swells: *N&C*, September 3, 1886.

10. [L. E. Cantwell] "Ned," " 'Earthquake Echoes,' 1886" (43/189), SCHS. The night of the earthquake, Cantwell and Tom Doyle made three separate raids on the store where Doyle worked to get more cigars.

11. Edward Wells, "Mem. of the Charleston Earthquake of 1886" (11/521C/1), 13, SCHS.

12. DuPré, Glidden, and Dawson experiences: Miriam DuPré to SMD, September 1, 1886, FWD Family Papers; *N&C*, September 3, 1886; FWD to SMD, September 2, 1886, FWD Family Papers.

13. St. Philip's a "total wreck": *N&C*, September 3, 1886.

14. Charles B. Rittenhouse memoir (43/2185), SCHS.

15. A. Toomer Porter, *Led On! Step by Step* (1898; rpt., Charleston: Home House Press, 2010), 362–63.

16. Mrs. William H. Lowndes to Miss Harriott Middleton, September 5, 1886, Cheves-Middleton Papers (12/165/15), SCHS. Mrs. Lowndes had heard that only fifty houses remained standing in Charleston.

17. *N&C*, September 3, 1886.

18. "Our Lightning Press: The Most Wonderful Printing Machine Ever Built," *N&C*, September 29, 1884.

19. Compositors as cowards: FWD to SMD, September 19, 1886, FWD Family Papers. *AC* typesetters in 1882: Melton Alonza McLaurin, *The Knights of Labor in the South* (Westport, Conn.: Greenwood Press, 1978), 64; Harold E. Davis, *Henry Grady's New South: Atlanta, a Brave and Beautiful City* (Tuscaloosa: University of Alabama Press, 1990), 186–87.

20. Susan Elizabeth Hough, *Earthshaking Science: What We Know (and Don't Know) about Earthquakes* (Princeton, N.J.: Princeton University Press, 2002), 56–61, and Bruce A. Bolt, *Earthquakes and Geological Discovery* (New York: Scientific American Library, 1993), 77.

21. Under the headline "A Tidal Wave," the *N&C* on September 3 reported accounts that "a wave of considerable height advanced up the Cooper River and overflowed not only the banks of the river but the country interiorly for about a mile." However, the paper acknowledged that little damage was caused. The next

day the N&C noted, "In most histories of earthquakes near the sea mention was made of a tidal wave." Miriam DuPré and her friends fled the beach at Sullivan's Island the night of the quake fearing that a tidal wave might be coming. Miriam DuPré to SMD, September 1, 1886, FWD Family Papers. Even as late as September 13, a long blast from the ship *City of Columbia* terrified women and children, who expected a tidal wave. N&C, September 15, 1886.

Of course, so-called tidal waves (tsunamis) have nothing to do with the tides. They are generated by offshore earthquakes and volcanoes and can travel thousands of miles before striking land. About 80 percent occur in the Pacific Ocean, though they have been known to strike in the Atlantic and Caribbean. Karl V. Steinbrugge, *Earthquakes, Volcanoes, and Tsunamis* (New York: Skandia America Group, 1982), 233–34, 236.

22. "The wives and daughters of prominent citizens" and drugstore clerk: *SMN*, September 17, 1886. A woman lost ability to speak: *NYW*, September 5, 1886. Smoaks Crossroads girl: *SMN*, September 13, 1886.

23. Many accounts of insanity were reported in "People Driven Crazy by Events of the Earthquake," *AC*, September 4, 1886 (Augusta city collector, daughter of factory worker, the family that jumped into Horse Creek, shoe salesman, the man who made the noose). Three women — Hagar, Amelia Bing, and Lucy Foster — were "frightened to death," according to the N&C, September 4, 1886. In reporting Angeline David's death, the paper explained, "The fright was so great that after an hour of violent struggling she died." N&C, September 3, 1886.

24. According to the N&C, the first shock "excited [Minnie Martus] greatly, and her family was surprised to hear her cry and scream. Since then she has gradually regained her speech, and now talks fluently." N&C, September 8, 1886. The account was inaccurate, as she had regained speech earlier that year. Martus became famous years later as "the waving girl" who greeted all ships arriving at Savannah. A statue of her stands on Savannah's riverfront. "Many chronic cases of partial paralysis": N&C, October 25, 1886.

25. *SMN*, Sept. 7 and 8, 1886. On September 6, 1886, the N&C reported, "The earthquake has apparently emboldened John Chinaman's principal article of food, the rats of Charleston." A gang of rats was said to be "holding a carnival of war" on Broad Street. Fish were "frightened to death": N&C, September 4, 1886.

26. Augustine Smythe to "My Wife," September 8 and 11, 1886 (originals, 24/8/9; typescript 30/29/1), SCHS.

27. Fire to "purify" the air: Myra C. Vaux letter, n.d., Stoney Family Correspondence, 1872–1886 (24/14/1), SCHS.

28. Dawson household: Miriam DuPré to SMD, September 1, 1886, and September 12, 1886, both in the FWD Family Papers; and Miriam DuPré to Mrs.

J. C. Hemphill, September 27, 1886, Hemphill Papers. In 1883 Charles H. Glidden was one of the founders of the Carolina Yacht Club and served as its first commodore. Robert P. Stockton, *The History of the Carolina Yacht Club, Charleston, South Carolina* (Charleston: Carolina Yacht Club, 2004), 6, 164, and 215.

29. C. E. [Charlotte Elizabeth] Hayden to Sidney, September 2, 1886, 1886 Earthquake folder (30/29/1), SCHS.

30. Severens, *Alice Ravenel Huger Smith*, 76–79.

Chapter Five. The Earthquake Hunters

1. Activities at *Constitution* and telegraph offices: *AC*, September 1 and 2, 1886.

2. The "Charleston Shocked!" headline appeared in the *AC*, September 1, 1886, "Extra Edition." *AC* sold 50,000 copies: *AC*, September 2, 1886.

3. Grady's report of his journey from Atlanta to Charleston ran in the *AC*, September 3, 1886. His article published on September 4 includes his impressions of Charleston and his decision to return home; the last part of this report is datelined September 4, Atlanta. Other accounts of his activities are in Raymond B. Nixon, *Henry W. Grady: Spokesman of the New South* (New York: Alfred A. Knopf, 1943), 4, 216, and Harold E. Davis, *Henry Grady's New South: Atlanta, a Brave and Beautiful City* (Tuscaloosa: University of Alabama Press, 1990), 50–51. Among the papers that printed Grady's account were the *New York World*, the *Cincinnati Enquirer*, and the *Raleigh News and Observer*. Davis, *Henry Grady's New South*, 57; Nixon, *Henry W. Grady*, 5.

4. FWD to SMD, September 2, 1886, FWD Family Papers.

5. *N&C*, August 29, 1886, 1; ibid., September 6, 1886.

6. *SMN*, September 3, 1886.

7. *NYH*, September 5, 1886.

8. *N&C*, September 23 and 28, 1886.

9. Walt McDougall, "Old Days on the World," *American Mercury*, January 1925, 22–23; Walt McDougall, *This Is the Life* (New York: Alfred A. Knopf, 1926), 177–79. The *NYW* ran stock sketches of Charleston buildings on September 3, 1886. McDougall's drawings of earthquake scenes and written accounts appeared on September 4, 5, 7–12, 14, 16, and 19, 1886.

According to *The World Encyclopedia of Comics*, Walter Hugh McDougall (1858–1938) was "in the forefront of several movements in the comics." Before being hired by Pulitzer, he had sold drawings to *Harper's Weekly*, *Puck*, and the *New York Graphic*, the first illustrated daily paper in America. He produced the first cartoon to be printed in color in a U.S. paper and the first color comic strip. His two-page spread in 1898 was "probably the largest single-panel cartoon in color in an American newspaper . . . and [he] once had front-page drawings in color in New York's *Herald, World,* and *American,* all on the same Sunday." Later he drew a number of comic strips, including *The Wizard of Oz,* with the help of *Oz* author L. Frank Baum. *The World Encyclopedia of Comics,* ed. Maurice Horn, rev. and updated (1976; rpt., Philadelphia: Chelsea House, 1999), 4:499.

10. *NYW,* September 7, 1886.

11. Scientists travel to Charleston: *AC,* September 1, 1886; *N&C,* September 6, 1886. Earthquake Commission: *N&C,* September 5, 1886.

12. Mendenhall was the first faculty member hired when Ohio State University was founded. Although he never attended college, he was offered an appointment as president of the school, but he turned it down. Dumas Malone, ed., *Dictionary of American Biography* (New York: Scribners, 1933) 6:530–31. Mendenhall set up earthquake stations: NOAA History: A Science of Odyssey, *C&GS Bulletin* 3/1924, http://www.history.noaa.gov/cgsbios/biom13.html (accessed September 24, 2010). Mendenhall's globe demonstration: *Grand Rapids (Mich.) Daily Democrat,* September 2, 1886.

13. Malone, *Dictionary of American Biography* 6:47–48; Emma P. McGee, *Life of W J McGee: Distinguished Geologist, Ethnologist, Anthropologist, Hydrologist, etc. in Service of United States Government* (Farley, Iowa: self-published, 1915). Born in Farley, Iowa, McGee was a sickly child, which his doctor attributed to his having a brain too big for his body. McGee, *Life of W J McGee,* 37–38.

14. The C. C. Jones photographs are often credited to John K. Hillers, head of the photography lab at the USGS. For an in-depth study of Jones's Charleston photographs and how they fit into the evolution of the USGS, see Robin Kelsey's chapter "C. C. Jones: The USGS Investigation of the Charleston Earthquake," in *Archive Style: Photographs and Illustrations for U.S. Surveys, 1850–1890* (Berkeley: University of California, 2007), 143–89.

15. McGee's experiences can be followed each day in the *N&C* and in the final USGS report, Clarence Edward Dutton, *The Charleston Earthquake of August 31, 1886* (U.S. Geological Survey Ninth Annual Report, 1887–88; rpt., Arlington, Va.: U.S. Geological Survey, 1979), 8 ("the bed was beating him"), 20 ("voices of the colored population"), 8 ("indescribable wail"), 22 ("a pretty severe quake"). The *N&C* was sure that although one-third of Summerville inhabitants had moved away, "the exodus would cease," and those who had fled would soon return, when they heard McGee's reassuring report. *N&C,* September 6, 1886.

16. Edward Wells, "Mem. of the Charleston Earthquake of 1886," p. 24 (11/521C/1), SCHS.

17. Bruce A. Bolt, *Earthquakes and Geological Discovery* (New York: Scientific American Library, 1993), 10–11.

18. *N&C,* September 16, 1886.

19. McDougall, *This Is the Life*, 177; *AC*, September 4, 1886.

20. *N&C*, September 15, 1886.

21. *NYW*, September 5, 1886; *N&C*, September 9, 1886.

22. *AC*, September 5, 1886.

23. Ibid.

Chapter Six. Aftershocks

1. *AC*, September 4, 1886.

2. Unless otherwise specified, all details of refugee sites are in *N&C*, September 7, 1886. The *N&C* claimed that Robb's Lot held "perhaps more colored people to the square foot than . . . any of the other camps of refuge in the city": *N&C*, September 10, 1886. Porter Academy: A. Toomer Porter, *Led On! Step by Step* (1898; rpt., Charleston: Home House Press, 2010), 393.

3. The *Delaware* arrived in Charleston the afternoon after the earthquake and found only one usable wharf. Carl McKinley, "A Descriptive Narrative of the Earthquake of August 31, 1886," in *Year Book — 1886. Charleston, So. Ca.* (Charleston: Walker, Evans and Cogswell, n.d.), 379. See also "An Ark of Refuge," *NYH*, September 9, 1886.

4. "Linguard Street washerwomen": *N&C*, September 16, 1886; *NYW*, September 17, 1886. "Dry as a carpet": [L. E. Cantwell] "Ned," " 'Earthquake Echoes,' 1886," 10 (43/189), SCHS.

5. Blacks staked "claims": *N&C*, September 4, 10, 1886. *N&C* delivery wagon: *N&C*, September 11, 1886. Blacks forbidden to enter Washington Square: Don H. Doyle, *New Men, New Cities, New South: Atlanta, Nashville, Charleston, Mobile, 1865–1910* (Chapel Hill: University of North Carolina Press, 1990), 303.

6. *N&C*, September 5, 1886.

7. *AC*, September 4, 1886.

8. Samuel Stoney to "My Dear Mother," September 3, 1886, Stoney Family Correspondence, 1872–1886 (24/14/1), SCHS.

9. *NYH*, September 3, 1886.

10. For more on sandblows and liquefaction, see Kerry E. Sieh and Simon Levay, *The Earth in Turmoil: Earthquakes, Volcanoes, and Their Impact on Humankind* (New York: W. H. Freeman, 1998), 237 and 301. Dog not scalded: *N&C*, September 24, 1886; see also McKinley, "Descriptive Narrative," 360, 366, 368–70.

11. McGee: *N&C*, September 9, 1886; Mendenhall: ibid., September 26, 1886. Mooney, Ind.: *NYW*, September 2, 1886. Wilmington, N.C.: *NYW*, September 4, 1886. Pondtown District, Ga.: *NYH*, September 8, 1886. Tybee Island, Ga.: *NYH*,

September 8, 1886; *NYW*, September 10, 1886; *N&C*, September 10, 1886. As late as October 12, 1886, the *NYW* ran an article from Charleston titled "Is a Volcano Forming?"

12. Edward Wells, "Mem. of the Charleston Earthquake of 1886," 24–25, (11/521C/1), SCHS.

13. *N&C*, September 4, 1886; Mrs. Daniel Huger Lesesne to Miss Harriott Middleton, Flat Rock, September 5, 1886, Cheves-Middleton Papers (12/165/15), SCHS.

14. *N&C*, September 5, 1886. Dr. Rose gave permission to convert the hall into a hospital: ibid., October 7, 1886. On September 6 "a colored woman..., suffering from a fracture of the skull and... dangerously ill" was moved, leaving only one patient at the hospital: ibid., September 7, 1886.

15. *N&C*, September 5, 1886.

16. Examples of Congress appropriating relief money after natural disasters: Gaines M. Foster, "The Nineteenth Century: Precedents," ch. 2 in *The Demands of Humanity: Army Medical Disaster Relief*, 6–22 (http://history.amedd.army .mil/booksdocs/misc/disaster/ch2.htm; accessed September 24, 2010). The first such appropriation took place in 1792 after a severe drought ruined the crops of the Creek Indians. Cleveland's response: *AC*, September 4, 1886; Allen Nevins, ed., *Letters of Grover Cleveland, 1850–1908* (Boston and New York: Houghton Mifflin, 1933), 119. The *SMN* on Cleveland's response: *SMN*, September 19, 1886.

17. Executive authorization for military tents: *NYW*, September 9, 1886. Prohibition on use of government property: *N&C*, September 21 and October 8, 1886. "Take the tents": *N&C*, August 31, 1887. Ohio governor: *N&C*, September 14, 1886.

18. *NYW*, September 4, 1886.

19. Ibid., September 6 and 7, 1886; Nevins, *Letters of Grover Cleveland*, 119.

20. *N&C*, September 3, 1886.

21. Ibid., August 30 and 8, 1885.

22. Augustine Smythe re neighbors (the Misses Gibbes): Smythe to "My Dearest Wife," September 13, 1886, Correspondence, 1880–1886, A. T. Smyth [*sic*] Papers (originals, 24/8/9; typescript, 30/29/1), SCHS. Smythe's reason for adding the "e" to his name: "Excerpts from the Wartime Correspondence of Augustine T. Smythe," *SCHM* 62 (January 1961), 27n.

23. *N&C*, September 4, 1886.

24. *The General Ordinances of the City of Charleston, South Carolina* (Charleston: Lucas and Richardson, 1895), 174–82.

25. Previous examples of relief: E. Merton Coulter, *George Walton Williams: The Life of a Southern Merchant and Banker, 1820–1903* (Athens, Ga.: Hibriten Press), 88–89; John B. Clark Jr., *Fire Protection in the Old South* (PhD diss., Uni-

versity of Kentucky, 1957), 1:881. Relief during Civil War, Freedman's Bureau: Coulter, *George Walton Williams*, 93 and 92.

26. *N&C*, September 4 and 5, 1886.

27. *SMN*, September 7, 1886; *NYW*, September 7, 1886; FWD to SMD, September 5, 1886, FWD Family Papers.

28. *Philadelphia Inquirer*, qtd. in *N&C*, September 4, 1886; *N&C*, September 5, 1886; City of Charleston Health Department, "Return of Deaths Within the City of Charleston, South Carolina, 1884–1887," CCPL.

29. *N&C*, September 5 and 4, 1886.

30. Minutes of the ERC, September 8, 1886, Earthquake Records, CCPL; *N&C*, September 8, 1886.

31. *Charleston City Directory, 1886*; "A Bullet Through His Brain," *N&C*, June 27, 1892.

32. *N&C*, September 7, 8, 10, 11, and 6, 1886.

33. *Charleston As It Is After the Earthquake Shock of August 31, 1886* (Charleston: n.p., 1886), 22; *N&C*, September 5, 1886.

34. FWD urged people to calm down and go back to work: *N&C*, September 8, 1886; McGee: ibid., September 9, 1886; Mendenhall: *NYH*, September 7, 1886. Irish immigrants: *NYW*, September 19, 1886. This account may have been the source of Jose Martí's claim that people watchful for tidal waves were living in trees. *La Nacion* (Buenos Aires, Arg.), October 14, 15, 1886.

35. A. Toomer Porter's experience: Porter, *Led On!* 395–97.

36. *N&C*, September 6, 9, 7, and 11, 1886.

37. Tillman background: Stephen Kantrowitz, *Ben Tillman and the Reconstruction of White Supremacy* (Chapel Hill: University of North Carolina Press, 2000); William J. Cooper, *The Conservative Regime: South Carolina, 1877–1890* (Baltimore, Md.: Johns Hopkins University Press, 1968), 177 and 179. Letter re not meeting again: BRT to FWD, August 24, 1886, FWD Family Papers. Tillman letters of August 28 and September 10, 1886: BRT to FWD, September 10, 1886, FWD Family Papers.

38. BRT to FWD, September 10, 1886, FWD Family Papers. The August 28 letter appeared in the *N&C*, September 16, 1886.

39. *N&C*, October 8, 1886; Anna Vanderhorst to Sam Stoney Sr., Stoney Family Correspondence.

40. Wells, "Mem. of the Charleston Earthquake," 2; Clarence Edward Dutton, *The Charleston Earthquake of August 31, 1886* (U.S. Geological Survey Ninth Annual Report, 1887–88; rpt., Arlington, Va.: U.S. Geological Survey, 1979), 102–3.

41. *N&C*, September 5, 1886.

42. Ibid.

43. Ibid.

44. *NYH*, September 5, 1886; *NYW*, September 5, 1886. Both the New York papers ran items on the mysterious pebbles the day after they fell, though neither took seriously the widespread rumor that they were volcanic in origin. Dawson chose not to cover the story at all, but he kept some of the pebbles on his desk. When the stories appeared in New York, he was forced to acknowledge the events: *N&C*, September 6, 1886; McKinley, "Descriptive Narrative," 360. McGee and Mendenhall: *NYH*, September 7, 1886.

45. "R. C. Richardson, Pressman, Dead," *N&C*, August 26, 1938; "Charleston Had Worst Shock 57 Years Ago Tonight," *N&C*, August 31, 1943. Richardson so admired his boss that he named his last son Francis Dawson Richardson (1890–1961).

46. *N&C*, September 5, 1886; FWD to SMD, September 17, 1886, FWD Family Papers. The compositors' concerns were supported when on September 10 the commission of engineers inspected the *N&C* offices and declared that "the north wall of the job office (Elliott Street) should be taken down." *N&C*, September 11, 1886.

47. FWD to SMD, September 19, 1886, FWD Family Papers; Miriam DuPré to SMD, September 12, 1886, ibid.; Miriam DuPré to Mrs. Hemphill, September 27, 1886, Hemphill Papers; Miriam DuPré to SMD, October 6, 1886, FWD Family Papers.

48. Miriam DuPré to SMD, September 12, 1886, FWD Family Papers.

49. Miriam DuPré to SMD, October 6, 1886, ibid.

50. Miriam DuPré to SMD, October 6, 1886, ibid.; FWD to SMD, January 4, 1887, ibid.

51. Wells, "Mem. of the Charleston Earthquake," 9–10.

52. "Badly demoralized" and "all fools": Stoney to "My Dear Mother," September 3, 1886. On September 5 a Charleston woman wrote a friend, "the police are utterly demoralized." Mrs. Daniel Huger Lesesne to Miss Harriott Middleton, Flat Rock, N.C., September 5, 1886, Cheves-Middleton Papers. Having lived through the earthquake, Frank F. Whilden remembered forty-four years later that gambling houses, barrooms, and whorehouses sprang up all over the city: "Describes Night Earthquake Rocked City on Anniversary," *N&C*, September 20, 1930. The *National Police Gazette* of September 25, 1886, printed a full-page engraving of Charleston prostitutes ("The Demi-Monde of Charleston") "temporarily converted from their wicked ways by the recent earthquake." Prisoners escaped, "experienced thieves": *N&C*, September 5, 1886.

53. *N&C*, September 5 (bar robbed and Unitarian Church), 9 ("a daring and enterprising thief"), 10 (stolen bedding and "all the colored encampments"), 23 (child's coffin), October 13 (fishing lines), 1886.

54. Wells, "Mem. of the Charleston Earthquake," 10.

55. Rifle companies volunteered to patrol: *N&C*, September 4, 1886; Diary of Julius M. Bacot, September 8, 1886, Bacot-Huger Collection (11/57/4), SCHS; Samuel Stoney Sr., to his wife, September 5, 1886, and to "My dear Mother," September 12, 1886, both in Stoney Family Correspondence.

56. *N&C*, September 5 and 4, 1886.

57. Columbia Board of Trade met trains, blacks "quickly disappeared," many refused to leave rail car: *N&C*, September 4, 1886; white women and children: ibid., September 7, 1886.

58. Earthquake excursions: *N&C*, September 5–7, 1886. Earthquake sand: ibid., September 18, 1886; *NYW*, September 19, 1886. The shop of Walker, Evans and Cogswell offered bottles of earthquake sand for 15 cents apiece or a case of twelve bottles, each with a different colored sand, for one dollar. WAC, Earthquake Scrapbook, WAC Papers, CLS. Disaster sightseeing was not new to Charleston. After the cyclone the summer before, excursion trains brought thousands of tourists to see the damage: *N&C*, August 31, 1885.

59. *N&C*, September 5 and 8, 1886.

60. *AC*, September 5, 1886. Henry Grady's September 5 boast that Atlanta sat safely on the "firm granite backbone" of the country was preceded by the claim of the *New Orleans Picayune* that New Orleans's location "on a cushion of mud and water" made it safer than cities situated on solid ground. Qtd. in *AC*, September 4, 1886.

61. *AC*, September 6, 1886.

62. Ibid., September 5, 1886.

Chapter Seven. An Angry God

1. *N&C*, September 6, 1886; [L. E. Cantwell] "Ned," "'Earthquake Echoes,'" 11 (43/189), SCHS.

2. T. P. Stoney to his mother, September 11, 1886, Stoney Family Correspondence, 1872–1886 (24/14/1), SCHS.

3. *N&C*, September 6, 1886.

4. *NYW*, September 19, 1886.

5. 1727 New England earthquake and Jonathan Edwards: *N&C*, September 11, 1886; George L. M. Marsden, *Jonathan Edwards: A Life* (New Haven, Conn.: Yale University Press, 2003), 120–22.

6. Marsden, *Jonathan Edwards*, 120–22.

7. Charles Edwin Clark, "Science, Reason, and an Angry God: The Literature of an Earthquake," *New England Quarterly* 28, no. 3 (1965): 340–62.

8. Prentice qtd. in ibid., 357.

9. Theodore E. D. Braun and John B. Radner, eds., *The Lisbon Earthquakes of*

1755: Representations and Reactions (Oxford, U.K.: Voltaire Foundation, 2005); Fredrick Golden, *The Trembling Earth: Probing and Predicting Quakes* (New York: Scribner's, 1983), 30; Voltaire, *Candide and Other Stories*, trans. Roger Pearson (New York: Everyman's Library, 1992), 14.

10. *N&C*, September 11, 1886.

11. Ibid., September 6, 1886.

12. Ibid., September 9, 1886.

13. Liberty County prophetess: *NYH*, September 8, 1886. For white antagonism to loud black worship services, see Shane White and Graham White, *The Sounds of Slavery: Discovering African American History through Songs, Sermons, and Speech* (Boston: Beacon Press, 2005), 130–31.

14. *N&C*, September 4, 1886.

15. Undated clipping in WAC, Earthquake Scrapbook, WAC Papers, CLS.

16. Details of the Matilda McKnight murder and the subsequent trials appeared the *N&C*, July 10, 1885, through August 25, 1885. Dr. William Crum was a co-owner of the *Palmetto Press*.

17. *N&C*, July 23, 1885.

18. Ibid., August 2, 1885.

19. Ibid., August 19, 1885.

20. Ibid.

21. Ibid., August 24, 1885.

22. Ibid., August 28, 1885.

23. For a full account of the 1885 cyclone, see *N&C*, August 26–September 7, 1885, and Carl McKinley, "The August Cyclone," appendix to *Year Book — 1885. Charleston, So. Ca.* (Charleston: News and Courier Book Presses, n.d.), 371–89 ("carnival of havoc": 373). On the hurricane as vengeance for the McKnight decision, see *The Centenary Souvenir, Containing a History of Centenary Church, Charleston, and an Account of the Life and Labors of Rev. R. V. Lawrence, Father of the Pastor of Centenary Church* (Charleston: n.p., 1885), xxviii.

24. The murder of Stephney Riley was first reported in the *N&C*, October 3, 1885. Unless otherwise noted, details of his killing come from the *N&C*, October 3–7 and November 11–17 and 23, 1885. See also John Hammond Moore, *Carnival of Blood: Dueling, Lynching, and Murder in South Carolina, 1880–1920* (Columbia: University of South Carolina Press, 2006), 143–44, and *Centenary Souvenir*, xxix–xxxi. On Riley's standing in the black community, see Bernard E. Powers, *Black Charlestonians: A Social History 1822–1885* (Fayetteville: University of Arkansas Press, 1994), 168, 175, and 224.

On Riley's early Democratic association and black hatred and persecution of him, see the *N&C*, October 5, 1885. Ten years before his murder Riley was "hunted through the streets of Charleston by a mob of colored men and women, who thirsted for his blood." A black political club, the Hunkidories, "smashed up his carriages, lamed his horses, and destroyed his harness." Whites gave him $5,000 to recoup his losses: *N&C*, October 4, 1885.

25. "There will be a rigid investigation . . .": *N&C*, October 3, 1885. On Dr. Amos Bellinger, including his service as jail physician, see Amos Northrop Bellinger file, Waring Historical Library, Medical University of South Carolina, Charleston. A Charleston merchant wrote in his diary, "The general belief is that it [the murder of Riley] was a case of silencing a family disgrace by death of one who knew." Jacob Schirmer diary (11/568/2), SCHS.

26. *Centenary Souvenir*, xxxvi.

27. *N&C*, November 23, 1885.

28. Ibid., November 14, 1885.

29. Ibid., July 2, 1886.

30. *NYF*, August 28, 1886. Though this piece was not signed, earlier and later articles by Heard appeared in the *NYF*. He was the only named correspondent from Charleston. News from his church always dominated the paper's coverage of the city, though activities at other churches were mentioned.

31. On Rev. William H. Heard, see his *From Slavery to the Bishopric in the A.M.E. Church: An Autobiography* (1924; rpt., New York: Arno Press, 1969), and A. W. Watson, "Rev. William H. Heard: Sketch of Pastor of Mt. Zion A.M.E. Church, Charleston, S.C.," *NYF*, May 7, 1887.

32. On Rev. George C. Rowe, see *Church Annual of Plymouth Congregational Church, 1925* (Charleston: Wainwright Printers, 1925), Special Collections, College of Charleston. Though Rowe had been installed at a Charleston church only recently, he had visited the city two years before for a meeting. The *N&C* had praised his speech then as "choicely worded and perfectly grammatical." *N&C*, November 16, 1884. On Rev. John Lewis Dart, see "John Lewis Dart, 1854–1915," S.C. biographical files "Dart family," South Carolina Room, CCPL. On Samuel W. McKinlay, see *N&C*, October 7 and 29, 1888.

33. On Dr. William D. Crum, see Willard B. Gatewood, "William D. Crum, A Negro in Politics," *Journal of Negro History* 3 (October 1968), 301–20; Sharon Cruz-Reidbord, "The Forgotten Crum Affair," *Carologue* (SCHS), summer 2000: 3.

Chapter Eight. Labor Day

1. *N&C*, September 6, 1886.

2. Melton Alonza McLaurin, *The Knights of Labor in the South* (Westport, Conn.: Greenwood Press, 1978); Jonathan Garlock, *Guide to the Local Assemblies of the Knights of Labor* (Westport, Conn.: Greenwood Press, 1982).

3. Garlock, *Guide to the Local Assemblies*, 480; *N&C*, August 12, 1886.

4. *N&C*, September 6, 1886.

5. Ibid., September 7, 1886; ERC Minutes, October 1, 1886, Records of the ERC.

6. N&C, September 14, 1886. General Huguenin's "lamp-post" remark reportedly first appeared in the *Charleston Dispatch* on September 13, 1886, copies of which no longer exist.

7. N&C, September 6, 1886.

8. Robert E. Weir, *Beyond Labor's Veil: The Culture of the Knights of Labor* (University Park: Pennsylvania State University Press, 1996), 310; *NYW*, September 7, 1886.

9. Labor Day in Charleston, FWD praised Knights as "moderate": N&C, September 7, 1886. No KOL foothold in South Carolina: McLaurin, *Knights of Labor in the South*, 5. The N&O said the Knights' actions "cannot be too highly recommended," as they could have demanded much more. N&O, September 11, 1886.

10. McLaurin, *Knights of Labor in the South*, 65, 47 ("giant killer"), 137 (Charleston Knights had asked for black organizer).

11. "The Dramas of Haymarket," http://www.chicagohistory.org.dramas/ (accessed August 27, 2010).

12. KOL in Augusta, Ga.: Melton A. McLaurin, "Early Labor Organizational Efforts in South Carolina Cotton Mills, 1880–1905," *SCHM* 72, no. 1 (January 1971): 44–59; McLaurin, *Knights of Labor in the South*, 68–73. "Utterly unreasonable": N&C, August 10 and 20, 1886. Russell to FWD: N&C, August 20, 1886.

13. N&C, September 17, 1886.

14. Ibid., September 9, 1886.

15. Ibid., September 14, 1886.

16. Ibid., September 7 and 8, 1886.

17. *Cleveland Gazette*, September 25, 1886, photocopy in "Earthquake, 1886," vertical files, CCPL; N&C, September 13, 1886.

18. N&C, September 8, 1886. Complicating matters further, a quarrel erupted among northern blacks over whether it was appropriate to perpetuate the color line by organizing a separate colored relief movement: *NYF*, September 11, 1886.

19. *The Position of the Colored Clergy Defined* (pamphlet), WAC, Earthquake Scrapbook, WAC Papers, CLS.

20. N&C, September 11, 7, and 9, 1886.

21. Ibid., September 8, 1886; *NYF*, September 25, 1886.

22. FWD: Enough paid work and "too lazy to work": N&C, September 9, 1886. Two men nearly killed: ibid., September 11, 1886. Five men thrown to ground: *NYH*, September 8, 1886. Cleaning bricks was hard, dirty work, and few volunteered for it. One black child cleaned a thousand bricks, for which he received $1.50. The N&C applauded the feat as an example to his race. "But," the reporter added in sympathy, "he was very tired at dark." N&C, September 14, 1886.

23. "Earthquake prices": *N&C*, September 12 and 20, 1886. Henry Lesesne: ibid., September 8 and 9, 1886.

24. FWD II to Frank Logan, Logan Papers.

25. For a different view of South Carolina Gov. Franklin Moses, see Benjamin Ginsberg, *Moses of South Carolina: A Jewish Scalawag during Radical Reconstruction* (Baltimore, Md.: Johns Hopkins University Press, 2010).

26. FWD supported Chamberlain: E. Culpepper Clark, *Francis Warrington Dawson and the Politics of Restoration: South Carolina, 1874–1889* (University: University of Alabama Press, 1980), 40–41, 58. FWD gave reasons to support Chamberlain: *N&C*, July 7–15, 1876.

27. E. Culpepper Clark, *Francis Warrington Dawson*, 68. For more on Mississippi in 1875 and 1876 see Nicholas Lemann, *Redemption: The Last Battle of the Civil War* (New York: Farrar, Straus and Giroux, 2006).

28. Alfred B. Williams, *Hampton and His Red Shirts: South Carolina's Deliverance in 1876* (Charleston: Walker, Evans and Cogswell, 1935).

29. On the Combahee River riots, see Eric Foner, *Nothing but Freedom: Emancipation and Its Legacy* (Baton Rouge: Louisiana State University Press, 1983), 92–102, and *N&C*, September 7, 8, 12, and 13, 1876.

30. Foner, *Nothing but Freedom*, 101.

31. Stephen Budiansky, *The Bloody Shirt: Terror after Appomattox* (New York: Viking, 2008); Lemann, *Redemption*, 172–73, 174. Hamburg is now a part of North Augusta, South Carolina.

32. "Barbarous in the extreme": *N&C*, July 10, 1876. Thomas Nast, "The 'Bloody Shirt' Reformed," *Harper's Weekly*, August 12, 1876.

33. *N&C*, July 11 and 12, 1876.

34. FWD, Gary, and Rhett: E. Culpepper Clark, *Francis Warrington Dawson*, 63–66; Williams, *Hampton and His Red Shirts*, 63–65, including Rhett's quotation.

35. FWD and dueling: E. Culpepper Clark, *Francis Warrington Dawson*, 63–66, 105–8; "would have had a duel": Williams, *Hampton and His Red Shirts*, 53; duel in Tennessee: FWD II to Frank Logan, February 8, 1949, Logan Papers; FWD knighted: E. Culpepper Clark, *Francis Warrington Dawson*, 108.

36. *N&C*, August 14–18, 1876.

37. E. Culpepper Clark, *Francis Warrington Dawson*, 67–68.

38. Riot in Charleston on September 6, 1876, Citadel Green: *N&C*, September 7, 8, 1876; Melinda Meek Hennessey, "Racial Violence during Reconstruction: The 1876 Riots in Charleston and Cainhoy," *SCHM* 86, no. 2 (April 1985): 104–5. Another black man who stood by the Republicans in 1876 was Moses Brown, who died in early September 1886 from injuries he received during the earthquake. He had been rewarded for his loyalty with a custodial position. "Brown, it will

be remembered, was one of the few staunch colored Democrats who stood the persecutions of their own race for their principles.... His widow is entirely helpless, but will doubtless receive support at the hands of those white men to whom her dead husband had been so staunch a friend." *N&C*, September 5, 1886.

Many years later, Charleston men would compare their experiences in the Civil War, the 1876 riots, and the earthquake, debating which was worst: Williams, *Hampton and His Red Shirts*, 119; C. Irvine Walker, *Carolina Rifle Club, Charleston, S.C.* ([Charleston]: n.p., 1904), 69.

39. "Beaten almost to a jelly": *N&C*, September 8, 1876; "Kill them! Kill them all!": Hennessey, "Racial Violence during Reconstruction," 104–5.

40. Mark M. Smith, "'All Is Not Quiet in Our Hellish County': Facts, Fiction, Politics, and Race — The Ellenton Riot of 1876," *SCHM* 95, no. 2 (April 1994): 143–55; Stephen Kantrowitz, *Ben Tillman and the Reconstruction of White Supremacy* (Chapel Hill: University of North Carolina Press, 2000), 74; Lemann, *Redemption*, 174.

41. Hennessey, "Racial Violence during Reconstruction," 107–9; Elise Pinckney, "The Cainhoy Riot as Remembered by Jim Alston," *SCHM* 86, no. 2 (April 1985): 158–60.

42. Broad Street riot: *N&C*, August 12, 1876; Williams, *Hampton and His Red Shirts*, 372; Walker, *Carolina Rifle Club*, 71.

43. Election of 1876: Walter Edgar, *South Carolina: A History* (Columbia: University of South Carolina, 1998), 402–6; E. Culpepper Clark, *Francis Warrington Dawson*, 60–69.

44. "The last battle of the Civil War": this is also the subtitle of Lemann's book, *Redemption*.

45. Fraud, eight-box law: See Hyman S. Rubin III, "Eight Box Law," in Walter Edgar, ed., *The South Carolina Encyclopedia* (Columbia: University of South Carolina Press, 2006), 292; Edgar, *South Carolina*, 414; Brooks Miles Barnes, "Southern Independents: South Carolina, 1882," *SCHM* 96 (July 1995): 230–51. Establishment of district 7 as the black district: Edgar, *South Carolina*, 415–16.

46. C. Vann Woodward, *Strange Career of Jim Crow* (1955; rpt., New York: Oxford University Press, 1974), 44.

Chapter Nine. "Bury the Dead and Feed the Living"

1. *NYW*, September 6, 1886; *N&C*, September 7, 1886; http://www.chriscunard.com/Etruria.php (accessed December 21, 2010).

2. WAC, Earthquake Scrapbook, WAC Papers, CLS.

3. Ibid.

4. Ibid.

5. Ibid.

6. *NYW*, September 6, 1886.

7. Ibid., reported the conversation with WAC about the numbers of black and white victims. On September 8, 1886, the *N&C* claimed that the statements attributed to WAC the day before "were wholly manufactured and unauthorized."

8. FWD to SMD, September 5, 1886, FWD Family Papers.

9. Richard B. McCaslin, *Portraits of Conflict: A Photographic History of South Carolina in the Civil War* (Fayetteville: University of Arkansas Press, 1994), 223, 224, and 308.

10. Russell R. Dynes, "The Lisbon Earthquake of 1755: The First Modern Disaster," in *The Lisbon Earthquake of 1755: Representations and Reactions*, ed. Theodore E. D. Brown and John D. Radner (Oxford, U. K.: Voltaire Foundation, 2005), 34–49.

11. Robert G. Spinney, *A History of Chicago* (DeKalb: Northern Illinois University Press, 2000), 104–7.

12. Mrs. Courtenay may have been out of town when her husband returned home. A telegram to her from Orangeburg, S.C., in one of his Earthquake Scrapbooks, CLS, invites her for a visit at this time. French consul: DeJardin-Courtenay Correspondence, 1879–1894 (microfilm 51/552), SCHS; originals are at CLS.

13. *N&C*, September 8, 1886.

14. Ibid., September 7, 10, and 11, 1886.

15. WAC correspondence, September 8, 1886, WAC Papers, SCL. Others in town also welcomed Courtenay's return; see, for instance, Diary of Julius M. Bacot, September 7, 1886, SCHS. Rev. A. Toomer Porter, a veteran of many crises, was more measured in his expectations. It was beyond the ability of one man, he wrote, to "bring order out of chaos." *N&C*, September 9, 1886.

16. *N&C*, September 8 and 11, 1886.

17. Allowance of food provided: ibid., September 9, 1886. This was considerably more generous than the standard allowance after the Chicago fire. See Chicago Relief, *First Special Report of the Chicago Relief and Aid Society* (Chicago: Culver, Page, and Hoyne, 1871), 14. First day of commissary: *N&C*, September 8 and 9, 1886. Applicants had to present documents: *N&C*, September 6, 1886. In four days, 21,000 packets: *N&C*, September 11, 1886.

In normal times, the almshouse provided daily rations to about 175 "outdoor pensioners," about 60 percent of them black. "Department of Charities," in *Year Book — 1886. Charleston, So. Ca.* (Charleston: Walker, Evans and Cogswell, n.d.), 103. By the end of the second week after the quake, about 80,000 single-day rations had been distributed, or almost 6,000 per day. *N&C*, September 20, 1886. A few people asked if they could redistribute their rations to those even more needy; permission was always granted. *N&C*, September 14, 1886.

18. Soup kitchen: *N&C*, September 10, 1886. Head chef (Augustus Harleston):

ibid., September 10, 11, and 12, 1886. One man "paralyzed with indecision": *NYW*, September 10, 1886.

19. *NYW*, September 10, 1886; *N&C*, September 24, 1886.

20. WAC reappointed original relief committee: *N&C*, September 9, 1886. Yates, Huguenin refused to continue on committee: *N&C*, September 13, 1886. WAC appointed new members: *N&C*, September 10 and 15, 1886.

21. ERC Minutes, September 11, 13, and 14, 1886, Records of the ERC.

22. *N&C*, September 7, 19, 13, and 11, 1886.

23. Ibid., September 14 and 9, 1886.

24. Post office: ibid., September 9, 1886. St. Philip's steeple: ibid., September 7, 1886. Calhoun Monument: ibid., September 6, 9, and 10, 1886.

25. Sum sent to Dawson: FWD to SMD, September 20, 1886, FWD Family Papers. Almost all donations were listed in the *N&C* and in the city's official "Records of the Executive Relief Committee for the Earthquake of 1886," South Carolina Room, CCPL. A ledger at the CCPL (box 1, folder 15) summarizes donations by city and state. Unless otherwise noted, the contributions mentioned in this chapter can be found there. Letters accompanying checks quoted in this chapter are held in other files, also at the CCPL. New York City, J. P. Morgan: *N&C*, September 8, 9, and 26, 1886. Eventually, Baltimore would send $30,092.29 and Philadelphia $55,583. Richmond: $5,000 raised to $10,000: *RD*, September 4, 1886.

26. Four Vanderbilts, John Jacob Astor, Jay Gould, Martin Van Buren: *Report of the Special Committee Appointed by the Chamber of Commerce of the State of New-York to Obtain Relief for the Sufferers by the Earthquake at Charleston, S.C.* (New York: Press of the Chamber of Commerce, 1886), CCPL. William Astor: *NYH*, September 22, 1886. New York City collection boxes: *N&C*, September 20, 1886. Joseph Pulitzer: *N&C*, September 4, 1886. John Kenyon: *NYW*, September 9, 1886. Bale of cotton from Georgia: *N&C*, September 8, 1886.

27. *N&C*, September 18, 1886.

28. S.C. Lunatic Asylum, nine-year-old girl: ibid., September 24, 1886. Material goods: ibid., September 3, 9, 22, and 25, 1886.

29. Charleston had suffered enough: *NYH*, September 2, 1886. "How to Wipe Out the Past": *Boston Herald*, rpt. in *N&C*, September 9, 1886. GAR officer: *National Tribune* qtd. in *N&C*, September 29, 1886. "The people of the North": *NYW* qtd. in Robin Kelsey, *Archive Style: Photographs and Illustrations for U.S. Surveys, 1850–1890* (Berkeley: University of California Press, 2007), 184–85.

30. GAR post offered to send troops, city acknowledged: *N&C*, September 11, 1886. Brooklyn GAR post, one-armed soldier: ibid., September 8, 1886. John Greenleaf Whittier: *Amesbury (Mass.) News*, rpt. in *N&C*, September 26, 1886. Edwin Booth: *N&C*, September 8, 1886. John Brown Jr. sent a $5.00 contribu-

tion to Major H. E. Young, who distributed it to the Confederate Home: *N&C*, March 2 and 11, 1887.

31. For more on the dynamics of North-South reconciliation from 1865 until 1900, see David W. Blight, *Race and Reunion: The Civil War in American Memory* (Cambridge, Mass.: Harvard University Press, 2001).

32. Deaths September 3–11: *N&C* regularly reported new deaths, but the official record of deaths was compiled by the Charleston Board of Health, records (including "Return of Deaths within the City of Charleston, South Carolina") at the CCPL.

33. Enterprise Railroad: *N&C*, September 10, 1886. Railroads donated boxcars: ibid., September 7 and 15, 1886. Stable for 150: *NYH*, September 8, 1886; *N&C*, September 10, 1886. *Amethyst*: *N&C*, September 7, 1886. *Wistaria*: *N&C*, September 15, 1886. On the *Wistaria*, see also *CW*, February 2, 1889, *N&C*, August 27, 1933. Other ships: *N&C*, September 8, 1886. Italian vessels: *N&C*, September 8 and October 6, 1886.

34. WAC re sewage issues before quake: see, for instance, *Year Book — 1880. Charleston, So. Ca.* (Charleston: News and Courier Book Presses, n.d.), 31, *1884*, 43–44, and *1885*, 62–63 ("A week! A month! A year!"), 62–63. Though the *N&C* complained on September 10 that Marion Square had no sanitary closets, on September 12 it proclaimed "excellent sanitary arrangements" at the park.

35. Camp supervisors, Marion Square hydrants: *N&C*, September 11, 1886. Linguard Street: ibid., September 16, 1886; *NYW*, September 17, 1886.

36. *N&C*, September 16, 1886.

37. *NYW*, September 13, 1886.

38. Rodgers resigned: *N&C*, September 16, 1886; *SMN*, September 11, 1886; *N&C*, September 29, 1886. Francis Rodgers had made his fortune in cotton and phosphates. His four-story brick mansion on Wentworth Street included a cupola that allowed him to scan the city for fires. Don H. Doyle, *New Men, New Cities, New South: Atlanta, Nashville, Charleston, Mobile, 1865–1910* (Chapel Hill: University of North Carolina Press, 1990), 234; "Mr. Francis S. Rodgers Dead," *N&C*, March 14, 1911. The building is now a hotel known as the Wentworth Mansion, with a restaurant named 1886 in one of the outbuildings.

39. *N&C*, September 8 and 29, 1886.

40. WAC authorized hiring police: *N&C*, September 8, 1886. Stockade plans: ibid., September 25, 1886. Colonel Rhett: *NYW*, September 13, 1886. Rhett was also well-known for having killed a fellow Confederate officer in a duel during the Civil War. C. Russell Horres Jr., "An Affair of Honor at Fort Sumter," *SCHM* 102 (January 2001): 6–26.

41. *N&C*, September 9 and 10, 1886.

42. "The trouble": Clelia Porcher: September 16, 1886, Frederick Adolphus Porcher papers, SCL. "Servant girls": N&C, September 11, 1886. Rumors re visiting black man: N&C, September 12, 1886.

43. N&C, September 8 and 9, 1886.

44. NYT, rpt. in N&C, September 20, 1886; W. T. Waters to WAC, WAC Papers, vol. 3, SCL.

45. N&C, September 11, 12, and 16, 1886.

46. Ibid., September 18 and October 5, 1886.

47. "Injudicious": N&C, September 9–11, 1886. Twelve canvassers chosen: ibid., September 19, 1886. Two-thirds of those helped were black: ibid., September 18, 1886. "Repressing Bummerism": NYH, rpt. in N&C, September 11, 1886.

48. Six black canvassers: N&C, September 12, 1886. Dart quotation: ibid., September 14, 1886. Heard quotation: NYF, September 25, 1886.

49. N&C, September 14, 16, and 20, 1886.

50. Knightsville: ibid., September 9, 1886. Member of Summerville Town Council (H. A. M. Smith): ibid., September 16, 1886. Some small communities near Summerville, including the all-black town of Lincolnville, were given relief by the Summerville committee, whose funds were provided by Charleston. Ibid., September 19, 1886. The Summerville Relief Committee soon wired a request that no more rations be issued to able-bodied men from Summerville, since they could get work at good wages in their own town: ibid., September 12, 1886. Mt. Pleasant and other communities asked for money: ibid., September 10 and 16, 1886.

51. N&C, September 8, 1886. The two black men on the Summerville committee were identified as "the Rev. Anthony Alston of the colored Baptist Church" and "the Rev. J. Sasportas of the colored Presbyterian Church."

52. N&C, September 9, 1886.

53. Harper's Weekly, September 11, 1886.

54. Charleston vultures: Arthur Mazyck and Gene Waddell, Charleston in 1883 (Easley, S.C.: Southern Historical Press, 1983), xvii. Market filled with refugees: N&C, September 16, 1886. Fishing fleet idle: N&C, September 11, 1886.

55. N&C, September 8, 1886.

56. Miriam DuPré to "Zay" (SMD), September 12, 1886, FWD Family Papers.

57. FWD to SMD, September 5, 1886, ibid.

58. Miriam DuPré to "Zay" (SMD), September 12, 1886, ibid. Lucile played Mozart at age four: N&C, January 13, 1888.

59. FWD to SMD, September 10, 1886, FWD Family Papers.

60. N&C, September 13, 1886, and August 31, 1886.

61. Ibid., September 13, 1886.

Chapter Ten. The Comforts of Science

1. Edward Wells, "Mem. of the Charleston Earthquake of 1886," (11/521C/1), 6, SCHS.

2. Clarence Edward Dutton, *The Charleston Earthquake of August 31, 1886* (U.S. Geological Survey Ninth Annual Report, 1887–88; rpt., Arlington, Va.: U.S. Geological Survey, 1979), 240–41.

3. L. R. Gibbes, in *Proceedings of the Elliott Society* 2 (July 1887): 153–71.

4. Frank Fisher, "June 1st, 1889: The Earthquake of August 1886" (unpublished), Frank R. Fisher Notes, 1882–1902, Special Collections, Marlene and Nathan Addlestone Library, College of Charleston.

5. James Lal Penick Jr., *The New Madrid Earthquakes* (Columbus: University of Missouri Press, 1981), xiv.

6. Ted Steinberg, *Acts of God: The Unnatural History of Natural Disaster in America* (New York: Oxford University Press, 2000), 4.

7. The earth resembled an apple drying, including references to Edward Seuss: Naomi Oreskes, *Plate Tectonics: An Insider's History of the Modern Theory of the Earth* (Boulder, Colo.: Westview Press, 2001), 4; Fredrick Golden, *The Trembling Earth: Probing and Predicting Quakes* (New York: Scribner's, 1983), 33, 142. President of British Geological Association (Sir William Dawson): *NYH*, September 19, 1886.

8. *NYH*, rpt. in the *N&C*, September 16, 1886.

9. "Recent Earthquake Literature," *Science* 8 (September 10, 1886), 242–43.

10. Woman in Lausanne: *N&C*, October 27, 1886. "If you destroy the sound": Records of the ERC, n.d.

11. History of the USGS: http://www.usgs.gov (accessed March 19, 2008). Crater Lake: *Grand Rapids (Mich.) Daily Eagle*, September 1, 1886. See also Stephen R. Mark, "Seventeen Years to Success: John Muir, William Gladston Steel, and the Creation of Yosemite and Crater Lake National Parks," National Park Service, U.S. Department of the Interior (http://www.nps.gov/archive/crla/steel .htm; accessed April 2, 2008). Dutton would later write the official USGS report on the Charleston quake.

12. California quake in 1812: Robert L. Kovach, *Early Earthquakes of the Americas* (Cambridge, U.K.: Cambridge University Press, 2004), 143. Long Island quake in 1884: "East Coast Earthquakes 1884" (http://www.gendisasters .com/data1/ny/earthquakes/eastcoast-earthquake-aug1884.htm; accessed April 2, 2008).

13. Earle Sloan hired: Carl McKinley, "A Descriptive Narrative of the Earthquake of August 31, 1886," in *Year Book — 1886. Charleston, So. Ca.* (Charleston: Walker, Evans and Cogswell, n.d.), 390. Sloan and Stoney: Samuel L. Stoney to

"My dear Mother," September 3, 1886, Stoney Family Correspondence, 1872–1886 (24/14/1), SCHS.

14. The N&C tracked Sloan's movements almost daily. See, for instance, N&C, September 11 (2,000-foot fissure), 15 (handcar), 16 (brick reservoir at gas works), 1886. Railroad trestle: NYW, September 19, 1886. Sloan's reports have been published in W J McGee, *First-hand Observations of the Charleston Earthquake of August 31, 1886, and Other Earthquake Materials: Reports of W J McGee [et al.]*, compiled and edited by Kenneth E. Peters and Robert B. Herrmann (Columbia: South Carolina Geological Survey, Division of Research and Statistical Services, South Carolina State Budget and Control Board, 1986).

15. Sloan's findings are reported in Dutton, *Charleston Earthquake*, 60, 61, 68. In his final report Dutton praises Sloan extensively for the quality of his work. Ibid., 210. Sloan later served for many years as the South Carolina state geologist.

16. Sloan wrote McGee: Dutton, *Charleston Earthquake*, 44. Theory of three foci confirmed: Pradeep Talwani, interviews by the authors, May 24, 2003, and May 17, 2004. Middleton Place Plantation: Elise Pinckney, " 'Still Mindful of the English Way': 250 Years of Middleton Place on the Ashley," *SCHM* 92, no. 3 (July 1991): 159. The main house and one of the two flanking buildings at Middleton Place had been destroyed by fire in a raid at the end of the Civil War; the earthquake brought down the ruins and drained the lakes.

17. James Dewey and Perry Byerly, "The Early History of Seismometry (to 1900)," USGS Earthquake Hazards Program, http://earthquake.usgs.gov/learn/topics/seismology/history/history_seis.php (accessed December 15, 2010); "Famous Scientists and Earthquake Detection," http://inventors.about.com/library/inventors/bljohnmilne.htm (accessed April 2, 2008).

18. Homemade seismoscope of Charleston judge (Patrick Gleason): N&C, September 16, 1886. Dr. Charles U. Shepard, in *Proceedings of the Elliott Society* (January 1888): 188–89. Seismograph an "earthquake shock indicator": see, for instance, N&C, September 16, 1886.

19. *New York Star*, rpt. in N&C, September 15, 1886.

20. Improvements in seismographs and seismoscopes: Golden, *Trembling Earth*, 66–69, 146–47; Bruce A. Bolt, *Earthquakes and Geological Discovery* (New York: Scientific American Library, 1993), 45–49; Dewey and Byerly, "Early History of Seismometry"; "Seismoscopes in Eighteenth Century Europe," " 'The Seismometer' of James Forbes," "Further Studies of Seismoscopes," and "The Invention of a Seismograph in Italy," all at About.com/library/inventors (accessed April 2, 2008). Images of a beautiful modern re-creation of the first seismoscope can be found in Bolt, *Earthquakes and Geological Discovery*, 44, and Frank W. Lane, *The Violent Earth* (Topsfield, Mass.: Salem House, 1986), 158–59.

21. Yale Observatory professor (Sherman): AC, September 2, 1886. Paris Ob-

servatory researcher (M. Daubree): *NYH*, October 10, 1886. Washington Monument seismoscope: *New York Star*, rpt. in *N&C*, September 15, 1886. Sloan trying to measure shocks: *N&C*, October 24, 1886.

22. Karl V. Steinbrugge, *Earthquakes, Volcanoes, and Tsunamis* (New York: Skandia America Group, 1982), 355; Bolt, *Earthquakes and Geological Discovery*, 154.

23. Talwani, interviews.

24. Moment Magnitude: Pradeep Talwani and Navin Sharma, "Reevaluation of the Magnitudes of Three Destructive Aftershocks of the 1886 Charleston Earthquake," *Seismological Research Letters* 70, no. 3 (May/June 1999): 360. The largest earthquake ever recorded was the 1960 Chilean quake, which registered an astounding 9.5 on the moment magnitude scale. The December 24, 2004, earthquake in the Indian Ocean, which was followed by deadly tsunamis, registered between 9.1 and 9.3.

25. U.S. Geological Survey, "The Severity of an Earthquake," http://pubs.usgs.gov/gip/earthq4/severitygip.html (accessed August 29, 2010).

26. Pradeep Talwani of the University of South Carolina has tracked the Charleston earthquake closely. See, for instance, Pradeep Talwani and William J. Schaeffer, "Recurrence Rates of Large Earthquakes in the South Carolina Coastal Plain Based on Paleoliquifaction Data," *Journal of Geophysical Research* 106, no. B4 (April 10, 2001): 6621–42.

Continental drift, plate tectonics: Golden, *Trembling Earth*, 88–90, 126; Kerry E. Sieh and Simon Levay, *The Earth in Turmoil: Earthquakes, Volcanoes, and Their Impact on Humankind* (New York: W. H. Freeman, 1998), 236–37; Steinbrugge, *Earthquakes, Volcanoes, and Tsunamis*, 6–7. Steinbrugge also includes on pages 9–10 a good description of P-waves, S-waves, Love waves, and Rayleigh waves; on page 104 he explains how various types of brick construction are affected by earthquakes.

27. The sedimentary deposits beneath the east coast can transmit seismic waves for thousands of miles: John J. Nance, *On Shaky Ground: An Invitation to Disaster* (New York: Morrow, 1988), 130. Structures built on soft deep soils often suffer more damage: Bolt, *Earthquakes and Geological Discovery*, 34.

28. Prehistoric sandblows: Talwani and Schaeffer, "Recurrence Rates," and Sieh and Levay, *Earth in Turmoil*, 237–38. Five-hundred-year intervals: Talwani and Schaeffer, "Recurrence Rates."

29. Woodstock fault, dogleg, plutons: Sieh and Levay, *Earth in Turmoil*, 236–37, 327; Talwani, interviews; Martin C. Chapman, J. R. Martin, G. Olgun, and B. Regmi, "Prediction and Geographic Information System (GIS) Mapping of Ground Motions and Site Response in Charleston, S.C. and Two Neighboring Counties: First Phase Development of a GIS for Seismic Hazard Evaluation," http://www.geol.vt.edu/outreach/vtso/charlestongis/report.html (accessed Sep-

tember 24, 2010). Fort Dorchester area: *A Compendium of Field Trips of South Carolina Geology with Emphasis on the Charleston, S.C., Area* ([Columbia]: South Carolina Department of Natural Resources, Geological Survey, May 23–24, 2000), 2, 5.

30. *NYH*, September 7, 1886; *N&C*, September 15 and 16, 1886.

31. *N&C*, September 16, 1886.

32. *NYH*, September 21, 1886.

33. *N&C*, September 23, 1886.

Chapter Eleven. Relief

1. Clelia Porcher to her daughter, September 7, 1886, Frederick Adolphus Porcher Papers, SCL; A. R. Alley, M.D., to William J. Cumming, September 12, 1886, Thomas John Cumming Collection, 1835–1886 (43/365), SCHS.

2. *N&C*, September 16, 1886; *SMN*, September 7, 1886.

3. Molsey Edwards, "rackety, rickety . . . house," carriage as weapon: *N&C*, September 16, 1886. Man found wife with another man, fish seller: ibid., September 23, 1886.

4. *N&C*, September 26, 1886.

5. Ibid., September 18, 22, and 20, 1886.

6. Ibid., September 22, 1886.

7. For a summary of the Chicago fire and relief efforts afterward, see Robert A. Cromie, *A Short History of Chicago* (San Francisco: Lexicos, 1984), 90–107. President Ulysses S. Grant sent $1,000 to Chicago to support the relief efforts: ibid., 90. As Charleston struggled with its many needs, the *New York World* suggested that the city of Chicago donate to Charleston whatever was left in its relief fund, which had totaled more than $5 million fifteen years before. Dawson applauded the idea. The Chicago fund was sacred, he said, but Chicago had long since recovered, and what better use for the money could there be than to help Charleston bounce back? Chicago apparently did not agree — no money from the fire fund ever arrived. *NYW*, rpt. in *N&C*, September 23, 1886.

8. *N&C*, September 27 and 17, 1886. A copy of the application form is in ibid., September 16, 1886.

9. *N&C*, September 16, 1886.

10. ERC Minutes, September 17, 1886, Records of the ERC.

11. Ibid., September 22, 1886; *N&C*, September 26, October 7, and September 30, 1886.

12. *NYH*, rpt. in *N&C*, September 22, 1886.

13. *N&C*, September 24, 1886.

14. ERC Minutes, September 29, 1886, Records of the ERC.

15. "No loss of any person": ibid., September 24, 1886; 750 applications, "of course claims": N&C, September 23, 1886. "Deserving widows," "Their future": Robert Adger to William E. Dodge, rpt. in the New York Tribune, September 23, rpt. in N&C, September 26, 1886.

16. Fast-track claims of women: N&C, September 24, 25, and 28, 1886. "Attend to their own": ibid., September 30, 1886. Most requests from working people: ibid., September 25, 1886. Petition for $5,800: ibid., September 29 and 30, 1886.

17. Inspectors, 50 dwellings/day: N&C, September 24, 25, and 22, 1886; 75 dwellings/day: ibid., September 29, 1886. "These people belong to the class": ibid., September 27, 1886. Applications "laid on the table": ibid., September 28, 1886.

18. New York architect (Arthur S. Jennings): N&C, September 8, 1886. On the mortar, see ibid., October 2, 1886. Spier, "We have a society": ibid., September 20, 1886. A recent study concluded that more than 80 percent of the damaged buildings in Charleston were made of brick, while only 7 percent of the wood-frame structures were damaged. Of these, 96 percent were located on made ground. Further, the authors determined that much of the structural damage resulted from liquefaction rather than shaking. Andrew Robinson and Pradeep Talwani, "Building Damage at Charleston, South Carolina, Associated with the 1886 Earthquake." Bulletin of the Seismological Society of America 73, no. 2 (April 1983): 633–52.

19. Buddensiek mortar: "The Gossip of New York," N&C, April 20 and 21, 1885. See ibid., September 14 ("We Want No More . . ."), 21, 30, October 2, 3, 5, 6, and 17, 1886. The "Buddensiek disaster," as it came to be known, was one of artist Walt McDougall's first big assignments. Walt McDougall, This Is the Life (New York: Alfred A. Knopf, 1926), 100.

20. G. E. Manigault, M.D., "The Earthquake at Charleston," in Clarence Edward Dutton, The Charleston Earthquake of August 31, 1886 (U.S. Geological Survey Ninth Annual Report, 1887–88; rpt., Arlington, Va.: U.S. Geological Survey, 1979), 228–30. Architect Jennings recommended English bond: N&C, October 2, 1886. Today, most masons use running bond, which omits the crosswise bricks altogether in the interest of saving material.

21. Manigault, "Earthquake at Charleston," 228–29.

22. College of Charleston: N&C, September 19, 1886. Unitarian Church: ibid., March 21, 1888. On October 4, 1886, the N&C noted that St. John's Lutheran Church, next door to the Unitarian Church, was built in 1816–18 and suffered little damage.

23. N&C, September 20 and 22, 1886.

24. Ibid., September 17, 1886.

25. Ibid., September 16 and 18, 1886.

26. Ibid., September 17 and 18, 1886.

27. Ibid., September 18, 1886.

28. Dr. Rose objected but fired employees: ibid., September 20, 1886. Subsistence Committee employment: ERC Minutes, September 18, 1886, Records of the ERC. Canvassers, delivery wagons laid off: N&C, September 26, 23, and 24, 1886. "All Bills": N&C, September 28, 1886.

29. N&C, September 29, 1886.

30. Booths empty, small businesses at Marion Square: ibid., September 12, 24, and 25, 1886. People sleeping on Battery benches: ibid., September 25, 1886. If finished with tents, notify committee: ibid., September 26, 1886. Lumber to be sold: ibid., September 25 and October 1, 1886.

31. N&C, September 22, 1886.

32. "Work, or Go to Jail": ibid., September 29, 1886. This editorial appeared while Dawson was out of town, so it could have been the work of J. C. Hemphill, his second-in-command, who often took over editorial writing when Dawson was absent.

33. FWD suggested hiring out-of-town workers: N&C, September 17, 1886. Word went out around country for workers: ibid., September 19 and 28, 1886. Fifty skilled bricklayers arrived: ibid., September 23, 1886. "Prominent citizens": ibid., September 19, 1886. Labor bureau, 85 workmen, "hundreds if not thousands": ibid., September 28, 1886. The next day the N&C reported that thirty "additional mechanics signed up."

34. Ten dollars: ERC Minutes, September 14, 1886, Records of the ERC. Recipients of immediate relief: "Register of Contributions to the Sufferers in Charleston by the Earthquake, 1886," Records of the ERC. Limit raised to $25.00: ERC Minutes, September 14, 1886, Records of the ERC. Staff of the CCPL have entered all data regarding home-repair relief into a database, available in its South Carolina Room, and at "The City of Charleston's Executive Relief Committee for the Earthquake of 1886: Money Vouchers for Work Done, September 1886 through June 1887," Records of the ERC, and at http://ccplarchive.wordpress.com.

35. "Register of Contributions." Though Mrs. Goutevenier's case was often discussed by the ERC, her name does not appear in their final printed report, The Earthquake, 1886; Exhibits Showing Receipts and Disbursements and the Applications for Relief with the Awards and Refusals of the Executive Relief Committee (Charleston: Lucas, Richardson and Co., 1887), Records of the ERC.

36. N&C, September 29, 1886; ERC Minutes, September 17, 1886, Records of the ERC.

37. Letter re "needy Africans": "Register of Contributions." Americans in China sent money, girls' soap bubbles: Letters to WAC, Records of the ERC. Irish lace makers: NYW, October 15, 1886.

38. New Orleans Amateur Opera Company: *N&C*, September 26, 1886. Elsa Von Blumen: *NYW*, September 21, 1886. Corpulents vs. Consumptives: *N&C*, September 26, 1886.

39. Ford's Grand Opera House: *NYH*, September 13, 1886. Nashville Grand Opera House, Philadelphia Academy of Music: *N&C*, September 26, 1886. *Umbria: Report of the Special Committee Appointed by the Chamber of Commerce of the State of New York* (n.p., n.d.), 11, copy in CCPL. (The *Umbria* was the sister ship of the *Etruria*, on which Mayor Courtenay had returned to the United States: http://cunard.com; accessed December 15, 2010.) Opera and theater companies across the country: *Report of the Special Committee*, 11.

40. By the time the relief books were closed, Atlanta had sent $1,501.00; in comparison, Savannah raised $6,740.64. Register of Donations Listed by State, box 1, folder 15, Records of the ERC. On September 4 the *Atlanta Constitution* claimed that more than $1,600 in relief had been subscribed through its offices; apparently, not all of that reached Charleston. Grady on Atlanta's strong foundation: see, for instance, *Atlanta Constitution*, September 1 and 4, 1886.

41. *Greenville (S.C.) News*, rpt. in *N&C*, September 22, 1886; Daniel Huger Bacot to Josephine Norton Rhett, September 28, 1886, Bacot Family Papers, 1860–1938, box 1, Special Collections, Marlene and Nathan Addlestone Library, College of Charleston.

42. *N&C*, September 25 and 22, 1886.

43. Ibid., September 12, 1886.

44. *City of Atlanta* visitors: *NYW*, September 13, 1886. 1500 excursionists: *N&C*, September 13, 1886.

45. Atlantic Coastline Railroad planned excursions: *N&C*, September 22, 1886. Rumors of tidal wave, trains with excursionists: ibid., October 3 and 4, 1886. "No one need be deterred": ibid., October 1, 1886. Tour groups, "monster" ACL trip: ibid., October 8, 1886.

46. *N&C*, October 8 and November 3, 1886.

47. Earthquake sand 50¢/bottle: *SMN*, September 18, 1886. In 1886, according to advertisements in the *N&C*, 50¢ would also buy a one-way train ticket to Savannah, a pair of boys' linen knee pants, a cheap pair of shoes, a corset, or a yard of wool fabric. When sand ran out, red pepper and ground coffee: *N&C*, October 4, 1886. "Cyclonic cigars," "cyclonic shakes": *N&C*, August 30, 1885. Earthquake beer: *Charleston As It Is After the Earthquake Shock of August 31, 1886* (Charleston: n.p., 1886), 60. Photo views before and after: *N&C*, October 1, 1886.

48. "Earthquake relics": *N&C*, October 1, 1886. Dime museums looking for "earthquake babies," black triplets: *N&C*, October 9, 1886. Three true earthquake babies: *SMN*, September 7, 1886. Earth and Quake: Augustine Smythe to his wife,

September 6, 1886, A. T. Smyth [*sic*] Papers (24/8/9), SCHS; he was writing about the children of Mrs. Elliott Welch.

49. September 21 shock: *N&C*, September 22 (*City of Monticello*, "It would have been a little thing," medical college wall collapsed) and 24, October 1 (dead fish), 1886. Man injured by falling wall: ibid., September 17, 1886.

50. *N&C*, September 27, 1886.

51. FWD: get ready for tourists: ibid., September 30, 1886. "Truly that is typical": *American* (Atlanta), March 16, 1889, in SMD scrapbook of FWD's murder (f:5323), FWD Family Papers.

52. Clara Barton visit: *N&C*, September 28 and 30, 1886; Elizabeth Brown Pryor, *Clara Barton: Professional Angel* (Philadelphia: University of Pennsylvania Press, 1987), 245–46.

53. History of Red Cross: Foster Rhea Dulles, *The American Red Cross: A History* (New York: Harper, 1950), 12, 26 (Michigan fires), 2; Clyde E. Buckingham, *For Humanity's Sake: The Story of the Early Development of the League of Red Cross Societies* (Washington, D.C.: Public Affairs Press, 1964), 15, 16 (European societies), 48 (U.S. branch to aid victims of natural disasters), 25 (floods). In its first twenty-three years of existence, the American Red Cross raised only about $2 million. Dulles, *American Red Cross*, 40.

54. Chicago chapter of Red Cross: *N&C*, September 28, 1886. "So great as to be beyond": Buckingham, *For Humanity's Sake*, 15. WAC escorted Barton and Hubbell: *N&C*, September 30, 1886.

55. Stephen B. Oates, *A Woman of Valor: Clara Barton and the Civil War* (New York: Free Press, 1994), 146, 180; Pryor, *Clara Barton*, 114.

56. "Entertwined": *N&C*, September 28, 1886; "fully covered" and silver dollars: ibid., September 30, 1886. In addition to her $100 contributions, Barton gave each City Hospital patient a silver dollar: Carl McKinley, "A Descriptive Narrative of the Earthquake of August 31, 1886," in *Year Book — 1886. Charleston, So. Ca.* (Charleston: Walker, Evans and Cogswell, n.d.), 91.

57. *N&C* speculated that new resources coming: *N&C*, September 30, 1886. Same as Blackville, Key West: Records of the ERC. Barton wrote mayor of Chicago: *N&C*, October 1, 1886.

Chapter Twelve. Waiting for the Apocalypse

1. *NYH*, September 21, 1886. The president of the Astronomical Meteorological Association, Walter J. H. Smith, would deny his support for Wiggins a week later: ibid., September 29, 1886.

2. Wiggins's biography: http://famousamericans.net/ezekielstonewiggins (ac-

cessed September 23, 2010) and John D. Reid, "A Most Unusual Person," http://www.anglo-celtic-connections.blogspot.com/2010/08/most-unusual-person.html (accessed September 23, 2010). Wiggins's assertion about dinosaurs at the bottom of the ocean resembles Jules Verne's *Journey to the Center of the Earth* (1864). Grocery ad: *Ottawa Citizen*, March 12, 1883.

3. *NYT*, February 10, 1883.

4. *N&C*, September 24, 1886.

5. Ibid.

6. Galveston: ibid., September 24, 1886. "The Poor People Rendered Frantic" and New Orleans country folk: ibid., September 25, 1886; in that issue, Wiggins was described as the "Terror of Texas Darkies." Traveling salesmen: ibid., September 16, 1886.

7. Farm laborers halted work, Liberty County prophetess: *NYH*, September 8, 1886. "Indignant enough": *NYW*, September 24, 1886.

8. *N&C*, September 27, 1886.

9. Savannah: ibid., September 27, 1886; *SMN*, September 30, 1886 (every shake was "good for fifty souls").

10. Augustine Smythe: Letter to "My own darling," September 29, 1886, A. T. Smyth [*sic*] Papers (24/8/9), SCHS. Sam Stoney: letter to "My Dears" [September 24, 1886; originally dated "Friday 10 A.M." and assumed by archivists to be September 10], Stoney Family Correspondence, 1872–1886 (24/14/1), SCHS.

11. *N&C*, September 26 and 25, 1886.

12. U.S. Naval Observatory astronomer (Professor Haul): *N&C*, September 25, 1886. English astronomer (Richard A. Proctor): *N&C*, September 27, 1886.

13. Charleston officers of Signal Corps: *N&C*, September 27, 1886. Canadian government: *NYW*, October 20, 1886.

14. Atlanta excursion: *N&C*, October 8, 1886. Policeman trembled, man ran for a block: ibid., September 26, 1886. Advertisement: ibid., September 22, 1886.

15. *N&C*, September 25 and 30, 1886.

16. Ibid., September 28 and 27, 1886.

17. Loch Ness–type "sea serpent": *SMN*, September 23 and 25, 1886. Wiggins said to have announced bottom of sea opened, Savannah scene: *SMN*, September 28, 1886.

18. *N&C*, September 24, 1886.

19. *SMN*, September 30, 1886.

20. *SMN*, September 29 and 30, 1886.

21. Wilkes County, Jacksonville: *SMN*, September 29, 1886. Hillman, Michigan: *NYH*, October 1, 1886. Whites complained "bitterly": *N&C*, September 30, 1886; Wiggins hoped to visit Charleston: *NYT*, September 25, 1886.

22. Small shock September 27 and "These shocks are guarantees": *N&C*, September 28, 1886. "Baby Quake": *N&C*, September 29, 1886.

23. *N&C*, September 30, 1886.

24. Ibid.

25. "It mayn't be too late yet": *SMN*, September 30, 1886. Michigan family: *NYH*, October 1, 1886. Dynamite factory: *N&O*, October 1, 1886.

26. September 23 storm, Galveston's Harbor Island, and the Colima volcano: *N&C*, September 30, 1886. The National Oceanic and Atmospheric Administration now ranks this hurricane as a category 4 storm and the fifth strongest to strike the U.S. mainland between 1851 and 2004: *Charleston Post and Courier*, September 22, 2005.

27. *N&C*, September 30, 1886, and *NYT*, October 1, 1886.

28. Scaffolds full: *N&C*, October 1, 1886. Charity straightened, portable house: ibid., September 29, 1886; Jacob Schirmer diary (11/568/2), 153, SCHS. Two shakes in Summerville: *N&C*, October 1, 1886. Thirty shocks since August 27: *N&C*, October 2, 1886. "Historical truth": *N&C*, September 30, 1886.

29. "Wiggins says he is descended": *NYW*, October 1, 1886. Wiggins soup: *N&C*, September 29, 1886.

30. Mark Twain's story about the 1865 earthquake is reprinted in Jelle Zeilinga de Boer and Donald Theodore Sanders, *Earthquakes in Human History: The Far-Reaching Effects of Seismic Disruptions* (Princeton, N.J.: Princeton University Press, 2005), 20–21. His comments on Wiggins appeared in the *N&C* and the *New York Sun*, September 30, 1886.

31. FWD to SMD, September 27 and 30, 1886, FWD Family Papers; Edward Wells, "Mem. of the Charleston Earthquake of 1886," 20 (11/521C/1), SCHS.

32. FWD's private secretary resigned: *N&C*, September 30, 1886. FWD asked for week off from committee, Morris Israel replaced him: ERC Minutes, September 27, 1886, Records of the ERC.

33. FWD to SMD September 19 ($5,000), October 18 (iron rods), 1886, FWD Family Papers. Throughout the city, iron rods were installed in many buildings in an effort to pull damaged walls slowly back together and stabilize shaky structures. The ends of the bolts were often covered with decorative iron plates that are still visible. These features have come to be known as "earthquake bolts," though they had also been used after the 1885 hurricane.

34. FWD to SMD, September 24, 1886, FWD Family Papers.

35. FWD to SMD, September 27, October 10 and 12, 1886, ibid. FWD was indebted to Jimmy Morgan for helping him out of several scrapes. For one of the most dramatic, an 1876 libel case against Dawson brought by Christopher Columbus Bowen, see E. Culpepper Clark, *Francis Warrington Dawson and the Poli-*

tics of Restoration: South Carolina, 1874–1889 (University: University of Alabama Press, 1980), 41–45, and Frank Logan, "Francis W. Dawson, 1840–1889: South Carolina Editor" (Master's thesis, Department of History, Duke University, 1947), 131–32.

36. The *N&C* ran many articles trumpeting the successes of the Mason Cotton Harvester in various tests during its development: see *N&C* for July 9 and 20, 1885; December 20, 1886; September 25, 1887; April 21 and June 23, 1888; and January 14, 1889.

37. *NYW*, rpt. in *N&C*, October 3, 1886.

38. Ibid.

39. President Cleveland "really mad": FWD to SMD, October 21, 1886, FWD Family Papers. Hampton "on the warpath": FWD to SMD, October 15, 1886, ibid. Dawson and Hampton had been feuding for at least ten years. Dawson felt that Hampton had often slighted him, while Hampton suspected Dawson of "wanting to rule the whole State." E. Culpepper Clark, *Francis Warrington Dawson*, 113.

40. FWD to SMD, October 11, 1886, FWD Family Papers; Hugh S. Thompson to FWD, October 19, 1886, ibid.

41. FWD to Grover Cleveland, October 12, 1886, FWD Family Papers.

42. FWD wrote *NYW*: *N&C*, October 16, 1886. President Cleveland sent money: *N&C*, October 5 and 27, 1886.

43. Hampton had given $148: *N&C*, September 22 and October 6, 1886; box 1, folder 15, Records of the ERC. On September 28 Butler had sent $50.00 from Paris: *N&C*, October 24, 1886. FWD apologized for any "annoyance": FWD to Grover Cleveland, October 12, 1886, FWD Family Papers. Butler "did not get mad the least": M. C. Butler to FWD, October 25, 1886, FWD Family Papers. FWD had loaned Butler $1,000: E. Culpepper Clark, *Francis Warrington Dawson*, 161–62. FWD had helped Butler with his finances a number of times; one observer called FWD and Butler "a pair of licentious creatures whose conduct would destroy any-body's respect for their positions." E. Culpepper Clark, *Francis Warrington Dawson*, 161.

44. *N&C*, October 6, 1886.

45. The city council authorized mayor to withdraw his request, telegram sent: *N&C*, October 6, 1886. "Too Grateful to be Greedy": ibid., October 8, 1886. Many newspapers applauded: rpt. in *N&C*, October 9, 1886. *New York Journal of Commerce* thought premature: rpt. in *N&C*, October 12, 1886.

46. Soup kitchen closed: *N&C*, October 10, 1886. Heard's article was signed and dated November 11, 1886; it ran in the *NYF* on November 27, 1886. Blacks starving along the Waccamaw River: *N&C*, October 5, 1886. Committee action:

N&C, September 12, 1886. Black ministers proposed "fasting, humiliation and prayer": *N&C*, October 13, 1886.

Chapter Thirteen. Rising from the Ruins

1. FWD to SMD, October 10, 1886, FWD Family Papers.

2. *N&C*, October 13 and 15, 1886.

3. The KOL assembly in Richmond: T. V. Powderly, *Thirty Years of Labor, 1859–1889* (Philadelphia: T. V. Powderly, 1890), 651–62; Melton Alonza McLaurin, *Knights of Labor in the South* (Westport, Conn.: Greenwood Press, 1978), 143–44. "The most important labor meeting": *NYH*, rpt. in *N&C*, September 22, 1886.

4. Qtd. in "Race and Racism at the 1886 Knights of Labor Convention," http://historymatters.gmu.edu/d/44 (accessed June 8, 2008).

5. *N&C*, October 8, 1886.

6. On September 25, 1886, the *N&O* ran an article titled "Bigot Barnum: . . . How He Abhors Democracy and Hates the Solid South." It quotes Barnum's warning about Cleveland's election. Charges that the troupe was a fraction of full show: *N&O*, September 26, 1886.

7. *N&C*, October 3, 1886.

8. The full breathless description of the Charleston performances (including all quotations) can be found in *N&C*, October 17, 1886.

9. The story of Jumbo can be found in Paul Chambers, *Jumbo: The Greatest Elephant in the World* (Hanover, N.H.: Steerforth Press, 2008) and Susan Wilson, "An Elephant's Tale" (www.tufts.edu/alumni/magazine/spring2002/jumbo.html; accessed June 11, 2008). Years later the *N&C* purchased a printing press named by the manufacturer "The Jumbo": "R. C. Richardson, Pressman, Dead," *N&C*, August 26, 1938.

10. *N&C*, October 17, 1886.

11. Ibid., October 31, 1886.

12. Christina Margaret Pagès, "Sixty-seven Years of Drama in Charleston, South Carolina, 1869–1936: A History of the Academy of Music" (PhD diss., Department of English, University of South Carolina, 1993), 1: 15 (quotation), 551, 552.

13. ERC Minutes, October 7, 1886, Records of the ERC.

14. FWD seeking disaster relief aid from legislature: *N&C*, October 8, 1886. Relief money from state would require constitutional amendment: ibid., October 1, 1886, *CDR* qtd. in ibid., October 8 and 13, 1886. Rep. Brawley wrote Sheppard: *N&C*, October 7, 1886. "Now is the hour for action": *N&C*, October 8, 1886.

15. General assembly would have to vote: *N&C*, October 8, 1886. Rep. Braw-

ley's plan: ibid., October 13, 1886. FWD re state's phosphate royalties: ibid., October 9, 1886. Courtenay, city council opposed, *"or even a century"*: ibid., October 11, 1886.

16. "Our people cannot afford": *Georgetown (S.C.) Enquirer,* October 20, 1886; as much the act of God as the destruction of houses: see *N&C,* December 10–13, 1886.

17. James Simons to "My dear Governor," October 4 and 8, 1886, Gov. John C. Sheppard Records, box 1, folder 26, SCDAH.

18. *N&C,* October 13, 1886.

19. Butler and Hampton made no move to encourage: ibid., October 14, 1886. "Coming of your own accord": Wade Hampton to Grover Cleveland, October 18, 1886, Grover Cleveland Papers, Library of Congress, qtd. in Walter Brian Cisco, *Wade Hampton: Confederate Warrior, Conservative Statesman* (Washington, D.C.: Brassey's, 2004), 297.

20. "Earthquake proof store": *N&C,* October 2, 1886. Citadel Square Baptist Church steeple: ibid., October 15, 1886. Bagging Factory, Chamber of Commerce building: ibid., September 23, 1886. Circular Church congregation: ibid., October 27, 1886. Heard received $250: William E. Dodge to WAC, October 4, 1886, WAC, Earthquake Scrapbook, WAC Papers, CLS; December 14 and 17, 1886, box 7, folder 4, Records of the ERC; *N&C,* October 27, 1887.

21. The first school reopenings were scheduled for October 4, as reported in the *N&C* on October 5: the Citadel, College of Charleston, and ten private schools run by Charleston ladies. Other openings continued until much later in the year. See the annual report of the school superintendent in *Year Book — 1886. Charleston, So. Ca.* (Charleston: Walker, Evans and Cogswell, n.d.), 147–68. Memminger School used Porter Academy: Schirmer diary (11/568/2), 155, SCHS. Plans to hold classes throughout the city: *N&C,* October 19, 1886.

22. "A new city is being built," "We have inspected": *N&C,* October 7, 1886. The Atlanta architect claimed the city was as well built as any other, except that so many of the buildings were very old. Unlike most observers, he felt that the modern buildings survived the earthquake in better shape than older ones. City council elected inspector of buildings: ibid., October 6, 1886.

23. *N&C,* October 27 and 21, 1886.

24. Drought: ibid., September 24, 1886. Windstorm: ibid., October 20, 1886. Hurricane hit Sabine Pass: ibid., October 16 and 17, 1886.

25. Sabine Pass hurricane, including all examples and quotations: *N&C,* October 16 and 17, 1886. FWD collected contributions, "The sufferers": ibid., October 16, 1886. Contributions were reported on October 22, 24, 27, and November 3 and 11, 1886. About a month after the storm, Clara Barton thanked her friends in

Charleston for their contributions to the Sabine Pass sufferers: ibid., November 18, 1886.

26. October 22 tremor, funeral service, wells, chimneys: *N&C*, October 23 and 24, 1886. Geysers in Summerville, ditches brimmed with water: ibid., October 24, 1886. "There are times": H. P. Walker Papers, October 7, 1886 (original, 24/274/9; typescript, 24/274/2), SCHS.

27. People returned to tents: *N&C*, October 23, 1886. Summerville officials voted to discontinue repairs: ibid., October 24, 1886. "Some one is being killed or injured": *NYF*, October 30, 1886; "there are many": *NYF*, November 6, 1886.

28. Earthquake felt in Columbus, Louisville, Jacksonville: *N&O*, October 23, 1886. These October 1886 shocks have been reevaluated by seismologists, who estimate that the first measured 5.1 on the moment magnitude scale, and the second 5.7; they have been assigned Modified Mercalli Intensity ratings of VII and VIII. Pradeep Talwani and Navin Sharma, "Reevaluation of the Magnitudes of Three Destructive Aftershocks of the 1886 Charleston Earthquake," *Seismological Research Letters* 70, no. 3 (May/June 1999). Miriam DuPré's experiences: Miriam DuPré to SMD, October 6, 1886, FWD Family Papers.

29. Cause of earthquake "far to the west": *N&C*, October 25, 1886; *Springfield Republican*: rpt. in *N&C*, October 28, 1886.

30. FWD to SMD, October 23, 1886, FWD Family Papers.

Chapter Fourteen. The Old Joy of Combat

1. *N&C*, October 8, 1886.

2. Ibid., November 4, 1886; *Charleston Recorder*, November 6, 1886, Avery Research Center for African American History and Culture, College of Charleston.

3. November 5 shock: *N&C*, November 6, 1886; *Charleston Recorder*, November 6, 1886. Black parents stormed Shaw School, students and teachers calm: *N&C*, November 7, 1886. Serious injuries: *NYF*, November 13, 1886. Earthquake drills: *N&C*, November 8, 1886.

4. *N&C*, November 14, 1886.

5. E. Culpepper Clark, *Francis Warrington Dawson*, 140. A photo of the tea set can be found in the FWD Family Papers. At the SCHS, a photocopy of the back of the same photo shows that it was inscribed by WAC, "I was the largest contributor to this gift and was subsequently very badly treated by recipient, without cause" (30/4 FWD), SCHS.

6. FWD to SMD, November 10, 1886, FWD Family Papers.

7. Standard time: Michael O'Malley, *Keeping Watch: A History of American Time* (New York: Penguin, 1990). On September 1, 1886, after the earthquake, articles in the *New York World* claimed one clock in Cincinnati stopped at 8:54, another in the same city at 9:16. In his report to the U.S. Signal Service, Professor

Mendenhall commented on the difficulty of calculating exact times in parts of the country where "so-called 'local time' is still adhered to." J. C. Mendenhall, "Report on the Charleston Earthquake," *Monthly Weather Review of the U.S. Signal Service* 14 (August 1886): 234. An article in *Science* acknowledged, "The general use of standard time has added greatly to the reliability of these observations" about the earthquake: "The Charleston Earthquake," *Science* (November 26, 1886): 472.

8. Regulator clock: *N&C*, September 13, 1886. Time 9:51.48: ibid., November 18, 1886. St. Michael's clock adjusted: ibid., October 30, 1887. The USGS conversions appear in its final report.

9. Committee on immediate relief closed its books: *N&C*, December 1, 1886. Relief figures: *The Earthquake, 1886; Exhibits Showing Receipts and Disbursements and the Applications for Relief with the Awards and Refusals of the Executive Relief Committee* (Charleston: Lucas, Richardson and Co., 1887). ERC presented final report: *N&C*, December 1, 1886.

10. ERC Minutes, December 21, 1886, Records of the ERC.

11. *N&C*, December 15, 1886.

12. Official thank-you: ibid., December 29, 1886. City printed 20,000 copies: ibid., January 1, 1887.

13. *N&C*, December 11, 1886.

14. Opposition to bill: ibid., December 18, 1886. FWD: reassessment fair: ibid., December 13, 1886. "Could Carolinians speak": ibid., December 11, 1886. "We had a hard day": A. T. Smythe to his wife, letterhead of the Senate Chamber, December 2, 1886, A. T. Smyth [*sic*] Papers (24/8/9), SCHS. State senate passed earthquake bill: *N&C*, December 2, 1886.

15. Grady at New England Society: Raymond B. Nixon, *Henry W. Grady: Spokesman of the New South* (New York: Alfred A. Knopf, 1943), 237–51; Joel Chandler Harris, *Henry Grady: His Life, Writings, and Speeches* (New York: Cassell, 1890), 15–16.

16. Nixon, *Henry W. Grady*, 249.

17. *NYF*, January 8, 1887.

18. Harold E. Davis, *Henry Grady's New South: Atlanta, a Brave and Beautiful City* (Tuscaloosa: University of Alabama Press, 1990), 178; *N&C*, December 28 and 29, 1886. For a comparison of Atlanta and Charleston during this time, see Don H. Doyle, *New Men, New Cities, New South: Atlanta, Nashville, Charleston, Mobile, 1865–1910* (Chapel Hill: University of North Carolina Press, 1990). S. Frank Logan referred to "Dawson's earthquake" in the title to chapter 11 (p. 248) of his 1947 thesis, "Francis W. Dawson, 1840–1889: South Carolina Editor" (Master's thesis, Department of History, Duke University, 1947).

19. *AC*, January 14, 23, and 28, 1887; Davis, *Henry Grady's New South*, 44.

20. FWD to SMD, November 15, 1886, FWD Family Papers.

21. N&C, December 11, 1886. Reid, an outspoken Republican, had visited Charleston after the earthquake and described the ruins: Doyle, *New Men*, 56. FWD to SMD, December 24, 1886, FWD Family Papers; N&C, December 24, 1886.

22. FWD to SMD, November 20, 1886, FWD Family Papers.

23. FWD to SMD, December 26, 1886, and January 3, 1887, ibid.

24. N&C, December 29, 1886. The office of city assessor was relatively new, having been established by Mayor Courtenay in 1884. The assessor was required to conduct an assessment every year.

25. N&C, December 29, 1886.

26. WAC to FWD, December 29, 1886, FWD Family Papers. Courtenay's note is scrawled on a scrap of paper, a hint of the rage felt by the mayor, who prized formality.

27. N&C, December 29, 1886.

28. Ibid., December 30, 1886.

29. WAC to J. C. Hemphill, April 9, 1890, Hemphill Papers.

30. FWD to SMD, December 28, 1886, FWD Family Papers.

Chapter Fifteen. Wrapped in the Stars and Stripes

1. FWD to SMD, February 2 and 14, April 28, and May 5, 1887, FMD Family Papers; "Talks by the Way," N&C, June 5, 12, 19, and 26, 1887.

2. Family's return: FWD to SMD, August 8, 1887, FWD Family Papers; with them came Hélène Burdayron: Deposition of "Marie Budeyron [*sic*]," March 26, 1889, Dawson Murder Papers (152.05.04.12), Mitchell and Smith Law Firm Collection, SCHS. People gossiped about Hélène: E. Culpepper Clark, *Francis Warrington Dawson and the Politics of Restoration: South Carolina, 1874–1889* (University: University of Alabama Press, 1980), 215–16; SMD to H. A. M. Smith, "Friday night" [1889], Dawson Murder Papers (152.05.04.18). Sarah hired new servants: Depositions of Cecile Reils, Jane Jackson, and Isaac Heyward, March 15, 1889, Dawson Murder Papers (152.05.04.13). Years later FWD's son would remember Cecile Reils as "Celia Seabrook": FWD II to Frank Logan, Logan Papers.

3. FWD II to Frank Logan, Logan Papers.

4. Sarah's fall from carriage: Charles East, ed., *Civil War Diary of Sarah Morgan* (Athens: University of Georgia Press, 1991), 333–37. Telepathic powers, spoke with the dead: E. Culpepper Clark, *Francis Warrington Dawson*, 29. Diary sewn into linen wrappings: East, *Civil War Diary of Sarah Morgan*, xxxiii. SMD's manuscript diaries and scrapbook of essays are now in RBMSCL, Duke. Dawsons rarely hosted: FWD II to Frank Logan, Logan Papers.

5. Ethel unhappy: See her diary from this period: box 80, FWD Family Papers. Warrington dreamed of writing: FWD II to Frank Logan, Logan Papers. A photo

of Warrington, age seven (about 1887, probably before he returned to Charles-ton), in lace collar and with hair curling below his shoulders, can be found in Pictures: Dawson Family Relatives, etc. (box 90, 23-F), FWD Family Papers.

6. FWD II to Frank Logan, Logan Papers. Logan wrote a 1947 master's thesis, "Francis W. Dawson, 1840–1889: South Carolina Editor" (Department of His-tory, Duke University), and interviewed FWD II extensively. He sent letters with questions, and Warrington, who lived in Paris, typed long, expansive, revealing responses.

7. FWD II to Frank Logan, Logan Papers.

8. *NYT*, April 2, 1887.

9. "No white religious meetings": *SMN*, September 2, 1887. Summerville couple predicted another earthquake: *N&C*, March 17, 1887. Passion play: *N&C*, August 31, 1887.

10. Number of buildings restored, new homes and businesses built, plastering done: "A Year Ago Today," *N&C*, August 31, 1887. Debris used as fill: ibid., Janu-ary 1, 1887. New hospital: ibid., July 26, 1887.

11. The full events of Calhoun Day were described in exhaustive detail in the *N&C*, April 27, 1887. "Baby unveilers": ibid., April 26, 1887. The newspaper ran articles about the ceremony almost daily for about two months leading up to the event. For more than a week afterward, enthusiastic reviews of the activities were reprinted from newspapers around the country. The story of the monu-ment's history is best told in Thomas J. Brown's "The Monumental Legacy of Calhoun," in *The Memory of the Civil War in American Culture*, eds. Alice Fahs and Joan Waugh (Chapel Hill: University of North Carolina Press, 2004), 130–56. "Calhoun and 'e wife": *N&C*, June 2, 1887. For African Americans' reaction to the monument, including the story of throwing rocks and brickbats, see Mamie Garvin Fields and Karen Fields, *Lemon Swamp and Other Places: A Carolina Memoir* (New York: Free Press, 1983), 57.

12. Electric lights installed: *N&C*, March 3 and April 6, 1887. In June the Charleston Electric Lightworks was taken over by the Charleston Light and Power Company: ibid., June 16, 1887. Marion Square: ibid., February 3, 1887; Washington Square: ibid., February 17 and April 6, 1887. Medical college rebuilt: the *N&C* reported on April 8, 1887, that the contract for the rebuilding was given out, though the work had already begun. Guard House: ibid., August 10, 1887; Jonathan Poston, *The Buildings of Charleston: A Guide to the City's Architecture* (Columbia: University of South Carolina Press, 1997), 168. Robb's Lot: *N&C*, March 14, 1887. Historic churches: the *N&C*, February 2, 1887, summarizes the damage to many Charleston churches. For information on the restoration of each church, see *N&C* articles: Bethel Methodist (October 29 and 31, 1887), Centenary Methodist (November 26, 1887), First Baptist (September 10, 1887),

Grace Episcopal (July 18, 1887), Kahal Kadosh Beth Elohim synagogue (February 15, 1887), St. Luke's Lutheran (October 8, 1887), St. Michael's (June 19, 1887), St. Philip's (February 28, June 26, and October 6, 1887), Second Presbyterian (October 10, 1887), Spring Street Methodist (March 3, 1888), Unitarian (April 23 and 25, 1887), Wesley Methodist Episcopal (September 12, 1887), Westminster Presbyterian (February 3, 1888). Plaques recognizing the restoration effort can still be seen at First (Scots) Presbyterian Church and St. Michael's. A plaque above the Broad Street entrance to the Confederate Home reads, "Ruined by the Earthquake 1886, Restored by the People of the Union 1887." City Hospital (old Workhouse) torn down: N&C, February 19 and March 12, 1887.

13. N&C, February 1, 1888, March 20, 1887, and February 18, 1888.

14. Earthquake fox: ibid., November 10, 1886; extra eggs: ibid., March 14, 1887; huckleberry bushes, rattlesnakes: ibid., June 16, 1887; milk cows ran dry: ibid., October 5, 1886.

15. Ibid., July 28–30, 1887.

16. President and Mrs. Cleveland invited: ibid., August 10, 11, September 12, 1887. Eckels objected: ibid., August 10, 1887. Atlanta's Piedmont Exposition invitation, Cleveland accepted: ibid., August 13, 1887; Paul Jeffers, An Honest President: The Life and Presidencies of Grover Cleveland (New York: W. Morrow, 2000), 198. Georgia's diamond industry was never significant, but it did exist. Cleveland declined: N&C, September 14, 1887. On October 26, 1887, the N&C would criticize Atlanta for "mismanaging" the president's visit.

17. N&C, August 18, 1887.

18. Railroads asked to offer special rates: ibid., September 22, 1887. Electrical circuit around Colonial Lake: ibid., October 31, 1887. Arc lights: ibid., November 1, 1887. Incoming trains doubled number of coaches: ibid., November 7, 1887. Trains and streetcar lines coordinated, purchase of a return ticket included harbor tour: ibid., November 1, 1887. Special guidebook: ibid., November 1, 1887. Academy of Music: ibid., November 4, 1887. Food displays: ibid., November 2, 1887.

19. Ibid., November 1, 1887.

20. An article in the N&C promoted Gala Week by explaining that since the end of the Civil War, "The colored citizen gets a good deal of enjoyment out of Independence Day, but the white citizen gets very little else than a 'lay-off.'" N&C, July 30, 1887. For more on Fourth of July celebrations in Charleston, see Walter Byron Hill, "Family, Life, and Work Culture: Black Charleston, South Carolina, 1880 to 1910" (PhD diss., University of Maryland College Park, 1989), 272–73.

21. Number of U.S. flags sold, "Everything on two wheels," "Quite the thing": N&C, November 1, 1887. Shoe stores, pies, and cakes: ibid., November 2, 1887.

"Charleston means to emphasize the fact," Charleston Tea Pot, flags of other nations: ibid., November 1, 1887.

22. Stars and Bars "full of bullet holes," "The display of this one relic": ibid., November 1, 1887. For more on the display of Confederate flags during this period, see David W. Blight, *Race and Reunion: The Civil War and American Memory* (Cambridge: Harvard University Press, 2001), 269, 276, 281, and 382. Jefferson Davis not invited: *NYT*, October 31, 1887.

23. *N&C*, November 1, 1887.

24. Ibid.

25. Two articles in the *N&C*, November 1, 1887, described the *N&C* decorations, as did another the next day, identifying Swinton Baynard as the designer and including "there was not." During Gala Week, the paper expanded from eight pages to twelve.

26. *N&C*, November 1 and 4, 1887.

27. Ibid., November 2, 1887.

28. "The People Went Wild," rowing match: ibid. Baseball game: ibid., November 5, 1887. The *N&C* in that article claimed, "If there is one thing that Charleston likes above all other things (barring an appropriation for the Jetties) it is a good game of ball." City people jammed the baseball stadium to standing-room-only capacity. "The cracks in the centre field fence were also occupied, while the reserved seats on the neighboring house tops, tree tops, fence tops and telegraph poles were all occupied." Chicago and St. Louis split the first two games. The third game was delayed a day when Charleston police pointed out that baseball games were not allowed on Sundays. Ibid., November 5–7, 1887. The Academy of Music operas were announced each day of Gala Week in the *N&C*, October 31, November 1–4, 1887.

29. *N&C*, November 4 and October 31, 1887.

30. Ibid., November 2 and 3, 1887.

31. Fantastic Parade: ibid., November 4, 1887. "Doubtless some of the old fashioned saints": *NYT*, October 31, 1887. Students at many medical schools and hospitals posed for photos with skeletons, but parading with them in public was rare: See John Harley Warner and James M. Edmonson, *Dissection: Photographs of a Rite of Passage in American Medicine, 1880–1930* (New York: Blast Books, 2009).

32. "War, pestilence": *N&C*, November 8, 1887. No doubt Dawson, who was quite straitlaced, would have agreed with the *N&C* reader who urged the organizers of the next year's event to avoid the rudeness shown in the 1887 Fantastic Parade: "I was quite disgusted at the depraved taste of some of our citizens who caricaturized themselves with female accoutrements. . . . Such behavior tends towards lowering morals and will lead to degradation. As for parading skeletons,

I consider it an outrage to the memory of our absent ones." *N&C*, November 19, 1888. However, the *N&C* offered no criticism, claiming, "The entire celebration was unmarred by a single untoward incident." That same day pledges for the next year's events were gathered. *N&C*, November 6, 1887.

Chapter Sixteen. Fault Lines

1. Carlyle McKinley, *An Appeal to Pharaoh: The Negro Problem, and its Radical Solution* (New York: Fords, Howard, and Hulbert, 1889), 13, 25, 13. McKinley's book went through three editions, the last in 1907.

2. McKinley, *An Appeal to Pharaoh*, 120.

3. Bruce E. Baker, "The 'Hoover Scare' in South Carolina, 1887: An Attempt to Organize Black Farm Labor," *Labor History* 40, no. 3 (1999): 282, 272.

4. *N&C*, June 28–30, August 4, 1887.

5. On Ida B. Wells, see Linda O. McMurry, *To Keep the Waters Troubled: The Life of Ida B. Wells* (New York: Oxford University Press, 1998). Wells published an account of her case in the *New York Freeman* in January 1885. For a record of other attempts by blacks to assert their legal right to enter segregated spaces in all parts of the United States after the passage of the Reconstruction Amendments and the Civil Rights Act of 1875, see Mark Stuart Weiner, *Black Trials: Citizenship from the Beginnings of Slavery to the End of Caste* (New York: Alfred A. Knopf, 2004), 216–28.

6. *NYT*, July 3, 1887; *AC* qtd. in *NYT*, July 3, 1887; *N&C*, August 1, 1887.

7. *N&C*, July 24, 1887.

8. Ibid., June 30, 1887. On Booker T. Washington, see Robert J. Norrell, *Up from History: The Life of Booker T. Washington* (Cambridge, Mass.: Belknap Press, 2009).

9. Heard won his case, "to furnish to passengers": *N&C*, February 17, 1888; "cease and desist": *N&C*, February 28, 1888. William S. Councill won his case against the Western and Atlantic Railroad Co. but was awarded no damages. *N&C*, December 4, 1887. For more on Councill, see Norrell, *Up from History*.

10. Episcopal diocese battle: Lyon G. Tyler, "Drawing the Color Line in the Episcopal Diocese of South Carolina, 1876 to 1890: The Role of Edward McCrady, Father and Son," *SCHM* 91 (April 1990): 121; *N&C*, May 15 and July 12, 1888. "The sooner we are rid": Schirmer Diary (11/568/2), 143, SCHS.

11. Legislature debated bills: *N&C*, December 17, 18, and 20, 1886. Farm workers leaving the state: see, for example, ibid., January 23–25 and 31, 1887.

12. Christopher Waldrep, *The Many Faces of Judge Lynch: Extralegal Violence and Punishment in America* (New York: Palgrave, 2002), 113.

13. Pickens County lynching: *N&C*, January 3, 5, 17, and 19, 1888. For more on

the case, see Bruce E. Baker, "Lynch Law Reversed: The Rape of Lula Sherman, the Lynching of Manse Waldrop, and the Debate over Lynching in the 1880s," *American Nineteenth Century History* 6, no. 3 (September 2005): 273–93.

14. *N&C*, January 19, 1888.

15. Ibid., August 29, 1887, and January 25, 1888.

16. Ibid., November 30 and December 1, 1887.

17. As late as September 1887 WAC supporters were still urging him to run: *N&C*, September 13, 1887. Some proposed supplementing his mayoral salary, hoping that would help change his mind: ibid., August 15, 1887.

18. Election of 1886: "A Democratic Walk-Over": *N&C*, November 3, 1886. Smalls claimed he received 7,000 legal votes, 1,000 more than Elliott: ibid., May 22, 1887. Smalls's supporters protested, and some members of the U.S. House took up the issue, but it wasn't resolved until the end of Congressman Elliott's two-year term. Though many voting discrepancies were found on both sides, Elliott's election — the margin reduced to 323 votes — was confirmed: *N&C*, January 11, 1889.

19. *N&C*, November 9, 1887.

20. Ibid., November 9 and 12 and December 12, 1887.

21. Ibid., November 12, 11, 13, and 15, 1887.

22. Ibid., November 28, 1888, December 2 and 5, 1887.

23. Ibid., December 2, 5, and 13, 1887.

24. Election results: ibid., December 14, 15, and 19, 1887. John M. Freeman, chairman of the city's Republican Party, later claimed that Rowe and Crum had actually won: *N&C*, December 15, 1887. United Labor Party threatened to "blow up the managers": *N&C*, November 15, 1887.

25. *CW*: E. Culpepper Clark, *Francis Warrington Dawson and the Politics of Restoration: South Carolina, 1874–1889* (University: University of Alabama Press, 1980), 211; John Hammond Moore, ed. and comp., *South Carolina Newspapers* (Columbia: University of South Carolina Press, 1988), 67. Rodgers retired from city council: *N&C*, December 19, 1887.

26. FWD II to Logan, Logan Papers; *CW*, February 8, 1888.

27. *CW*, February 18, 1888.

28. The *N&C*'s circulation drive can be seen, for instance, in the *N&C*, January 1, 1888.

29. *CW*, February 18, March 1–8, 10, 1888.

30. On April 22, 1888, the *N&C* printed a long humorous account of the case with African American dialect and Walt McDougall–like illustrations. Case went to court June 20: *N&C*, June 21, 1888. McDow implicated in insurance fraud: FWD II, "Memorandum on the Murder of Captain F. W. Dawson, March

12, 1889, and the Trial of Dr. T. B. McDow, June 24–30, 1889," Dawson Family Writings, FWD Family Papers.

31. On Henry Flagler, see David Leon Chandler, *Henry Flagler: The Astonishing Life and Times of the Visionary Robber Baron Who Founded Florida* (New York: Macmillan, 1986) and Sidney Walter Martin, *Florida's Flagler* (1949; Athens: University of Georgia Press, 1982).

32. For a summary of the campaign for a tourist hotel, see E. Merton Coulter, *George Walton Williams: The Life of a Southern Merchant and Banker, 1820–1903* (Athens, Ga.: Hibriten Press, 1976), 206–18. Dawson called on Charleston businessmen to build a new hotel: *N&C*, May 26, 1888; description of May 31 meeting: *N&C*, June 1, 1888.

33. Name "The Eden" proposed: *N&C*, June 1, 1888. Charleston as Eden: see, for example, the editorial in ibid., November 2, 1887. Company applied for a charter: ibid., June 21, 1888. Pledgers failed to sign papers: ibid., July 10, 1888. Canvassing committee went door to door: ibid., June 9 and 13, 1888. Architect hired: ibid., July 21, 1888.

34. Articles about yellow fever appeared regularly in the *N&C* beginning August 10, 1888.

35. Charleston collected money for the Jacksonville sufferers: *N&C*, September 7, December 7, 1888; *CW*, September 11, 1888. Seven trained nurses sent: *N&C*, December 8, 1888. Benefit concert: *N&C*, October 4, 1888. Black churches took up collections and "We know from experience": *NYA*, October 6, 1888. The *New York Freeman* changed its name to the *New York Age* in October 1887.

36. Railroads quarantined all passengers leaving the fever district: *CW*, August 13 and 16, 1888. Visitors from fever district would be arrested: ibid., August 16, 1888. Several articles in the *CW*, though not the *N&C*, told of people being sent to a quarantine station: *CW*, August 13 and 28, September 1, 1888. "Scouring the city day and night": *CW*, September 5, 1888; man tried to visit sick father: *CW*, September 1, 1888.

For more on the 1888 yellow fever epidemic and the strong-arm tactics used by cities and states to control the disease, see Margaret Humphries, *Yellow Fever and the South* (New Brunswick, N.J.: Rutgers University Press, 1992). Humphries points out that yellow fever was viewed above all as a "commercial problem," since outbreaks could shut down commerce for months at a time and discourage investment in southern enterprises. Officials often resorted to cover-ups or outright lies in an attempt to prevent panics and quarantines that would interfere with business.

37. Congress voted $100,000 to relieve suffering: *CW*, September 20, 1888. FWD took defeat personally: see Don H. Doyle, *New Men, New Cities, New South: At-*

lanta, Nashville, Charleston, Mobile, 1865–1910 (Chapel Hill: University of North Carolina Press, 1990), 171. FWD and the *N&C* tried to revive the hotel project; see, for instance, *N&C*, January 14 and 18, May 19, 22, and 23, 1889. Planning for a grand tourist hotel continued in 1892–93, and again in 1894, but for years no hotel was built. Coulter, *George Walton Williams*, 216. "The cyclone and earthquake taught the people": *N&C*, September 3, 1888. Jacksonville epidemic ended in early December: J. A. Mulrennan Jr., "Mosquito Control: Its Impact on the Growth and Development of Florida," *Journal of the Florida Medical Association* 73 (1986): 310, 311.

38. *N&C*, June 11, 1888.

39. On Benjamin Harrison, see Charles C. Calhoun, *Benjamin Harrison* (New York: Henry Holt, 2005). Quotations on 29.

40. Thomas Adams Upchurch, *Legislating Racism: The Billion Dollar Congress and the Birth of Jim Crow* (Lexington: University of Kentucky Press, 2004), 19 and 17; *N&C*, October 1, 1888.

41. *N&C*, November 16, 1887.

Chapter Seventeen. Standing over a Volcano

1. *N&C*, May 18, 1888. On the Clemson endowment, see E. Culpepper Clark, *Francis Warrington Dawson and the Politics of Restoration: South Carolina, 1874–1889* (University: University of Alabama Press, 1980), 176–77.

2. Historian Walter Edgar describes the Dawson-Tillman relationship: "Had it not been for the *News and Courier* in 1885, it is probable that Ben Tillman would have remained nothing but an unhappy upcountry farmer. The Charleston newspaper, with its statewide circulation, gave him a forum and credibility." Walter Edgar, *South Carolina: A History* (Columbia: University of South Carolina Press, 1998), 434. July 20 rally, "spew his slime," "ring rule": *N&C*, July 21, 1888.

3. *N&C*, August 4 and 5, 1888.

4. Ibid., August 13 and 14, 1888.

5. Filler lines: *CW*, August 8 and 9, 1888, with similar squibs on many other dates; "The Lord High Executioner": ibid., August 18, 1888; "tell us how to get rid of the incubus": ibid., August 24, 1888.

6. *N&C*, August 29 and 30, 1888.

7. Tillman's reference to Dawson as a Colossus was a favorite misquoting of Shakespeare's *Julius Caesar*; years later he would use almost the same phrase to complain about President Theodore Roosevelt. Qtd. in Edmund Morris, *Theodore Rex* (New York: Random House, 2001), 430.

8. Pro-FWD rally: *N&C*, August 30, 1888.

9. *CW*, August 30, 1888.

10. Ibid.

11. *N&C*, August 31, 1888.

12. SMD: "on that fateful night": "Biographical Sketch Written by Mrs. Francis W. Dawson (Sarah Morgan Dawson) in 1894 at the Request of J. T. White for the *National Cyclopedia of American Biography*," 14, FWD Family Papers. FWD instructed staff to avoid mentioning BRT's name, "editorial snuffers": FWD to James C. Hemphill, September 11, 1888, Hemphill Papers.

13. *CW*, September 1 and 11, 1888.

14. Swinton Baynard moved to the *World*: *N&C*, September 24, 1888. Hemphill looking for employment, Snowden moved to *World*: E. Culpepper Clark, *Francis Warrington Dawson*, 212. *N&C* lost 600 subscribers: SMD "Note," May 24, 1898, FWD Family Papers.

15. FWD appealed to Siegling re finances: FWD II to Frank Logan, Logan Papers. "In the extremity of horror and distress": ibid. Sarah claimed Siegling put in far less money than Frank: "Siegling: A Crime which is now Being Expiated: Statement of the Question Between General Siegling and Myself, February 4, 1890," FWD Family Papers. In addition, FWD II claimed that his father had paid for *N&C* employees' salary increases out of his own pocket. FWD II to Frank Logan, Logan Papers.

16. *CW*, September 28, 1888.

17. "Have the Democratic citizens": *CW*, October 5, 1888; Reformers appointed committee to watch: *N&C*, October 6, 1886; ward 1 voters, similar ticket: *CW*, October 4, 1888. Reformers' letter to the poll managers: *N&C*, October 6, 1888.

18. *N&C*, October 7, 1888; FWD II to Frank Logan, Logan Papers.

19. Heard moved to Philadelphia in August 1888: *N&C*, July 30, 1888. "Ignorant, dishonest and spiteful Republicans": ibid., October 19, 1888.

20. *N&C*, October 29, 1888.

21. Ibid., October 15, 1888.

22. Ibid., November 6, 1888.

23. Democrats' mass meeting of the upper wards: ibid., November 1 and 3, 1888; *CW*, November 1 and 2, 1888.

24. The business-license uprising was covered regularly in the *N&C* and the *CW* after November 2. Warrants served and men settled: *CW*, November 13, 1888; jailed in separate building: *CW*, November 3, 1888; gift baskets: *N&C*, November 5, 1886; McGrath retained: *CW*, November 3, 1888; protesters released: *N&C*, November 15, 1888. The business-license issue was also raised before the earthquake: see, for instance, the merchants' petition in *N&C*, August 13, 1886. City council passed an ordinance requiring the licenses in December 1886: *N&C*, December 18, 1886.

25. FWD II to Frank Logan, Logan Papers.

26. "Lightning fast" telegraphic updates and stereopticons: *N&C*, November 3, 6, and 8, 1888. *World's* stereopticon show: *CW*, November 5, 6, and 8, 1888.

27. *N&C*, November 7, 1888; *CW*, November 7, 1888.

28. *CW*, November 9, 1888.

29. *N&C*, November 8, 1888.

30. Ibid.

31. Ibid.

32. Ibid., November 7, 1888.

33. Discussion of fair elections: *CW*, November 9, 1888. FWD "preparing to go": *CW*, November 24, 1888; "It Is About Time for You, Captain Dawson": *CW*, November 1, 1888. Job offer in Midwest, "if the community went against him": FWD II to Frank Logan, Logan Papers.

34. "Certainly earthquakes and Republican national victories": *N&C*, November 16, 1888; FWD stomach pain: Clark, *Francis Warrington Dawson*, 214. *World's* stereopticon show: *CW*, November 20, 21, 23, and 24, 1888. "Free, Gratis, and for Nothing" and Gala Week a "failure": *CW*, November 23, 1888.

35. Anniversary of end of slavery: *N&C*, January 1, 1889. The various Emancipation Day celebrations contained many of the same elements as Gala Week. The Columbia, S.C., parade featured a "colored trades display" while the one in Orangeburg included a "fantastic parade and fireworks": *N&C*, January 2, 1889.

Chapter Eighteen. Killing Captain Dawson

The murder of Francis W. Dawson was almost the only story covered in both the *News and Courier* and the *Charleston World* in the first several days after it took place, March 13–16, 1889, and then again during the subsequent trial, June 25–July 5, 1889. The information in this chapter is based primarily on those accounts. Other valuable newspaper stories appeared in the *New York Times*, *New York Age*, and the *Columbia (S.C.) Daily Register*.

Of the many secondary accounts of the murder, the best include E. Culpepper Clark, *Francis Warrington Dawson and the Politics of Restoration: South Carolina, 1874–1889* (University: University of Alabama Press, 1980), 215–19; John Hammond Moore, *Carnival of Blood: Dueling, Lynching, and Murder in South Carolina, 1880–1920* (Columbia: University of South Carolina Press, 2006), 84–100; and Thomas K. Peck, "The Killing of Captain Dawson, 1889" in *Charleston Murders*, 71–107, ed. Beatrice St. J. Ravenel (New York: Duell, Sloan, and Pearce, 1947). A Charleston novelist described Dawson's death in fiction, including the gossip that circulated around town: Robert J. Molloy, *An Afternoon in March* (Garden City, N.Y.: Doubleday, 1958).

Sarah Morgan Dawson wrote an account of the murder "For Ethel and Warrington," which can be found as "The Narrative of Sarah Morgan Dawson: Book No. 1," box 73, FWD Family Papers.

As an adult, FWD II added to his mother's reminiscences, revealing secrets he had kept for sixty years. His handwritten manuscripts can be found in box 73, FWD Family Papers. His original account was titled "Memorandum in re Sarah Morgan Dawson's Narrative Record of her Husband's Last Days as Recorded by Her in Two Ms. Notebooks, deposited with other Francis W. Dawson papers at Duke University." It was dated July 27, 1946; he updated it on February 9, 1949. He published a version as "Son of Editor Sheds New Light on Murder in 1889," in the *News and Courier Sunday Magazine*, August 24, 1958, 1-C, soon after the Peck chapter in *Charleston Murders* was published.

Depositions taken by Julian Mitchell and H. A. M. Smith for the trial can be found in the Dawson Murder Papers, Mitchell and Smith Law Firm Collection, SCHS. In folder 152.05.04.12 are depositions by George W. Harper, Emma Drayton, Moses Johnson, and Marie Budeyron [*sic*; Burdayron's was taken by Gabriel Manigault, who spoke French]. In folder 152.05.04.13 are depositions by Julia Smith and Dawson family employees Isic [*sic*] Heyward, Jane Jackson, Grace Managault, and Cecile Riels. Folder 152.05.04.13 also contains the police report dated March 16, 1889, of the investigation of the Nunan Street house where McDow tried to take Hélène.

1. McDow's affair with Julia Smith: *CDR*, March 14 and 15, 1889. The second article also claims that Katie McDow had earlier moved out of the McDow house on Rutledge Avenue because of Smith. The account of McDow's plan to kill his wife and father-in-law: Memorandum, Detective M. J. McManus to Chief of Police Joseph Golden (152.05.04.13), Mitchell and Smith Law Firm Collection.

2. *CDR*, March 16, 1889.

3. FWD applied for a loan, "sharpness of competition": FWD memo, February 9, 1889, FWD Family Papers. FWD "could not afford to die": *CDR*, March 16, 1889.

4. Marie Lewis lived next door: FWD II to Frank Logan, Logan Papers. In his "Memorandum in re Sarah Morgan Dawson's Narrative," Warrington mentions the telephore and seeing McDow while they were playing.

5. On the trial of the Pickens lynchers, see *N&C*, March 10 and 11, 1889. Dawson's editorial on the lynchers, "A Distinction with a Difference," appeared on March 11, 1889. "Had Lula Sherman been white," "the genuine sense": Bruce E. Baker, "Lynch Law Reversed: The Rape of Lula Sherman, the Lynching of Manse Waldrop, and the Debate over Lynching in the 1880s," *American Nineteenth Century History* 6, no. 3 (September 2005): 273–93.

6. The proof copy of McDow's letter on cremation, with FWD's note "Kill this,"

can be found in SMD Scrapbook. The *CW* had run an editorial about the desirability of cremation on February 24, 1888.

7. Private Gordon was described as being of mixed race in *NYT*, June 30, 1889. In Charleston he would have been considered black.

8. Sarah had expected Frank to be killed in part because it had almost happened in the past. FWD II reported years later two accounts of his father fighting off attackers: FWD II to Frank Logan, Logan Papers.

9. William Watts Ball, *The State That Forgot: South Carolina's Surrender to Democracy* (Indianapolis: Bobbs-Merrill, 1932), 173–74.

10. The report of the autopsy, signed by Middleton Michel, M.D., "Examination of the Body of Capt. F. W. Dawson, March 14, 1889": Dawson Murder Papers (152.05.04.14), Mitchell and Smith Law Firm Collection.

Chapter Nineteen. The Trial

1. *N&C*, March 13, 1889.

2. Cleveland telegram: March 18, 1889, FWD Family Papers. FWD "fearless spirit": *Boston Evening Record*, March 13, 1889, SMD Scrapbook.

3. "Bad, bad, bad": *Charleston Daily Sun*, March 13, 1889, in FWD I Scrapbook (f:5323), FWD Family Papers. The reports of the "chips of flesh," the smaller set of footprints, and the hat in the privy all appeared in *CDR*, March 15, 1889.

4. On Andrew G. McGrath, see Dumas Malone, ed., *Dictionary of American Biography* (New York: Scribners, 1933), 6:203–4. On Asher Cohen, see his obituary, *N&C*, October 11, 1904.

5. *N&C*, March 15, 1889.

6. Events from the day of the funeral and the service appeared in the *N&C* on March 14, 1889. There are no known extant copies of the *CW* for March 13–16, 1889. Ribbon in FWD's buttonhole: FWD II to Frank Logan, Logan Papers. Naturalization papers in FWD's pocket: FWD II to Frank Logan, Logan Papers.

7. *NYT*, March 13, 1889; *NYA*, March 23, 1889.

8. *N&C*, March 15, 1889; *NYT*, March 15, 1889.

9. *CW*, April 2, 1889.

10. FWD II to Frank Logan, Logan Papers.

11. *CW*, March 25 and April 1, 1889.

12. McDow's history: *N&C*, March 15, 1889; *CDR*, March 13 ("bawdy house"), 14 (blackballed), 1889. Mrs. Fair: SMD to Herbert Barry, January 12, 1898, FWD Family Papers.

13. On William St. Julien Jervey, see "Former Solicitor Has Passed Away," *N&C*, December 18, 1913. On H. A. M. Smith, see Malone, *Dictionary of American Biography*, 6:276–77; Alexander Moore in *The Historical Writings of Henry A. M.*

Smith: Articles from the South Carolina Historical (and Genealogical) Magazine (Spartanburg, S.C.: Reprint Co., 1988), 1:xi–xiii.

14. SMD badgered Smith with advice: Sarah's letters to Smith are included in the Mitchell and Smith Law Firm Collection (152.05.04.18), SCHS. (All quotations are in letters dated only "Friday.")

15. Lavinia Drum to Miriam DuPré, March 15, 1889, FWD Family Papers.

16. SMD to H. A. M. Smith, Mitchell and Smith Law Firm Collection.

17. SMD to H. A. M. Smith, "Thursday," ibid.

18. Almost verbatim transcripts of each day's trial proceedings appeared the next day in the *N&C* and the *CW* (day 1 covered June 25, 1889; day 2 covered June 26, 1889; etc.). Quotations are taken from those accounts, which are nearly identical.

19. On Judge Joseph Brevard Kershaw, see Malone, *Dictionary of American Biography*, 5:359–60.

20. Jury foreman Arthur Middleton was identified as an insurance agent in *NYT*, June 30, 1889.

21. A photo of Dawson with ink marks showing where his face was scratched in McDow's attempt to bury the body can be found in the Dawson Murder Papers, Mitchell and Smith Law Firm Collection (152.05.04.16).

22. E. Culpepper Clark, *Francis Warrington Dawson and the Politics of Restoration: South Carolina, 1874–1889* (University: University of Alabama Press, 1980), 227.

23. "That settles it!": *N&C*, July 2, 1889; *CDR*, June 29, 1889. This last article claims that blacks in Charleston regarded the verdict as a "victory over the white race."

Epilogue. Rebuilding the Walls

1. Black jurors "intend to do what is right": *SMN*, rpt. in *N&C*, July 1, 1889; blacks "are not safely to be trusted": *NYW*, July 1, 1889, rpt. in *N&C*, July 3, 1889.

2. *CW*, July 7, 1889.

3. "I have plenty of friends": *NYW*, July 15, 1889, copy in SMD Scrapbook. Charleston Club incident: *CDR*, July 1, 1889; SMD wrote next to a copy of this article, "George Trenholm," SMD scrapbook. WAC to Asher Cohen, July 1, 1889, Asher D. Cohen Papers (Mss. 1034–54), Special Collections, Marlene and Nathan Addlestone Library, College of Charleston. Courtenay mentions that he read the account in the *Charleston World*. "It was a great thing": Mary Esther Middleton Lowndes to her sister Harriott Middleton, May 15, 1894, Harriott Middleton Family Papers (373/01 [1894]/03), SCHS. "What a sad commentary": Robert Chisolm to H. A. M. Smith, June 28, 1889, Mitchell and Smith Law Firm Collection (152.05.04), SCHS.

4. SMD's marginalia, SMD Scrapbook.

5. Grace King on SMD: Grace King, *Memories of a Southern Woman of Letters* (New York: Macmillan, 1932), 206–7. A huge crowd gathered to gawk: Emma Middleton to Harriott Middleton, n.d., Cheves-Middleton Papers, SCHS.

6. Among the stocks owned by FWD was 40 percent of the *N&C*: letter from FWD marked "Confidential," February 9, 1889, FWD Family Papers. Cover letter from the insurance company, SMD Scrapbook. "Shame! Shame!": SMD to J. C. Hemphill, March 1, 1890, Hemphill Papers.

7. Jimmy Morgan on Charleston's "fiendish hatred" for FWD: James Morgan to SMD, June 30, 1889, FWD Family Papers.

8. Incident between Hélène, Warrington, and SMD, including Hélène's firing: FWD II, "Memorandum in re Sarah Morgan Dawson's Narrative Record of her Husband's Last Days as Recorded by Her in Two Ms. Notebooks, deposited with other Francis W. Dawson papers at Duke University," July 27, 1946, updated February 9, 1949, box 73, FWD Family Papers; and FWD II, "Son of Editor Sheds New Light on Murder in 1889," *News and Courier Sunday Magazine*, August 24, 1958, 1-C.

9. SMD felt life was "a daily crucifixion": SMD to H. A. M. Smith, Mitchell and Smith Law Firm Collection (152.05.04.18).

10. King, *Memories of a Southern Woman*, 208.

11. SMD's original Civil War diaries are held in the FWD Family Papers.

12. *State*, rpt. in *N&C*, October 29, 1891.

13. FWD II to Frank Logan, Logan Papers.

14. Gladys McDow "stopped growing": FWD II to Frank Logan, Logan Papers. Gladys McDow Hibbett, *Winds of Memory* (Philadelphia: Poetry Publishers, 1934) includes poems about Charleston and Tennessee ("state of my adoption"), and others dedicated to her mother and to her father. It was illustrated by Charleston artist Antoinette Rhett. At least one of the poems first appeared in the *N&C*.

15. New York attorney (T. McCants Stewart) in 1885: Don H. Doyle, *New Men, New Cities, New South: Atlanta, Nashville, Charleston, Mobile, 1865–1910* (Chapel Hill: University of North Carolina Press, 1990), 302–3.

16. Henry M. Stanley on *An Appeal to Pharaoh*: His letter was reprinted in later editions of the book; a photocopy of the handwritten letter can be found in the file Biography: McKinley, South Carolina Room, CCPL.

17. Harrison qtd. in Charles C. Calhoun, *Benjamin Harrison* (New York: Henry Holt, 2005), 89.

18. *NYA*, May 25, 1889.

19. On *Plessy v. Ferguson*, see Mark Stuart Weiner, *Black Trials: Citizenship from the Beginnings of Slavery to the End of Caste* (New York: Alfred A. Knopf,

2004), 214–15. Plessy's defense was supervised by Albion Tourgee, a northern carpetbagger who was the target of Carlyle McKinley's argument in *An Appeal to Pharaoh*: Weiner, *Black Trials*, 236.

20. On South Carolina's 1895 constitution: Walter Edgar, *South Carolina Encyclopedia* (Columbia: University of South Carolina, 2006), 217. Smalls: "for no other purpose": in Paul Escott and David R. Goldfield, eds., *Major Problems in the History of the American South: Documents and Essays*, vol. 2, *The New South* (Lexington, Mass.: Heath, 1990), 182. Tillman: "We stuffed ballot boxes" in Frances Butler Simkins, *Pitchfork Ben Tillman, South Carolinian* (1944; rpt. with a new intro. by Orville Vernon Burton, Columbia: University of South Carolina Press, 2002), xxiv. W. E. B. Du Bois, *Black Reconstruction in America* (1935; New York: Atheneum, 1992), 30.

21. There are no known extant copies of Rev. George Rowe's *Charleston Enquirer*. On Rev. John Dart, see "John Lewis Dart 1854–1915," Biography: "Dart Family," South Carolina Room, CCPL. Dart exchange with Tillman: Stephen Kantrowitz, *Ben Tillman and the Reconstruction of White Supremacy* (Chapel Hill: University of North Carolina Press, 2000), 258.

22. On Rev. William Henry Heard, see his autobiography, *From Slavery to the Bishopric in the A.M.E. Church: An Autobiography* (Philadelphia: AME Book Concern, 1924; rpt., New York: Arno Press, 1969), 73–95; and "Bishop W. H. Heard, Clergyman 67 Years," *NYT*, September 14, 1937.

23. Willard B. Gatewood, "William D. Crum, A Negro in Politics," *Journal of Negro History* 3 (October 1968): 301–20; Walter Byron Hill, "Family, Life, and Work Culture: Black Charleston, South Carolina, 1880 to 1910" (PhD diss., Department of Philosophy, University of Maryland College Park, 1989), 375–80.

24. Tillman qtd. in Edmund Morris, *Theodore Rex* (New York: Random House, 2001), 210; *N&C* qtd. in Gatewood, "William D. Crum," 312.

25. Gatewood, "William D. Crum," 320.

26. Doyle, *New Men*, 309–10; William D. Smyth, "Blacks and the South Carolina Interstate and West Indian Exposition," *SCHM* 88 (October 1887): 211–19.

27. Alice R. Huger Smith and D. E. Huger Smith, *The Dwelling Houses of Charleston, South Carolina* (Philadelphia: J. B. Lippincott, 1917). On the Charleston Renaissance, see Harlan Greene and James Hutchisson, eds., *Renaissance in Charleston: Art and Life in the Carolina Low Country, 1900–1940* (Athens: University of Georgia Press, 2003).

28. Josephine Pinckney, *Great Mischief* (New York: Viking Press, 1948).

SELECTED BIBLIOGRAPHY

Though hundreds of documents and letters about the earthquake can be found in many archives, collections in the following institutions were of particular importance: Charleston County Public Library; Charleston Library Society; Avery Research Center for African American History and Culture, College of Charleston; the Special Collections, Marlene and Nathan Addlestone Library, College of Charleston; Rare Book, Manuscript, and Special Collections Library, Duke University, Durham, N.C.; South Carolina Department of Archives and History, Columbia; South Carolina Historical Society, Charleston; and South Caroliniana Library, University of South Carolina, Columbia.

Charleston Earthquake of 1886

Charleston As It Is After the Earthquake Shock of August 31, 1886. Charleston: n.p., 1886.

Dutton, Clarence Edward. *The Charleston Earthquake of August 31, 1886.* U.S. Geological Survey Ninth Annual Report, 1887–88. Reprint, Arlington, Va.: U.S. Geological Survey, 1979.

The Earthquake, 1886; Exhibits showing Receipts and Disbursements and the Applications for Relief with the Awards and Refusals of the Executive Relief Committee. Charleston: Lucas, Richardson and Co., 1887.

Kelsey, Robin. "C. C. Jones: The USGS Investigation of the Charleston Earthquake." In *Archive Style: Photographs and Illustrations for U.S. Surveys, 1850–1890,* 143–89. Berkeley: University of California Press, 2007.

McGee, W J. *First-hand Observations of the Charleston Earthquake of August 31, 1886, and Other Earthquake Materials: Reports of W J McGee [et al.].* Compiled and edited by Kenneth E. Peters and Robert B. Herrmann. Columbia: South Carolina Geological Survey, Division of Research and Statistical Services, South Carolina State Budget and Control Board, 1986.

McKinley, Carl[yle]. "A Descriptive Narrative of the Earthquake of August 31, 1886." In *Year Book — 1886. Charleston, So. Ca.,* 343–441. Charleston: Walker, Evans and Cogswell, n.d.

Mendenhall, J. C. "Report on the Charleston Earthquake." *Monthly Weather Review of the U.S. Signal Service* 14 (August 1886).

Proceedings of the Elliott Society. Vol. 2 (July 1887).

Robinson, Andrew, and Pradeep Talwani. "Building Damage at Charleston,

South Carolina, Associated with the 1886 Earthquake." *Bulletin of the Seismological Society of America* 73, no. 2 (April 1983): 633–52.

Stockton, Robert P. *The Great Shock: The Effects of the 1886 Earthquake on the Built Environment of Charleston, South Carolina.* Easley, S.C.: Southern Historical Press, 1986.

Talwani, Pradeep, and Navin Sharma. "Reevaluation of the Magnitudes of Three Destructive Aftershocks of the 1886 Charleston Earthquake." *Seismological Research Letters* 70, no. 3 (May/June 1999): 360–67.

Earthquakes

Boer, Jelle Zeilinga de, and Donald Theodore Sanders. *Earthquakes in Human History: The Far-Reaching Effects of Seismic Disruptions.* Princeton, N.J.: Princeton University Press, 2005.

Bolt, Bruce A. *Earthquakes.* New York: W. H. Freeman, 2000.

———. *Earthquakes and Geological Discovery.* New York: Scientific American Library, 1993.

Clark, Charles Edwin. "Science, Reason, and an Angry God: The Literature of an Earthquake." *New England Quarterly* 38, no. 3 (1965): 340–62.

Golden, Fredrick. *The Trembling Earth: Probing and Predicting Quakes.* New York: Scribner's, 1983.

Hough, Susan Elizabeth. *Earthshaking Science: What We Know (and Don't Know) about Earthquakes.* Princeton, N.J.: Princeton University Press, 2002.

Nance, John J. *On Shaky Ground: An Invitation to Disaster.* New York: Morrow, 1988.

Oreskes, Naomi. *Plate Tectonics: An Insider's History of the Modern Theory of the Earth.* Boulder, Colo.: Westview Press, 2001.

Penick, James Lal, Jr. *The New Madrid Earthquakes.* Columbus: University of Missouri Press, 1981.

Sieh, Kerry E., and Simon Levay. *The Earth in Turmoil: Earthquakes, Volcanoes, and Their Impact on Humankind.* New York: W. H. Freeman, 1998.

Steinbrugge, Karl V. *Earthquakes, Volcanoes, and Tsunamis.* New York: Skandia America Group, 1982.

Talwani, Pradeep, and William J. Schaeffer. "Recurrence Rates of Large Earthquakes in the South Carolina Coastal Plain Based on Paleoliquifaction Data." *Journal of Geophysical Research* 106, no. B4 (April 10, 2001): 6621–42.

Visvanathan, T. R. "Earthquakes in South Carolina 1698–1975." Bulletin 40, South Carolina Geological Survey, 1980.

City of Charleston

Fraser, Walter J. *Charleston! Charleston! The History of a Southern City*. Columbia: University of South Carolina, 1989.

The General Ordinances of the City of Charleston, South Carolina. Charleston: Lucas and Richardson, 1895.

Mazyck, Arthur, and Gene Waddell. *Charleston in 1883*. Easley, S.C.: Southern Historical Press, 1983.

Powers, Bernard E. *Black Charlestonians: A Social History 1822–1885*. Fayetteville: University of Arkansas Press, 1994.

Severens, Martha, ed., *Alice Ravenel Huger Smith: An Artist, a Place, and a Time*. Charleston: Carolina Art Association, Gibbes Museum of Art, 1993.

Yuhl, Stephanie E. *A Golden Haze of Memory: The Making of Historic Charleston*. Chapel Hill: University of North Carolina Press, 2005.

Reconstruction, Redemption, and the New South

Avary, Myrta Lockett. *Dixie after the War*. Boston: Houghton Mifflin, 1937.

Baker, Bruce E. "The 'Hoover Scare' in South Carolina, 1887: An Attempt to Organize Black Farm Labor." *Labor History* 40, no. 3 (1999): 261–82.

———. "Lynch Law Reversed: The Rape of Lula Sherman, the Lynching of Manse Waldrop, and the Debate over Lynching in the 1880s." *American Nineteenth Century History* 6, no. 3 (September 2005): 273–93.

Barnes, Brooks Miles. "Southern Independents: South Carolina, 1882." *SCHM* 96 (July 1995): 230–51.

Blight, David W. *Race and Reunion: The Civil War and American Memory*. Cambridge: Harvard University Press, 2001.

Brown, Thomas J. "The Monumental Legacy of Calhoun." In *The Memory of the Civil War in American Culture*, edited by Alice Fahs and Joan Waugh, 130–56. Chapel Hill: University of North Carolina Press, 2004.

Budianski, Stephen. *The Bloody Shirt: Terror after Appomattox*. New York: Viking, 2008.

Coulter, E. Merton. *George Walton Williams: The Life of a Southern Merchant and Banker, 1820–1903*. Athens, Ga.: Hibriten Press, 1976.

Doyle, Don H. *New Men, New Cities, New South: Atlanta, Nashville, Charleston, Mobile, 1865–1910*. Chapel Hill: University of North Carolina Press, 1990.

Foner, Eric. *Freedom's Lawmakers: A Directory of Black Officeholders during Reconstruction*. Rev. ed. Baton Rouge: Louisiana State University Press, 1996.

———. *Nothing but Freedom: Emancipation and Its Legacy*. Baton Rouge: Louisiana State University Press, 1983.

———. *Reconstruction: America's Unfinished Revolution*. New York: Harper and Row, 1988.

Gatewood, Willard B. "William D. Crum, A Negro in Politics." *Journal of Negro History* 3 (October 1968): 301–20.

Heard, William H. *From Slavery to the Bishopric in the A.M.E. Church: An Autobiography*. Philadelphia: AME Book Concern, 1924. Reprint, New York: Arno Press, 1969.

Hennessey, Melinda Meek. "Racial Violence during Reconstruction: The 1876 Riots in Charleston and Cainhoy." *SCHM* 86, no. 2 (April 1985).

Kantrowitz, Stephen. *Ben Tillman and the Reconstruction of White Supremacy*. Chapel Hill: University of North Carolina Press, 2000.

Lemann, Nicholas. *Redemption: The Last Battle of the Civil War*. New York: Farrar, Straus and Giroux, 2006.

McKinley, Carlyle. *Appeal to Pharaoh: The Negro Problem, and its Radical Solution*. New York: Fords, Howard and Hulbert, 1889.

Moore, John Hammond. *Carnival of Blood: Dueling, Lynching, and Murder in South Carolina, 1880–1920*. Columbia: University of South Carolina Press, 2006.

Norrell, Robert J. *Up from History: The Life of Booker T. Washington*. Cambridge, Mass.: Belknap Press, 2009.

Osthaus, Carl R. *Partisans of the Southern Press: Editorial Spokesmen of the Nineteenth Century*. Lexington: University of Kentucky Press, 1994.

Pike, James Shepherd. *The Prostrate State: South Carolina under Negro Government*. 1873. Reprint, New York: Harper and Row, 1968.

Porter, A. Toomer. *Led On! Step by Step*. 1898. Reprint, Charleston: Home House Press, 2010.

Simkins, Francis B., and Robert H. Woody. *Pitchfork Ben Tillman, South Carolinian*. 1944. Reprint, with a new introduction by Orville Vernon Burton, Columbia: University of South Carolina Press, 2002.

———. *South Carolina during Reconstruction*. Chapel Hill: University of North Carolina Press, 1932.

Smith, D. E. Huger. *Mason Smith Family Letters, 1860–68*. Columbia: University of South Carolina Press, 1950.

Tyler, Lyon G. "Drawing the Color Line in the Episcopal Diocese of South Carolina, 1876 to 1890: The Role of Edward McCrady, Father and Son." *SCHM* 91 (April 1990): 107–24.

Upchurch, Thomas Adams. *Legislating Racism: The Billion Dollar Congress and the Birth of Jim Crow*. Lexington: University of Kentucky Press, 2004.

Waldrep, Christopher. *The Many Faces of Judge Lynch: Extralegal Violence and Punishment in America*. New York: Palgrave Macmillan, 2002.

Weiner, Mark Stuart. *Black Trials: Citizenship from the Beginnings of Slavery to the End of Caste.* New York: Alfred A. Knopf, 2004.

Williams, Alfred B. *Hampton and His Red Shirts: South Carolina's Deliverance in 1876.* Charleston: Walker, Evans, and Cogswell, 1935.

Woodward, C. Vann. *The Strange Career of Jim Crow.* 1955. Reprint, New York: Oxford University Press, 1974.

Dawson Family

Clark, E. Culpepper. *Francis Warrington Dawson and the Politics of Restoration: South Carolina, 1874–1889.* University: University of Alabama Press, 1980.

Dawson, Francis Warrington, II. "Son of Editor Sheds New Light on Murder in 1889." *News and Courier Sunday Magazine,* August 24, 1958, 1-C.

East, Charles, ed. *The Civil War Diary of Sarah Morgan.* Athens: University of Georgia Press, 1991.

Randall, Dale B. J. *Joseph Conrad and Warrington Dawson: The Record of a Friendship.* Durham, N.C.: Duke University Press, 1968.

Roberts, Giselle, ed. *The Correspondence of Sarah Morgan and Francis Warrington Dawson.* Athens: University of Georgia Press, 2004.

Labor History

Garlock, Jonathan. *Guide to the Local Assemblies of the Knights of Labor.* Westport, Conn.: Greenwood Press, 1982.

McLaurin, Melton A[lonza]. "Early Labor Organizational Efforts in South Carolina Cotton Mills, 1880–1905." *SCHM* 72, no. 1 (January 1971): 44–59.

———. *The Knights of Labor in the South.* Westport, Conn.: Greenwood Press, 1978.

Snowden, Yates. *Notes on Labor Organizations in South Carolina 1742–1861.* Columbia: University of South Carolina Press, 1944.

Weir, Robert E. *Beyond Labor's Veil: The Culture of the Knights of Labor.* University Park: Pennsylvania State University Press, 1996.

INDEX

The abbreviations FWD and SMD stand for Francis Warrington Dawson and Sarah Morgan Dawson respectively.

Summerville Relief Committee, 287n50
Summerville Town Council, 115
Sumter, S.C., 203
Sumter Guards, 189
Sweegan, Edward F., 59, 196–97

Taft, William Howard 255
Taft, W. W., 103
Talwani, Pradeep, 130
Ten Mile Hill, S.C., 47, 49, 50, 120, 143; earthquake at, 2
Terre Haute, Ind., 2
Texas, 57
Thompson, Hugh S., 158
Thompson, Seth, 174
Thurman, Allen G., 202
tidal waves. *See* tsunamis
Tilden, Samuel, 99
Tillman, Benjamin R., 2, 12, 64–65, 95, 167, 211–13, 245, 254, 255; attacks FWD, 204–10
Tillman, George, 65
Tom Thumb (elephant), 163–64
Tourgee, Albion, 317n19
tsunamis (tidal waves), 36, 53, 56, 63, 290n24; in Indonesia (2006), xii; rumors of, 23, 36, 63, 143
Turner, Nat, 216
Twain, Mark, 155
Tybee Island, Ga., 56
typesetters' union, 35

Umbria (ship), 142
Union Wharf, 26
Unitarian Church (Charleston, S.C.), 33, 70, 137, 305n12; on night of earthquake, 22
United Labor Party, 197–98
United Press, 44
United Umbrella and Walking Stick Dressers, 87–88
University of Virginia, 123
U.S. Army Signal Corps, 48, 149, 172

U.S. Congress, 94, 253; provides local relief, 57, 202
U.S. Department of the Army, 57
U.S. Department of the Navy, 57
U.S. flag, 186–87
U.S. Geological Survey (USGS), 48, 122, 123, 124, 173, 216; Division of Volcanic Geology, 121–22
U.S. Marine Hospital, 166–67
U.S. Naval Observatory, 150
U.S. post office, 30, 106–7, 138, 163
U.S. Supreme Court, 254
U.S. Treasury Department, 136

Van Buren, Martin, 107
Vanderbilt family, 107
Victoria, Queen, 58, 158
Viett's marble yard, 50
Virginia state penitentiary, earthquake at, 2
volcanoes: Colima, Mexico (1886), 154; fears of, 55–56, 67; Krakatoa (1883), 36
Voltaire, 74–75
Von Blumen, Elsa, 142
Von Santen's, 188
vultures (buzzards), 115–16

Wadmalaw Island, S.C., 113, 123
Wagener, F. W., 184
Wagener, F. W., and Company, 190
Waldrop, Manse, 194–95
Walker, Evans, and Cogswell, 188, 278n58
Walker, Keitt, 21–22, 29
Wando Phosphate Company, 189–90
Washington, Booker T., xiii, 192, 193, 256
Washington, D.C., 1, 125
Washington Monument (Washington, D.C.), 125, 127
Washington Race Course, 18
Washington Square Park, 54, 63, 76, 91, 105, 109, 110, 112, 154, 205, 253; electric